CLINICAL APPROACHES TO BASIC AND CARDIAC INTENSIVE CARE

Dr. Gunadhar Padhi

BLUEROSE PUBLISHERS
India | U.K.

For permissions requests or inquiries regarding this publication,
please contact:

BLUEROSE PUBLISHERS
www.BlueRoseONE.com
info@bluerosepublishers.com
+91 8882 898 898
+4407342408967

ISBN: 978-93-5741-655-9

Cover design: Muskan sachdeva
Typesetting: Pooja Sharma

First Edition: July 2023

Preface

It is my honor and pleasure to introduce this book on Intensive Care, a project that has been a long-time aspiration of mine. As an intensivist, I have dedicated my career to caring for critically ill patients and advancing the field of critical care medicine. This book is a reflection of that dedication, and I am proud to present it to the medical community.I would like to begin by acknowledging the unwavering support and encouragement of my family throughout this journey. Their love and patience allowed me to dedicate the necessary time and energy to bring this project to fruition. I am also grateful for the valuable contributions of my dear students, who have inspired me with their enthusiasm and curiosity. Their passion for learning has pushed me to constantly strive for excellence.I am indebted to my seniors and colleagues, whose guidance and expertise have been instrumental in shaping my understanding of Intensive Care medicine. Their mentorship has been invaluable, and I am grateful for their unwavering support.Lastly, I would like to thank my patients, who have taught me the importance of compassionate care and the impact that it can have on recovery. Their experiences have provided the inspiration for many of the concepts discussed in this book.I hope that this book will serve as a useful resource for healthcare providers and contribute to the advancement of Intensive Care medicine.

Editor's Note

In the fast-paced and ever-evolving field of medicine, it is crucial for healthcare professionals to stay updated with the latest knowledge and advancements, especially in critical care. We are delighted to present "Text Book of Basics of Critical Care Management and Cardiac Intensive Care" a book that serves as an exceptional guide for both medical students and seasoned experts in the field.

This comprehensive resource offers a wealth of information on critical care management and cardiac intensive care, covering a wide range of relevant topics. Whether you are a medical student seeking a solid foundation in critical care or an experienced practitioner looking to expand your knowledge and enhance your skills, this book is an invaluable companion.

The book provides a well-structured and organized approach to critical care medicine, delivering essential concepts and practical guidance. From the initial assessment and monitoring of critically ill patients to the intricate management of complex cases, the authors have meticulously compiled a comprehensive overview of the field. The inclusion of real-world case studies and examples adds a practical dimension, allowing readers to apply their knowledge to realistic scenarios.

One standout aspect of this book is its emphasis on compassionate treatment and patient-centered care. The authors recognize that while technical expertise is essential in critical care, a holistic approach that prioritizes empathy and understanding is equally vital. The book encourages healthcare professionals to view patients not only as medical cases but as individuals with unique needs, values, and fears. By highlighting the importance of patient-centered approaches, the book equips readers with the tools to provide not just excellent medical care, but also compassionate and empathetic support.

"Text Book of Basics of Critical Care Management and Cardiac Intensive Care" has the potential to significantly impact the field of critical care medicine. Its detailed exploration of fundamental issues and emerging trends provides readers with a deeper understanding of the complexities involved in managing critically ill patients. This, in turn, will contribute to improved patient outcomes and enhanced quality of care.

I commend the authors for their dedication and expertise in compiling this exceptional resource. Their wealth of experience and commitment to advancing critical care medicine shines through the pages, making this book an indispensable asset for healthcare professionals and trainees alike.

In conclusion, "Text Book of Basics of Critical Care Management and Cardiac Intensive Care" is a must-have book for anyone seeking to expand their knowledge and expertise in critical care and cardiac intensive care. Its comprehensive coverage, emphasis on patient-centered care, and potential to advance the field make it an essential addition to every medical professional's library. We wholeheartedly recommend this book as a valuable resource that will undoubtedly enhance the practice of critical care medicine.

Dr. Saurabh Kr Das, Editor
Senior Consultant, Department of Critical Care Medicine, Max Super Speciality Hospital

Dr Khadake Swapnil M., Associate Editor
Intensivist, Apollo Hospitals, Navi-Mumbai.

Recommendation

I highly recommend the book "Text Book of Basics of Critical Care Management and Cardiac Intensive Care" for anyone seeking in-depth knowledge and guidance in the field of critical care medicine. This book provides a comprehensive overview of the principles, strategies, and best practices involved in managing critically ill patients. Authored by experienced healthcare professionals and experts, "Text Book of Basics of Critical Care Management and Cardiac Intensive Care" delves into various aspects of critical care, including the assessment and monitoring of patients, resuscitation techniques, ventilator management, hemodynamic support, infection control, and ethical considerations in critical care settings. The book combines theoretical concepts with practical insights, making it a valuable resource for healthcare professionals, trainees, and students alike. Furthermore, I would like to praise Dr. Gunadhar Padhi for his remarkable expertise and dedication as a Critical Care Specialist for over 16 years. Dr. Padhi's extensive experience in the field undoubtedly reflects his profound understanding of the complexities involved in critical care management. His commitment to providing high-quality care to critically ill patients is commendable, and his expertise has likely positively impacted numerous lives. Dr. Gunadhar Padhi's vast experience and dedication, coupled with his contributions to critical care medicine, make him an invaluable asset to the healthcare community. It is through the tireless efforts of professionals like Dr. Padhi that the field of critical care continues to advance, leading to improved patient outcomes and enhanced quality of care. Overall, I wholeheartedly recommend "Text Book of Basics of Critical Care Management and Cardiac Intensive Care" as an essential resource for healthcare professionals, and I applaud Dr. Gunadhar Padhi for his impressive achievements and valuable contributions to the field of critical care medicine.

Dr Sanjay Choudhry
Practicing Intensivist
Mayo Clinic (USA)

Contents

Part 1

Basics of ICU

Chapter 1:

Basic Concepts of Critical Care

When Dr. W. E. Dandy established a 3-bed unit at the Johns Hopkins Hospital in Baltimore for postoperative neurosurgery patients, it became the very first ICU in the United States. Due to a staffing shortage after World War II, patients were stationed together in recovery rooms that resembled today's Intensive Care units. The establishment of respiratory care units all across the nation was prompted by the introduction of mechanical ventilators in the 1950s [1].

Critically unwell patients need medical attention right away. The detection, ongoing monitoring, evaluation, and treatment necessary to manage a critical illness is known as "emergency and critical care." Reviving unstable patients while giving them time to recuperate or experience the effects of particular medicines to enhance outcomes and prevent death is the main goal of emergency and critical care [2]. When we refer to emergency anssd critical care, we mean care given to all critically sick patients in a wide sense. Therefore, emergency and critical care can be given anywhere in the hospital, including the emergency room, the intensive-care unit (ICU), high-dependency units, post-operative recovery units, and general wards to patients who are critically ill upon arrival or who were stable but later deteriorated [3].

A multidisciplinary and interprofessional specialty devoted to the comprehensive care of individuals with, or at risk of developing, severe, life-threatening organ dysfunction is known as Intensive Care, sometimes known as critical care. A variety of technologies are used in Intensive Care to maintain failing organ systems, including the kidneys, cardiovascular system, and lungs. The main objective of Intensive Care is to avoid further physiologic worsening while the underlying illness is treated and resolved. While the area of expertise has developed expert knowledge in the proper treatment of disorders like sepsis and Acute Respiratory Distress Syndrome (ARDS), its common expertise is the pathophysiology and assistance of organ dysfunction [4].

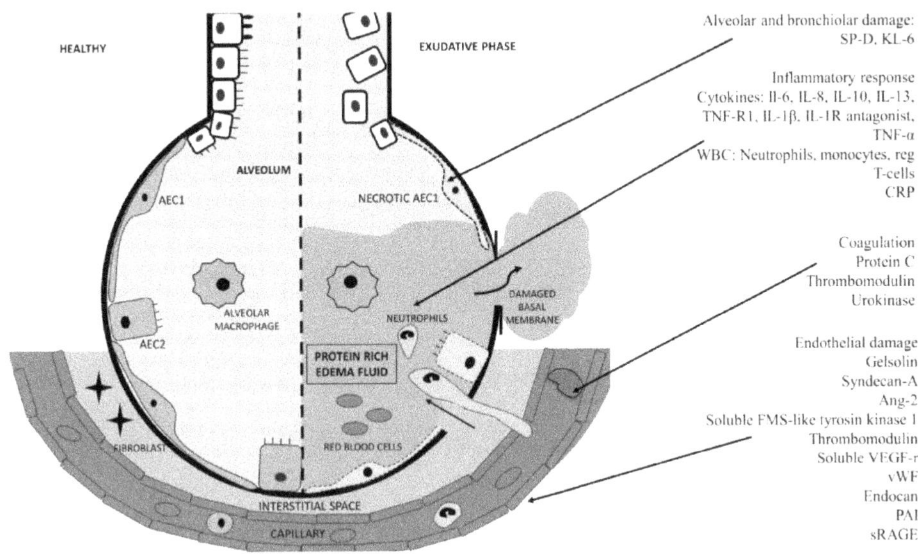

Figure 1.1: Acute Respiratory Distress Syndrome

Intensive Care is a unique medical specialty in several nations, with a specific training program that begins after medical school graduation. Aspiring intensivists frequently complete extra training in Intensive Care after finishing a master's degree in another field, such as anesthesia, pulmonology, surgery, pediatrics, or emergency medicine [2,4].

Providing skilled interprofessional care, Intensive Care is more than just a clinical specialty. It involves a wide range of professionals, including doctors, respiratory therapists, nurses, physiotherapists, microbiologists, ethicists, pharmacists, social workers, spiritual care providers, and many more [5].

ICU patients are a fairly diverse group, but they all require care that is more acute than that provided to most hospital patients. Patients in the ICU frequently need ventilatory or cardiovascular assistance, invasive monitoring, and close nurse and doctor watch. Larger hospitals typically separate patients into two categories: surgical patients and medical ICU patients. Subspecialty units like trauma surgery units, cardiac surgery units, coronary care units, neurology ICUs, and burn care units have been created as a result of the severity of these patients' illnesses and the degree of illness-specific understanding required to care for them [6,7].

The significant international variation that exists currently in the capability of caring for the sickest patients within the healthcare system must be recognized in order to establish a global concept of an Intensive Care unit (ICU). We acknowledge that Intensive Care is not an absolute term, but rather a relative one described in regard to the realities of a specific healthcare system which can vary based on available resources and strategies to care. We group the factors that make care intensive and stratify ICUs based on their ability to provide that care [8].

Five elements can be used to categorize the elements that distinguish intensive clinical care from normal clinical care and contribute to its intensity [9,10].

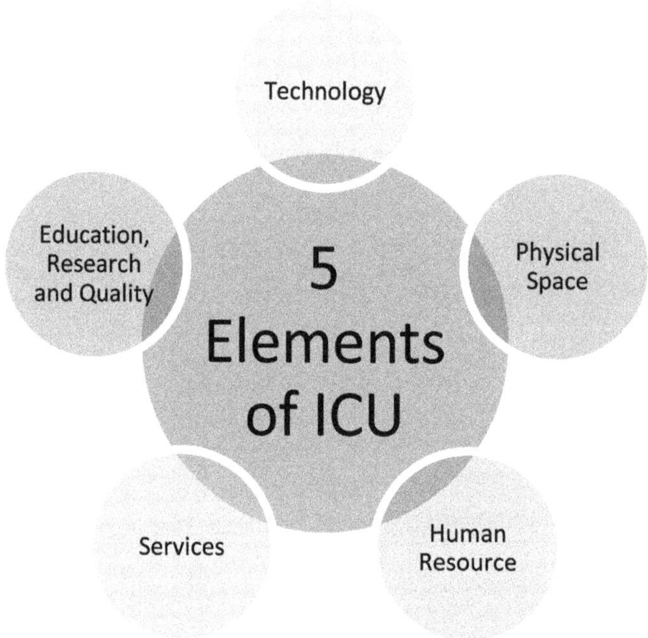

Figure 1.2: Five elements of ICU that make it different from usual clinical care

- Technology for monitoring and assistance:

  One important aspect that distinguishes ward-based hospital treatment from Intensive Care treatment is the capability to do constant monitoring of the patient's physiological status. Transcutaneous oxygen saturation monitoring, non-invasive monitoring of blood pressure and heart rate, and continuous EEG or ECG monitoring are examples of non-invasive monitoring. Invasive monitoring involves intracranial pressure monitoring and hemodynamic monitoring. Data should indeed be constantly displayed so that everyone involved in the patient's care has easy access to it, and it should be documented so that physicians can watch for trends and react appropriately [10].

  The ICU offers a variety of respiratory support capabilities ranging from delivery of supplemental oxygen through a mask or high-flow system of oxygen to traditional and non-conventional mechanical ventilatory techniques, in some of the ICUs it may include extracorporeal membrane oxygenation (ECMO), and Extracorporeal carbon dioxide removal ($ECCO_2R$). In addition to mechanical cardiac support with intra-aortic balloon counterpulsation or ventricular assist devices and ECMO to give tissue oxygenation, hemodynamic support can also be mostly pharmaceutical and is directed by data derived from constant monitoring of hemodynamic parameters. Both nutritional support administered orally through a feeding tube or through parenteral route. The patients are often provided renal assistance in the form of continuous or intermittent renal replacement treatment. Pain and anxiety relief, as well as delirium prevention and treatment, are constant needs [9,11].

- Physical Space:

The existence of a distinct geographic area inside a hospital or healthcare center in which the sickest patients can always be cared for is essential to the concept of an ICU, despite the fact that critical care is progressively provided outside the actual boundaries of an ICU. To maximize the benefits for all patients, a dedicated physical area facilitates the concentration and effective sharing of skills and technologies [12]. An ICU's physical layout should allow for the appropriate number of ICU beds to be comfortably accommodated. To enable assessment of the patient, management, and reliable and successful execution of infection control measures, each bed must have access from all sides. Each patient should receive care in a room with just one bed, if possible. Each room needs to include a sink, as well as design elements that allow for and facilitate quick access to monitoring equipment, ventilators, and dialysis machines. A natural lighting source light is preferred, and oxygen and a vacuum system—preferably from an integrated system—should be provided [12,13]. A negative-pressure chamber or a pressure regulated chamber with the ability to isolate individuals with airborne infections or immunocompromised patient should be included in the ICU. For mixing and distributing medications as well as cleaning and storing used equipment like bronchoscopes and ventilator circuits, separate facilities should be made available. Data from individual patient monitoring devices should be reproduced at a central nursing station. Regardless of whether the records are kept on paper or electronically, the ability to capture and understand patient data throughout time must be available [12].

The physical space requirements for an ideal Intensive Care Unit (ICU) can vary depending on various factors such as the number of beds, specific equipment needs, and local regulations. These are approximate values and it's always best to consult with healthcare professionals and local regulations for specific requirements.

According to Ministry of Health and Family Welfare, Government of India, National Accreditation Board for Hospitals & Healthcare Providers (NABH) and Indian Society of Critical Care Medicine (ISCCM), these are guidelines regarding specifications of physical space:

Total Floor Area: The total floor area required for an ICU can range from 200 to 400 square feet per bed, depending on the level of care provided. This includes space for patient beds, equipment, circulation areas, and workstations for healthcare staff.

Patient Bed Space: Each ICU bed should have a clear area of around 150 to 200 square feet to accommodate the bed, medical equipment, and provide space for healthcare professionals to attend to the patient.

Circulation Space: Sufficient circulation space should be provided within the ICU to allow for easy movement of patients, healthcare staff, and medical equipment. A width of 8 to 10 feet for corridors is generally recommended.

Handwashing and Sanitization Facilities: Adequate handwashing and sanitization facilities should be available within the ICU to promote good hygiene practices. This includes sinks, soap dispensers, and hand sanitizers conveniently located for both staff and patient use.

Support Areas: The ICU should have designated areas for staff and equipment support, such as nursing stations, medication preparation areas, storage rooms for supplies and equipment, and restrooms for staff.

Ventilation and Environmental Control: Proper ventilation and environmental control systems are crucial in an ICU. The area should have adequate heating, ventilation, and air conditioning (HVAC) systems to maintain a comfortable and controlled environment, including temperature and humidity regulation. Negative-pressure rooms may be required for certain isolation needs.

Safety and Security: The ICU should have appropriate safety features, including emergency exits, fire safety systems, and security measures to ensure patient and staff safety.

It's important to note that these are general guidelines, and the specific requirements may vary based on factors such as the level of care provided (e.g., general ICU, cardiac ICU, neonatal ICU), local regulations, and specific healthcare facility standards. Consulting with healthcare architects, engineers, and professionals experienced in designing ICUs would be beneficial to ensure compliance with local regulations and optimal functionality of the ICU space.

- Human resources:

The clinical staff that provides care in an ICU is highly skilled, multidisciplinary, and interdisciplinary. By virtue of a more intensive and direct engagement between team members and the critical patient, the treatment it offers is much more intensive than that given elsewhere within the hospital [14,1]. The most important human resource in the team is the registered and trained doctors who has proper qualification and training for handling ICU patients and different cases. This should also be divided into senior doctors and juniors doctors. In the context of an Intensive Care Unit (ICU), the roles and responsibilities of senior doctors and junior doctors can vary depending on the specific healthcare system, hospital policies, and staffing arrangements. However, the following can be a general understanding of their typical roles:

Senior Doctors:

Attending Physicians/Consultants: These are experienced doctors who are responsible for overseeing the care provided in the ICU. They have completed their medical training and usually hold specialist qualifications. Attending physicians provide overall supervision, make important medical decisions, and ensure high-quality patient care. They often lead the multidisciplinary team in the ICU and may have administrative or teaching responsibilities.

ICU Specialists/Intensivists: These doctors have received additional training in critical care medicine and specialize in the management of critically ill patients. They are often responsible for making complex medical decisions, coordinating the patient's care, and ensuring adherence to evidence-based practices. Intensivists work closely with the ICU team and provide expertise in managing patients with severe illnesses or injuries.

Junior Doctors:

Residents/Registrars: These are doctors who have completed their medical degree and are pursuing further training in a specific medical specialty, such as internal medicine, anesthesia, or emergency medicine. In the ICU, residents or registrars may rotate through the unit as part of their training. They participate in patient care under the supervision of senior doctors, assist with procedures, perform medical assessments, and communicate with patients and their families. They also help with documentation and contribute to the ongoing management of patients.

Interns/House Officers: These are doctors who have recently graduated from medical school and are in their first year of supervised practice. In some healthcare systems, interns or house officers may also rotate through the ICU. They typically assist the senior and junior doctors, learn essential clinical skills, and gain exposure to the critical care environment. Their responsibilities may include basic patient assessments, documentation, and performing certain procedures under supervision.

The team taking care of the ICU patients should include trained ICU nurses, respiratory therapist who handles the mechanical ventilator system, physiotherapists who support mobility and rehabilitation, nutritionists with expertise in parenteral and enteral feeding needs of complex patient populations and pharmacists with special expertise in drug-drug interactions. Other human resource that can aid in increasing the efficiency of the ICU management is social worker who can assist with the requirements of both patients and their families may be included on the team in addition to doctors and nurses [14]. (The sentence is too long, difficult to understand)

- Services provided in critical care:

In addition to meeting the immediate needs of individual patient care, an ICU is also identified by the services that it offers. The ICU at the hospital has the knowledge base, technological facilities, and human resource ability for the management of critical patients who are acutely unstable. It can assess, support, and resuscitate the patient with the most cutting-edge equipment available. An ICU, however, also contributes to the whole healthcare system. It might act as a referral hub for smaller hospitals without ICUs. In a bigger community, it might offer specialized services like advanced trauma care, complex respiratory failure management, neurologic assistance, and monitoring, which are not offered by other ICUs. The administration of patients on hospital beds or in the emergency room is increasingly being done by the ICU team [15].

- Education, research, and quality improvement:

  A functioning ICU has an intrinsic responsibility to continuously enhance care delivery based on an assessment process of the deficiencies of the service it delivers and the evolving body of knowledge that guides the best care, just like any other specialized component of the healthcare system. This area falls within the purview of ongoing quality improvement. It also has a responsibility to support the evaluation of best practices in healthcare and the dissemination of that knowledge, which fall within the purview of research and education, respectively. Although the degree to which an ICU may engage in improving quality, education, and research will vary, doing so should be a goal for all ICUs because doing so ultimately results in better patient care and improved outcomes [16].

Classification of ICU:

The majority of ICU classification frameworks employ a numerical scale, with 3 being its highest level. Following this precedence, we categorize Intensive Care units as primary, secondary, and tertiary.

Primary ICU (level 1): In this, the personnels with minimum critical care training are present. Mostly these personnels have practical training who may not have received official training in an affiliated or recognized institution. These personnels are easily accessible and approachable by the common people, specially in the town or suburb regions. The nurse-patient ratio is higher than it is on a typical ward of the same facility since nurses have some ICU experience, either with or without extra training. Although not always a member of the ICU team, other specialists are accessible within the hospital. The device has the ability to continuously monitor the ECG as well as monitor transcutaneous saturation of oxygen and vitals non-invasively on an intense basis [17].

Organ support is only allowed to provide by the administration of supplementary oxygen via a mask, non-invasive positive pressure ventilation, or short-term invasive mechanical ventilation. Simple mechanical ventilation may also be used to manage in case of a stable chronic ventilated patient. A level 1 ICU is housed in a specific area of the hospital. The unit exclusively serves patients inside the hospital and has a minimal quality improvement program, however, it may not frequently participate in research [17].

Secondary ICU (level 2): A Level 2 ICU's staff consists of doctors with specialist training in medicine, anesthesia, emergency medicine, surgery, pediatrics, and other fields who may additionally have formal ICU training from affiliated center or recognized institution. Additional to this, staff members may have specific Intensive Care coaching. During the day, staff members are on-site or close by, and during the evenings and weekends, they are instantly accessible by telephone or in person to manage emergencies.

Nurses with specialized training in Intensive Care provide 24-hour nursing care; the nurse-to-patient ratio is greater than in other hospital sections but is normally no less than 1:3. A dedication to inter-professional practice is demonstrated by the frequent multidisciplinary rounds and the presence of allied health care providers who are either already on the ICU team or easily accessible [17,18].

It is possible to track vital signs continuously, including transcutaneous saturation levels of oxygen (SpO2), central venous pressure, and blood pressure. Blood Gas Analyzer can also be included here. Endotracheal intubation, positive pressure breathing, the administration of vasoactive drugs, and renal replacement therapies are all examples of organ support techniques. Anyone can use the facilities easily and staff improvement programs are continuously run to keep the staffs updated with the current guidelines of management. A rigorous quality improvement program with regular reviews of procedures and problems exists in a level 2 Intensive Care unit. It acts as a referral hub for nearby hospitals without specialized ICU resources [18].

Tertiary ICU (level 3): The critically ill patient is managed with the most advanced care in a level 3 ICU. It is staffed by medical practitioners with Intensive Care training, either as a stand-alone specialty or after completing comprehensive training in another field. A staff physician, nurse, or Intensive Care trainee provides on-site coverage around the clock. Nurses with further training in Intensive Care, are only able to deliver nursing care in Critical Care Unit. Usually, the nurse-to-patient ratio should be kept at 1:1 or 1:2, however, it depends on the severity of the patient. The care of patients is aided by additional specialized personnel such as respiratory therapists, pharmacists, physiotherapists, dietitians, and microbiologists [19].

It's possible to get additional specialized services like invasive neurological monitoring and ECMO. A third-level ICU frequently acts as a teaching facility for trainees in Intensive Care and actively engages in clinical research and quality-improvement initiatives. It acts as a regional referral hospital for seriously ill patients, and it is anticipated that it will have procedures in place for pandemics and other emergencies where a sudden spike in demand might be anticipated. Patients requiring contact or airborne precautions can use the unit's isolation facilities. It offers an integrated outreach program that can offer assistance to patients in the emergency room or on the ward. A formal ICU follow-up program is ideal [20].

Neglected emergency and critical care:

There are a number of causes to worry that urgent and critical care may be overlooked. Firstly, as opposed to the severity-related "horizontal" strategy of critical and emergency care, the approach used by the majority of medical specialties and healthcare systems is often "vertical," prioritizing diagnosis-related and specialty-related care. In hospitals, both in limited settings and in high-resource settings' general wards, low staffing levels, equipment shortages, and inadequate understanding or awareness of critical care and emergency care can occur. These factors can contribute to a failure to recognize critical illness and an under-prioritization of emergency and critical care. Secondly, there are no generally accepted criteria or standards for identifying a critical illness or for providing emergency and Intensive Care. Thirdly, expensive and high-tech care provided in Intensive Care units (ICUs) can be confused with critical and emergency care [21].

Essential Emergency and Critical Care (EECC):

We suggest a new emphasis on Essential Emergency and Critical Care (EECC) to enhance the treatment of the critically ill (EECC). Treatment that all critically sick patients should obtain in all hospitals around the world" is how we describe EECC. EECC is a concept that should play a significant role in universal health coverage because it is affordable, suitable for use in all nations and environments, and intended for patients regardless of their age, gender, underlying diagnoses, medical specialization, or location. EECC consists of a number of procedures and therapies as well as system-wide standards for their delivery [20,21].

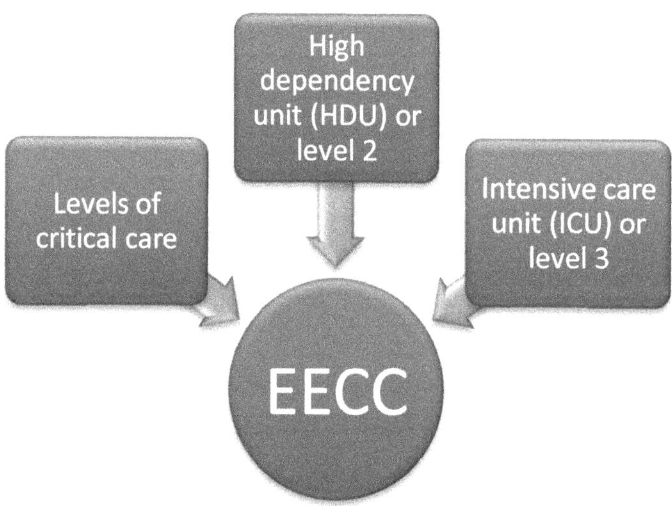

Figure 1.3: Components of EECC

The fundamental level of critical and emergency care, or EECC, has to be offered in all settings. The type of supplementary care that is necessary or feasible will depend on the resources that are available. EECC is not the type of care needed for terminally ill patients or when a patient's condition is so bad that recovery is thought to be impossible. Even while the choice to provide palliative care rather than EECC can be difficult, it is nonetheless crucial, and the implementation of EECC must not cause patients who have no chance of a full recovery to suffer anymore [22].

Levels of critical care: [290].

A wide range of cutting-edge observation and organ support capabilities are available in contemporary critical care medicine. These are based on the layout and range of each individual unit.

High dependency unit (HDU) or level 2:

Admission for single-organ support should not call for a specialized critical care nurse for every patient (invasive ventilation excluded). It enables the close observation of patients who are experiencing or at risk of experiencing organ failure:

- respiratory: arterial blood gasses, non-invasive ventilation
- cardiovascular: invasive arterial pressure monitoring, low dose vasopressors
- renal: certain renal replacement therapies, close fluid balance control

Intensive Care unit (ICU) or level 3:

Admission for advanced monitoring or multi-organ support requires at least one specialized critical care nurse for every patient:

- Respiratory: extracorporeal membrane oxygenation (ECMO), invasive and non-invasive ventilation, or removal of carbon dioxide (ECCO2R) in selected centers.
- cardiovascular: vasopressor and inotropic support, ventricular assist devices, intra-aortic balloon pump, advanced cardiac output monitoring, ECMO.
- renal: renal replacement therapies.
- neurological: monitoring of intracranial pressure, advanced neurological monitoring, EEG.

Post Critical Care: The critical care staff continues to be involved even after an ICU patient is discharged, and many units are building procedures to guarantee excellent in-patient follow-up, with some hospitals even setting up RaCI (Recovery after Critical Illness) clinics. These could aid in comprehending, reducing, and preventing the negative long-term impacts of critical disease. It is only lately that the long-term burden and decline in quality of living post-critical illness are being understood, despite more patients surviving until hospital discharge.

Bedside critical care scoring systems:

Florence Nightingale raised this topic for the first time in 1863, marking the beginning of the evaluation of medical treatment outcomes. Initial critical illness outcome prediction relied on the clinicians' subjective assessment. In order to assess the efficacy of treatment strategies, Intensive Care units (ICUs) and their rapid proliferation produced a need for quantifiable and clinically pertinent surrogate outcome measures. As a result, scoring systems have been devised and used for this purpose. The fate of patients in Intensive Care depends on a number of variables that exist on the patient's first day in the ICU and later on during their stay there [23].

A scoring system typically consists of two components: a score (a number indicating the severity of the condition), and a probability model (an equation giving the probability of hospital death of the patients). The capacity of scores or scales to be used for comparing different patient groups for the purposes of treatment, triage, or comparative analysis is improved by a model, which aids in decision-making [24,25].

Acute physiology and chronic health evaluation (APACHE), the simplified acute physiology score (SAPS), and the mortality prediction model (MPM) are the most used scoring methods that use data gathered on the first ICU day to produce scores (MPM). Others, like the Three-Day Recalibrating ICU Outcomes (TRIOS), Sequential Organ Failure Assessment (SOFA), Organ Dysfunction and Infection System (ODIN), Logistic Organ Dysfunction (LOD) Model, and Multiple Organs Dysfunction Score (MODS) are repetitive and collect data every day for the duration of the ICU stay or for the first three days. **Scores might be objective or subjective** [24].

The following are some examples of typical ICU grading systems (for the adult population):

- APACHE II - Acute Physiology and Chronic Health Evaluation II
- ODIN - Open Data INteroperability Network
- SOFA - Sequential Organ Failure Assessment
- SAPS II - Simplified Acute Physiology Score II
- MPM II - Mortality Probability Models II
- MODS - Multiple Organ Dysfunction Syndrome
- TRIOS - Treatment and Rehabilitation in Orthopaedic Sports Medicine Intervention Study
- GCS - Glasgow Coma Scale

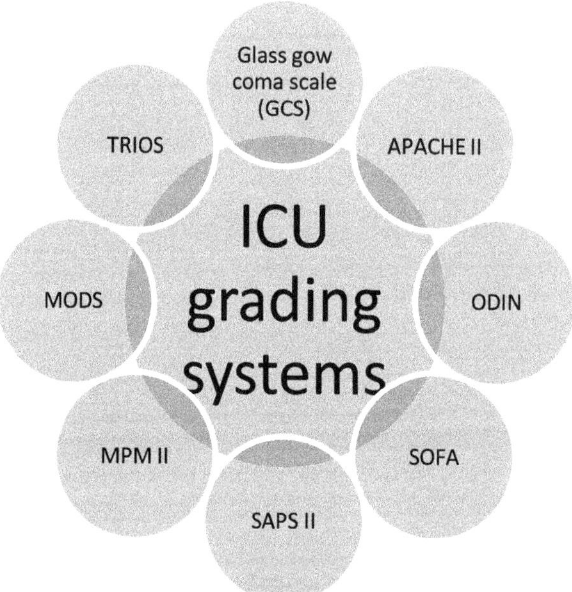

Figure 1.4: Scoring system available for evaluation of patients in ICU setup

APACHE II: According to William Knaus in 1981, APACHE-1 consists of 33 parameters The seriousness of disease classification system, APACHE II, was created in 1985 utilizing a database of ICU patients from North America. In order to offer an overall assessment of disease severity, a point score based on the results of 12 regular physiological measurements (collected within the first 24 hours of admission), age, and prior health condition is used. Based on these measurements, an integer score between 0 and 71 is then calculated; higher scores indicate a more serious illness and a higher probability of passing away. A variable receives zero points if it hasn't been measured. The APACHE II score is used to predict mortality rates in hospitals [23].

SAPS II: The severity of ICU patients is measured using the SAPS II scale, which was first introduced in 1993 by Le Gall et al. The model has 17 variables: 3 disease-related variables, 3 age-related variables, 12 physiological variables, and the type of admission. The range of the SAPS II score is 0 to 163 points (0-116 points for physiological variables, 0-17 points for age, and 0-30 points for previous diagnosis). Following that, logistic regression is used to calculate the probability of mortality. Six admission characteristics were added to SAPS II in order to construct the standardized mortality ratio or the performance measure of ICU: age, sex, length of ICU inpatient stay, patient location prior to ICU, clinical category, and presence or absence of drug overdose [26].

MODS: The degree of multiple organ failure as a result of critical illness is assessed using the MODS. It includes a score based on the failure of six organs. The scale ranged from 0 to 4 (maximum of 24). After totaling the scores, hospital mortality is then estimated. Both when used as a prognostic indicator on the initial day of ICU admission and when computed over the course of the ICU stay as an outcome measure, this score showed a graded correlation with the ICU mortality rate [27].

SOFA: The European Society of Intensive Care Medicine developed the SOFA system during a consensus meeting in 1994, and it underwent additional revision in 1996. Based on information about the severity of organ failure in six organ failures, this score was created to rate the severity of a patient's disease on a scale of 0-4. The lowest mortality is indicated by one failure and a respiratory failure [28].

LODS: Six organ failures were identified and 12 variables were investigated when Le Gall et al. first suggested the LODS in 1996. The model has undergone numerous tests. It is very likely that the hospital result will differ between the LODS on day 3 and day 1 of the hospital stay. The LODS was created to provide a single score that could quantify the severity of various organ dysfunctions [29].

MPM II: Lemeshow et al. were the first to describe MPM II. The MPM II model directly estimates the likelihood of hospital death. There have been four models put forth: MPM II upon admissions and at 24, 48, and 72 hours. Based on information from admission and after the initial 24 hours in the ICU, the first version of this model was created to predict mortality after hospital discharge. Later, further models were created with information from 48 to 72 hours following ICU admission. This model makes use of mechanical ventilation as well as acute diagnosis, a few physiological variables, and chronic health status [30].

ODIN: The ODIN system was proposed in 1993 by Fagon et al. The prognosis is differentiated based on the type of failure; the greatest mortality rates were discovered to be linked with liver failure, accompanied by hematological and renal derangements, and the lowest with respiratory impairment and infection. This contains data documented within the first 24 hours of ICU admission if there is any inclusion or lack of impairment in six organs plus one infection [31].

TRIOS: In order to predict hospital generosity in ICU patients who were hospitalized for longer than 72 hours, Timsit et al. presented a composite score, the TRIOS, in 2001 utilizing daily SAPS II and LODS [32].

GCS: The GCS is a common instrument for determining the severity of a brain injury and for quickly determining the state of awareness in a patient who has been harmed. To assist in assessing the state of consciousness in infants and children, a modified verbal and movement version has been created [33]. The GCS assesses three primary components: eye-opening response, verbal response, and motor response. Each component is assigned a score ranging from 1 to 4 or 6, with a higher score indicating a more favorable neurological status. The scores are then combined to give an overall GCS score, which can range from 3 (indicating deep unconsciousness) to 15 (indicating full consciousness). By using the GCS, healthcare providers can gauge the severity of a patient's brain injury, monitor changes over time, and make informed decisions regarding further diagnostic tests, treatment strategies, and potential interventions. The GCS is particularly valuable in emergency departments, intensive care units, and other critical care settings where prompt assessment and management of patients with traumatic brain injury, stroke, or other neurological conditions are paramount.

Chapter 2:

Common Problems in ICU Patients

Patients in intensive-care units (ICUs) who are critically sick, face numerous risks because of the sophisticated therapy needed to address their severe illnesses. Indwelling device-related healthcare-associated infections (HAIs) cause several problems. These side effects include central line-associated bloodstream infection (CLABSI), catheter-associated urinary tract infection (CA-UTI), and ventilator-associated pneumonia (VAP). Patients in the surgical ICU (SICU) frequently experience the complication of surgical site infection (SSI). Vein thromboembolism (VTE), which includes deep-vein thrombosis (DVT) and pulmonary embolism (PE), is another frequent consequence [34].

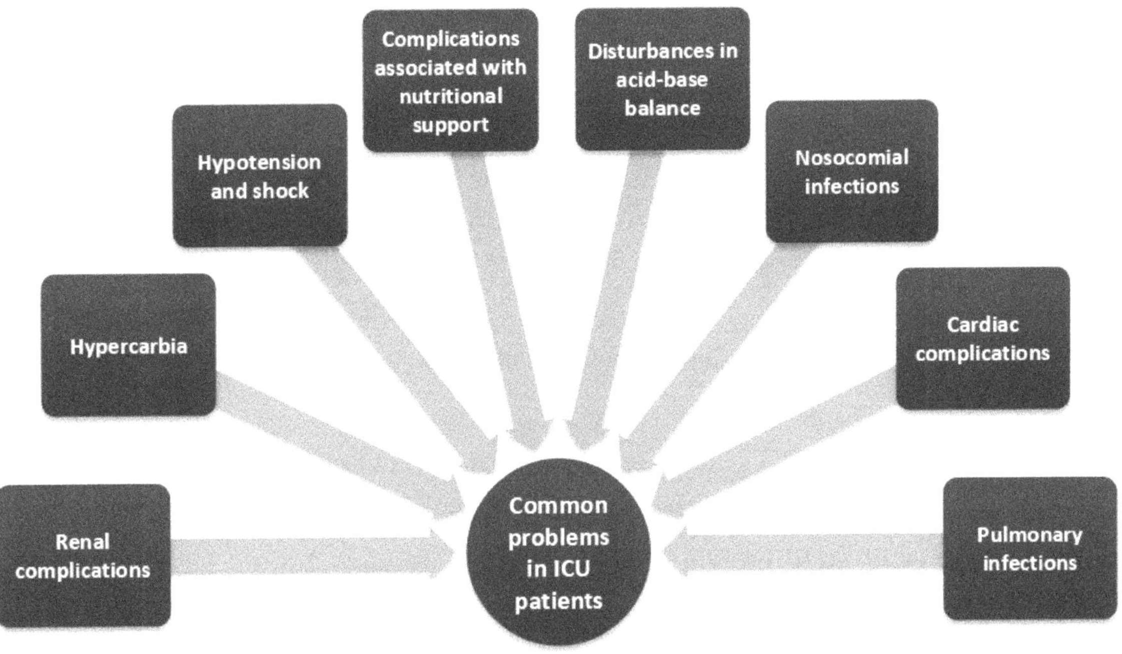

Figure 2.1: Common problems in ICU patients

Pulmonary infections: Acute respiratory failure (ARF), a frequent issue in Intensive Care units (ICUs), is the result of numerous illness conditions. ARF problems can result from techniques employed to support the patient's respiratory system. Intubation, hypoproteinemia, and the administration of wide spectrum intravenously (IV) given antibiotics all contribute to the dangerous and frequently fatal condition known as nosocomial pneumonia. Early ambulation and prophylaxis of low-dose heparin can help prevent pulmonary embolism, a common but challenging to diagnose-ICU issue. Mechanical ventilation complications such as pulmonary barotrauma, including pneumothorax and pneumomediastinum, are quite dangerous. With measures that lower mean airway pressure, such as sedation, modest inflationary pressures, and the lowest potential positive end-expiratory pressure (PEEP), barotrauma can be somewhat avoided [34].

Cardiac complications: Arrhythmia development in the ICU is a frequent issue that results from both the underlying illness of the patient and the ICU's own care. The electrocardiographic characteristics of five typical ICU arrhythmias are illustrated in the section on cardiac problems. Patients with chronic lung disease, ischemic or hypertensive disease, rheumatic heart disease, and other conditions may experience atrial fibrillation (AF). Cardioversion and digoxin are the best treatments for AF patients who are not stable, although digoxin IV followed by optional electrical or chemical cardioversion helps control AF patients who are stable. The causes and treatments of atrial flutter are the same as those of atrial fibrillation [35].

Nosocomial infections: ICU patients are more likely than ward patients to contract nosocomial infection (18.3% versus 6.7%, respectively). The lungs, urinary tract, and bloodstream are the three most typical infection sites, accounting for 85.5% to 90.2% of all infections. Urinary tract infections (UTIs) are more likely to occur with bladder catheterization, breaches in the closed system, unhygienic staff, aging, and deadly illnesses [36].

ICU complications including primary nosocomial bloodstream infections are terrifying. Patients are especially vulnerable if they have IV lines or other blood-stream devices, are on antibiotics, corticosteroids, or hemodialysis, have burns injuries, or neutropenia, or are older or have cutdowns. 50.4% of IV line infections are caused by S. aureus; other gram-negative bacteria have been linked to contaminating the IV infusate itself; and Pseudomonas is often the cause of diseased arterial lines. Bloodstream infections require comprehensive, frequent empiric treatment [36].

Patients with intubations or tracheostomies who are taking antibiotics and have hypoalbuminemia are more likely to develop nosocomial pneumonia. The majority of this pneumonia—50%—are brought on by different gram-negative bacteria, 13.5% by S. aureus, and anaerobes or H. influenza—less frequently. Nosocomial pneumonia typically requires empiric treatment [36].

Renal complications: 3.8% of ICU patients and 11.5% of people who have respiratory failure experience acute renal failure. Septic shock, hypotension, hemorrhagic shock, aminoglycoside therapy, and the consumption of contrast media are the most common causes of renal failure. Aminoglycosides pose a special issue because they are frequently prescribed to individuals who are at risk for renal failure due to other conditions like sepsis or hypotension. Renal failure prevention measures are essential since such ICU patients have a high mortality rate. To avoid sepsis, endotracheal tubes, Foley catheters, and intravenous lines need to be carefully maintained. In order to preserve renal perfusion in all types of shock, intravascular volume must be swiftly restored. In all critically ill patients, gastrointestinal bleeding prevention measures must be implemented [34].

In cases of acute renal failure, dialysis can save lives, but it also comes with a unique set of risks. Hemodialysis side effects include access-related infections, severe electrolyte imbalance, air embolism, muscle spasms, and hemodynamic instability. Organ perforation, ascites, and peritonitis are only a few of the many local issues that peritoneal dialysis is linked to. Metabolic abnormalities, hypotension or hypertension, sepsis, atelectasis or hydrothorax, and protein deficiency are just a few of the systemic issues that might arise during peritoneal dialysis [34].

Disturbances in acid-base balance: Medical treatment in the ICU is directly caused by certain acid-base imbalances. The most typical acid-base imbalance seen in hospitalized patients is metabolic alkalosis. The dangers include steroids, nasogastric suctioning, hypoproteinemia, diuretics, hyperalimentation, and overventilation in patients with documented CO_2 retention (posthypercapnic). Since metabolic alkalosis patients have a death rate of around 65%, the underlying cause must be corrected in addition to treating the condition with hydrochloric acid, acetazolamide, hemodialysis, or ammonium chloride. In the ICU, metabolic acidosis becomes less frequent. However, enteral feedings can result in diarrhea and low serum bicarbonate, and iatrogenic ketoacidosis can happen during hyperalimentation [35].

Complications associated with nutritional support: ICU patients can't eat or absorb nutrition, and doctors don't always pay more attention to their requirement for protein-calorie substitution, which leads to starvation. Lengthy hospital stays and the need for mechanical ventilation are both related to malnutrition in hospital patients. Since malnutrition affects 50.2% of ventilated patients, patient with chronic obstructive pulmonary disorder looks to be especially vulnerable to it. Malnutrition can result in failure to wean, infection, and increased death [34].

However, nutritional replacement itself comes with its own set of issues. Although the enteral route is an efficient delivery technique, it can also result in tube obstruction, aspiration, severe diarrhea, and gram-negative bacterial colonization of the stomach. However, compared to delivery by the parenteral route, metabolic abnormalities are far less common. TPN necessitates meticulous attention to the small elements of everyday care. There are three main categories of TPN problems. (1) Phlebitis, Barotrauma, arrhythmias, etc. can occur as a result of gaining catheter access. (2) Hyperlipidemia, hypolipidemia, ketosis, alterations in vitamin or electrolyte levels, hypoventilation brought on by elevated CO_2 generation, and other metabolic abnormalities. (3) Sepsis affects about 7.2% of TPN patients, and infection is dangerous, frequently occurring consequence [34,35].

Hypotension and shock: When a patient is hospitalized in the Intensive Care unit (ICU), hypotension is frequently one of the common symptoms of an underlying distributive, obstructive, hypovolemic, or cardiogenic shock with a frequency ranging from 47.6% to 72.3%. The typical approach to treating hypotensive episodes focuses on increasing preload, contractility, and/or afterload. The treatment of hypotension can be difficult and complicated due to the diversity of its origins and manifestations [37,38].

Hypotension is linked to acute kidney injury (AKI), myocardial infarction, and death in ICU patients with distributive shock. With increasing hypotension severity and duration, these correlations become stronger. In the overall ICU population, hypotension has also been recognized as a risk factor for AKI [39].

Acute circulatory collapse with insufficient or improperly distributed tissue perfusion leading to generalized cellular hypoxia is referred to as shock. Instead of achieving predetermined hemodynamic targets, circulating blood must satisfy the metabolic needs of the tissues. The best way to tell if there is shock present is to look for signs of decreased end-organ perfusion. An early shock is temporarily compensated for by switching from aerobic metabolism to anaerobic metabolism. As a consequence of this anaerobic metabolism, lactate builds up. Cellular and later tissue necrosis are the end results of hypoxia. Organ failure results from the loss of adequate tissue, and multiple organ failure follows when there is global hypoperfusion. The purpose of resuscitation is to stop the shock from getting worse and to get the circulation back to a point where it can supply the body's tissues with the oxygen they need [40].

Tissue hypoperfusion triggers the activation of compensatory mechanisms. Acute activation of the adrenergic autonomic nervous system. Preload on the heart is increased by venoconstriction; arterial blood pressure is maintained by vasoconstriction of all auxiliary arterial beds; and myocardial contractility is increased. Once the compensatory mechanisms are exhausted or the autonomic nervous system is not able to respond appropriately, hypotension develops [40].

Cardio-surgical critical care unit (ICU) patients who experience shock suffer from a dangerous condition with a high mortality and morbidity rate. The key to reversing the shock state and improving the patient's result is a prompt diagnosis of the underlying disease and treatment interventions. Therefore, the first six hours of treatment are of utmost significance. The phrase "golden hours" is also used to describe this time frame. Though early hemodynamic treatment approaches were achieved, some patients may have suffered multiple organ dysfunction that lasted longer than the first six hours, which makes it ideal to reverse shock at this time. This time frame is sometimes known as "the silver days,"[41].

Patients who are in shock should ideally be recognized at triage and moved to the resuscitation room. High-flow oxygen should be administered to all patients, IV access should be established, and basic monitoring should be implemented (continuous ECG, pulse oximetry, and non-invasive blood pressure) [40].

Hypoxia: Hypoxia is a condition in which the body's tissues do not have access to enough oxygen to maintain healthy homeostasis. This can be caused by either inadequate blood flow to the tissues or low levels of oxygen in the blood (hypoxemia). Acute, chronic, or chronic and acute types of hypoxia can manifest and range in severity from moderate to severe. The body's reaction to hypoxia varies; although some tissues can withstand certain types of hypoxia or ischemia for a longer period of time, other tissues are severely injured by low oxygen levels [42].

Hypoxia is caused by hypoventilation in ICU patients it may be due to: [43]

- Airway obstruction can be distant, as in chronic obstructive pulmonary disease or bronchial asthma, or proximal, as in laryngeal edema or foreign body inhalation (COPD).
- Respiratory drive is impaired, as in coma or profound sedative instances.
- Limited mobility of the chest wall, such as that caused by obesity hypoventilation syndrome, ankylosing spondylitis, large ascites, or circumferential burns.
- Neuromuscular conditions such as phrenic nerve damage, amyotrophic lateral sclerosis, muscular dystrophy, and myasthenia gravis.

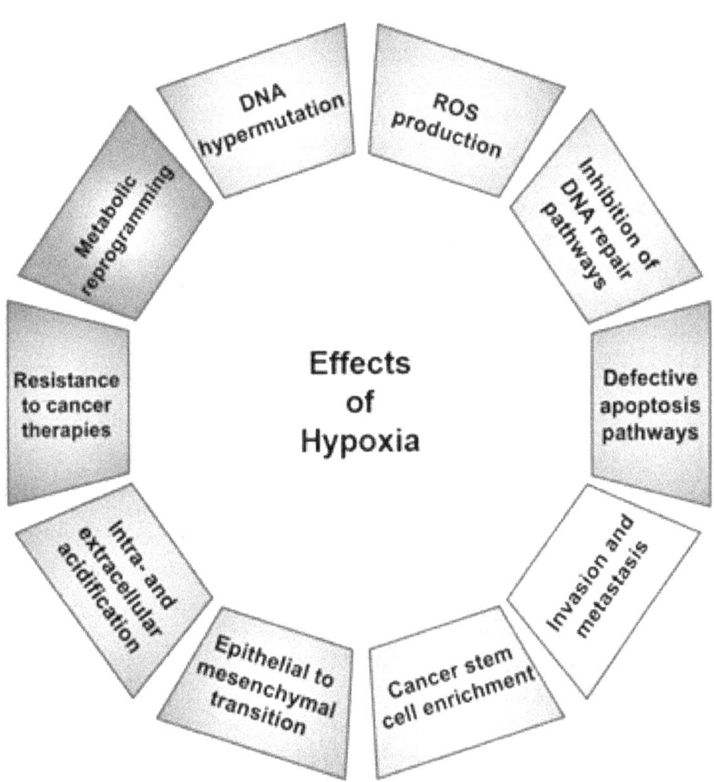

Figure 2.2: Pathological effects of Hypoxia

Hypoventilation comprises elements that lower the alveolar oxygen content, whether as a result of airway obstruction or a rise in the partial pressure of alveolar gases apart from oxygen. One illustration is carbon dioxide. Also, profound drowsiness can decrease respiratory rate, leading to hypoventilation, and ankylosing spondylitis or obese hypoventilation syndrome can limit chest wall motion [42].

In alveoli, an elevation in one gas' partial pressure will come at the expense of all the other gases that make up the air; for example, a rise in carbon dioxide's partial pressure causes a fall in oxygen's partial pressure, both in the alveoli and in the arterial blood. Adding more oxygen is a simple way to treat this kind of hypoxemia [42].

In the treatment of respiratory distress in critically ill patient, mechanical ventilation is a crucial tool. For the treatment of respiratory failure brought on by a variety of clinical diseases, including chronic obstructive pulmonary disease (COPD), acute respiratory distress syndrome (ARDS), sepsis, pneumonia, and asthma, mechanical ventilation is necessary. Although it has the potential to save lives, mechanical ventilation is also known to have a number of hazards and side effects. Hypotension, respiratory distress ("fighting the ventilator"), a resulting rise in airway pressure, ventilator-associated pneumonia (VAP), ARDS, and endotracheal tube issues are only a few of the consequences of mechanical ventilation. One of the main aims of mechanical ventilation is to ensure proper oxygenation. However, patients who are receiving mechanical ventilation frequently have hypoxia events that might have a variety of causes and need to be thoroughly assessed [44,45].

Hypercarbia: A rise in blood carbon dioxide is what defines hypercarbia. Despite the fact that there are numerous causes of hypercarbia, provided the respiratory drive and functioning of lungs are not impaired, the body is typically able to make up for it. When this balancing act fails, respiratory acidosis happens. In order to maintain pH balance, many individuals with chronic hypercarbia brought on by lung illness and adequate renal function will retain larger levels of bicarbonate. The terms hypercapnia and hypercarbia are frequently used interchangeably [46].

Hypercarbia can have a variety of reasons. First, hypoventilation causes insufficient elimination of carbon dioxide from the body. The causes of hypoventilation include inadequate respiratory drive through the depression of the central nervous system (CNS), insufficient respiratory muscle function, and ventilation-perfusion mismatch. Second, an excessive generation of carbon dioxide (CO_2) with insufficient respiratory adjustment. In humans, the final byproduct of metabolism is CO_2. Beyond only being a metabolic waste product, it has a variety of biochemical and physiological impacts. Excess production can occur in severely ill patients for a variety of reasons, including fever, thyroid illness, sepsis, metabolic acidosis, and others [47]. Third, exposure to exogenous carbon dioxide. Insufflation of CO_2 is frequently employed throughout a variety of surgical operations. This can result in hypercarbia and the consequent circulatory problems, despite generally being tolerated well. Fourth, persistent hypercarbia in a pulmonary disease context. This type of ventilation failure frequently develops gradually, giving the kidneys time to compensate [48].

One of the frequent reasons for admitting individuals to Intensive Care is acute respiratory failure. To help with the treatment of respiratory failure, the majority of these patients need mechanical ventilatory support. In the past, blood gases were kept within normal limits via mechanical ventilation. This frequently called for exerting strong inspiratory pressures, which it was later shown aggravated lung damage and respiratory failure. On mechanical ventilation, a technique of lowering inspiratory pressures appeared to lower mortality. Hypercapnic acidosis and hypercapnia development are two outcomes of this breathing method [49,50].

It is unclear how acidosis and hypercapnia affect patients who are critically ill. Some medical professionals think hypercapnic acidosis can guard against lung injury and death on its own, without the need for low-volume ventilation. In fact, they have proposed that critically ill patients with abrupt respiratory failure may benefit from supplementary carbon dioxide (CO_2)-induced hypercapnia [51].

The consequences of severe hypercapnia, as defined by $PCO_2 > 50$ mmHg, were independently related with greater ICU mortality as well as higher comorbidities such as barotrauma, renal failure, and cardiovascular dysfunction in individuals with acute respiratory distress syndrome (ARDS). Gastrointestinal, acute cerebral injury, pulmonary, sepsis, trauma, cardiac, and renal causes of admission to ICU were among the disease criteria of mechanically ventilated patients in which hypercapnic acidosis was also found to be individually linked with higher mortality [52,53].

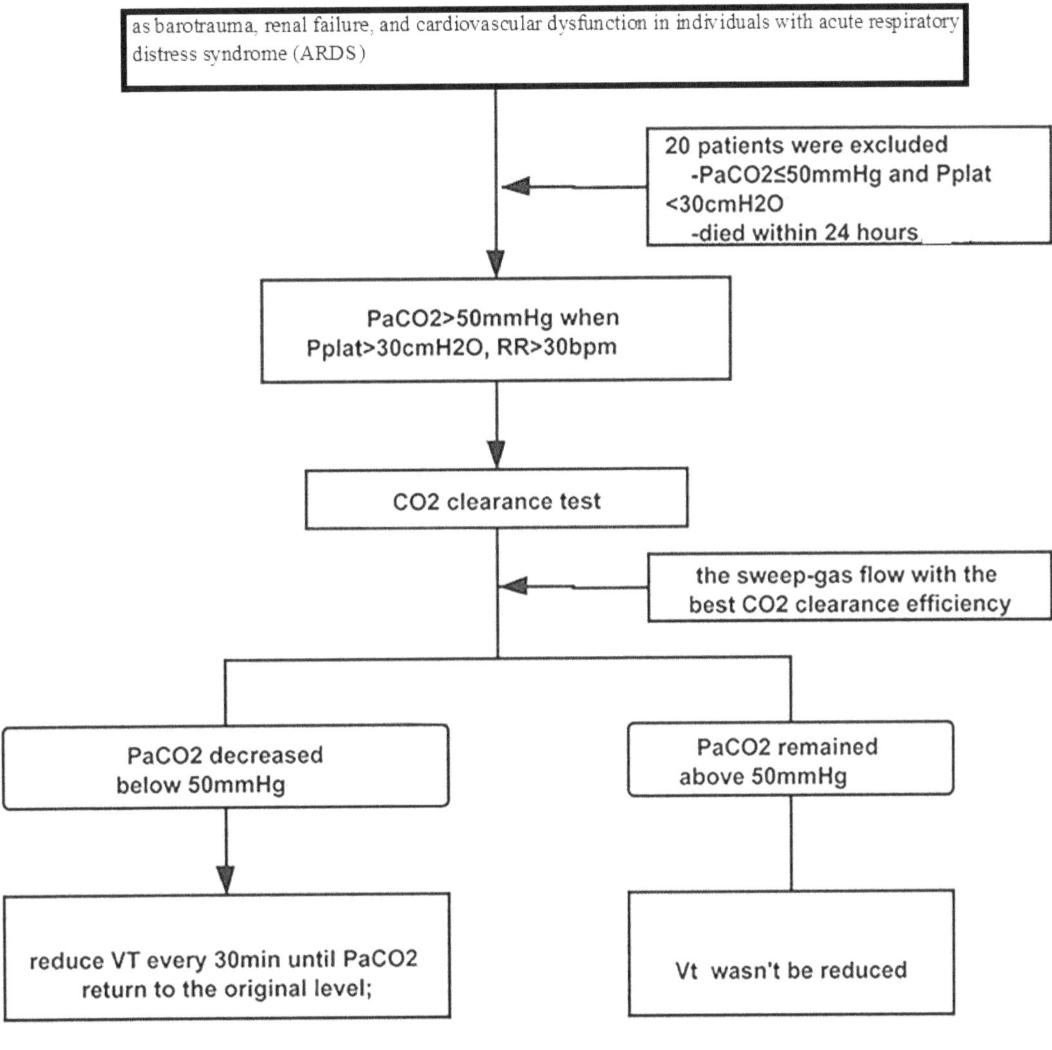

Figure 2.3: Consequences of severe hypercapnia

There are several treatments for hypercapnia that can be used:

As hypoventilation is frequently the cause of hypercarbia, increasing ventilation is the main course of treatment. Non-invasive positive pressure ventilation is the first-line treatment for a patient who is breathing. This is often given by a full-face mask with bilevel positive pressure air settings in hospital settings. If ventilation is delivered effectively, CO2 levels should start to rise within a few minutes to many hours. The next course of action is mechanical ventilation and intubation if non-invasive ventilation is unsuccessful in treating the hypercarbia, the individual is unable to breathe, or if its usage is contraindicated. After this broad treatment with additional ventilation, the root problem can be addressed with further care [53].

Mechanical ventilation: To increase mortality, decreased tidal volume ventilation was effective. This was thought to be caused by both the concomitant hypercapnia with decreased tidal volume ventilation and a decrease in injury to the lung with low tidal volumes. The best mechanical ventilation control should continue to be the principal strategy for preventing or treating hypercapnic acidosis [54].

- Raising the minute ventilation: The care of hypercapnic acidosis may benefit from modifications to the way standard mechanical ventilation is delivered, including optimizing the settings by raising respiratory rate (and minute ventilation) as advised by the ARDS network [55].
- Decrease in dead space ventilation: Hypercapnia is brought on by dead space ventilation, which has also been linked to higher mortality. In individuals with hypercapnic respiratory failure, attempts to decrease physiological dead space are generally easy to execute. Other techniques that could decrease dead space include changing the ventilation circuit [56,58].
- Decrease in physiological dead space: It has been demonstrated that prolonging the end-inspiratory pause will help ARDS patients remove more hypercapnia. A decrease in physiological dead space was the cause of the PCO2 drop. Throughout respiration, CO2 diffusion is time-dependent. Lengthening the end-inspiratory pause extends the time allowed for CO2 removal by alveolar gas exchange [57].

For a separate reason, severe asthma exacerbations are also permitted with permissive hypercarbia. Higher respiratory rates are unable to fully exhale due to bronchospasm, which can result in increasing air entrapment with deteriorating respiratory and hemodynamic effects. Extracorporeal carbon dioxide removal (ECCO2R) is a form of treatment for individuals with severe hypercarbia who are unable to respond to the aforementioned therapies or who are unable to tolerate them. It is a new type of life support that removes carbon dioxide straight from the blood [59,60].

Oliguria: Numerous critically ill patients exhibit oliguria, which was one of the earliest "biomarkers" of acute kidney impairment (AKI). Despite the discovery of numerous new AKI indicators, oliguria is still crucial for clinical purposes. Urinary output (UO) is a component of the diagnostic standards for AKI in all systems. Oliguria is most frequently described as a urine production of less than 0.5 ml/kg over a period of six hours, while other time periods and cut-offs have been documented that range from one to twenty-four hours [61,62].

One must determine if oliguria is the result of a normal physiological reaction or an underlying disease process while examining its genesis. Physiological oliguria can happen for a variety of reasons, such as antidiuresis brought on by hypovolemia, after extended periods of fasting from liquids and food, and during ultra-endurance sports where some athletes have oliguria both during and for a few hours after the event. In addition, post-operative non-critically unwell patients commonly encounter transient oliguria, which is frequently accompanied by vasopressin production and sympathetic nervous system activity because of pain or nausea [62].

However, oliguria can develop in critically unwell patients through a variety of pathophysiological routes. First, there is the neuro-hormonal pathway that affects kidney function by stimulating the sympathetic nervous system, which in turn causes the renin-angiotensin-aldosterone system (RAAS) to operate more actively, vasopressin levels to start rising, and the tubuloglomerular feedback system (TGF) to become active. This causes sodium and water retention, decreased renal filtration, and systemic vasoconstriction [63].

Reduced renal blood flow may result from both relative (hemodynamic disturbances) and absolute (hypovolemia) decreases in effective blood volume (RBF). However, a decrease in glomerular filtration rate is rarely caused by this fall in RBF alone (GFR) [63].

Management of oliguria is a stepwise approach:

- Hemodynamic stabilization (1): In order to get sufficient renal blood flow in an oliguric individual, hypovolemia must first be ruled out and treated, albeit caution should be exercised to prevent volume overload. It is best to stay away from starches because they can harm osmotic tubules. Balanced crystalloids are preferred when a substantial fluid volume is required for fluid resuscitation. UO should be kept an eye on when a patient starts to get oliguria. Hourly urine screening is not just doable in ICU patients, who frequently have catheters, but it should also be done on normal wards [65].
- Response to furosemide stress and diuretics (2a): The responsiveness to diuretics may be assessed if the patient is still oliguric after obtaining the proper volume and hemodynamic condition. Although diuretics are currently regularly administered to oliguric patients, a systematic method should be adopted to maximize their diagnostic efficacy [66].

  Predicting which patients may advance to a greater stage/severity of illness is a frequent challenge while managing patients who are either at risk or who have AKI. The furosemide stress test (FST), a standardized evaluation of the functional integrity of the tubule, is a tool that can be used for risk stratification. It goes without saying that it's crucial to carefully monitor the patient's heart rate and blood pressure throughout an FST to ensure that they are not hypovolemic. Additionally, the FST may prove to be a helpful tool for decision-making when starting renal replacement therapy (RRT) [67].

- Biomarkers (2b): To determine the likelihood that AKI is the underlying cause of oliguria and to direct the best therapeutic course of action, biomarkers may be employed [68].
- AKI (4): Oliguria patients should generally follow the treatment recommendations for AKI. Nephrotoxic medications should be stopped for individuals who are at high risk of AKI, and the status of volume and (renal) perfusion pressures should be controlled and closely watched, possibly through invasive monitoring [69].
- Management of volume overload (5): Peripheral edema and a rise in the central venous pressure (CVP), which is measured sonographically by the vena cava inferior diameter, are two potential symptoms of fluid overload. Diuretics may be administered to patients who respond to them in order to maintain fluid balance and prevent volume overload [70].

Diarrhea: Between 2.5% and 95.7% of critically ill individuals have been observed to experience diarrhea. This large range results from the absence of an Intensive Care unit-wide definition (ICU). It might be challenging to distinguish between changes in stool consistency or frequency and genuine diarrhea (the passing of much more than three watery bowel motions every 24 hours) (eg, looser stools). What is deemed to be "a normal bowel habit" also varies greatly, ranging from 2 to 3 bowel movements each day to three bowel movements each week. It is difficult to characterize diarrhea and to determine what might be "abnormal" in the ICU setting because of this "normal fluctuation" [71,72].

Diarrhoea is defined by the WHO as passing 3 or even more watery stools per day. Although this concept is straightforward and easy to use at the bedside, in actual ICU practise, physicians hardly ever use it. The quantity of stools is not always a reliable predictor of colonic transit time, according to a critique of the WHO definition. In critically ill patients, enteral nutrition, prokinetics, antifungal medication, and antibiotics may increase the risk of diarrhoea. Enteral nutrition is frequently blamed for diarrhoea when there is weak evidence to inform ICU clinicians of other probable aetiologies; feeds are thus stopped. Although enteral nutrition is the recommended form of nutrition supply in the ICU, needless feeding interruptions may increase protein and calorie deficiencies if diarrhoea is mistakenly thought to be related to enteral nutrition [72,73]

There are numerous other potential causes of diarrhoea than feeding, which is frequently blamed for it. [74,75]

- The lack of fiber in formulas for tube feedings, drugs
- physiological effects of stress or the critical illness itself, and others.
- Changes in gut flora resulting from the use of antibiotics decreased gut motility, and antacids.
- Medications (mainly that contain magnesium and sorbitol).

Diarrhea can make a patient more uncomfortable, harm their skin, and take up valuable nursing time. In addition, diarrhea increases the chance of faecal contamination of surrounding wounds or central venous catheters that have been implanted through the femur. Along with the financial implications that diarrhoea has on staffing personnel and the usage of commodities like linen, such illnesses may increase hospital costs. The adjustments needed to care for an unstable patient who has diarrhoea are the most serious because they can result in a life-threatening episode of instability. Constipation in Intensive Care unit (ICU) patients may lengthen the length of time spent in the ICU and contribute to issues like eating intolerance and difficulties weaning ventilation [76,77].

Management: When healthy people switch to an enteral diet exclusively, considerable bowel function alterations take place. Studies indicating that those taking enteral tube feeding (ETF) have an aberrant gastrointestinal function, such as diarrhea, support this. As a result, understanding tube feeding formulae is crucial while creating an EN plan [78].

- EN formula: Patients who are fed through an enteral tube most usually use polymeric formulations. These recipes include nonhydrolyzed versions of the macronutrients protein, lipids, and carbohydrates [78].

  The primary macronutrient in the majority of enteral formulae is carbohydrates, which can be obtained from sources such as corn syrup solids, maltodextrin, and hydrolyzed cornflour. Although these formulae often don't contain gluten or lactose, they sometimes do. Patients with chronic diarrhoea, pancreatic illness, or other malabsorptive disorders may want to investigate peptide formulations. Long-chain fatty acids and medium-chain triglycerides are the two forms of fat available (MCTs) [78].

- Formulas based on fibre: Diarrhea can be less frequent when enteral formulations with fibre are used. Humans do not digest fibre; instead, it ferments in the colon and is categorised as either soluble or insoluble. While soluble fibre absorbs water and makes stool soft, insoluble fibre works as a bulking agent that speed up the rate at which the stool travels through the intestines. Blends of soluble and insoluble fibres are frequently used in enteral formulations. According to reports, these mixtures promote the production of stool and faecal short-chain fatty acid contents. Prebiotic fibres, most frequently inulin, oligofructose, and fructooligosaccharides have been added to some feeding formulae [78].

- Feed delivery: Continuous feeding is the recommended method for EN delivery in critically ill patients since it allows for a lower feed rate. Even though the feed rate has been linked to diarrhoea, an observational research conducted in Spain found no connection between the feed rate or osmolality and the condition. Continuous feeding can limit delivery to 50%–60% of the specified volume since interruptions are frequently seen in critical care settings, which can affect how adequate the feeding is. Bolus or intermittent feeding can be employed to create free feeding periods. As a result of intermittent or bolus eating, nutrition goals are attained more quickly and without experiencing any changes in bowel habits like diarrhoea. This form of feeding is often only used for medically stable patients who have feeding tubes that terminate in the stomach [78].

Delirium and agitation: Delirium is defined as a sudden shift in mental state or a mood swing that is accompanied by changed levels of consciousness, disorganised thinking, and impaired awareness. It's sometimes described as a severe state of confusion. Most instances of delirium start out suddenly, especially in the Intensive Care unit.

The American Association of Retired Persons commissioned an executive summary on potentially preventable injuries, which identified delirium as one of the six main reasons for injuries correlated with hospitalisation in patients over 65 years of age. Delirium is a common expression of acute brain dysfunction in critically sick patients and is associated with poor short-term outcomes as well as the potential for unfavourable consequences years after ICU discharge [79,80].

Despite delirium's high incidence in the ICU, doctors sometimes overlook it or mistake its symptoms for depression, dementia, or ICU syndrome. According on psychomotor behaviour, delirium can be divided into subgroups, and the high incidence of hypoactive delirium among critically ill patients likely plays a role in physicians' failure to recognise delirium. Reduced responsiveness, disengagement, and apathy are characteristics of hypoactive delirium, whereas restlessness, agitation, and emotional instability are characteristics of hyperactive delirium [81].

In the therapeutic environment, a variety of pharmaceutical medications are used to treat delirium, including steroids, statins, antipsychotics, benzodiazepines, melatonin, opioids, and dexmedetomidine. Non-pharmacological interventions are those that don't include any sort of therapeutic medical intervention. Non-pharmacological therapies include physical therapy (mobilization), occupational therapy, sleep promotion therapy (sound and light sleep therapy), cognitive rehabilitation, and family participation. Non-pharmacological interventions try to prevent or minimise delirium [82,83]

After a critical illness, cognitive deficits are widespread, and individuals who have delirium do poorly cognitively once they are discharged. This impairment is still there after a year and is on par in severity with mild traumatic brain injury patients. Symptoms of psychological distress are frequently felt following serious sickness. Despite the fact that depressive symptoms are common following a critical illness, it is still not entirely known how delirium is related. Even a year following discharge, physical function is frequently diminished as assessed by daily living activities (ADL). A definite dosage response exists, with prolonged delirium time resulting in lower function [84,85].

A psychomotor disorder called agitation is defined by a significant increase in both physical and psychological activity, which is frequently followed by a lack of control over actions and a disorganized state of mind. Delirium and anxiety, two conditions that frequently occur in the Intensive Care unit (ICU), are the root cause of this issue. As a result, it occurs frequently in the ICU setting, especially in older patients, and may be brought on by a variety of internal (metabolic diseases, drugs, encephalopathy associated with sepsis, etc.) as well as external (environmental variables) reasons (discomfort, noise, pain, and so on). In the ICU, agitation itself may be harmful since it can affect patient care, increase metabolic demands, and ultimately increase morbidity and death [86,87].

In addition to agitation, the ICU may also experience a number of mental problems, such as delirium, and anxiety. It is currently unknown if these mental states represent a range in the seriousness of the cerebral damage or whether they convey different varieties of brain malfunction. Anxiety is a generalised feeling of fear that is unrelated to a genuine external threat. Due to the multiple stressful scenarios that take place in this environment, this sensation is anticipated to happen in the ICU [88,89].

These symptoms must be thoroughly examined and diagnosed before agitation, anxiety, or delirium in the ICU is treated. In order to determine whether there is a connection between the now observed and the patient's pre-existing mental state, the physician must first be aware of it. The patient's current mental state is objectively assessed in the second phase [86].

In order to prevent mild anxiety in ICU patients, non-pharmacological treatment must be prioritized. Examples of non-pharmacological treatment include reassurance, a comfortable bed position, voiding a painfully full bladder, and so on [88].

First, all potential causes of the mental disease (hypoglycemia, hyponatremia, etc.) must be addressed before beginning symptomatic medication treatment. Second, it is important to keep in mind that certain medications that are frequently used to treat agitation (such as benzodiazepines) may, on their own, result in or exacerbate psychological or cognitive disorders. Third, in order to select the right medication, the treatment's goals (such as easing discomfort, lowering anxiety, improving sleep rhythm, managing delirium, etc.) must be well specified. Fourth, in order to prevent the risks of both under- and over-sedation, the amount of sedative as well as the therapeutic goal whenever a delirious person is managed must be strictly adjusted and frequently checked by objective criteria (scores and scales) [88,89].

Drowsiness: For the body and mind to regenerate, sleep is essential. Physiological rest is produced by nocturnal sleep, which causes the nervous system to slow down and the muscles to regenerate. Patients with sleep difficulties do not experience this regeneration, which leaves them with cognitive deficiencies and physical exhaustion. Noise, discomfort, pain, medication given in the Intensive Care setting, and the kind of mechanical ventilation have an impact on the nocturnal sleep of ICU patients. Since sleep evaluation is inherently subjective, it might be challenging to carry out in an Intensive Care unit. Due to speech difficulties, patients are unable to give accurate descriptions of their perceived level of rest and the things that bother them the most [90,91].

The term "sleep disturbance" refers to perceived or actual changes in overnight sleep (including quantity and quality), which are followed by impairment in the following day. Even though sleep disturbances might be sudden and short-lived, they frequently happen repeatedly. It is well established that poor sleep quality and disturbance lower cognitive function and quality of life (QOL). In addition, insomnia can make sadness, anxiety, and discomfort worse. ICU patients' sleep is characterized by interrupted nocturnal sleep, ineffective sleep, and protracted sleep onset (sleep latency). ICU patients' sleep cycles are said to be brief, frequently interrupted by arousals, and equally spaced out throughout the day and night [92].

A significant portion of ICU patients have trouble falling or staying asleep, have a lengthy sleep latency, and wake up frequently, all of which add to their physical and mental discomfort. More than 50% of ICU survivors continued to have worse disturbed sleep or disrupted sleep patterns several months after leaving the hospital compared to their pre-hospital patterns [93].

Critically ill individuals may experience sleep abnormalities as a result of underlying injury or sickness, underlying primary sleep problems, therapeutic/diagnostic procedures, and environmental factors. Existing sleep disorders can make ICU-related sleep disturbances worse. On the other hand, several sleep problems might result from underlying medical conditions[94].

Sleep disturbance is a result of therapeutic interventions and diagnostic procedures that are required (such as drugs and surgery), as well as their side effects (such as drowsiness and discomfort). It is crucial to take drug use into account as a factor in critically ill patients' disturbed sleep. Analgesic and sedative combinations that are used to support mechanical breathing are the most often prescribed drugs that affect sleep. Numerous sleep disorders have also been linked to the use of gastric protection, cardiovascular, antidepressant, anti-infective, and anticonvulsant medications [94].

Dyssynchrony breathing, sedation, ventilation mode, discomfort from the endotracheal tube, and stress resulting from communication hurdles can all further impair sleep in ventilated patients. Careful consideration of sedative medications and mechanical ventilation techniques are among the steps taken to increase comfort, quantity, and quality of sleep. Sleep disturbances in critically sick patients are caused by environmental factors such as activities encountered in patient care, diagnostic tests, and the absence of nocturnal cues. According to patient reports, noise disrupts sleep, particularly conversational noise, but also noise from ventilators, television, alarms, phones, and beepers [95].

A thorough examination of each patient's medication regimen and its effects on sleep is the first step in the pharmacological therapy of sleep disturbance in the Intensive Care unit. Many ICU patients are given drugs to sustain blood pressure, increase cardiac and/or urine output, or improve oxygen supply in general. These substances can have a negative impact on sleep-wake cycles because they work through a number of neurotransmitter pathways, modulators, and receptors that are linked to alterations in cortical activation. Therefore, it is important to stop taking any sleep-disrupting medications that were begun in the ICU as soon as possible. A medication dose decrease may be necessary for sedatives and analgesics to increase the quantity and quality of sleep [96].

Although frequently recommended for the management of sleep disorders, benzodiazepines change the architecture of sleep. Because of its beneficial therapeutic profile— no active metabolites, a short half-life, water solubility, and availability intravenously or subcutaneously—midazolam, a short-acting benzodiazepine, is frequently used within ICUs for procedural sedation and sedatives of ventilated patients [97].

Environmental measures, alternative therapies, and cognitive-behavioral interventions can all be considered as non-pharmacologic methods for enhancing sleep. Cognitive therapy seeks to lessen dysfunctional attitudes and beliefs that interfere with the start and maintenance of sleep. The promotion of sleep in critically ill individuals can be helped by nurse-driven interventions like as music, massage, therapeutic touch, and relaxation. The majority of environmental sleep disruption therapies focus on diurnal illumination, habits, and arranging an uninterrupted time for a good sleep in addition to noise suppression or filtration [97].

Paralytic ileus: The term "paralytic ileus" refers to a situation in which the myenteric (Auerbach's) and submucous (Meissner's) plexus experience neuromuscular failure, resulting in motor function paralysis of the digestive system. Due to a functional obstruction caused by the gut's inability to transfer peristaltic waves, liquids and gas can accumulate inside the intestine. The stomach and colon may also be affected, however, the small intestine is more commonly impacted. The resulting stasis causes the colon to fill with fluid and gas, which causes distension, a reduction in bowel sounds, vomiting, and complete constipation [98,99].

Disorders of gastrointestinal (GI) movement are frequent side effects of serious illness. A complicated combination of neurohormonal stimulus and feedback including several hormones and peptides controls GI motility. Sedation, anticholinergics, analgesics, immobilization, enteral feeding, surgery, spinal and head traumas, inflammatory processes, and sepsis can all affect GI motility in the critical care unit. Constipation, stomach distension, discomfort, vomiting, and nausea are some of the symptoms of hypomotility diseases of the GI tract, which can also lead to morbidities such as food intolerance, insufficient nutrient, and medicine absorption, and longer hospital stays. Irregularities in gut transit (IGT) are frequently described as ileus or constipation, however, these labels do not fully describe all GI tract issues that might result in impaired transit [100].

For critically ill patients, the best pharmaceutical regimen for the treatment and prevention of constipation has not yet been identified. There are various sorts of laxatives that can be utilized, but each has drawbacks. Sodium phosphate, magnesium hydroxide, and magnesium citrate are examples of saline laxatives (also known as osmotic's). Saline laxatives may result in volume overload and electrolyte imbalances in patients who have renal impairment or cardiac dysfunction because of salt, magnesium, or phosphorus absorption. Poorly absorbed sugars like lactulose, polyethylene glycol, and sorbitol are examples of other osmotic laxatives. Constipation in severely unwell individuals has been linked to dehydration. Osmotic laxatives can impair hemodynamic status in individuals who already have intravascular fluid depletion because they work by pulling fluid into the gastrointestinal system and potentially reducing intravascular volume [101].

Coagulopathy: Coagulopathies are frequent in critically sick patients, and if recognized early on and managed in a goal-directed, risk-adjusted way, associated consequences may be avoided. A key component of patient blood management is optimizing hemostasis to reduce blood loss, which has a substantial impact on mortality and morbidity. Being a predictor of both the requirement for major blood transfusions and mortality, coagulation disorders frequently occur or develop in Intensive Care unit patients that a critical care physician must manage [102]. These deviations can be as straightforward as isolated thrombocytopenia or as intricate as multisystem coagulation disorders. One of the most important management techniques for preventing any procedure or perioperative bleeding in critically unwell patients is monitoring bleeding risk. Critically ill patients are more likely to bleed for a wide range of reasons such as underlying health diseases like liver or kidney disease, concurrent anticoagulant medicines, poor platelet function, factor deficits, and factor inhibitors [103,104].

When the coagulopathy is undifferentiated or attributable to conditions like sepsis and DIC, fresh frozen plasma (FFP) can be used to treat the factor deficits. When it is known that a specific factor insufficiency and/or an anticoagulant are the cause of the coagulopathy, factor concentrates are employed. In a patient who needs volume resuscitation in addition to several other treatments to treat coagulopathy, plasma transfusion might be helpful. It's crucial to keep these patients' temperatures at 35°C, ionized calcium concentrations over 1.1 mmol/L, and pH levels above 7.25. To enhance the distribution of blood components (packed blood cells, packed blood cells, fresh frozen plasma in set ratios, along with cryoprecipitate if the fibrinogen is 2.0 g/L), one must also activate a systematic transfusion therapy with a local large transfusion procedure [105,106].

Arrhythmias and chest pain: Arrhythmias are a common issue that intensivists deal with. They are a significant cause of morbidity and prolonged hospital stays. The vast majority of individuals with structural cardiac disease are at risk for arrhythmias. An insult such as infection, hypoxia, cardiac ischemia, an excess of catecholamines (exogenous or endogenous), or electrolyte abnormalities may be the cause of an arrhythmia in a particular patient. Correction of these abnormalities is part of management, along with medical treatment aimed at the arrhythmia itself. Arrhythmias' physiological effects are influenced by the basic cardiac function as well as their ventricular response rate and length [107].

In individuals with remarkably constant stroke volumes, bradyarrhythmias may reduce cardiac output attributable to heart rate alone, and loss of an atrial kick may result in a massive rise in pulmonary pressures in individuals with diastolic dysfunction. Similar to this, tachyarrhythmias can cause myocardial ischemia as well as hypotension by decreasing diastolic filling and cardiac output. It is obvious that the patient's heart function and physiology determine the effect of a particular arrhythmia in a certain circumstance. Similarly to this, the emergency and treatment type is decided by both the underlying heart condition and the physiological consequence of the arrhythmia [107].

Everyone agrees that bystander first assistance, defibrillation, and advanced life assistance are crucial for patients who experience cardiac arrest owing to ventricular tachyarrhythmias to have a positive neurologic prognosis. Only when (1) early warning signs are identified, (2) the emergency medical services system is activated, (3) basic cardiopulmonary resuscitation, (4) defibrillation, (5) management of the respiratory system and ventilation, and (6) intravenous drug administration happens as quickly as possible can be the best survival rate from cardiac arrest be achieved. The best method for treating ventricular fibrillation seems to be open-access defibrillation, which places automated exterior defibrillators in the control of trained laypeople [108].

A considerable rise in life expectancies has been linked to the use of automated exterior defibrillators by basic life support ambulance personnel or first responders in early defibrillation programs. Patients in Intensive Care units were advised to take medications like sotalol, lidocaine, procainamide, amiodarone, or magnesium to treat ventricular tachyarrhythmias. Amiodarone appears to be more effective than other antiarrhythmic medications for treating a variety of cardiac arrhythmias, including atrial fibrillation and malignant ventricular tachyarrhythmias [108].

A frequent complaint, chest pain can have a wide range of potential causes, some of which can be fatal. Visceral pain frequently exhibits a hazy distribution pattern, making it difficult for the patient to pinpoint where the pain is located. For instance, ischemic heart discomfort can occur in the left or right shoulder, mouth, or left arm. Visceral discomfort may also manifest as signs of vomiting and nausea. Chest discomfort is the second most frequent complaint in the emergency room and accounts for about 5% of all visits. Always take into account potentially fatal causes of chest pain, such as pneumothorax, acute coronary syndrome, pulmonary embolism, and aortic dissection, when examining a patient for chest pain [109].

Tachypnea: Breathing too quickly is referred to as tachypnea. An average adult should breathe between 12 and 20 times each minute. A child's resting respirations might occur at a rate higher than those of adults. There may not always be a pathogenic cause for tachypnea. Tachypnea, for instance, can result from exertion. Sepsis, diabetic ketoacidosis, and respiratory conditions such as carbon monoxide poisoning, pneumonia, pleural effusion, pulmonary embolism, chronic obstructive pulmonary disease, or asthma are some pathogenic reasons for tachypnea (COPD). Tachypnea can also be brought on by other medical conditions such as allergies, anxiety, and aspiration to foreign bodies [110].

The root cause of tachypnea should indeed be addressed while treating it. Infants who arrive owing to a newborn's temporary tachypnea can be treated with supplemental oxygen, and in some circumstances, they might need to spend a while in the neonatal critical care unit. Patients may be given an inhalation medication to dilate and widen the alveoli in obstructive lung disease if the tachypnea is brought on by asthma or COPD. If pneumonia is the cause of tachypnea, antibiotics should be taken to treat bacterial pneumonia; however, viral pneumonia can be managed supportively without the use of antibiotics [111,112].

Fever: One of the most crucial vital signs for all patients, including those in Intensive Care units, is temperature (ICU). In the Intensive Care unit, fever or hypothermia frequently require further physical assessments, investigations, and therapy modifications. According to the American College of Critical Care Medicine, a single temperature of 101 degrees Fahrenheit or 38.3 degrees Celsius is considered a fever in an ICU patient (ACCCM). Rarely occurring in acute care settings, hyperpyrexia or hyperthermia is a temperature of more than 105.8 degrees F (or 41 degrees C) [113]. Different definition for immuno competant and immuncompromised

Either an infectious or non-infectious cause could be the cause. In the ICU, infections are the main cause of fever episodes. Ventilator-associated pneumonia, surgical site infections, catheter-related bloodstream infections, catheter-related urinary tract infections, and bacteremias of many origins, including the aforementioned causes, are examples of common infectious causes [114].

Management: Patients who have suspected illnesses should begin empirical antibiotic therapy after receiving the necessary cultures. When sepsis is detected, antibiotics must be started as soon as possible, particularly in cases of septic shock. The right dosage of antibiotics must be administered for the right amount of time. Source management needs to be implemented right away after finding the infection's source. This covers the removal of intravascular devices, urinary catheters, and the drainage of empyemas and abscesses [115]..

Antipyretics lower the hypothalamic thresholds for controlling body temperature, hence lowering body temperature. According to research, fever reduces the growth of bacteria, boosts cytokine secretion, and activates macrophages, neutrophils, and T cells in infected patients. Fever, however, can have some negative consequences. There is evidence that it raises metabolism and consequently oxygen consumption. It has been demonstrated that lowering the temperature will lower lactate concentrations in septic individuals. It is unknown if the expense of pyrexia is related to adverse results. Furthermore, it is without a shadow of a doubt that fever raises mortality in brain damage. For controlling the temperature in the ICU, the majority of physicians favor acetaminophen over aspirin. The enteral/oral route is preferable over the intravenous formulation because of the superior absorption of enteral acetaminophen unless the enteral route is a contraindication [116].

Infection control practices:

Healthcare professionals and patients alike should be extremely concerned about hospital-acquired infections (HAIs). By eliminating such infections, efforts must be made in making hospitals as safe as feasible, taking into account mortality, morbidity, lengthening the duration of stay, and expense [185].

General measures in controlling infections:

Isolation: the ICU patients are screened for infections like Neutropenia and immunological disorder, Skin rashes, Diarrhea, Known carriers of an epidemic strain of bacterium, and Known communicable disease [186].

There are two types of isolation: [187]

- Protective isolation: preventing opportunistic infections in immunocompromised or neutropenic individuals through protective isolation
- Source isolation: To reduce the risk of infection spreading to other patients or personnel, colonized or infected individuals should be isolated at the source.

Hand hygiene: The single most efficient way to stop the horizontal transmission of illnesses among hospitalized patients and medical staff is "hand cleanliness," which is the most frequent method of organism transmission [187].

Five moments of hand hygiene by the world health organization- when and why to follow: [187]

- Before handling patients: in order to protect the patient from harmful micro-organisms through your hands.
- Before the aseptic process: to protect the patients from micro-organisms including the patient's own.
- Following exposure to body fluids: in order to protect yourself and the environment of the health care facility from infectious organisms.
- As soon as the patients are touched: in order to protect yourself and the environment of the health care facility from infectious organisms.

Follow standard precautions: Regardless of a patient's illness condition, standard precautions include appropriate preventive actions to be used at all times [187]

- Gloves: When handling mucous membranes, and non-intact skin, and when conducting sterile operations including artery, central line, and Foley catheter placement, sterile gloves should be used after completing hand hygiene.
- Gown: Wear a gown during procedures that could result in splashes of blood, bodily fluids, secretions, or excretions to avoid soiling of clothes and skin. Only aseptic procedures necessitate the use of the sterile gown; otherwise, a clean, non-sterile gown will do.
- Mask, eye protection/face shield: When performing procedures or providing patient care that could result in sprays or splashes of blood, body fluids, etc., cover your eyes, nose, and mouth by using a mask, appropriate eye protection (eyeglasses are not sufficient), or a face shield.

Airborne precautions: [187]

- Disease-causing bacteria, such as Mycobacterium tuberculosis (pulmonary/laryngeal), herpes zoster (shingles), varicella zoster virus (chickenpox), rubella virus, and measles, can be suspended in the air as microscopic particles, aerosol, or dust and continue to be contagious over time and space.
- Utilize negative-pressure ventilation to isolate.
- Entering the isolation chamber requires wearing respiratory protection.
- Usage of a disposable N-95 respirator mask, which snugly encloses the mouth and nose to provide protection from both big and small droplets of liquid. Everyone who enters the room, including visitors, must wear this.

Droplet precautions: [187]

- Isolation is necessary.
- Usage of a disposable N-95 respirator mask, which snugly encloses the mouth and nose to provide protection from both big and small droplets of liquid. Everyone who enters the room, including visitors, must wear this.
- Limit the patient's transportation.

Use of certain tactics targeted at preventing particular nosocomial illnesses: [188]

The prevention of certain nosocomial infections in critically ill patients is the focus of numerous techniques in addition to the usual and transmission-based precautions. The most significant of these are catheter-related bloodstream infections (CRBSI), ventilator-associated pneumonia (VAP), and urinary tract infections (UTIs).

Modern trends in treating VAP: The term "VAP" refers to a parenchymal lung infection that manifests itself either when a patient is receiving mechanical ventilation or within 48 hours of that treatment ceasing. About 11% to 21% of patients who received more than 48 hours of mechanical ventilation experience the development of VAP, which has been regarded as the main cause of nosocomial infection in the ICU. The VAP has also been linked to higher morbidity, longer periods requiring mechanical breathing, longer stays in the Intensive Care unit, and higher hospital expenses [189,188]

The difficulty in diagnosing VAP and the potential negative effects on health and finances make preventative initiatives necessary. A "ventilator bundle" suggested by the Institute for Health care Improvement includes a number of these tactics (IHI). Stress ulcer prophylaxis,thromboembolism prophylaxis, daily sedative interruption, and daily assessment of patients' readiness to wean from mechanical breathing were all part of the initial ventilator bundle that IHI suggested in 2004. IHI launched a further treatment in May 2010 called daily chlorhexidine oral care [188,190]

The systematic review found that it was unclear whether a 45-degree bed head elevation was beneficial or detrimental in terms of the incidence of clinically suspected or microbiologically confirmed VAP, in contrast to the meta-analysis, which found that patients positioned semirecumbently at 45-degree had a markedly decreased frequency of clinically diagnosed Ventilator - associated pneumonia in comparison to supinely positioned patients. The period of mechanical ventilators has been shown to reduce with everyday sedation breaks and extubation readiness assessments, theoretically lowering the risk of VAP [191].

A silver-coated endotracheal tube, subglottic secretion drainage (SSD), the material used for the endotracheal tube cuff, continuous lateral rotation therapy (CLRT), cuff pressure monitoring, saline instillation before endotracheal suctioning, positive end-expiratory pressure (PEEP), tracheostomy, multimodality chest physiotherapy, and position of patient during transportation are additional methods to prevent VAPs [188].

Modern Trends in Prevention of CLABSI:

CLABSI is defined by the CDC NHSN as the recovery of a pathogen from a blood culture in a person who had a central line at the time of the infection or during the 48-hour window prior to the positive blood culture, and there was no indication of infection at another site. The length of hospital stays is longer when there are CLABSIs [192].

The Keystone study, which was published in 2006, demonstrated that adoption of a standardized CLABSI preventive bundle might significantly lower CLABSI rates throughout the whole state of Michigan. Since then, the majority of hospitals have started using this set of five interventions, which consists of HH, maximum barrier precautions during insertion, chlorhexidine skin antisepsis, selecting the best catheter placement, and daily line necessity reviews with fast removal of unneeded lines [193].

There are other additional interventions that can be used to lower CLABSI rates, but for the time being, the CDC only advises using them in environments where the rates are unacceptably high. Despite the use of the CLABSI prevention bundle, CLASBI rates still exist. The use of dressings made of chlorhexidine-impregnated sponges, daily washing with chlorhexidine,anti-infective lock therapy are some of these approaches, and antimicrobial-coated central venous catheters [188].

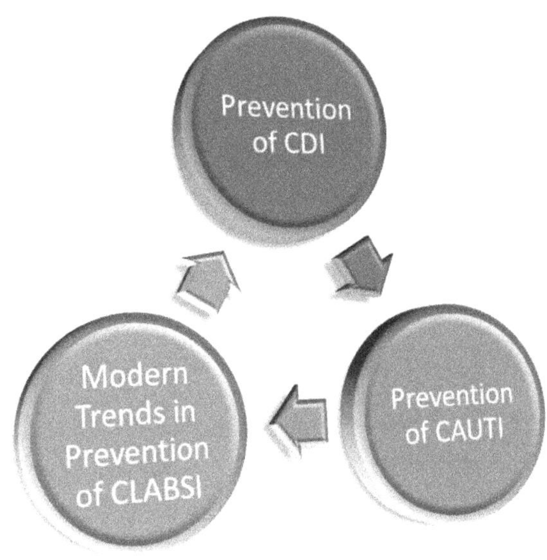

Figure 2.4: Modern Trends in Prevention of CLABSI

Prevention of CAUTI:

The most frequent HAI, accounting for 42.5% of all nosocomial infections, is a urinary tract infection (UTI). In medical and surgical ICUs, it accounts for 2.43% of nosocomial infections and is virtually invariably connected to an indwelling urine catheter. The CAUTIs are linked to longer hospital stays and higher healthcare expenses. Several recommendations have been made for preventing CAUTIs. These recommendations include reducing the use of urinary catheters while taking into account alternatives to indwelling catheters, maintaining a closed drainage system, and early catheter removal, inserting catheters aseptically [194,195]

Prevention of CDI:

The CDI is the most prevalent type of nosocomial infectious diarrhea and is linked to higher rates of mortality, longer stays in Intensive Care units, and higher costs. Older age, the use of proton pump inhibitors, recent hospitalization, antibiotics, chemotherapy, numerous comorbid conditions, the use of glucocorticoids, HIV, patients on hemodialysis, abdominal surgery, inflammatory bowel diseases, and the use of enemas are risk factors related with CDI. The proliferation of a particular C difficile strain appears to be responsible for the rising incidence of CDI [196].

The main sources of patient encounter to C difficile in hospitals are contaminated environments and the hands of health care providers. Adequate implementation of infection control measures is essential for avoiding this spread. In respect to HH, there is proof that washing with water and soap is more effective than alcohol-based products in eliminating C. difficile spores since alcohol is inert to the spores. When caring for patients with CDI, isolation precautions include donning gloves and a gown and putting the individual in a private room. The effectiveness of gowns is found to be insufficient, however the use of gloves has been demonstrated to be effective in reducing the transfer of C. difficile spores. In addition to infection prevention practices, antimicrobial stewardship programmes and restricting the use of unnecessary antibiotics have been linked to reductions in the frequency of CDI [197].

C difficile spores can be effectively eliminated by disinfectants that contain chlorine. Hydrogen peroxide vapor, copper-coated surfaces, and UV light decontamination are all used in the environmental decontamination of C. difficile [198].

Chapter 3:

Monitoring and Evaluation in Critical Care Management

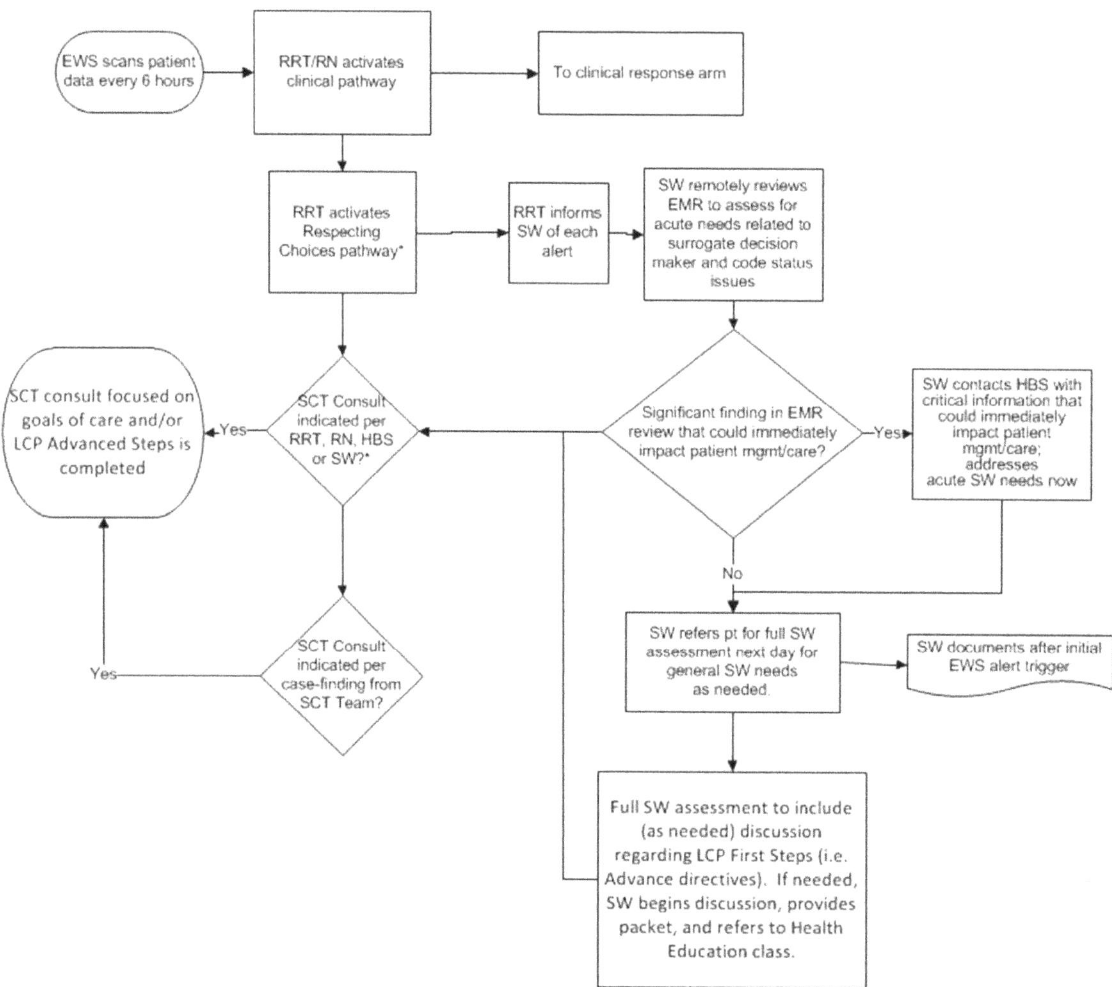

Figure 3.1: Early identification of critical patients before reaching the critical care unit. [EWS, early warning system, EMR, electronic medical record; pt, patient; LCP, life care planning; HBS, hospital based specialist; RN, registered nurse; RRT, rapid response team; SCT, supportive care team; SW, social worker]

Anemia: Patients who are very ill or injured frequently have anemia. Upon admission, almost two-thirds have hemoglobin levels below 12 g/dl, and by day eight, 97% have anemia. Anemia is a result of two essential processes in severe sickness and injury: a shorter RBC circulatory average life expectancy and decreased RBC production [117]. Phlebotomy losses, hemolysis, seeping at wounded sites, invasive operations, and gastrointestinal bleeding are some factors that shorten life expectancy. The average daily blood loss during diagnostic phlebotomy in critically ill patients ranges from 40 to 70 ml, exceeding the healthy replacement rate. Another cause of ongoing occult blood loss is the GI tract's compromised mucosal integrity. Nutritional inadequacies and the "anemia of inflammation" are the two main causes of decreased RBC production [118].

Anemia, whether acute or chronic, necessitates compensatory actions, which add additional stress to critically ill patients, who many already have cardiovascular disease. In healthy individuals who are at rest, an acute isovolemic fall in hemoglobin concentration to as low as 5 g/dl causes a gradual rise in stroke volume, heart rate, cardiac index, and oxygen extraction without showing any signs of tissue hypoxia. Due to cellular alterations brought on by the transcription of genes aiding hypoxic survival, like those controlled by hypoxia-inducible factor (HIF), even more, severe anemia may be acceptable with chronicity [119].

Management:

Blood transfusion: RBC transfusions have historically been used to treat anemia in patients with serious illnesses. When an ICU stay lasts more than a week, more than 70.2% of all patients require transfusions. The use of transfusions is a contentious topic in critical care medicine [120].

To increase the tissue supply of oxygen and carbon dioxide elimination in the volume-replete, the non-hemorrhaging patient is the main purpose of transfusion. Changes in hemoglobin will have a substantial impact because oxygen delivery is mostly governed by cardiac output, hemoglobin concentration, and oxygen saturation [121].

Acute lung injury (ALI) and transfusion-related acute lung injury (TRALI), transfusion-associated circulatory overload (TACO), transfusion-related immunomodulation (TRIM), transfusion reactions, transfusion-transmitted infections, and transfusion-related acute lung injury (TRALI), among others, are potential side effects of allogeneic blood that could increase the risk of nosocomial infection and death [121].

Erythropoiesis stimulating agents (ESA): A high prevalence of thrombotic events was linked to erythropoietin. According to Jelkmann et al., this may be because ESAs take time to take action or because the essential patients are resistant to ESAs and need a high dosage (2013). As a result, only critically ill patients with a concurrent medical condition (renal disease) or trauma victims are found to benefit from ESAs [120].

Blood substitutes: These are also referred to as oxygen carriers, although research on them has not yielded any encouraging findings. There are two categories of developed oxygen carriers:

- Hemoglobin-based oxygen carriers without cells (HBOCs).
- based on fluorocarbons.

Numerous negative effects of HBOCs include nephrotoxicity, decreased perfusion, and elevated risks of myocardial infarction and fatalities. Additionally, their 12- to 48-hour intravascular half-life has restricted their use to the most severe cases of acute hemorrhage in surgical or trauma patients [121].

Iron therapy: Iron sequestration and reduced intestinal absorption cause iron-restricted erythropoiesis in critically sick patients. This shows that iron therapy may have a role, namely intravenously. The effectiveness of this form of treatment has been questioned, though, because iron has been linked to the virulence and proliferation of the bacteria that cause nosocomial infections, and lowering iron levels may be the body's defense mechanism against sepsis [122].

Glycemic control: With the published findings from the study by van den Berghe and colleagues, which found that surgical critical care unit patients who were managed according to a strict glucose control protocol had higher rates of survival, especially in comparison to those managed based on the standard practise at the time, the story of glycemic control in critically ill patients gained momentum. the notion that glucose control may be more crucial than previously believed for all ICU patients, not just those with documented diabetes, has drawn the attention of intensivists worldwide. The outcomes prompted the creation of new technologies to continually detect and monitor blood glucose levels in ICU patients as well as strategies to handle the tighter glucose control now being sought after [123].

There is a chance that certain acute changes in the characteristic being measured could go undetected if monitoring is just intermittent. Depending on how frequently data are taken, intermittently monitoring the glucose has limited capacity to precisely perform trends and follow the impact of treatments. Continuous glucose monitoring (CGM) for blood glucose levels may, by enabling earlier therapeutic strategies, help decrease the frequency of hyper- as well as hypoglycemic episodes, which are known to be involved with worse patient outcomes, as well as glucose variability, which is another factor that has been linked to worse outcomes. Decreased nursing workload may be another benefit of constant monitoring [123].

Even in patients without diabetes, hyperglycemia in the critically ill is an established condition. Modifications in insulin sensitivity, cytokines, and counter-regulatory hormones work in concert to cause the stress response. Additional factors may include sickness/infection, overeating, drugs (such as corticosteroids), inadequate insulin, and/or volume depletion. Acute hyperglycemia can have a negative impact on fluid balance (via dehydration and glycosuria), inflammation, immunological and endothelial function, and outcome. Although there are a number of effective and safe insulin infusion regimens for treating hyperglycemia, the majority of cumulative research does not establish a link between acute hyperglycemia and unfavorable outcomes in the medical critical care unit [124].

Nutrition: As part of the majority of therapeutic interventions, monitoring the outcomes of medical interventions and the accomplishment of the therapeutic goals necessary to judge their efficacy is necessary. No intensivist would consider administering fluids and norepinephrine to treat shock situations without first checking blood pressure to titrate therapy and afterward employing more sophisticated monitoring equipment in the most difficult cases [125,126].

For a number of reasons, it is important to evaluate the metabolic response during nutrition therapy. The most significant factor is that patients may suffer injury and have their physiologic balance altered by incorrect nutrition therapy. The refeeding syndrome is a severe instance of a life-threatening condition associated with the beginning of feeding (RS). The metabolic, viral, and muscular difficulties brought on by under or overfeeding, as well as an uneven supply of nutrients such as insufficient electrolytes, fat, or vitamins, are other less obvious effects. An organized approach incorporating protocols and standardized operating procedures (SOPs) used for organizing, starting nutritional therapy, and spotting difficulties is crucial for ensuring enough nutrition [127].

The primary objectives of nutrition therapy monitoring in critical illness are: [128]

- to ensure that the proper nutritional support is selected and provided as prescribed and planned
- to ensure that approximated energy and protein needs are met
- to detect or avoid early any potential complications
- to analysis findings of feeding; and
- to help detect electrolytes or deficiencies of micronutrients in patients at risk due to special losses (such as drains, renaissance, etc). or any pathologies (e.g. major burns).

Analgesia: The evaluation of the patient's other necessities, the subjective and/or objective estimation of the critical factors (such as pain, agitation, and level of consciousness), and the titration of therapy to meet predetermined goals are all necessary for the effective management of sedation and analgesia in the Intensive Care unit (ICU) setting. It is crucial to understand that patient needs can vary based on the clinical situation, and that therapy aims for any particular patient are likely to shift over time. Therefore, it is essential to accurately measure pain, sedation, agitation, and other related variables using validated tools that are simple to use, accurate, precise, and sufficiently robust to encompass a wide range of behaviors in order to achieve patient comfort and ensure patient safety, including avoiding excessive or prolonged sedation [129].

Evaluation of pain and analgesia: The best pain evaluation is necessary for adult critical care facilities because 35% to 55% of nurses are observed to underestimate the patient's discomfort. In critically ill adults, inadequate pain evaluation as well as ineffective pain management that results can have serious physiologic repercussions. For instance, pain raises the burden on the myocardium, which increases the risk of myocardial ischemia, or it can cause splinting, atelectasis, and a sequence of events that can result in pneumonia. The greatest way to gauge pain is by patients ' self-report, specifically when utilizing a 0–10 numeric pain rating scale. However, due to cognitive dysfunction, drowsiness, paralysis, or mechanical ventilation, many critically sick individuals are unable to speak properly.

Observable indications, both physiological and behavioral, have been addressed as pain-related behaviors in this population when a patient is unable to communicate themselves [129]..

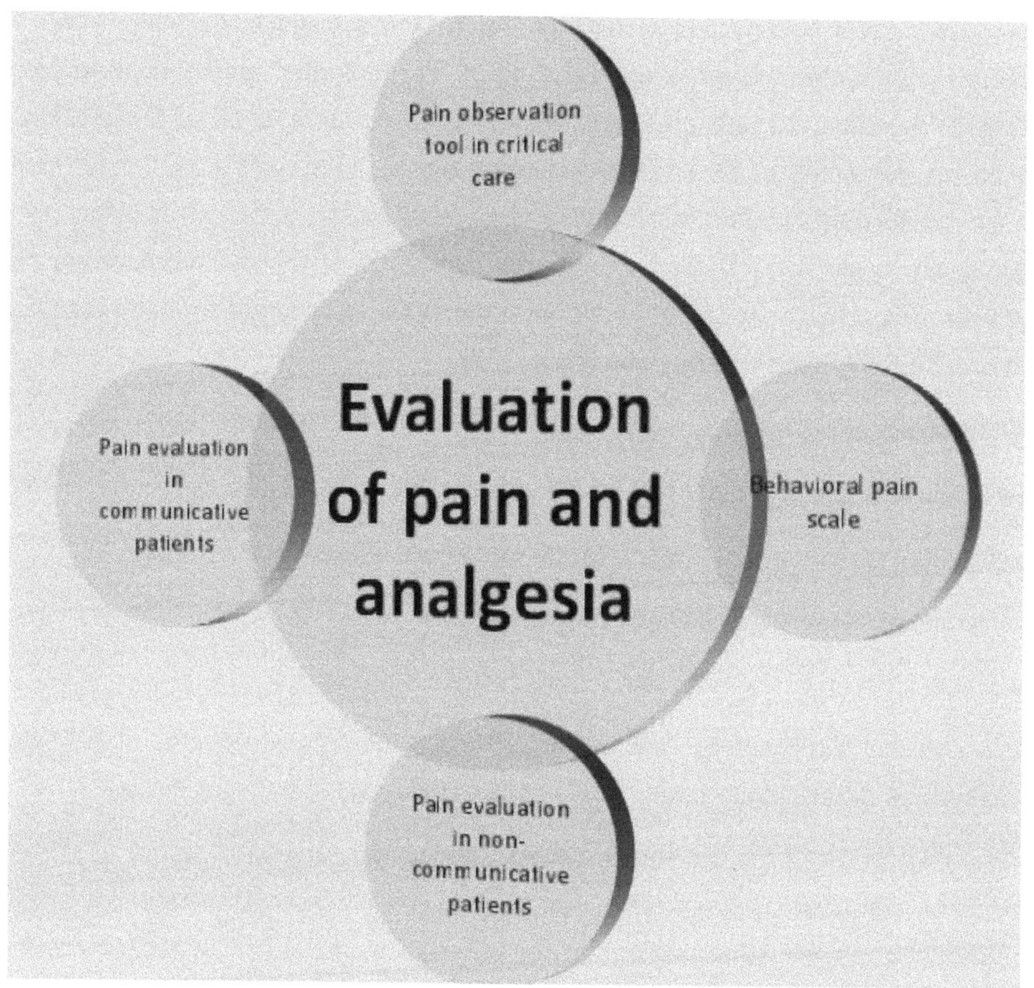

Figure 3.2: Evaluation of pain and analgesia

Pain evaluation in communicative patients: The Numeric Pain Range (NPS), which is widely used in a number of therapeutic contexts, uses verbal agony ratings on a scale ranging from 0 to 10, with 10 representing the worst pain ever experienced. It has been successfully applied to assess pain in geriatric patients, changes in the intensity of pain, assessment of reducing pain, and assessment of pain in older individuals, in addition to evaluating assess procedural pain in communicative critically sick patients [130].

Pain evaluation in non-communicative patients: To assess the level of pain in noncommunicative patients, a range of measures concentrating on behavioral and physiological signs of pain are being utilized, although there is little proof of their reliability and validity in severely sick patients. The Face, Leg, Activities, Crying, Consolability Observation Tool [FLACC] scale, and the Comfort scale were created and validated in the pediatric population before being employed in adult critical care settings. Despite the fact that noncommunicative critically sick adults share with infants, babies, and preverbal toddlers the inability to express their distress, several behavioral elements of these strategies designed for children do not apply to adults [131].

Behavioral pain scale: Behavioural pain scale (BPS) ratings are determined by identifying typical pain behaviors, such as agitation, grimacing, rigid limbs, and ventilator asynchrony, that are seen during uncomfortable operations. It has been shown that the behavioral pain scale consistently correlates well with the nurse's management of pain and the patient's self-reported pain intensity [132].

Pain observation tool in critical care: This tool recognizes common pain notations and observations and was developed through retrospective chart reviews and observations among ICU clinicians. The final score is based on four domains: facial expression, muscle tension, gestures, and ventilator compliance (or vocalization for patients who are not intubated). The maximum score for each of these ranges from 0 to 2. This rating system is straightforward and quick to calculate. It has been tested internally and among users, both when the patient is at rest and after being repositioned [132].

Analgesics:

Opioids: Because they are so highly effective, so affordable, and so relatively simple to administer, opioids are the first-line analgesics for mild to severe pain. The only painkillers that can be delivered by any method are opioids. Unfortunately, inappropriate use of opioids may result in adverse effects, such as nausea, constipation, respiratory depression, vomiting, tolerance, and physical dependency, which can have harmful implications in critically ill patients. Particularly after surgery, ileus, and opioid-induced bowel dysfunction can lengthen hospital stays and raise morbidity. According to clinical practise standards, iv opiates should be used as the primary optiion of treating non-neuropathic analgesia in critically ill patients [133].

Morphine: Because of its low cost, superior analgesic efficacy, and euphoric impact, morphine has historically been the chosen medication for treating immediate pain in the postoperative period. Because morphine's metabolites can have long-lasting effects in patients with kidney impairment, high initial doses and fixed dosage schedules should be avoided. Additionally, it is challenging to titrate the delivery of opioids in hemodialysis patients due to the poorly studied pharmacokinetics of these drugs. Morphine pharmacokinetics may change in critically ill patients as a result of altered binding affinity of protein brought on by cancer, renal impairment, and liver failure [134].

Fentanyl: Due to its increased lipophilicity, fentanyl, a synthetic opioid, has an efficacy that is 100 times higher than iv morphine. While extended treatment through multiple boluses or continuous infusion of fentanyl results in a buildup in those compartments and a longer half-life, its short half-life for bolusing (30–60 min) is caused by its fast redistribution into the periphery (9–16 hours). Fentanyl is safest in renal failure since it is metabolized in the liver and there are no active metabolites. Fentanyl was not linked to the release of histamine, either. Fentanyl has been suggested as the preferred analgesic in critically ill patients with hemodynamic instability because of these factors [135].

Hydromorphone: A semi-synthetic opioid called hydromorphone is more powerful than morphine but less euphoric. The sole hydromorphone metabolite that is eliminated renally is hydromorphone-3-glucuronide (H3G). In patients with renal illness, H3G hydromorphone has an enhanced safety profile compared to morphine because it lacks active metabolites that operate at opiate receptors. There is absolutely no relationship with histamine release, similar to that of fentanyl [136].

Oral opioids: Enteral opioid delivery is favored if individuals can tolerate the medicine because it is practical, non-invasive, and typically cheaper. If used properly, controlled release drugs like oxycodone can lessen the troughs in analgesic effects that are associated with short-acting oral opioids. In a recent trial, individuals randomly assigned to take oral opioids had pain at levels comparable to those who took patient-controlled iv morphine following cardiac surgery, with fewer morphine-equivalent dosages [137].

Non-opioid analgesics:

Dexmedetomidine and clonidine: Dexmedetomidine has indeed been utilised as an additional analgesic and sedative in critical care patients without having a depressive effect on the respiratory system. Dexmedetomidine, which has a 2 hour elimination half-life and a 6 minute half-life, has a greater affinity for α-2 receptors than clonidine. More crucially, there is growing evidence in favour of its usage in patients who are being mechanically ventilated in order to facilitate extubation. Dexmedetomidine in the ICU has been shown in numerous studies to lower the incidence of delirium. Dexmedetomidine has an opioid-sparing action as an analgesic, which helps individuals with morbid obesity and obstructive sleep apnea in particular. Due to central sympathetic suppression, bradycardia and hypotension are the most often reported side effects [138].

Ketamine: Ketamine has been an important component of perioperative pain management in patients who required high doses of opioids and in cases where opioid hyperalgesia was present. Studies have also demonstrated a significant decrease in opioid intake in the first 24 hours when administered as an adjuvant, without the need for an increase in side effects, demonstrating the role of subanaesthetic dosages of ketamine in the avoidance of opioid tolerance in perioperative patients. An intraoperative ketamine injection can be prolonged in the ICU for patients who are opioid-tolerant and undergoing major surgery for better analgesia. Ketamine has bronchodilatory effects as a result of catecholamine release and is not linked to respiratory depression. Ketamine should not be used in people with psychosis since it causes hallucinations and dreams [139].

Lidocaine: An analgesic as well as an anti-inflammatory, lidocaine is an amide local anaesthetic. It has been demonstrated that a lidocaine infusion administered in an Intensive Care setting works well as an adjuvant to an opioid analgesic during the first 24 hours following surgery [140].

Acetaminophen: An useful painkiller for mild to severe pain is acetaminophen. It has a favourable adverse impact and a 20%–30% opioid-sparing action [141].

Regional anesthesia in ICU: There are many benefits of adding regional anaesthesia to an analgesic regimen in the ICU, including a decrease in opioid-induced side effects, the ability to wean patients from mechanical breathing earlier, enhanced analgesia, and a quicker recovery of bowel function. Additionally, it has been demonstrated that neuraxial blocks lower the risk of cardiorespiratory issues and venous thromboembolism in postoperative patients [142].

Electrolyte levels:

The most frequent clinical issues in the context of critical care include fluid and electrolyte abnormalities. Serious burns, trauma, infection, brain injury, and heart failure are examples of critical illnesses that cause changes in electrolyte and fluid homeostasis. Activation of hormonal systems including the vasopressin and renin-angiotensin-aldosterone system, as well as tubular damage brought on by ischemia or nephrotoxic kidney injury, including renal insult brought on by a variety of drugs used in critical care, are a few potential reasons. The diagnosis and management of fluid and electrolyte abnormalities should also take into account the improper delivery of fluids and electrolytes [143]

Fluid management: The treatment of patients who have sepsis or hypovolemic shock must include volume resuscitation. To make up for the intravascular volume deficit and to reduce problems linked to hypovolemia like hypotension, tachycardia, acute renal injury, and multi-organ failure, enormous volumes of intravenous fluid are typically provided. Physicians should keep in mind that specific oxygenation and hemodynamic parameters, such as central venous pressure, mean arterial pressure, and central venous oxygen saturation should be used to assess the hemodynamic response to vasopressors and volume resuscitation rather than relying solely on signs and symptoms [143].

Fluid intake and output should generally be monitored regularly, and leakage into "third spaces" should indeed be considered. Chest radiographs, physical examination results, and vital signs are all crucial in determining the patient's volume status. It may be helpful to perform invasive monitoring of the pulmonary capillary wedge pressure and central venous pressure [143].

Hyponatremia: Patients hospitalized in the Intensive Care unit frequently have clinical problems related to changes in plasma sodium levels. The occurrence of dysnatremia is linked to a poor prognosis and is frequently developed when a patient is brought to the Intensive Care unit. Low plasma [Na+] is caused by a relative water surplus and a kidney that is unable to eliminate electrolyte-free water. Nearly all patients in the ICU have compromised urine dilution, which is necessary for the kidney to remove extra water [144].

The most frequent occurrence of hyponatremia symptoms is a sharp drop in plasma [Na+] to 125 mEq/L. Seizures and comas are typically brought on by a sharp drop in plasma [Na+] to below 110 mEq/L. Acute cerebral edema is the most dreaded consequence in a patient with symptomatic hyponatremia [144].

Euvolemic hyponatremia without symptoms does not need immediate treatment since brain cells have evolved to hypoosmolality if there are no symptoms. The first stage in management should be to identify and address reversible causes [144]

Loss of both solutes and water with a relatively greater loss of solutes—leads to hypovolemic hyponatremia. It is frequently seen in a patient who was using thiazide as an antihypertensive drug and was on a minimal salt diet. withdrawal of thiazide and replacement of deficit volume eliminates the stimulus for vasopressin secretion and starts water diuresis [144]

When the body retains both waters as well as a solute, but the retention of water is more than the solute, hypervolemic hyponatremia results. Numerous instances of hypervolemic hyponatremia are linked to severe and occasionally irreversible heart, liver, or kidney failure. Treatment of underlying conditions, limitation of salt and water consumption, and use of loop diuretics are all beneficial. Extracorporeal ultrafiltration has repeatedly been demonstrated to alleviate congestion, reduce the need for diuretics, and correct hyponatremias in individuals with decompensated heart failure who experience severe hyponatremia [143].

Hypernatremia: Hypernatremia is a serious risk for patients in the Intensive Care unit. The use of sodium bicarbonate solutions in the treatment of metabolic acidosis is a predisposing factor, as are renal water loss due to a kidney disease-related concentrating defect, the usage of diuretics, or solute diuresis from urea or glucose; gastrointestinal fluid losses due to nasogastric suction and lactulose presidency; and water losses due to fever, drainages, and open wounds. Traumatic brain injury can be complicated by acute diabetes insipidus with hypernatremia, which can arise 5–10 days after the damage and go away in a few days to a month [144].

Identification of the symptoms, identification of the underlying water metabolism flaws, adjustment of volume irregularities, and adjustment of hypertonicity are all necessary for the detection and treatment of hypernatremia. Changes in mental health status, such as agitation, irritability, lethargy, confusion, and somnolence, are the main symptoms. If a patient is able to converse, they could express extreme thirst. Due to prior knowledge of these diseases, doctors can effectively replace urine water loss and prevent the onset of dangerous hypernatremia in polyuric patients who undergo examination for faults in urinary concentration [145].

In patients who get a lot of saline or bicarbonate throughout their illness, hypervolemic hypernatremia is not rare and is frequently iatrogenic. Removing too much sodium from the body is a necessary component of hypervolemic hypernatremia treatment. Exogenous sodium sources ought to be avoided unless medically necessary. To induce a negative sodium balance, loop diuretics with replenishment of free water may be useful. Renal replacement therapy is typically the only appropriate treatment in this situation since hypervolemic hypernatremia is frequently an iatrogenic consequence that only manifests when renal function is impaired. Reduce sodium concentration in the hemodialysis solution's composition [144].

Prior to replacing the water deficit in individuals with hypovolemic hypernatremia, the effective circulation volume deficit should be corrected, especially in those who have hypotension and overt indications of hypovolemia. In addition to giving isotonic sodium chloride, the root cause of a fluid loss should be found and treated. In order to effectively treat euvolemic hypernatremia, the water deficit must be made up, and the continuous loss of hypotonic fluids must be reduced [144].

Hypokalemia: Low dietary potassium consumption, transfer into the intracellular compartment, potassium loss from the extrarenal system, and potassium loss from the kidneys are the main causes of hypokalemia. Medicines that are frequently given in the ICU are linked to hypokalemia. Most of the neuromuscular signs and symptoms of hypokalemia include nausea, paralysis, vomiting, weakness, constipation, weakness of the respiratory muscles, and rhabdomyolysis. Cardiac arrhythmias are the most frightening side effects of hypokalemia, especially in people with myocardial infarction/ischemia, hypertension, or heart failure [145].

In all circumstances, oral potassium supplementation is preferred, excluding emergency situations. Parenteral potassium replenishment should only be used in patients who have severe hypokalemia and electrocardiographic abnormalities. A central venous catheterization is necessary for rapid potassium infusion (i.e., > 10–20 mEq/hr), as phlebitis and vein damage can result from infusion through a peripheral line. The initial therapy should be between 40 and 80 mEq in size. Dextrose infusion causes insulin secretion and hinders the extracellular K+ deficit from being corrected quickly, hence parenteral K+ replenishment should be administered in the form of dextrose-free vehicles. If hypokalemia persists despite appropriate supplementation, hypomagnesemia and hypocalcemia should be found and treated [145].

Hyperkalemia: Predisposing variables for hyperkalemia in critically ill patients include renal failure, adrenal insufficiency, insulin resistance and deficit, and tissue injury from burns, rhabdomyolysis, or trauma. Numerous pharmaceuticals used in the ICU, such as beta-blockers, renin-angiotensin-aldosterone system inhibitors, heparin and its derivatives, potassium-sparing diuretics, trimethoprim, and non-steroidal anti-inflammatory drugs, can also result in hyperkalemia [146].

The hyperkalemia treatment plan is dependent on the existence of urgent circumstances. If there is any electrocardiographic abnormalities that can be attributed to hyperkalemia, emergency care should come first. The first line of treatment to counteract the depolarizing effects of hyperkalemia is intravenous calcium gluconate. Albuterol may be administered intravenously or breathed. As evidence on the efficacy of sodium bicarbonate are conflicting, it should be avoided by patients with extracellular fluid overload and is typically not the first option in the management of hyperkalemia [146].

Following acute care, potassium elimination from the body should be a part of hyperkalemia long-term therapy. Dialysis is a useful treatment, particularly for people with renal failure. The potassium-lowering effects of sodium polystyrene sulfonate take a while to manifest, and they can also lead to salt retention and intestinal necrosis. The causes of potassium excess, such as muscle damage and tissue ischemia, should be identified and effectively addressed [146].

Hyperphosphatemia: Critical illnesses like open heart surgery and Gram-negative sepsis have been linked to hypophosphatemia. In severely ill patients in the ICU, hypophosphatemia is known to occur in roughly 28% of cases. Hypophosphatemia (plasma phosphate concentration 2.5 mg/dL or 0.81 mmol/L) can be brought on by phosphate shifting to intracellular space, increased renal phosphate losses, and decreased intestinal phosphate absorption. The use of diuretics, drunkenness, acute respiratory alkalosis, diabetic ketoacidosis, inadequate body phosphorus storage, vomiting or gastrointestinal losses, and critical illness all predispose people to hypophosphatemia [147].

Given the potential negative effects of hypophosphatemia, plasma phosphorus levels in critically ill patients should indeed be kept within the normal range (2.5-4.5 mg/dL). The severity of the hypophosphatemia and the existence of symptoms will determine how it is treated. If the gastrointestinal tract is healthy, mild-to-moderate hypophosphatemia (1–2.5 mg/dL) without any symptoms can be administered orally with phosphate supplementation. Intravenous phosphate should be administered to address symptoms or severe hypophosphatemia (1.0 mg/dL) [147].

Hypocalcemia: Of the most typical electrolyte abnormalities seen in the ICU is hypocalcemia. As many as 90percent of a total of critically sick patients have been reported to have low total calcium levels, while the incidence of hypocalcemia as evaluated by ionized calcium is thought to be around 15-20%. Patients receiving ICU treatment have a higher mortality rate when they have hypocalcemia. Hypoparathyroidism, vitamin D insufficiency, hypomagnesemia, trauma, sepsis, acute and chronic renal failure, complexing with albumin, citrate, or administered phosphate are among the most typical causes of hypocalcemia. It has been suggested that one of the main causes of hypocalcemia in trauma patients is the dilution of plasma brought on by the injection of large volumes of iv fluids in a resuscitative effort [148].

To treat acutely symptomatic severe or moderate hypocalcemia, intravenous calcium should be administered as calcium chloride or calcium gluconate. For routine calcium preservation and replenishment, calcium gluconate should be chosen instead. Since calcium chloride offers 3 times greater elemental calcium compared to calcium gluconate, use of calcium chloride should be limited to urgent and emergent conditions. The therapy of serious and symptomatic hypocalcemia is urgent. To reduce symptoms at first, 1,000 mg of calcium chloride or 3 g of calcium gluconate may be administered over ten minutes. It may be necessary to administer calcium continuously while closely checking serum calcium levels at least every six hours. Due to the potential risk of cardiac arrhythmias, the infusion rate shouldn't be higher than 0.8–1.5 mEq/min. Typically, 1-2 g of calcium gluconate is dissolved in 100 mL of either 5% dextrose or 0.9% sodium chloride and administered as an intermittent bolus over the course of 30 to 60 minutes. Until calcium levels in serum have returned to normal, the dose may be administered again every 6 hours as necessary [148].

Other acid-base and electrolyte problems are frequently present with hypocalcemia. If hypocalcemia is not adequately rectified by frequent calcium treatment, hypomagnesemia should indeed be sought out and treated. Hypocalcemia should be treated first when metabolic acidosis is present since treating acidosis lowers the concentration of ionised calcium, which can lead to issues like tetany or cardiac collapse. To prevent calcium carbonate precipitation, distinct intravenous lines should be used to give calcium salt and bicarbonate solution [148].

Hypomagnesemia: Critically sick patients typically exhibit hypomagnesemia, which has been estimated to occur in the ICU up to 50% of the time. Seizures, comas, torsades de pointe arrhythmias and even death can occur as a result of severe hypomagnesemia. Corresponding electrolyte disorders including hypocalcemia and hypokalemia are linked to hypomagnesemia. In critically ill patients, the mean serum magnesium concentration should be kept at 1.5 mg/dL or above. To prevent fatal cardiac arrhythmias, patients with acute myocardial infarction may need larger amounts (i.e., > 1. 8mg/dL). The objectives of therapy ought to be to reduce or eliminate symptoms, bring the level of serum magnesium back to 1.6–2.5 mg/dL, and prevent hypermagnesemia [149].

In critically ill patients who have severe or symptomatic hypomagnesemia, intravenous administration is preferable. The duration of the infusion is crucial since magnesium diffuses slowly into tissues and is rapidly removed by the kidneys, with close to 50 percent of the total of magnesium being infused being expelled into the urine. Individuals with renal impairment should be given a reduced dose to prevent hypermagnesemia. Oral replacement can be used to treat mild hypomagnesemia [149].

Volume status: One of the main challenges in providing care for the severely ill is the assessment and management of intravascular volume. In line with recommendations for treating several shock states, patients with hypotension are frequently revived with intravenous crystalloid fluid [150]. Preload, or the stressed venous volume, is raised therapeutically with the intention of increasing cardiac output and stroke volume. output. Large-volume resuscitation encourages tissue edema, fluid extravasation, and endothelial damage. Along with gradual organ malfunction and death, rising interstitial fluid and extravascular lung water are also linked [151].

Principles in evaluating the volume responsiveness:

Static pressure and volume variables: The initial indices to help predict volume response were static measurements of volumes and pressure. These include surrogates derived through echocardiography as well as the central venous and pulmonary artery occlusion pressures (PAOP) [152].

Heart-lung interactions and dynamic variables: Researchers proposed changes in preload indices caused by an intrathoracic change in pressure while mechanical breathing as indicators of volume responsiveness when the shortcomings of static methods became apparent. The need for mechanical ventilation and rigorous use restrictions have tempered initially encouraging results, but these dynamic characteristics do play a role in predicting fluid responsiveness in some settings [152].

Volume challenges: More recently, a method for estimating fluid responsiveness has emerged: the utilization of simulated or tiny volume challenges. The passive leg raise (PLR) temporarily boosts venous return as an "auto-bolus" and mobilizes about 300 mL from the lower limbs. This provides a chance to quantify cardiac output or a hemodynamic parameter. Preload reserve is suggested at a threshold degree of improvement. The reversible action may prevent the need for an unneeded fluid bolus. PLR is useful for patients who have spontaneous breathing or dysrhythmia because it has been thoroughly verified [153].

Techniques used for predicting volume responsiveness:

Central venous pressure: CVP measurement is a well-known marker that directs fluid management. Although a central venous catheter must be implanted for CVP monitoring, it is quite simple to perform in the emergency room. Obtaining a CVP is still often used in the treatment of individuals with septic shock. The insertion of a central venous catheter entails a risk of mechanical issues and infection. Central lines are frequently installed in the ED, however, they require a lot of resources [154].

Pulmonary artery occlusion pressure: By using thermodilution, pulmonary artery catheters can monitor both cardiac output and PAOP. As pulmonary artery catheterization does not enhance patient outcomes and poses the risk of mechanical and infectious problems, its use has been reduced. Notably, fluid responsiveness has not been demonstrated to be predicted by PAOP levels. Lung ultrasound can be used to measure PAOPs non-invasively; the lack of widespread sonographic B-lines points to an occlusion pressure with less than 18 mmHg. During resuscitation, repeated lung ultrasounds may be used to assess fluid tolerance. If sonographic B-lines are absent, a physician can assume there is no interstitial edema and continue with a planned bolus [155].

Inferior vena cava measurements: It has been suggested that inferior vena cava (IVC) ultrasound readings could be used as a tool to help direct fluid management. IVC ultrasonography has been widely used in emergency departments since it is non-invasive and reasonably simple to do. The caval index, also known as the % compressibility of the IVC (cIVC), has indeed been proposed as a prediction of preloaded reserve in addition to providing an estimate of CVP. Although IVC size may act as a stand-in for CVP, it has not been shown to be a reliable indicator of fluid responsiveness. Varying tidal volumes and variations in intrathoracic pressure are examples of patient characteristics that may have contributed to this finding [156].

Flow time: The time needed for the cardiac cycle to reach systole is known as flow time. The time is converted to heart rate (FTc) units by dividing the systole time by the square root of the systole time. An esophageal Doppler monitor is primarily used to measure aortic flow time. Esophageal Doppler monitors are poorly tolerated by individuals who are not intubated, and proper measurement acquisition may be operator-dependent. Aortic flow time is highly unrealistic for any ED applications due to the restricted indications and variable performance of FTc [157].

Variation in pulse pressure: The difference between the greatest and minimum pressures experienced during a respiratory cycle, divided by their mean, is known as pulse pressure variation (PPV). It is a dynamic variable created by variations in intrathoracic pressure during mechanical ventilation. Positive pressure reduces right heart stroke volume to the absolute minimum on inspiration by increasing right ventricular afterload and decreasing right ventricular preload. In turn, the left ventricle's preload is reduced, and after a brief delay, the left heart's stroke volume also declines. The introduction of dynamic variables, such as PPV, provided a new method for measuring fluid responsiveness once it was realized that static predictors of fluid responsiveness were incorrect [158].

Stroke volume variation: Similarly to PPV, the SVV principle relies on the relationship among variables in stroke volume throughout the respiratory cycle. To determine the stroke volume, a commercial monitoring program and arterial catheter examine the contour of the pulse pressure. Pulse contour analysis is another method for calculating SVV, and a commercial apparatus is required for measurement. Similar restrictions apply to SVV as PPV, including the need for controlled tidal volumes, mechanical ventilation without spontaneous breathing, and the absence of dysrhythmia. SVV is not practicable for the ED due to the resources needed and usage restrictions [159].

Plethysmographic variation index (PVI): The respiratory cycle-induced variability in the plethysmograph waveform is measured by the plethysmographic variation index (PVI), which employs a modified pulse oximeter. A commercial instrument is used to assess the PVI, which has the benefit of being non-invasive. PVI measurements show a sufficient capacity to predict volume response in individuals who are intubated with no spontaneous respiratory effort and tidal volumes >8 mL/kg, which suggests that they share limitations with PPV and SVV. Although these requirements limit to use in the ED setting, PVI has indeed been successfully applied to ED patients, which is noteworthy. PVI may be an effective technique for patients who fit the strict application criteria [160].

Echocardiography:

Static echocardiographic parameters: A number of echocardiographic pressure and volume data, such as estimates of PAOP and CVP and the end-diastolic area of the left or right ventricles, have been suggested to predict fluid responsiveness. Additionally investigated as a volume responsiveness indicator is the end-diastolic ventricular area. The end-diastolic area has not been shown to be a reliable indicator of how the body will react to volume increase, according to numerous research [161].

Dynamic echocardiographic parameters: Using echocardiography to monitor the changes in stroke volume is a highly accurate way to forecast preload reserve. Transthoracic echocardiography can be used to calculate the velocity-time integral (VTI) of aortic blood flow, which can be used to calculate the stroke volume. Patients that are volume responsive can be easily identified by variations in stroke volume brought on by passive leg raising [162].

Chapter 4:

Pain Management, Organ Support

Pain: Patients in critical care units (ICUs) continue to frequently report feeling pain. More than half of patients in the ICU feel pain at some point, and the rates of unmanageable pain are still too high. Patients may feel pain for a variety of reasons, including an underlying health condition, tubes, catheters, medical treatments, or immobility. Unabated pain can make it difficult to fall asleep, is a major cause of stress, and is frequently associated with painful memories in patients. According to a study, 50% of ICU patients experience pain after being discharged from the hospital [163]. Pain treatment presents numerous special considerations and problems for ICU practitioners. Patients who are critically ill frequently have several systemic disease states, necessitating quick assessments and modifications to treatment regimens. Additionally, a large number of patients in the ICU are unable to speak coherently, either as a direct consequence of their illnesses or injuries or as a result of the necessity for intubation and sedation. These factors combined make it challenging to identify and treat potentially painful illnesses [164]. After ICU treatment, a significant majority of survivors experience cognitive, mental, and/or physical handicaps; post-Intensive Care syndrome (PICS) and PICS may continue to cause pain for years after ICU discharge [165].

A number of physiological reactions to pain include tachycardia, anxiety, diaphoresis, and catabolism. Elevated renin-angiotensin-aldosterone axis stimulation, tachypnea, increased bowel movements, and the synthesis of many cytokines are all consequences of this. Additionally, it is thought that pain may contribute to immune system dysfunction, hypercoagulable states, altered glycemic management, acute restrictive respiratory physiology, patient-ventilator dyssynchrony, and disturbed sleep quality [166].

Pain is a distressing sensory and emotional experience that is connected to, or symbolized by, potential or actual tissue damage. Even if this definition covers pain as a whole, it is still useful to categorize pain according to its features in order to better target therapy and advance research into particular pain states. In order to do this, the International Association for the Study of Pain has divided pain into five categories: (1) origin; (2) system suffering dysfunction; (3) length and pattern of occurrence; (4) severity; and (5) location of the body that is involved [167,168]

In the ICU, short-duration stimuli either with or without a certain degree of chronicity are the main causes of pain. The brain afferent (nociceptive) signals that have developed as a result of tissue damage are simply activated in this pathophysiologic mechanism. It's crucial to keep in mind that the patient's acute pain in the ICU may be caused by both the underlying disease or damage and iatrogenically derived discomfort from treatments including monitor implantation, surgery, and immobility [169].

The division of pain into the two groups most frequently observed in this setting (1) acute postoperative or posttraumatic pain and (2) neuropathic pain—is particularly beneficial for the ICU clinician. This straightforward classification can be used to direct therapy strategies and is efficient enough to be applied to the immediate care of these patients. The patient's communication ability in the Intensive Care unit frequently limits the subjective perception of pain the patient. ICU pain is primarily somatic in nature. This kind of pain is frequently described as dull and aching, is frequently well-localized, and responds well to treatments like opioids and nonsteroidal anti-inflammatory drugs (NSAIDs), which are the basis of Intensive Care unit (ICU) pain control [170,171].

Visceral pain is frequently seen in the Intensive Care unit and may result from suboptimal bowel management or underlying gastrointestinal pathology. Anticholinergics should be taken into consideration if patients are not reacting well to conventional somatic pain treatments because opiates and NSAIDs often do not function well for this subtype. Although less well understood in the ICU, neuropathic pain should be taken into account, particularly in patients who have lengthy hospitalizations or injuries that directly affect neurovascular structures [172].

Assessment of pain:

Physiology-based scales: Although physiological indicators and levels of pain can be correlated, care should be taken when using a therapeutic approach based on physiology. With increasing degrees of discomfort, heart rate, and blood pressure rise, but it's important to remember that these variations could also happen for other physiological (or pathophysiologic) causes. On the other hand, these physiologic abnormalities may not change when pain is not adequately managed [173].

Pain is described as an "unpleasant sensory and emotional experience connected with potential or actual tissue injury, or described in terms of such damage" by the International Association for the Study of Pain. The first issue is that any patient who has had Intensive Care shouldn't be able to express how much pain they are feeling, so it is essential to differentiate between a patient who can speak and one who cannot. Vital signs alone have been regarded as inadequate indications of pain (raised blood pressure, increased heart rate, altered breathing rate). Pupillometry processed EEG data, and changes in the Bispectral Index are a few contemporary techniques that have been suggested for the assessment and scoring of pain, although more research is required to evaluate these [174].

Improper management of pain or overtreatment of painful conditions are problems in the ICU. Uncontrolled pain can result in post-traumatic disorder, increased length of stay in the ICU, pulmonary problems, and patient-ventilator asynchrony. Over-treating pain can result in delirium, respiratory depression, prolonged mechanical ventilators, hemodynamic impairment, prolonged cognitive impairment, and more. The requirement of controlling pain and stabilization of underlying medical issues simultaneously must be better understood by patients and professional caregivers [174]

Since the patient's self-report of pain is regarded as the "gold standard," doctors should always make an effort to obtain an initial estimate of the patient's level of discomfort. The 2013 Japanese Pain Agitation and Delirium (J-PAD) guidelines and the 2013 Pain Agitation and Delirium (PAD) guidelines published by The American College of Critical Care Medicine (ACCM) both advocate (grade + 1B) routine pain monitoring (every 4 hours) for adult patients in the ICU. A 0-10 visually enlarged horizontal numeric rating scale (NRS) was found to be the most reliable and practical of the five pain intensity rating scales studied by Chanques and colleagues, who compared them with over 100 ICU patients. The PAD and J-PAD have not yet endorsed the use of the behavioral pain scale (BPS) or the Critical-Care Pain Observation Tool (CPOT), although the Federacion Panamericana e Iberica de Sociedades de Medicina Crtica y Terapia Intensiva (FEPIMCTI) recommendations do [175,176].

Figure 4.1: Numeric Rating Scale is used in rating the pain perception by asking the patient to circle and rate his or her pain according to the his or her perception of severity

Management of pain

In the ICU setting, it can be challenging to distinguish between pain management and sedative. Identifying and treating any potential root causes of agitation, like delirium, pain, hypotension, hypoxemia, or withdrawing from alcohol and other substances, as soon as feasible is advised (grade 1B) by the FEPIMCTI and J-PAD guidelines. Based on numerous recommendations, the Richmond Agitation-Sedation Scale (RASS) and Sedation-Agitation Scale are the most accurate and trustworthy sedation evaluation measures for gauging the degree and quality of sedation in adult ICU patients. It is advised to utilize dexmedetomidine, midazolam, or propofol. The main suggestions of evidence-based guidelines are summarized as follows: [176]

- The pain assessment should not be done using vital signs.
- Light levels of sedation should be done than deep levels.
- The administration of analgesia should be done before starting the painful procedures.
- Use of the "care bundle" involves using an interdisciplinary team approach, the "analgesia first" sedation method, promoting sleep, creating day-night routines, and controlling pain, agitation, and delirium.

The preferred analgesic for critically ill individuals with non-neuropathic pain is an opioid. According to the equianalgesic table, the effects of all intravenous opioids are the same. The first-line recommendation for treating pain in ICU patients is intravenous opioids. Numerous factors, including the pharmacodynamic and pharmacokinetic characteristics of the medicine, influence the best opioid to use and the dosage that is appropriate for each individual patient. Meperidine should never be administered to patients in Intensive Care units. The reason stems from meperidine metabolism, common renal disorders in Intensive Care units, probable pharmacological interactions with inhibitors of monoamine oxidase and selective serotonin reuptake inhibitors, and finally from the neurotoxic effects of meperidine. The evidence supporting the consumption of one opioid over another, with the exception of meperidine, is relatively weak [177].

Opioid use must be controlled; otherwise, patients in Intensive Care units may experience serious and negative side effects. Respiratory depression, vomiting, nausea, physical dependency, tolerance, and constipation are some of the more frequent adverse effects. Bowel dysfunction and ileus may emerge as an adverse effects, which may lead to a lengthy hospital stay and higher morbidity. It stands in contrast to real practices, which emphasize quick post-operative recovery and ileus prevention throughout the perioperative phase [178].

Fentanyl has a shot-like effect when taken as a single dose due to redistribution. Hence, it must be taken into account that its long half-life of elimination can determine its buildup when administered in high doses over extended periods of time. Given that fentanyl is metabolized in the liver by generating inactive metabolites, it must be taken into account that it is safe for patients with renal failure. Due to these factors, fentanyl has been suggested as the preferred analgesic in patients present in ICU, particularly in cases of impairment of hemodynamic variables [179].

Alfentanil and remifentanil both have advantageous kinetics when used in individuals with organ failure. When compared to the combination of midazolam and morphine, studies have shown that the combination of propofol and alfentanil shortened the time required for extubation and for ICU discharge. The fast elimination of remifentanil does not dependent on renal function [180].

The combination of opioids and adjuvant drugs is beneficial in ensuring improved analgesia and minimizing negative effects. Non-opioid analgesics can decrease the need for the prescription of opioids in ICU patients while also increasing the overall effectiveness of analgesia. According to reports, opioids combined with adjuvants can help ICU patients experience less discomfort. Because of their risk of organ toxicity (mainly liver and kidney), non-opioids use is mostly constrained. Additionally, numerous studies have shown that intravenous acetaminophen combined with opioids for the treatment of postoperative pain in major and cardiac surgery is safe and efficient. For instance, combining opioids with 1 gram of iv paracetamol every six hours during elective cardiac surgery enhances analgesia and cuts down on extubation delays [181].

NSAIDs give analgesia that is comparable to acetaminophen, but they should be utilized cautiously in individuals who have congestive heart failure, kidney damage, or who are at high risk of bleeding. Dexmedetomidine can keep patients in the Intensive Care unit (ICU) in a light to moderate state of sedation, even if they are undergoing protracted mechanical breathing. When dexmedetomidine and midazolam were compared, dexmedetomidine was found to be able to shorten the duration of mechanical ventilation. providing a better way for patients to express their discomfort. Dexmedetomidine can lessen the need for opioids in critically ill patients because of its opioid-sparing action. For rehabilitation to be successful, appropriate post-operative and post-trauma treatment of pain is also essential [182].

In ICU, pain is a common symptom of Guillain-Barré syndrome (GBS), yet it is frequently mismanaged. In a recent study, carbamazepine and gabapentin were able to demonstrate a pain decrease in GBS patients, however, the evidence was few and of extremely poor quality. Other specialized medications, such as iv methylprednisolone combined with iv immunoglobulins (IVIG), may hasten the patient's recovery but have little impact on neuropathic pain from the condition [183].

Patients in Intensive Care units (ICUs) go through a lot of diagnostic and therapeutic treatments every day. The authors reported that removing a chest tube, removing a wound drain, and inserting an arterial line were the most painful procedures. According to a recent randomized controlled research, the most effective method for providing analgesia is to administer 1% lidocaine subcutaneously [184].

Sedation protocol in ICU

Sedation: In the ICU setting, sedative drugs are usually prescribed primarily to alleviate anxiety and agitation, which can be brought on by a wide range of different conditions (eg, dyspnea, delirium, mechanical ventilation, lack of sleep, and untreated pain). When used properly, sedatives can improve patient care and increase patient safety; however, lengthy mechanical ventilation and cognitive problems are just a couple of the short- and long-term side effects of their use. Determining the purpose of sedation is therefore crucial because it may influence the choice of sedative and help establish the goal of sedative use [221,222].

General principles of sedation:

National medical associations and monitoring organizations have embraced the universal goal of ensuring patient comfort and safety. An already noticeable sympathetic stress response, which includes increased oxygen consumption, increased endogenous catecholamine activity, hypercoagulability, tachycardia, immunosuppression, and hypermetabolism is made even more pronounced in critically sick patients by pain and worry [221]. Additionally, unattended pain and anxiety can result in extreme agitation and the removal of life-saving medical equipment (such as intravenous lines and endotracheal tubes), endangering both the patient and medical professionals. In the immediate aftermath of the incident as well as in the future, when long-term repercussions like posttraumatic stress disorder (PTSD) may manifest, this may also significantly increase physical and psychological stress [223]. Therefore, analgesics and sedatives are used to provide comfort, promote patient safety, and lower the response to stress; however, oversedation frequently happens and is linked to longer stays on ventilators and in the critical care unit (ICU), a higher need for radiological assessments of mental health status, and a higher likelihood of developing brain dysfunction; therefore, the correct balance of analgesia and sedatives must be given to avoid these side effects [224].

Due to hemodynamic instability, medication interactions, altered protein binding, and compromised organ function, patients in the ICU have uncertain pharmacodynamics and pharmacokinetic properties. This makes it more challenging to receive the benefits of hypnotic and analgesic drugs without suffering the negative effects of their side effects. The use of sedatives is particularly complicated by drug buildup from continual infusions, tachyphylaxis, and redistribution, necessitating methods to stop systemic drug accumulation. The exact medical condition requiring therapy must be identified and regularly assessed in order to establish the optimum analgesic and sedative treatment plan [223,224].

Arousal monitoring: There are various ICU arousal scales that are utilised to deliver patient-specific, goal-directed therapy. The Richmond Agitation-Sedation Scale and the Riker Sedation-Agitation Scale are the two most often utilized arousal scales [225]. These scales can offer a therapeutic potential when utilized properly, which may result in a reduction in the dosage of sedative drugs and a shorter stay on mechanical ventilation. Arousal assessment, however, is a component of every critically sick patient's neurological examination and shouldn't be solely associated with the prescription of sedative medications [226].

Delirium monitoring: Delirium is now understood to be a manifestation of brain organ malfunction. It is an abrupt fluctuating shift in mental status characterized by inattention and changing levels of consciousness [227]. Up to 80% of cases can occur in the ICU, and they cancause long-term cognitive impairment. Delirium is linked to the use of sedative drugs and increases morbidity, mortality, length of hospital stay, and expense [228].

Sedation protocols: Sedation protocols are frequently used in ICU settings and offer a standardized framework that directs the monitoring and administration of sedatives. Their sole use has been linked to noticeably better patient outcomes. The most suitable providers to apply the sedation protocols are nurses, secondarily because of their more regular attendance at the patient's bedside. In fact, protocols delivered by nurses have been demonstrated to enhance patient outcomes [229].

Arousal monitoring devices, sedative dosage guidelines, spontaneous waking trials connected to spontaneous breathing trials, and early mobilization therapy should all be essential components of sedation regimens. The period of mechanical breathing, the length of stay in the Intensive Care unit, and the prevalence of post-traumatic stress disorder (PTSD) have all been demonstrated to be decreased by spontaneous waking trials (daily stoppage of sedation) [230,231].

Utilizing sedatives (especially lorazepam) has been linked to PTSD, and both PTSD and depression have been linked to the number of days spent sedated. While negative memories of their ICU experience may make survivors feel more depressed, PTSD is more frequently linked to having delusional memories rather than accurate ones of the ICU stay. Deep sedation may have long-lasting cognitive and neuropsychological impacts, as shown by the fact that patients who remember their time in the Intensive Care unit (ICU) have much fewer cognitive impairments than patients who have full amnesia [231].

Organ support: Multiple organ failure (MOF), which has an incidence of more than 31%, is becoming more common in critically ill patients on a yearly basis. The death rate in patients with later stages of MOF is still unacceptably high despite great therapeutic progress. Recent studies show that more than 61% of these individuals died during their stays in the Intensive Care unit. 21% of patients in the ICU had liver failure. More than 49% of critically ill patients experience acute kidney damage (AKI), which is more frequently linked to different types of liver illness. Increased morbidity and death in these patients are largely a result of AKI. Up to 31% of patients suffering from acute liver failure who stay in the ICU also have respiratory failure [200].

Air way and respiratory support: Many severely ill patients will require some kind of advanced respiratory support while they are being admitted. It is important to remember that starting mechanical breathing could result in severe patient morbidity. On the other hand, it shouldn't be put off until the patient is in critical condition. Technical approaches, albeit frequently incorporating input from a range of disciplines, most critically the physiotherapist, do not substitute good quality fundamental respiratory therapy [290]

High flow oxygen: is currently often utilized in the ICU, for single system ward-based assistance during surgery, and for medical and surgical patients. Patients are given very high volumes of warmed humidified oxygen at a predetermined oxygen percentage through a nasal or facial interface using an air-oxygen blender. By generating a tiny amount of positive end expiratory pressure (PEEP) and flushing away dead space gasses, large flows of up to 60 liters/min are believed to minimize work of breathing and enhance respiratory mechanics. In conjunction with humidification, this prevents the mucous membranes from drying out, improves tolerability, and speeds up secretion clearance. In comparison to non-invasive ventilation or face mask oxygen, high flow nasal cannula (HFNC) has been proven to be helpful in the therapy of patients suffering from severe acute hypoxic respiratory failure [290]

Non-invasive ventilation (NIV): is a type of breathing assistance that does not require endotracheal intubation. Positive airway pressure is most frequently applied through a facial interface using either continuous positive airway pressure (CPAP) or bi-level positive airway pressure (BiPAP). The term "CPAP" stands for continuous positive airway pressure during the respiratory cycle. This is comparable to PEEP in patients receiving invasive ventilation. The advantages include a decrease in the work of breathing, the correction of pulmonary shunt, the reversal of hypoxia through alveolar recruitment, and a decrease in cardiac afterload (via reduced left ventricular transmural pressure). Either a snug-fitting facemask or a specific CPAP hood or helmet are used to administer CPAP. Pressure injury must be avoided at all costs, especially to the nasal bridge.

Invasive ventilation: requires tracheal intubation of some kind. When compared to the controlled environment of an elective theatre list, securing the airway in critically sick patients presents considerable extra complications. This may be caused by severe physiological disturbances (often accompanied by a rapid decline), the presence of anatomical challenges (such as airway burns), outside factors (such as cervical in-line stabilisation in trauma), intense time constraints, less-than-ideal positioning, unfamiliar environments, and a lack of equipment and assistance. Therefore, for patient safety, meticulous planning and appropriate communication of airway plans are essential [290].

Prone ventilation, ECMO, and extracorporeal carbon dioxide removal (ECCO2R) are examples of advanced respiratory support treatments. Prone ventilation may reduce mortality in patients with severe acute respiratory distress syndrome (ARDS) [290].

The repeated inflation and deflation of collapsed lung areas (atelectrauma), as well as the induction of inflammatory mediators, are all ways that mechanical ventilation can cause lung injury. These mechanisms are most likely responsible for barotrauma and volutrauma (biotrauma). Extrapolating from ventilatory care in ARDS, a lung-protective ventilation technique has now been widely implemented in clinical practice [291].

Cardiovascular instability, pneumonia, or ventilator-associated lung injury, complications from prolonged immobilisation and sedative use, and oxygen toxicity in the critical care unit are all complications of mechanical ventilation. Tracheal intubation-related complications include damage to lips, teeth, and vocal cords. Equipment-related complications include ventilator malfunction or contamination [290].

Extracorporeal assistance is now often used in the treatment of individuals with liver failure. These therapies are typically recommended for critically ill individuals who have different types of organ failure as a bridge to recovery or transplantation. The majority of published data are accessible for cutting-edge dialysis devices such as liver support systems, even though traditional renal replacement modalities are often employed in everyday clinical practice among patients with liver failure [200].

With nearly the same rate of organ malfunction for the cardiovascular, renal, pulmonary, and central neurological systems, there is mounting evidence that many organs are equally and simultaneously implicated in critical disease [201]. This is due to the fact that, regardless of the location of the original insult, syndromes such as sepsis and acute respiratory distress syndrome (ARDS) frequently have a considerable impact on a number of distant organs. In addition, dysfunction in one organ is frequently linked to dysfunction in other organs [200].

A sophisticated and well-articulated therapeutic approach that encompasses pharmacological and organ-specific preventative and supportive interventions is necessary for critically sick patients with acute kidney injury (AKI) in the presence of multiple organ dysfunction syndrome (MODS). Although little is known about how different organ support therapies interact with native organs and other organ support systems, they are currently employed in the ICU [202].

The clinical illness known as acute kidney injury (AKI), which has a complex etiology and a varied clinical course, is recognized as being heterogeneous. Stage 1 AKI occurs in about 50% of patients at some time in their ICU stay, although stage 2 and stage 3 AKI occur far less frequently and only about 10% of patients need renal replacement therapy (RRT). Further organ damage may result from AKI. In contrast, AKI might be viewed as a secondary "bystander," especially in the presence of many pre-existing comorbidities and chronic illnesses [203].

It has been established that renal disease is independently related with mortality, regardless no matter whether the kidneys are the primary cause or are only incidentally implicated in distal organ dysfunction. In fact, it is believed that a significant portion of the mortality risk in people with MODS results from intricate relationships between the actual insult, the triggering of inflammation, and the repercussions on distant organs [204]. Death is independently correlated with the level of organ dysfunction; when RRT is required, mortality might exceed 50%. The fate of other organs may theoretically be affected as well if AKI is prevented by early detection of persons at risk or delaying the advancement of its severity [205].

Some of the authors of the current research recently expressed the opinion that extracorporeal organ support encompasses all therapies that include drawing blood from the patient and processing it using particular tools and methods (ECOS). This was done to set apart ECOS, a collection of systems that are being used more frequently in the context of MODS and severe illness, from conventional mechanical ventilators and isolated cardiac support (such as ventricular assistance devices or whole artificial hearts). For renal support, RRT has been utilized frequently in a variety of ICU settings for even more than three decades [201].

Extracorporeal carbon dioxide removal (ECCO2R) and veno-venous extracorporeal membrane oxygenation (VV-ECMO) are currently being utilized more frequently at the bedside for lung support, but patients who need circulatory and gas exchange support may benefit from veno-arterial ECMO (VA-ECMO). Fractionated plasma separation and adsorption (Prometheus), Molecular Adsorbent Recirculating System (MARS), or animal hepatocytes (e.g. extracorporeal liver assist device; ELAD) or a bio-artificial system that combines plasma separation with perfusion of bio-reactors filled with human are examples of additional artificial organ supports. Other artificial organ supports may also include haemoperfusion or liver support (in the context of specific intoxications or endotoxaemia) [201].

The kidney during extracorporeal organ support

More than 70.5% of patients who received ECMO are developing AKI and similar proportions are projected for ECCO2R. It is believed that the high incidence of AKI during extracorporeal lung support and MCS is the result of numerous variables, including underlying disease and seriousness, concomitant diseases, pre-existing kidney injury and possible detrimental effects of lung support and MCS on renal function [206].

In cardiogenic shock VA-ECMO provides appropriate end-organ circulation during low cardiac output, which is a prevalent cause of AKI, the favorable benefits of ECMO and ECCO2R may be connected to the early rectification of blood gas abnormalities and reduction in ventilator-induced lung injury (a type-1 cardiorenal syndrome). Prolonged pre-hypoxia and hypercapnia, hypoperfusion, ischaemia-reperfusion injury, an increased risk of bleeding, contact of artificial membrane with blood, haemodynamic instability, improper placement of the cannula resulting in venous interference/hypoperfusion, and iatrogenic plaque rupture during arterial cannulation are just a few of the potentially harmful renal effects. For patients with heart failure and their overall outcomes after receiving ECMO, pulmonary hypertension and elevated right atrial filling pressures have been recognized as risk factors [205]..

Support of multiple organ dysfunction and Renal Replacement Therapies (RRT)

RRT, the most widely used type of organ support therapy globally, is necessary for 10 to 15 percent of ICU patients and is the sole method of treatment for severe AKI. Acute RRT practice is allegedly not standardized, and there is great heterogeneity among centers throughout the world. Early RRT has been suggested in conjunction with ECCO2R in a variety of ICU settings for conditions like fluid overload, hypercapnic acidosis, and mediator removal [206]

Fluid balance: The care of critically ill patients revolves around optimizing fluid balance. High blood flow patients who use ECMO are especially vulnerable to fluid overload since fluids are frequently given in considerable volumes to prevent cannula suction. Extracellular fluid volume should be normalized because extended ECMO use is linked to fluid overload. In patients with severe ARDS, specific procedures have been recommended to achieve negative fluid balance while ECMO. By removing more sodium per unit volume than diuretic therapy, early renal assistance in the manner of extracorporeal ultrafiltration instead of RRT by hemodialysis may be able to resolve fluid excess. This may enhance cardiopulmonary function and lengthy results, as well as make nutritional assistance and medication distribution easier [206].

Mediator removal: The most well-known mediator of lung damage following AKI is plasma interleukin-6. High interleukin-10 levels are a significant predictor of worse outcomes in patients with ARDS getting VV-ECMO and also in patients with cardiogenic shock receiving VA-ECMO treatment [204].

In patients suffering ARDS, either with or without ECMO, cardiogenic shock, and/or AKI, blood-purification procedures such as plasma adsorption, high-volume haemofiltration, high cut-off haemofiltration, plasma filtration, and hemoperfusion offer a potential therapeutic advantage. This is assumed to be because of their capacity to eliminate cytokines and inflammatory mediators, reduce macrophage and monocyte activity, and inactivate circulating sepsis-related pro-apoptotic proteins [206].

Furthermore, RRT (especially with large effluent dosages) necessitates continuous monitoring to prevent hypokalaemia and hypophosphatemia, in contrast to the native kidney, which can control the depletion of electrolytes and minerals. Antibiotics and other drugs are lost along with enhanced solute clearance, which can negate the positive effects of blood-purification methods. Extracorporeal ultrafiltration reduces the likelihood that this will happen. RRT, however, could result in a negligible decrease in catecholamines [207].

The current gold standard of therapy for ARDS patients is protective ventilation. It has been proposed to further decrease the pulmonary, renal, and systemic inflammatory response brought on by ventilator-induced lung injury by lowering the plateau pressure to 25 cmH2O and the tidal volume to 4 ml/kg, which may enhance clinical outcomes. RRT and ECCO2R may be coupled in a single treatment to enable "super-protective" settings and the decrease of vasopressor needs in patients with ARDS who are experiencing AKI. ECCO2R may be required to treat respiratory acidosis related to poor minute ventilation [80]. In order to maintain pH and RRT in conjunction with ECCO2R in patients suffering from severe respiratory acidosis, more intrusive ECCO2R devices with greater blood flow rates (> 750 ml/min) are required [207].

In severely ill patients, hemodynamic imbalance during RRT is a common problem. During organ support, hypotensive episodes may worsen organ hypoperfusion and impair organ recovery. The most popular approach available globally to avoid haemodynamic instability in patients who received different types of organ support while using vasopressors is continuous RRT with varying ultrafiltration rates [202] Automatic biofeedback methods have been suggested as a way to keep the plasma refilling rate and ultrafiltration rate in check while avoiding haemodynamic instabilities during RRT. In such systems, ultrafiltration rate and dialysate conductivity would be continuously adjusted in response to variations in the volume of blood and vitals. By limiting the transfer of heat from the dialysate, cooler dialysate encourages vasoconstriction and may lessen myocardial stunning, a condition that has recently been demonstrated to occur in patients with AKI receiving RRT [204].

Oxygen therapy in ICU

A significant number of patients admitted to the critical care unit are due to respiratory illnesses. The lungs are exceptional in that they are both open to the outside world and, as a component of the cardiopulmonary circuit, are visible to the entire body's circulatory system. It seems sense, in light of these characteristics, that inhaled medicines serve as treatments for a variety of illnesses found in critical care [209]. The parenchyma of lung, airways, and vasculature have all been specifically targeted by a variety of medical devices and pharmacological formulations. The utilization of inhaled medicines in critical care, heliox, including high-flow nasal cannulae (HFNC), nitric oxide, bronchodilators and steroids, prostacyclins, and antibiotics are some [208].

HFNC: The normal flow rates for using standard nasal cannulae to administer oxygen are 2-4 L/min. Since there is significant dilution with ambient air at these low flows, the percentage of inspired oxygen (Fi O2) is less than 0.4 L/min [210]. Dry oxygen inhalation can be quite uncomfortable at flows more than 6 L/min. Although unheated bubbling humidifiers can be utilized, they are ineffective and lose effectiveness as the flow rate increases. The HFNC system is is made up of nasal prongs, a heated humidifier, a flow metre, and an air-oxygen blender that is set up to produce a high airflow [209].

An accurate Fi O2 can be achieved at high flows due to the limited entrainment of ambient air possible with an HFNC's high gas flow (60 L/min). The strong flow also flushes out expired gas from the upper airway, thereby increasing the amount of inspired oxygen on the subsequent inhalation. Compared to traditional oxygen therapy, the gas is more comforting because it has been warmed and humidified. Compared to other devices, HFNC appears to be less frequently associated with reports of dyspnea. A facemask might not be as comfortable as HFNC [210]..

Lowering dead space requires flushing the upper airway with HFNC. This effect lowers the amount of minute ventilation needed, which is consistent with the frequent observation that HFNC causes a lower respiratory rate than other methods. The high gas flow lessens inspiratory resistance, which could help to lessen the intensity of the dyspnea. Treatment of severe hypoxaemic respiratory failure that cannot be corrected by reduced oxygen flows is the most sensible application for HFNC [211].

Heliox: A mixture of helium and oxygen is called heliox (usually in helium: oxygen ratio of 80:20 or 70:30). Although there is little data to support its utility, this gas has been administered to patients with a variety of respiratory disorders for many years. With potential uses for obstructive lung and partial upper airway obstruction illnesses including asthma and COPD, Heliox's low density gives it a special place in the Intensive Care scenario. Inhaling heliox might make breathing easier and make it easier to transfer aerosolized medications to the distal airways. As helium predominates in the combination, the use of heliox is restricted to individuals with low Fi O2 requirements. The potential benefit of heliox is constrained as the oxygen-to-helium ratio rises (and the helium percentage falls) [212]..

By lowering the Reynolds number, heliox's low density helps the transition from turbulent to laminar flow. Reducing turbulent flow requires less pressure to produce the same total flow, reducing the labor required to breathe. Possible reductions include intrinsic PEEP, partial pressure of carbon dioxide (PaCO2), and hyperinflation. Higher alveolar ventilation or reduced carbon dioxide production due to reduced work of breathing could both be contributing factors to the drop in PaCO2 [213].

Since it may enable the movement of small-size drug particles and better flow across partially obstructed airways, heliox has been proposed as a driving gas for nebulized pharmaceuticals. As a result, it might effectively deliver medications to distant airways. In mechanically ventilated patients who have severe asthma, mild hypoxemia, and progressive dynamic hyperinflation and who have not responded to conventional treatments, heliox may be investigated [212]. Due to the potential impact that helium's characteristics may have on flow measurements, care must be taken to ensure that the ventilator being used is compatible with heliox. Heliox cannot be used with ventilators that use hot-wire flow sensors due to helium's high thermal conductivity. Heliox may also be used to treat patients with ARDS, according to scant preclinical research. Following extubation, heliox has been demonstrated to reduce the work of breathing [214]. Although more research is required, the utilization of heliox as a driving gas for nebulized drugs shows promise and may be used for patients who are severely ill and have the worst obstruction. Finally, heliox cannot yet be suggested as a first-line therapy for patients with asthma on mechanical ventilators, even if it would be advantageous for some individuals with severe acute asthma to avoid intubation [213].

Hypoxemic respiratory failure treated with inhaled nitric oxide

Colorless and odorless nitric oxide (NO) is a gas that is recognized to be hazardous in cigarette smoke and an environmental problem. L-arginine has converted into NO endogenously in endothelial cells through the action of the enzyme NO synthase. By quickly diffusing across alveolar cells to the nearby smooth muscle of pulmonary arterioles, where it stimulates cyclic GMP, inhaled NO (iNO) produces local pulmonary vasodilation [215]. The high affinity that NO has for the blood's hemoglobin prevents systemic effects. iNO is considered safe at concentrations lower than 80 ppm. At greater concentrations, however, methemoglobinemia, impaired platelet aggregation, pulmonary edema, and the production of nitrogen dioxide in the gas delivery system can occur [216]. The formation of deadly nitrogen dioxide is amplified by high oxygen concentrations and long periods of time that nitrogen oxide spends in the gas delivery system. In order to avoid rebound pulmonary hypertension, the medicine should be tapered off gradually after administration because it inhibits endogenous NO production [217].

Hypoxaemic respiratory failure treated with inhaled prostacyclins

Endothelial cells secrete endogenous prostacyclin, a prostaglandin belonging to the eicosanoid family of lipids. It serves as a vasodilator and a platelet activation inhibitor. Cyclic AMP (cAMP) is upregulated by prostacyclin, causing relaxation of smooth muscles and consequent vasodilation. Long used to treat pulmonary hypertension, intravenous synthetic prostacyclin analogs have a non-selective vasodilatory effect [218,219]. As the vasodilating effect is preferable to well-ventilated regions of the lung, inhaled prostacyclins have a more focused pulmonary vasodilatory effect and can significantly lower pulmonary artery pressure, improve oxygenation, and improve right ventricular function, through improved ventilation-perfusion matching [220].

Data interpretation in critical care

Humans have been intrigued by thinking machines for a very long time because of their potential to fundamentally alter civilization. As society has become more digitalized and vast volumes of data have accumulated, a new lexicon has developed. Big data was created as a result of the size of data collecting, and the subject of data science was created as a result of the union of statistics and computer science required to fully utilize this new resource [233]. Statistical modeling evolved into machine learning, and as new, advanced machine learning techniques achieved unheard-of performance, the term artificial intelligence (AI) became increasingly common. Two major factors—affordable, accessible high-performance computer technology and a data explosion—are fundamental to the development of these new technologies. The latter is frequently assumed [234].

The goal of critical care medicine is to treat unstable, high-acuity patients, especially those who have multiple organ failure; as a result, constant physiologic monitoring is the distinguishing feature of the Intensive Care unit (ICU). The ICU is a remarkably fertile field for the spread of big data technology given the nearly complete digitization of health care. By providing huge cohorts for knowledge discovery and causal inference, advances that make use of this wealth of data promise to strengthen our currently very brittle evidence base and will serve as the foundation for the subsequent generation of clinical decision support tools [235]

The first resource of this kind was the Multiparameter Intelligent Monitoring in Intensive Care (MIMIC) database. The Medical Information Mart for Intensive Care (MIMIC-III) database has been created and updated over the past 20 years by the MIT Laboratory for Computational Physiology (LCP). High-resolution, multi-modal, de-identified data from 53 342 unique hospitalizations at the Beth Israel Deaconess Medical Center (BIDMC) in Boston, Massachusetts, are included in the MIMIC-III database. Vitals recordings & waveforms, test results, clinical notes, diagnostic summaries, and given interventions, including medicine, are just a few examples of the data. Many of the data must be extracted from the text format, however, some are quantitative or organized [234].

A potent method for assessing cerebral function in comatose and obtunded critically ill patients is continuous EEG monitoring (CEEG). Due to the volume of data produced during monitoring and the requirement for almost immediate analysis of a patient's EEG patterns, the continuing analysis of CEEG data is a major undertaking. Technical feasibility for CEEG surveillance in the Intensive Care unit has been achieved thanks to advancements in digital EEG data collecting, computer processing, data transfer, and data display. Focused examination of EEG epochs of potential relevance is becoming more and more possible thanks to a number of quantitative EEG tools including Fourier analysis and amplitude-integrated EEG as well as other data analysis techniques like computerized seizure identification [236].

Setting up alarms in ICU

Clinical alarms from various medical equipment, which are rapidly expanding, are a new problem in Intensive Care units as a result of the growth of medical technology (ICUs). A new alarm hazard issue is being brought on by medical device (clinical) alarms, which are intended to alert medical workers when a participant's condition veers outside of the normal range [237].

Critical factors that influence how quickly critical care nurses respond to bedside alarm investigations include visibility to physiological data, waveform settings, and false alarm detection. As a result, the efficiency of alarm systems in an ICU depends on the direct engagement of nurses in configuring the monitors and effectively handling alarming limitations [238]. Due to the rising incidence of nurse attrition and an inexperienced workforce, the ideal one-to-one nurse-to-patientratio is currently not a realistic expectation. Modern ICUs have technologically improved clinical alarms installed to help the nurses, however, the nurses must appropriately evaluate the clinical alarms [239].

To evaluate the number of alarms from medical equipment applied to the patient, alarm-generating devices, as well as the alarm-setting state of patient monitoring and mechanical ventilators, a Baillargeon instrument was modified. Alarm noises were counted manually, and anytime an alarm rang, both the medical instruments that were responsible for it and its causes were noted. Based on Baillargeon's research, alarms were separated into genuine and erroneous categories [240].

Overuse of clinical alarms can result in an alarming danger, which includes alarm fatigue, inappropriate alarm use, and applying the same alarm range to all patients. While device flaws previously put patients' safety in jeopardy, alarms recklessly created by the exponential rise in the number of medical gadgets now do the same [238]. Clinical alarms in ICUs and background noise were determined to be over 80 dB, which is comparable to the noise produced by a pneumatic drill in an operating room. In addition to the noise issue that alarms cause, ICU nurses could find it challenging to differentiate between alarms for urgent intervention and other alarms since various equipment manufacturers employ various types of alarms [241].

Alarm fatigue occurs when a high volume of clinical alerts overwhelms medical professionals; primary causes of alarm fatigue include excessive usage of patient monitors, incorrect alarm-setting ranges, and false (positive) alarms [241]. False alarms are the most problematic of these since they frequently occur, which can have the "cry wolf" effect and lead nurses to misinterpret important alarms and fail to act appropriately. Additionally, it can reduce the dependability of an alarm system and discourage nurses from using alarm gadgets. Therefore, it is crucial to handle medical device alarms well and create effective solutions that can lower false alarm rates [242].

Feeding in ICU:

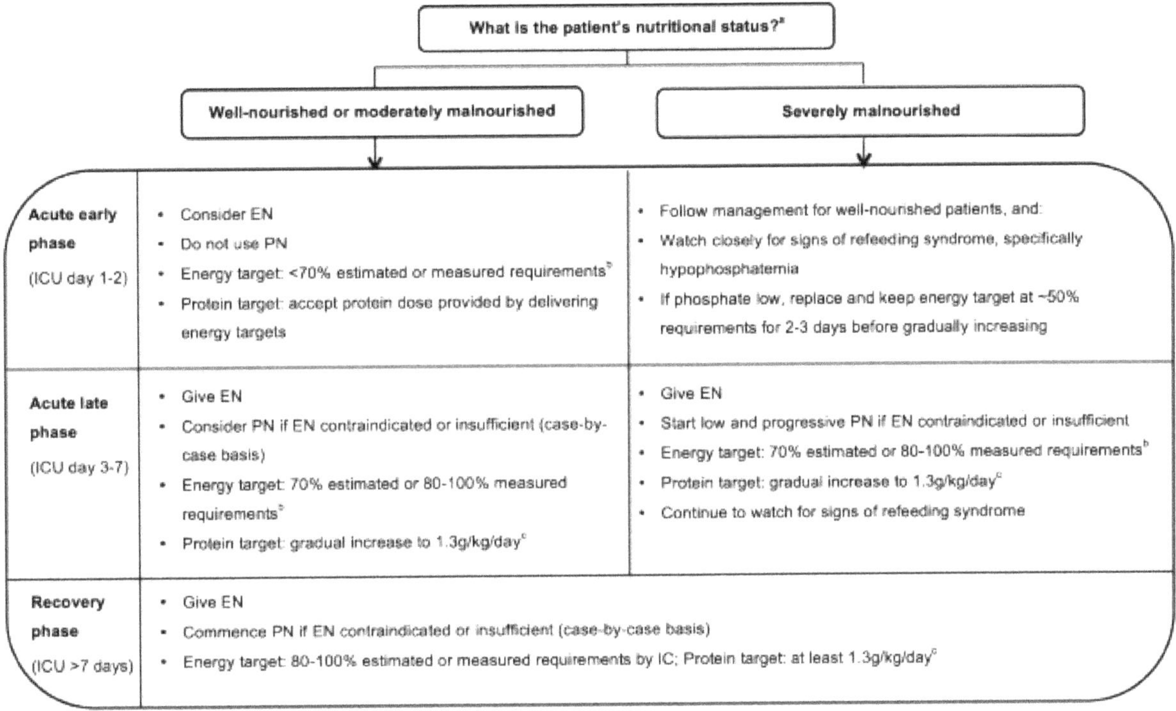

Figure 4.1: Nutrition in critical care

It is impossible to stress the importance of nutrition in critical care settings. Patients with critical illness frequently exhibit a catabolic stress state and a systemic inflammation response. Multi-organ dysfunction, higher infectious morbidity, and extended hospital stays are frequent complications [243]. It has been demonstrated that adequate nutrition interventions can modify immunological responses favorably and reduce the metabolic reaction to stress. In critically ill patients, nutritional therapy stops the further metabolic decline and lean body mass loss. The use of nutrition support in critically ill patients has been drawn to and valued because of the reduction in hospital stay length, morbidity rate, and improvement in patient outcomes [244].

Patients who are critically unwell experience a variety of physiometabolic alterations. The danger of malnutrition may rise as a result of these changes. The deteriorating clinical state is made more difficult by reduced overall calorie and protein intake. Multiple organ dysfunction, mortality, and shock may be brought on by an increase in sepsis, an increase in inflammatory biomarkers, and a metabolic imbalance. A thorough evaluation of critically sick patients will aid in selecting the nutritional support plan and enhance patient outcomes [245].

To meet the patients' needs for macro- and micronutrients, nutritional support becomes crucial. Based on the evaluation of gastrointestinal functionality and hemodynamic status, the route of feeding delivery (enteral or parenteral) must be chosen. This will eliminate the hazards brought on by improper feeding methods. Early enteral nutrition (EEN) has been demonstrated to have a number of advantages while also lowering the risk of problems in critically ill patients [243]. Appropriate time of introduction, volume, and form of nutrition all have an impact on the health outcomes of patients in the Intensive Care unit (ICU). Early nutrition intervention is defined as starting feeding within 24-48 hours of a serious illness. Depending on whether the nutritional adequacy goals are met, EN can be started either orally or by tube feeding [244].

Reduced peristalsis, mesenteric ischemia, and gastrointestinal hypoperfusion, may be seen in critically ill individuals. In patients with unstable hemodynamics (HD), EN may cause intestinal ischemia. Therefore, before beginning EN, clinical monitoring of gut function is crucial. The risk of problems such as gut ischemia in critically sick patients receiving two or even more vasopressors/inotropes in high dosages increases with the accidental beginning of EN [245]. As a result, there is still uncertainty over when EN should start. When a patient is receiving stable or lowering vasopressor dosage and has received sufficient volume support in HD unstable patients, EN should be started. The recommended course of action in these circumstances is trophic feeding (10–20 mL/h) to start nutrition [244].

Route of nutrition:

In critically ill patients, enteral (EN) rather than parenteral (PN) nutrition is preferred. The method used to give nutrients affects how well a nutritional intervention works. The enteral route is more physiological and offers nutrient value without compromising gut structural-functional integrity or the variety of intestinal microbes. Due to its potentially poorer nutritional requirements, EN has limitations during the acute illness phase and gastrointestinal dysfunction. Conversely, with PN, the desired nutritional requirement is better secured, although the main problems still include hyperglycemia, infectious complications, and hyperalimentation [246].

- Tube feeding: Enteral feeding is the method of choice for individuals with a functional gastrointestinal tract who are unable or unwilling to eat. Modern nasogastric (NG) feeding employing tiny tubes, percutaneous endoscopic gastrostomy feeding, and nasojejunal feeding are all examples of enteral tube feeding methods [247]. It is preferable for NG tubes to start enteral nutrition for the majority of surgical Intensive Care patients. In cases of late gastric emptying and slow intestinal motility, certain individuals might not be able to tolerate gastric feeding. Postpyloric eating may be beneficial for these patients [248].

  In patients receiving tube feeding, "nutrient content" and "microbiological safety" are crucial considerations. One of the frequent yet comparatively underappreciated risk factors for the onset of Clostridium difficile colitis is lengthy enteral tube feeding with minimal meals [249]. By keeping formula feeds sterile, feeding-related nosocomial infections in critically ill patients can be avoided [250].

  When EN is given to ICU patients, overfeeding is less likely to happen than underfeeding. Underfeeding is typically not advised in critically ill patients. Patients with feeding resistance, however, can be underfed [251,252]. Additionally, purposeful underfeeding of obese patients with BMIs greater than 30 kg/m2 may improve metabolic outcomes and shorten ICU stays [253].

Micronutrients: Critical disease is characterized by severe redox abnormalities that can result in a systemic inflammatory response syndrome, mitochondrial malfunction, and multi-organ failure. Micronutrient deficits may be caused by past malnutrition, the severity of the present illness, and the side effects of different therapy regimens and procedures. Such inadequacies may lead to decreased immunity, impaired wound healing, and increased morbidity and death. Therefore, additional vitamins and trace elements are a crucial therapeutic nutrition intervention to assist lessen the aforementioned difficulties [254].

Nutrition in hepatic failure: There are dietary myths about nutritional interventions in liver illnesses, particularly in the Indian context. Patients with hepatic encephalopathy and end-stage liver failure frequently experience malnutrition (HE). Malnutrition affects this patient population due to inadequate food intake, hypermetabolism, increased protein losses, inflammation, and decreased nutrient synthesis/absorption. In these people, nutritional inadequacies should be made up. The first dietary restriction to stop the development of edema and ascites is sodium restriction. Strict limitations, however, might result in protein-calorie malnutrition. In patients with ascites, sodium intake should be limited to 2 g per day [255].

Nutrition in traumatic brain injury: There is hypercatabolism and hypermetabolism in TBI, which increases the risk of malnutrition, muscular atrophy, weight loss, and negative nitrogen balance. Early dietary support maintains body weight and muscle mass while reducing the release of catabolic hormones. EN should be tried as quickly as volume resuscitation is finished and the patient is HD stable. In rehabilitation settings, EN might help TBI patients recover [256].

Nutrition in respiratory compromised: The lung condition known as chronic obstructive pulmonary disease (COPD) is characterised by a persistent, increasing restriction of airflow. Up to 60% of critically ill COPD patients with acute respiratory failure (ARF) have been observed to be malnourished. Low fat-free mass and decreased body weight are known to be bad prognostic indicators. Osteoporosis is a concomitant disease with COPD that is frequently seen. N nutrition and ventilation are fundamentally connected. Giving patients with clinically stable COPD modest, regular feeds without changing the composition of micronutrients helps achieve the best oral nutrition intervention efficacy [257].

Nutrition in acute kidney injury: AKI refers to a sudden decline in kidney function that makes it difficult to manage fluid, electrolyte, and acid-base balance. Protein-energy waste, which raises the risk of morbidity and mortality in AKI, is caused by hypercatabolism and lean body mass loss. A considerable amount of protein is catabolized in critically ill individuals with AKI, and their carbohydrate and lipid metabolisms are aberrant. Due to greater protein and micronutrient losses, this is especially challenging in AKI individuals on continuous renal replacement treatment [258].

Rules of FASTHUG not to forget:

The FASTHUG acronym was introduced as a standardised method to assist ICU doctors in making sure that all crucial requirements of care for critically ill patients were satisfied in 2005 [259]. The prevalence of ventilator-associated pneumonia was subsequently demonstrated to drop once the FAST HUG technique was used in a surgical ICU. Though generally well regarded, several physicians have altered the mnemonic to better fit their own ICU procedures [260]. It should be noted that the FAST HUG mnemonic was not intended to recognise drug-related issues frequently encountered in the ICU. As a result, we came up with the modified mnemonic FASTHUG-MAIDENS as a systematic, organized method of spotting drug-related issues in the ICU [261].

Abbreviation	Full forms	Abbreviation	Full forms
F	Feeding	M	Medication reconciliation
A	Analgesia	A	Antibiotics or anti-infectives
S	Sedation	I	Indications for medications
T	Thromboprophylaxis	D	Drug dosing
H	Hyperactive or hypoactive delirium*	E	Electrolytes, hematology, and other laboratory results
U	Stress ulcer prophylaxis	N	No drug interactions, allergies, duplications, side effects
G	Glucose control	S	Stop dates

*In the original version of the FASTHUG mnemonic, H was for "head of the bed elevated".

Figure 4.2: Fullforms of FASTHUG-MAIDENS

Description of FAST HUG MAIDENS:

F denotes feeding: Parenteral nutrition, sips of fluids, tube feeding, no oral intake, and diet as tolerated, are just a few of the ways that patients in the Intensive Care unit (ICU) may get nourishment. Due to the variety, there are several options to optimise drug therapy, like switching from the parenteral to the oral or vice versa based on the patient's feeding method. Alternative dosage forms, such as a liquid formulation or an immediate-release form, could be suggested for sustained-release drugs that are delivered in a form that is unable to crushed in order to reach equal total daily dosages. The pharmacists should determine that whether issue is due to a medicine if the patient is having large gastric residual volumes and is having trouble with enteral feeding [262].

A denotes analgesia: Analgesia is frequently needed by patients in the Intensive Care unit to alleviate pain from a variety of causes, surgery, including trauma, or other underlying medical disorders. A pain scale makes it simple to evaluate pain, and the patient's level of discomfort should be regularly monitored. The ideal dose of analgesic to administer to a patient is sufficient (to ensure that pain is not a problem), but not overwhelming. Additionally, the pharmacist can evaluate the patient's condition and offer recommendations for the best way to administer analgesic drugs, such as infusions, regularly spaced intermittent dosages, or longer-acting forms mixed with as-needed doses [263].

S denotes sedation: Sedation shares many of the same problems as analgesia outlined above. Midazolam and lorazepam are two examples of the benzodiazepines that are frequently used in the ICU as sedatives, however there may be circumstances in which a sedative-hypnotic may be preferable. Depending on the clinical context and the patient's score on a sedation scale, the pharmacists should be involved in decision making to start, stop, and alter the dosage of sedative drugs. Propofol, for instance, may be appropriate if the patient simply needs brief sedation. If, however, prolonged sedation is required, benzodiazepines might be a better choice [264].

T denotes thromboembolic prophylaxis: Nearly all ICU patients should get some kind of thromboembolic prophylaxis. However, certain medical factors may prevent some seriously ill patients from getting chemical thromboembolic prophylaxis (e.g., active gastrointestinal or intracranial bleeding). The pharmacist can work with these patients to develop a schedule for when to start taking the proper thromboembolic preventive drugs. Unfractionated heparin, low-molecular-weight heparins, intravascular filters, and sequential compression devices are some of the several prophylactic therapeutic options [265].

H denotes hypoactive or hyperactive delirium: In some form, delirium affects the majority of critically sick patients while they are in the Intensive Care unit. Delirium that is left untreated can lengthen a patient's time in the Intensive Care unit and increase expenditures, mortality, and moridibty. The pharmacist can detect the presence of delirium with the aid of tools like the Intensive Care Delirium Screening Checklist or the Confusion Assessment Method for the ICU. When delirium is identified, locating probable drug-related causes of delirium is frequently used in the search for the reason (and for methods to address the cause). Treatment options may include supportive and environmental strategies, as well as, in most cases, some type of pharmacological intervention using an antipsychotic medication [266].

U denotes stress ulcer prophylaxis: Stress ulcers can occur in ICU patients who are getting mechanical ventilation, hence the proper preventative drugs should be given. Proton pump inhibitors and Antagonists for histamine receptor are the medications most frequently prescribed for this indication. The pharmacist should make sure the patient is taking a preventive medication and should assist in choosing the best suitable medication in light of the patient's medical background. The pharmacist should reconsider whether the preventive agent can be stopped after the patient's condition becomes better and there is no longer risks for stress ulcers [267]..

G denotes glycemic control: In the Intensive Care unit, controlling blood glucose levels is a crucial component of patient care. The large selection of insulin regimens or oral hypoglycemic medications that are available can be used by the pharmacist to help choose the most suitable pharmacological regimen, which will assist keep blood glucose levels within the patient's target range [268].

M denotes medication reconciliation: Any patient who is admitted to the hospital will receive care that includes medication reconciliation. In order to maintain continuity of treatment, this process includes examining the medications the patient was taking before to admission and determining which prescriptions should be continued. Medication reconciliation should ideally be done before discharge, with each level or location change in care, and upon admission to any patient care unit. Acute medical circumstances prevent many people from restarting drugs they were taking before to admission. Finding stopped medications for which there is a strong possibility of experiencing symptoms of withdrawal is a crucial concern as well (e.g., benzodiazepines and selective serotonin reuptake inhibitors). In order to minimise difficulties, these medications should often be restarted as soon as feasible [269].

A denotes antibiotics or antinfectives: Patients who are admitted to the ICU are either already infected or have a higher risk of becoming infected while there. Because of this, pharmacists can be extremely important in antimicrobial stewardship. When cultures and susceptibility information are available, de-escalating treatments and choosing the best antimicrobial drug are examples of stewardship efforts. Before selecting a regimen, it is important to take into account factors including medical history (such as concurrent renal or hepatic impairment), allergies, recent use of antibiotics, and recent hospital admission. Additionally, the regimen's effectiveness and safety should be assessed, and the dosage or agent combinations should be changed as necessary [262].

I denotes indication for medications: It is common for patients to be treated with a significant number of drugs, the majority of which are started throughout their ICU stay, given the complex nature of treatment provided in the ICU. Every day, the pharmacist should check all routinely prescribed and as-needed medications to make sure they all have the right indications. To lower the chance of adverse events, drug interactions, errors in medications, and cost, any medicine that is no longer needed should be stopped [262].

D denotes drug dosing: Hepatic and renal function might fluctuate a lot in severely ill patients. To prevent accumulation of drug while ensuring adequate dosages are used to accomplish desired clinical end points, the pharmacist is in a prime position to recommend dose modifications based on clinical factors, particularly indications of hepatic and renal function. To avoid underdosing, it's crucial that the pharmacist continuously evaluates and modifies doses when the patient's condition starts to get better [262].

E denotes electrolytes, hematology, and other laboratory tests: The everyday management of critically ill patients includes blood tests. Pharmacists should keep an eye on individuals for drug-related causes of abnormal electrolyte levels, haematological findings, or other laboratory values and talk to the other members of the healthcare team about treatment options. Additionally, the pharmacist may suggest starting or stopping the use of minerals, nutrients, blood, and fluid products, depending on the situation [262].

N denotes no drug interactions, duplication, allergies, or side effects: The risk of drug interactions rises with the number of medications that a typical ICU patient takes. Therefore, it's critical to quickly identify clinically significant actual and potential drug-drug, drug-laboratory, drug-food interactions and to suggest an alternative course of treatment. Additionally, the pharmacist should do an evaluation to identify whether a patient's reaction to a certain drug is due to an intolerance or a true pharmaceutical allergy if the patient appears allergic to it. After the evaluation, the pharmacist can help by making recommendations for alternatives or keeping an eye out for negative drug responses [262].

S denotes stop dates: Not all medications that a doctor prescribes to a patient are intended to be taken forever. Examples of medications that might need a stop or review date include corticosteroids and anti-infective treatments, but this list is not exhaustive. The pharmacist and other healthcare professionals should talk about how long patients should take their prescriptions for [262].

Chapter 5:

Managements of Parameters in Critical Care Management

The goal of patient observation is to identify organ malfunction and provide instructions for restoring and maintaining tissue oxygen delivery. As the response to critical illness is significantly correlated with outcome, monitoring is an important component of the care of the ICU patient in the emergency department. This study focuses on the methods that screen critically ill patients inside the emergency department since it is crucial to understand the limitations of monitoring devices and monitored data as well as the possibility of dangers from invasive monitoring [283].

The eventual aim of monitoring in critically ill patients is to improve oxygen delivery to the tissues in order to prevent or treat organ failure and cellular damage. A number of frequently measured variables help to track oxygen delivery because it is a function of blood oxygen level and cardiac output. Blood oxygen content is connected to hemoglobin level and oxygen saturation, which can both be easily measured and watched, whereas cardiac output is the product of heart rate and stroke volume (also easily measured and monitored). Critically ill patients receive early goal-directed care in the emergency room, which lowers mortality [283].

End tidal carbon dioxide monitoring:

The location of the tracheal tube in a major airway is verified via measuring the end tidal carbon dioxide (ETCO2). The inability to detect carbon dioxide when cardiac output is present implies that the tube is placed in the esophagus. Other helpful data is also provided by continual carbon dioxide tracking. Capnometry is the measuring of carbon dioxide exhaled, and the most straightforward way to do this is to connect a disposable colorimetric detector to the tracheal tube. Carbon dioxide exhalation can be detected semi-quantitatively using a pH-sensitive indicator strip. Purple denotes the lack of carbon dioxide, whereas yellow represents a CO2 content of much more than 2%, suggesting proper placement of the tube in the upper airways [284].

Capnography, which continuously displays the ETCO2 wave, provides more thorough information. Electronic capnometry measures the quantity of CO2 inhaled using infrared light absorbance, which has an inverse relationship to the amount of infrared light communicated. The patient's breathing apparatus may be connected directly to the monitor, or a steady sample of gas may be routed to the capnometer.

Although sidestream devices are smaller, lighter, and more flexible than mainstream monitors, they respond more slowly—between one and two seconds—and there is a chance that the measured CO2 values will be a little lower [284].

Nevertheless, the capnometer is frequently used to check on the quality of ventilation, for instance, when moving patients with head injuries. A few situations, such as those after mouth-to-mouth resuscitation, inadequate bag-valve-mask ventilation (resulting in stomach distension), and after consuming carbonated beverages, have been linked to false-positive capnometry after oesophageal intubation. Before utilizing a colorimetric capnometry, at least six ventilations should be performed because carbon dioxide is dissipated within 10-15 seconds of administering ventilation [284].

Pulse oximetry:

A finger or ear probe is used in pulse oximetry, a continuous, non-invasive method of measuring arterial hemoglobin oxygen saturation. Pulsatile blood flow allows red and infrared light to pass through the tissue. The ability of deoxygenated and oxygenated hemoglobin to absorb red light (with wavelengths between 600 and 750 nm) and infrared light (with wavelengths between 850 and 1000 nm) differs: oxygenated hemoglobin absorbs more infrared light than deoxygenated hemoglobin, which in turn absorbs more red light than oxygenated hemoglobin. Because the absorption spectra of carboxyhemoglobin, oxyhaemoglobin, and methaemoglobin, are similar, pulse oximeters cannot discriminate between these dyshemoglobinemia and oxyhaemoglobin because the SpO2 overstates the oxygen saturation [285].

Central venous pressure monitoring:

A potentially helpful but sometimes misunderstood method for determining the intravascular volume status of critically unwell patients is central venous pressure (CVP). Despite the fact that the CVP is helpful for directing fluid therapy in critically ill patients, individual CVP readings have poor relationships with intravascular volume. Internal jugular or subclavian veins are the typical locations for central venous catheter insertion. The intravascular volume, patient posture, venous tone, cardiac valvular disease, and intrathoracic pressure are all factors that affect normal CVP, which is highly varied [286].

The transmural vascular pressure, which is intravascular pressure minus extravascular pressure, is what determines the ventricular preload, although the CVP transducer only detects intravascular pressure. Significant clinical problems including airflow blockage or increased dead space ventilation cause changes in the capnography waveform (as seen with pulmonary embolism). The intrathoracic pressure is typically close to zero towards the end of expiration during spontaneous breathing, hence the CVP should be assessed at this point [286].

Monitoring the continual central venous oxygen saturation:

It has been shown that patients with a wide range of critical diseases, such as heart failure and sepsis, have a worse result when the pulmonary artery mixed with venous oxygen saturation (SvO2) is lowered. This measurement is recommended as a helpful marker of tissue oxygenation. However, the insertion of a pulmonary artery catheter (PAC), which is relatively intrusive and linked to a number of problems, is necessary for this assessment. The usage of PACs is decreasing, and non-invasive cardiac output monitoring is gradually taking their place [287].

Monitoring of temperature:

As part of a severely ill patient's care, temperature monitoring is an essential but frequently overlooked task. Hypothermia impairs all organ functions, increases blood loss due to coagulopathy, and produces coagulopathy. Rewarming causes vasodilation and shivering, which enhance cardiovascular instability. These patients frequently have significant oxygen debt, which is made worse by shivering. Hypothermia causes an increase in adrenergic responses, which raises the risk of heart morbidity [288].

Vasoconstriction and reduced cardiac output have an impact on peripheral temperature, which represents tissue perfusion. The bladder, esophagus, rectum, or tympanic membrane can all be used to measure core temperature. The greater gradient between core and skin temperature that occurs in shock serves as a helpful, non-specific indicator of how well resuscitation is working. Thermistors are frequently used to check internal temperatures and work on the theory that resistance changes with temperature. Non-invasive tympanic thermometers can be used to quickly determine core temperature, however they are not always accurate in patients who are seriously unwell. The downside of the oesophageal and urinary bladder procedures is that they can only be used on sedated or intubated patients, or on individuals who have a urinary catheter, respectively [288].

Urine output:

An excellent indicator of the sufficiency of splanchnic perfusion, renal function, and cardiac output is hourly urine production. In order to facilitate monitoring during resuscitation, a standard urine flow threshold of 0.5 ml/kg/h is utilized; a urine flow that is below this denotes insufficient resuscitation [283].

How to write a critical care daily note:

A patient note is a clinical record that a hospital doctor creates to describe a patient's condition as well as the doctor's evaluations and treatment strategy. A daily note is written for each patient by the attending physician, who is primarily in charge of their treatment. These notes are a part of the official health record for billing and legal reasons and are referred to by other doctors when treatment is shared or transferred. In order to write a progress note, a doctor must collect, examine, and comment on both past and present patient data, including, information from medical rounds, lab results, medications, tests, procedures to assess patient health, as well as choose pertinent details to include in the note at hand [272,273].

The Intensive Care Unit (ICU) doctors that we researched do not use the documentation aspects of current Electronic Medical Record (EMR) systems, for the reasons that we discuss below. Current EMR systems provide facilities for producing and tracking progress notes. Oral briefings by fellows, residents, nurses, as well as data queries on EMR systems, are used to collect patient data; however, various technologies are used to track patients' progress. They include pertinent patient information into a progress note using general document processing tools like Microsoft Word and at least one other documentation tool, such as paper, custom software, or self-made macros, to help them monitor and record progress [271].

Creating notes in ICU: The process of writing a note involves developing patient assessments and care plans. The patient databases, earlier patient notes, printed lab reports, oral presentations, and written records of residents and fellows are just a few of the sources from which doctors gather factual information. They also consult EMR systems. We discovered that a significant portion of the note-making process in the Intensive Care unit took place in the context of cooperative group discussion and question-answering, frequently during a procedure known as "medical rounds." As prior research on information searching in ICUs reveals, during these group talks, doctors asked a variety of questions to ascertain the status of a patient and formulate a plan for their treatment [271].

Clinical data sources can provide some answers, but many also incorporate organizational or experiential knowledge that physicians learn through conversations with other clinicians and through their own observations. Clinical patient data located in the EMR system is also recorded; however, because of the structure and additional task switching required during rounds, data lookups are done separately, with placeholders for information being added as they go. The majority of these placeholders are due to gaps in resident reports as well as the lack of data on the devices used throughout rounds [271].

Typically, a patient note is not added to the patient data right away once it is written. Between the time the note is produced and the time it is filed to the record, the doctors predicted that up to eight hours may pass during which they will continue to monitor the patient's condition. The doctors monitor patient data all day long, including test results, ventilator settings, and vital signs in order to analyze a pattern of readings, spot anomalies, and modify assessments and plans for patient care as necessary [271].

How to do quick bedside evaluation and examination of critical care patients:

In order to diagnose and treat critically ill individuals, laboratory testing gives crucial information. Such tests could be carried out close to the patient or in a main clinical laboratory. Testing done "near the patient" can take place either there or at the patient's bedside (for example, in the stat lab in the Intensive Care unit [ICU]) [274].

Advantages of bedside testing: Because bedside monitoring reduces the turn - around time for receiving laboratory findings, patients can now be treated in real time. Because precise results can be provided right away, bedside testing may help reduce the need for unnecessary therapies. Both hypoglycemia and hypokalemia are examples of this. Many clinicians take a blood sample when hypoglycemia is suspected, test it for glucose, and then start treating the patient while they wait for the findings of the lab [275]. Hypertonic glucose, however, hurts and harms veins. Within a matter of minutes, a bedside blood glucose analysis can be completed, and therapy can safely wait while waiting for the findings. Additionally, additional diagnostic procedures can begin right away if the glucose concentration is normal, without having to wait for a normal outcome from the laboratory environment [276].

Arrhythmias that develop while surgery or in Intensive Care units may be a sign of hypokalemia. However, treatment with potassium is commonly postponed because of pending laboratory findings due to the fact that many individuals also are at threat for hyperkalemia (i.e. because of hypercatabolism, renal failure, or tissue injury). Potassium analysis at the bedside can help with quick diagnosis and targeted treatment [275].

Rapid lab results might also be helpful for cardiac arrest patients. Since hypocalcemia and hypokalemia are uncommon causes of cardiac arrest, it is not recommended that you treat all individuals who experience cardiac arrest with these medications. An early diagnosis, however, may be crucial for the minority people in whom these electrolytes result in the arrest [274].

Additionally, bedside testing may shorten hospital stays in the ICU and lower expenditures. Weaning time, lCU stay, overall hospital stay, and hospital costs all decreased as a result of bedside monitoring. Numerous possible sources of laboratory error could be reduced with the use of bedside testing. Since blood is taken, tests can indeed be measured and findings recorded right at the patient's bedside, minimizing errors caused by improper labeling and transportation. Medical professionals and patients both favor bedside testing. Because results can be retrieved right away while a doctor is on the scene, treatment can begin right away or be changed, which saves time [274].

Bedside laboratory tests conducted are:

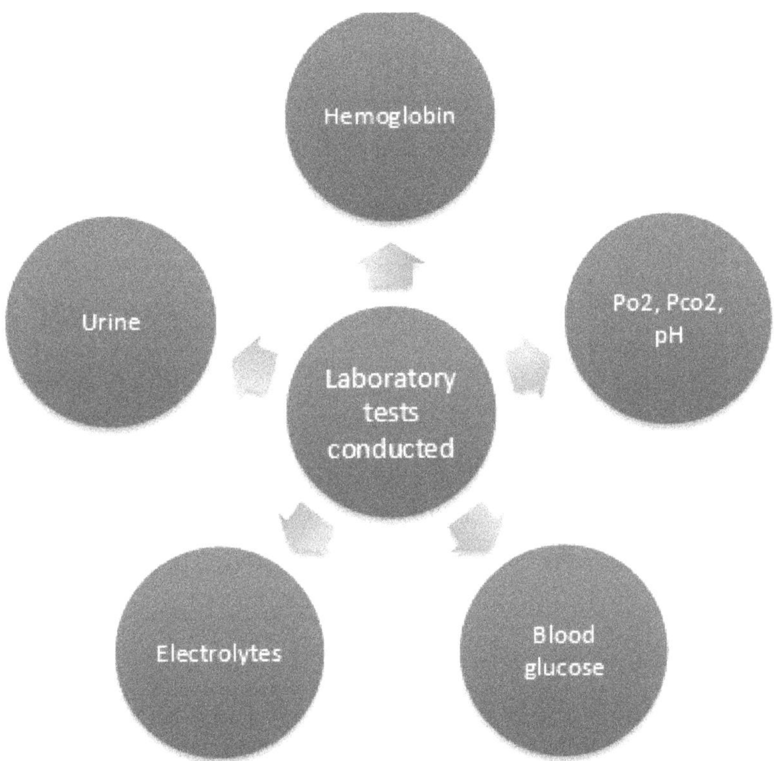

Figure 5.1:Bedside Laboratory Tests

Po2, Pco2, pH: The preservation of ventilation, tissue oxygenation, and proper acid-base balance is a top priority in critical care units. In critical care units, a variety of diseases and medications may interact with these procedures. A variety of factors can cause life-threatening changes in ventilation, acid-base balance, and oxygenation within a short amount of time. It is thought that early diagnosis of these changes may enhance patient treatment [277].

The most popular continuous oxygen monitoring method used today, pulse oximetry detects oxyhemoglobin saturation. There are also accessible transconjunctival and transcutaneous oxygen sensors. These devices assess the cutaneous or conjunctival surface's oxygen tension. However, they are not commonly used since they are less trustworthy and linked to a number of issues [278].

Blood glucose: In severely ill patients, bedside blood glucose monitoring may be very helpful. It makes it possible to precisely diagnose and treat hypoglycemia. Bedside blood glucose analysis can reduce hospital stays and expenditures for patients hospitalized with diabetic ketoacidosis. It is also beneficial in evaluating hyperglycemic patients and for optimizing insulin therapy. Typically, dry-chemistry reagent sticks (dipsticks) are used for bedside blood glucose measurement [279].

Electrolytes: Patients who are seriously unwell frequently experience electrolyte changes. The elements potassium, ionized sodium, calcium, phosphorus, and magnesium are the ones that change the most frequently. In severely ill patients, total calcium measurements do not accurately reflect ionized calcium levels, making them less useful for calcium status monitoring [280]. Magnesium rarely leads to serious issues on its own (that is, without concurrent increases in potassium or calcium). Although variations in sodium and phosphorus can have serious consequences, these ions often fluctuate slowly enough (over hours) that "central laboratory" monitoring is sufficient. Following the injection of diuretics, insulin, or epinephrine, potassium levels may vary significantly and quickly [281].

Hematocrit or hemoglobin: Even in patients who are actively bleeding, hematocrit and/or hemoglobin levels rarely vary quickly enough to call for routine bedside testing. Rapid evaluation can occasionally help the bleeding patient receive blood replacement therapy, nevertheless [274].

Urine testing: There are numerous tests available for urinalysis. These examinations are simple to carry out, quick, affordable, and helpful for patient screening. Screening can reduce the need for pointless tests and reduce hospital expenses. The majority of tests employ calorimetric techniques, and errors in procedure or user behavior may lead to inaccuracy. Screening patients with anomalies in antidiuretic hormone secretion and determining the causes of oliguria may benefit from measuring the osmolality or specific gravity of their urine. When evaluating patients with diabetes mellitus and determining the reasons for polyuria, urine glucose and ketones are helpful. Urine leukocyte esterase and nitrites can be used to test patients for urinary tract infections [282].

Chapter 6:

Critical Care Management in Patients with Other Conditions

A multidisciplinary approach is necessary for the Intensive Care unit's management of critically ill patients. Surgeons must be familiar with the fundamentals of Intensive Care medicine in order to handle their own critically sick patients and because there are known risks associated with critical care surgery [290].

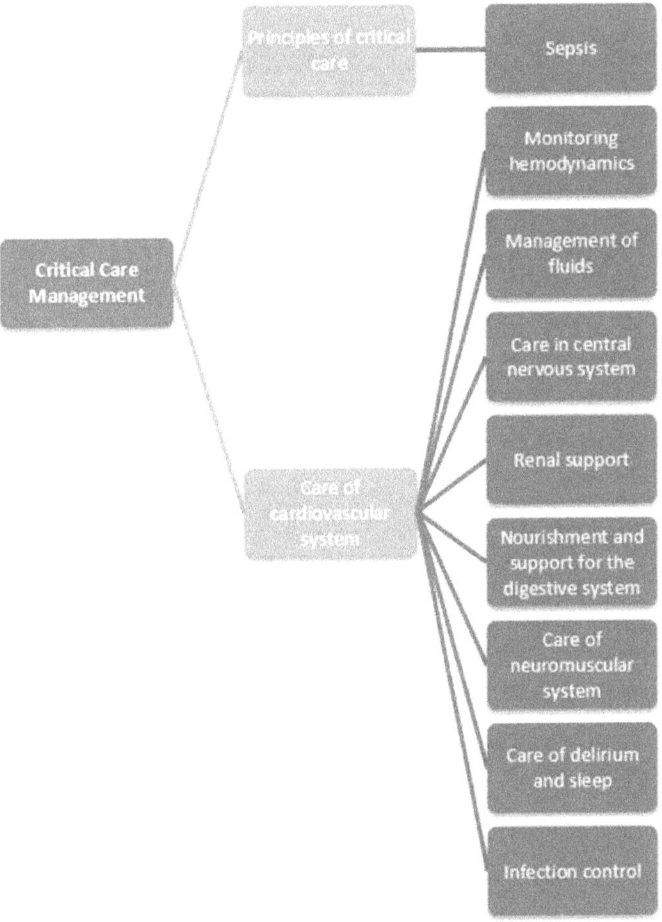

Figure 6.1: Critical Care Management in patients

Principles of critical care:

The method of caring for patients who either have life-threatening disorders or are at danger of developing them is known as critical care. High staffing ratios, sophisticated monitoring, and organ support can be provided in the critical care unit (ICU), a separate geographic entity, to reduce patient morbidity and death. However, providing efficient Intensive Care necessitates a comprehensive strategy that goes beyond the ICU. Preventative measures, a multidisciplinary approach before and during an ICU stay, early warning and response systems thorough follow-up, and high-quality palliative care are all necessary [290].

For guidance on specific patient care issues such the treatment of the surgical condition, nutrition, wound care, and treatment of anticoagulation in the postoperative period, the surgeon's position inside the critical care team is vital. Additionally, the surgeon and critical care physician must work together to make strategic decisions on the overall treatment of surgical patients and have a responsibility to explain these decisions to patients and family members. The patient and family should discuss difficult issues regarding the requirement for treatment restrictions and the identification of ineffective and burdensome treatments with both teams [290]

Sepsis: A significant majority of ICU patients either develop sepsis at the time of their admission or as a complication while they are in the ICU due to sepsis, which is a major cause of mortality and morbidity worldwide. The definition of sepsis is "life-threatening organ malfunction brought on by an abnormal host response to an infection." Sepsis complicated by hypotension in spite of volume resuscitation and elevated blood lactate >2 mmol/L is known as septic shock [291].

The main principles of progressive sepsis care are:

- Early sepsis recognition
- Adequate, balanced recognition
- Prompt detection of the source
- Control of source in appropriate time
- Efficient and early control with antimicrobials
- haemodynamic support, high-quality supportive care, and considering adjunctive therapies.

Care of cardiovascular system:

The goal of hemodynamic treatment for critically ill patients is to maximize oxygen delivery to the various organ systems and tissue perfusion. The use of vasoactive medications based on frequent monitoring of changes in the cardiovascular system and appropriate hydration management are the foundations of this strategy [292].

Monitoring hemodynamics: The assessment of hemodynamic abnormalities in critical illness is famously challenging due to their complexity. Clinicians need to combine complex information from numerous sources and take into account pathophysiological insults to both microcirculation and macrocirculation [292].

Management of fluids: Restoring a sufficient circulation volume to ensure tissue perfusion is the aim of fluid management. Endothelial injury and capillary leakage, however, can cause considerable tissue oedema that can impair the passage of nutrients and oxygen. When a patient is admitted to the ICU, having a cumulatively positive fluid balance has been linked to worse clinical outcomes. Therefore, fluid management involves striking a careful balance between many, possibly at odds requirements, and the significance of regularly checking the fluid balance cannot be emphasized [292]

Short- to medium-term acting medications called vasopressors and inotropic medicines are used to improve cardiac output or vascular tone in a range of critical disease conditions. They are employed as a stopgap measure until the disease process resolves and sufficient cardiovascular function restores. Vasopressors cause peripheral blood vessels' smooth muscles to contract, increasing both the systemic vascular resistance and the constriction of venous capacitance vessels. Most frequently, a rise in blood pressure is the reported net effect. Norepinephrine, metaraminol, epinephrine, dopamine (through -adrenoceptor action), vasopressin, and phenylephrine are examples of commonly used vasopressors [293].

The myocardium's increased contractility as a result of inotrope use raises cardiac output. Epinephrine, dopamine (through -adrenoceptor actions), milrinone, and dobutamine are some types of inotropes that are frequently used (a phosphodiesterase inhibitor). A more recent inotrope called levosimendan acts by raising myocardial sensitivity to calcium [293].

Care in central nervous system: Patients with spinal or intracranial pathologies require neuroprotective care (e.g. ischaemic strokes, traumatic brain injury, spinal cord ischaemia, intracranial bleeds). It necessitates a multisystem treatment, with careful ventilation and hemodynamic support being of utmost importance. Modern imaging and monitoring technologies, such as those that measure intracranial pressure or neurological function, can now be used to guide therapy choices. Extracranial illness processes also run the potential of resulting in secondary brain damage, which may be prevented. Targeted temperature control and the prevention of hyperthermia are two examples that could help patients who survive cardiac arrest outside of a hospital have better neurological outcomes [294].

Renal support: With a mortality rate of up to 67.6% in the general ICU population, acute kidney damage (AKI) is a serious consequence of critical illness that provides a considerable diagnostic challenge for the Intensive Care staff. In critical illness, prerenal factors (hypertension, sepsis, decreased cardiac output) frequently act as the primary precipitant of AKI. However, during the ICU stay, renal failure frequently develops complex, for instance due to parenchymal destruction from nephrotoxic medications. Post-renal causes are uncommon in seriously unwell patients. AKI is treated with prompt diagnosis, appropriate fluid administration, hemodynamic support, and eradication of underlying and contributory causes. To maintain fluid, electrolyte, and metabolic waste product balance when AKI is severe, renal replacement treatment (RRT) may be required [290].

Indications of renal replacement in critical care are:

- oliguria/anuria
- Pulmonary edema
- Increased hyperthermia
- Overdosing with toxins
- Uncompensated metabolic acidosis.

Nourishment and support for the digestive system: When patients are admitted to the ICU, many of them are malnourished. Their capacity to tolerate the physiologic stresses of severe disease is significantly impacted by this. Additionally, serious illness can have a direct impact on gut health and disrupt nutritional balance. Malnutrition can raise the risk of infection, promote slow healing of wounds, and cause muscle mass loss. Therefore, it is essential to improve patient outcome to conduct a full nutritional assessment upon entrance to identify high-risk individuals and to provide nutritional support promptly [295].

There has been much debate on the best method of nutritional support. Prokinetics are widely used to aid enteral feeding, which frequently requires nasogastric or nasojejunal feeding tubes (metoclopramide and erythromycin). Parenteral nutrition is typically given through a central vein and offers a different approach in cases of chronic gut failure. Both treatments have a lot of complications attached to them. Early enteral feeding is currently preferred over early parenteral nutrition because it has more dangers and less clear advantages for patients [295].

Care of neuromuscular system: Patients who are critically ill frequently experience severe muscle weakness. Along with specific disease entities (such as Guillain-Barré syndrome and myasthenia gravis) that may necessitate critical care admission, many patients may develop myopathies, neuropathies, or a combination of the two. These conditions are frequently referred to as ICU-acquired weakness (ICUAW). Muscular atrophy due to lack of use, multiple organ failure syndrome, exposure to certain medicines (such as corticosteroids and neuromuscular blocking agents), starvation, and infection all play a part. This is a typical finding in patients who have endured a serious postoperative complication, including an anastomotic leak; these patients frequently needed numerous admissions to the operating room and necessitated substantial organ support [296].

Care of delirium and sleep: The patient's normal sleep-wake cycle is frequently severely disturbed while they are suffering from a critical disease. On the Intensive Care unit, it might be challenging to maintain the appropriate state of daytime alertness and nighttime sleep. The underlying disease process, drug side effects, frequent interventions, discomfort, artificial organ support, and loud noises and bright lights are all contributing factors. Therefore, efforts to lessen the negative effects of sleep disturbance concentrate on reducing the aforementioned risk factors and promoting good sleep hygiene by restoring a normal circadian rhythm. Additionally, some departments use pharmaceutical strategies like melatonin, sedation breaks, and analgesia-based sedation regimes. Understanding the psychological effects of serious sickness and recovery can help the patient, their loved ones, and their return to work following discharge [297].

Careful evaluation is necessary if delirium develops in a postoperative patient since it could be the initial indicator of a surgical complication such an anastomotic leak or the onset of postoperative pneumonia. Patients who exhibit a hypoactive delirium need to have a high index of suspicion because their symptoms are less obvious than those of a hyperactive delirium patient who is agitated. In order to keep the patient and staff safe, management is based on the type (hyperactive, hypoactive, or mixed) and includes addressing the underlying cause, avoiding precipitants, assuring the patient, as well as prudent and focused pharmacological therapy [297].

Infection control: Patients who are in critical condition are more likely to get infections caused by multi-resistant germs. These "super bugs" are frequently prevalent only in a particular nation, hospital, or critical care unit. Stewardship of antibiotics plays a significant role in the daily care of critically ill patients. It's crucial to make sure the proper prophylaxis is administered intraoperatively to surgical patients [298].

Focusing on screening, prevention, and avoiding cross-contamination are essential elements of efficient infection control. It is crucial that the visiting team in the critical care unit adhere to local standards, such as using the appropriate personal protective equipment (PPE) when evaluating patients. The majority of the precautions are similar to those taken in other hospital rooms, but specific precautions taken in critical care units include selective gut removal of contaminants in ventilated patients, separation of infectious patients, common microbiology input to minimize the use of antibiotics, and meticulous asepsis during the insertion and ability to handle of invasive lines [298].

References

- Gutsche JT, Kohl BA. Who should care for Intensive Care unit patients? Crit Care Med. 2007 Feb;35(2 Suppl):S18-23. doi: 10.1097/01.CCM.0000252907.47050.FE. PMID: 17242601.
- Reisner-Senelar L. The birth of Intensive Care medicine: Bjorn Ibsen's records. Intensive Care Med 2011 Jul;37(7):1084-6.
- Vachon F. Histoire de la réanimation médicale française: 1954–1975. Reanimation 2011;20(1):72-8.
- Safar P, DeKornfeld T, Pearson J, et al. Intensive Care unit. Anesthesia 1961;16:275.
- Weil MH, Tang W. From Intensive Care to critical care medicine: a historical perspective. Am J Respir Crit Care Med 2011 Jun 1;183(11):1451-3.
- Halpern NA, Pastores SM. Critical care medicine in the United States 2000-2005: an analysis of bed numbers, occupancy rates, payer mix, and costs. Crit Care Med 2010 Jan;38(1):65-71.
- Adhikari NK, Fowler RA, Bhagwanjee S, Rubenfeld GD. Critical care and the global burden of critical illness in adults. Lancet 2010 Oct 16;376(9749):1339-46.
- Murthy S, Leligdowicz A, Adhikari NK. Intensive Care unit capacity in low-income countries: a systematic review. PLoS ONE 2015;10(1):e0116949.
- Mundy CJ, Bates I, Nkhoma W, Floyd K, Kadewele G, Ngwira M, et al. The operation, quality and costs of a district hospital laboratory service in Malawi. Trans R Soc Trop Med Hyg 2003 Jul;97(4):403-8.
- Gray IP, Carter JY. An evaluation of clinical laboratory services in sub-Saharan Africa. Ex africa semper aliquid novi? Clin Chim Acta 1997 Nov 6;267(1):103-28.
- Mollura DJ, Azene EM, Starikovsky A, Thelwell A, Iosifescu S, Kimble C, et al. White Paper Report of the RAD-AID Conference on International Radiology for Developing Countries: identifying challenges, opportunities, and strategies for imaging services in the developing world. J Am Coll Radiol 2010 Jul;7(7):495-500.
- Smith ZA, Ayele Y, McDonald P. Outcomes in critical care delivery at Jimma University Specialised Hospital, Ethiopia. Anaesth Intensive Care 2013 May;41(3):363-8.

- Dare L, Buch E. The future of health care in Africa. BMJ 2005 Jul 2;331(7507):1-2. (14) L'Her P
- Valentin A, Ferdinande P. Recommendations on basic requirements for Intensive Care units: structural and organizational aspects. Intensive Care Med 2011 Oct;37(10):1575- 87.
- Ferri M, Zygun DA, Harrison A, Stelfox HT. Evidence-based design in an Intensive Care unit: end-user perceptions. BMC Anesthesiol 2015;15:57.
- Caruso P, Guardian L, Tiengo T, Dos Santos LS, Junior PM. ICU architectural design affects the delirium prevalence: a comparison between single-bed and multibed rooms*. Crit Care Med 2014 Oct;42(10):2204-10
- Adhikari NK, Fowler RA, Bhagwanjee S, Rubenfeld GD. Critical care and the global burden of critical illness in adults. Lancet. 2010;376(9749):1339–1346. doi: 10.1016/S0140-6736(10)60446-1.
- Kause J, Smith G, Prytherch D, Parr M, Flabouris A, Hillman K. A comparison of antecedents to cardiac arrests, deaths and emergency Intensive Care admissions in Australia and New Zealand, and the United Kingdom—the ACADEMIA study. Resuscitation. 2004;62(3):275–282. doi: 10.1016/j.resuscitation.2004.05.016.
- McQuillan P, Pilkington S, Allan A, Taylor B, Short A, Morgan G, Nielsen M, Barrett D, Smith G, Collins CH. Confidential inquiry into quality of care before admission to Intensive Care. BMJ. 1998;316(7148):1853–1858. doi: 10.1136/bmj.316.7148.1853.
- Vincent JL, Marshall JC, Namendys-Silva SA, Francois B, Martin-Loeches I, Lipman J, Reinhart K, Antonelli M, Pickkers P, Njimi H, et al. Assessment of the worldwide burden of critical illness: the Intensive Care Over Nations (ICON) audit. Lancet Respir Med. 2014;2(5):380–386. doi: 10.1016/S2213-2600(14)70061-X.
- Murthy S, Leligdowicz A, Adhikari NK. Intensive Care unit capacity in low-income countries: a systematic review. PLoS One. 2015;10(1):e0116949. doi: 10.1371/journal.pone.0116949.
- Schell, C. O., Wärnberg, M. G., Hvarfner, A., Höög, A., Baker, U., Castegren, M., & Baker, T. (2017). The global need for essential emergency and critical care. *Critical Care, 22.*https://doi.org/10.1186/s13054-018-2219-2
- Knaus WA, Draper EA, Wagner DP, Zimmerman JE. APACHE II: A severity of disease classification system. Crit Care Med. 1985;13:818–29.
- Bouch DC, Thompson JP. Severity scoring systems in the critically ill. Contin Educ Anaesth Crit Care Pain. 2008;8:181–5.
- Champion HR. Trauma scoring. Scand J Surg. 2002;91:12–22.

- Le Gall JR, Lemeshow S, Saulnier F. A new Simplified Acute Physiology Score (SAPS II) based on a European/North American multicenter study. JAMA. 1993;270:2957–63.
- Marshall JC, Cook DJ, Christou NV, Bernard GR, Sprung CL, Sibbald WJ. Multiple organ dysfunction score: A reliable descriptor of a complex clinical outcome. Crit Care Med. 1995;23:1638–52.
- Vincent JL, Moreno R, Takala J, Willatts S, De Mendonça A, Bruining H, et al. The SOFA (Sepsis-related Organ Failure Assessment) score to describe organ dysfunction/failure. On behalf of the Working Group on Sepsis-Related Problems of the European Society of Intensive Care Medicine. Intensive Care Med. 1996;22:707–10.
- Le Gall JR, Klar J, Lemeshow S, Saulnier F, Alberti C, Artigas A, et al. The logistic organ dysfunction system. A new way to assess organ dysfunction in the Intensive Care unit. ICU Scoring Group. JAMA. 1996;276:802–10.
- Lemeshow S, Teres D, Avrunin JS, Gage RW. Refining Intensive Care unit outcome prediction by using changing probabilities of mortality. Crit Care Med. 1988;16:470–7.
- Fagon JY, Chastre J, Novara A, Medioni P, Gibert C. Characterization of Intensive Care unit patients using a model based on the presence or absence of organ dysfunctions and/or infection: The ODIN model. Intensive Care Med. 1993;19:137–44.
- Timsit JF, Fosse JP, Troché G, De Lassence A, Alberti C, Garrouste-Orgeas M, et al. Accuracy of a composite score using daily SAPS II and LOD scores for predicting hospital mortality in ICU patients hospitalized for more than 72 h. Intensive Care Med. 2001;27:1012–21.
- Castello FV, Cassano A, Gregory P, Hammond J. The Pediatric Risk of Mortality (PRISM) Score and Injury Severity Score (ISS) for predicting resource utilization and outcome of Intensive Care in pediatric trauma. Crit Care Med. 1999;27:985–8.
- To KB, Napolitano LM. Common complications in the critically ill patient. Surg Clin North Am. 2012 Dec;92(6):1519-57. doi: 10.1016/j.suc.2012.08.018. PMID: 23153883.
- Sawyer RG, Leon CA. Common complications in the surgical Intensive Care unit. Crit Care Med. 2010 Sep;38(9 Suppl):S483-93. doi: 10.1097/CCM.0b013e3181ec68c9. PMID: 20724882.
- Wollschlager CM, Conrad AR, Khan FA. Common complications in critically ill patients. Dis Mon. 1988 May;34(5):221-93. doi: 10.1016/0011-5029(88)90009-0. PMID: 3286162.
- S. Trzeciak, A.E. Jones, J.H. Kilgannon, B. Milcarek, K. Hunter, N.I. Shapiro, *et al.* Significance of arterial hypotension after resuscitation from cardiac arrest Crit Care Med, 37 (11) (2009), pp. 2895-2903.

- L.W. Lehman, M. Saeed, G. Moody, R. Mark Hypotension as a risk factor for acute kidney injury in ICU patients Comput Cardiol, 37 (2010), pp. 1095-1098
- van der Ven, W. H., Schuurmans, J., Schenk, J., Roerhorst, S., Cherpanath, T. G. V., Lagrand, W. K., Thoral, P., Elbers, P. W. G., Tuinman, P. R., Scheeren, T. W. L., Bakker, J., Geerts, B. F., Veelo, D. P., Paulus, F., & Vlaar, A. P. J. (2022). Monitoring, management, and outcome of hypotension in Intensive Care Unit patients, an international survey of the European Society of Intensive Care Medicine. Journal of Critical Care, 67, 118–125.https://doi.org/10.1016/j.jcrc.2021.10.008
- Graham, C. A., & Parke, T. R. J. (2004). Critical care in the emergency department: shock and circulatory support. *Emergency Medicine Journal*, *22*(1), 17–21.https://doi.org/10.1136/emj.2003.012450
- Hauffe, T., Krüger, B., Bettex, D., & Rudiger, A. (2016). Shock Management for Cardio-surgical Intensive Care Unit Patient: The Silver Days. *Cardiac Failure Review*, *2*(1), 56-62.https://doi.org/10.15420/cfr.2015:27:2
- Mesarwi OA, Loomba R, Malhotra A. Obstructive Sleep Apnea, Hypoxia, and Nonalcoholic Fatty Liver Disease. Am J Respir Crit Care Med. 2019 Apr 01;199(7):830-841.
- Zhang F, Niu L, Li S, Le W. Pathological Impacts of Chronic Hypoxia on Alzheimer's Disease. ACS Chem Neurosci. 2019 Feb 20;10(2):902-909.
- Mahmood, N. A., Chaudry, F. A., Azam, H., Ali, M. I., & Khan, M. A. (2013). Frequency of hypoxic events in patients on a mechanical ventilator. *International Journal of Critical Illness and Injury Science*, *3*(2), 124-129.https://doi.org/10.4103/2229-5151.114272
- Keith RL, Pierson DJ. Complications of mechanical ventilation. A bedside approach. Clin Chest Med. 1996 Sep;17(3):439-51. doi: 10.1016/s0272-5231(05)70326-9. PMID: 8875006.
- Pisani L, Corcione N, Nava S. Management of acute hypercapnic respiratory failure. Curr Opin Crit Care. 2016 Feb;22(1):45-52.
- Petersson J, Glenny RW. Gas exchange and ventilation-perfusion relationships in the lung. Eur Respir J. 2014 Oct;44(4):1023-41.
- Raveling T, Bladder G, Vonk JM, Nieuwenhuis JA, Verdonk-Struik FM, Wijkstra PJ, Duiverman ML. Improvement in hypercapnia does not predict survival in COPD patients on chronic noninvasive ventilation. Int J Chron Obstruct Pulmon Dis. 2018;13:3625-3634.
- Hillman D, Singh B, McArdle N, Eastwood P. Relationships between ventilatory impairment, sleep hypoventilation and type 2 respiratory failure. Respirology. 2014 Nov;19(8):1106-16.

- Hsieh MJ, Yang TM, Tsai YH. Nutritional supplementation in patients with chronic obstructive pulmonary disease. J Formos Med Assoc. 2016 Aug;115(8):595-601.
- Gutt CN, Oniu T, Mehrabi A, Schemmer P, Kashfi A, Kraus T, Büchler MW. Circulatory and respiratory complications of carbon dioxide insufflation. Dig Surg. 2004;21(2):95-105.
- Bräunlich J, Dellweg D, Bastian A, Budweiser S, Randerath W, Triché D, Bachmann M, Kähler C, Bayarassou AH, Mäder I, Geiseler J, Köhler N, Petroff D, Wirtz H. Nasal high-flow versus noninvasive ventilation in patients with chronic hypercapnic COPD. Int J Chron Obstruct Pulmon Dis. 2019;14:1411-1421.
- Abdo WF, Heunks LM. Oxygen-induced hypercapnia in COPD: myths and facts. Crit Care. 2012 Oct 29;16(5):323.
- Acute Respiratory Distress Syndrome Network Brower RG, Matthay MA, et al. Ventilation with lower tidal volumes as compared with traditional tidal volumes for acute lung injury and the acute respiratory distress syndrome. N Engl J Med 2000; 342: 1301–1308.
- Laher AE, Buchanan SK. Mechanically Ventilating the Severe Asthmatic. J Intensive Care Med. 2018 Sep;33(9):491-501.
- Morelli A, Del Sorbo L, Pesenti A, Ranieri VM, Fan E. Extracorporeal carbon dioxide removal (ECCO2R) in patients with acute respiratory failure. Intensive Care Med. 2017 Apr;43(4):519-530.
- Barnes T, Zochios V, Parhar K. Re-examining Permissive Hypercapnia in ARDS: A Narrative Review. Chest. 2018 Jul;154(1):185-195.
- Adrogué HJ, Madias NE. Alkali Therapy for Respiratory Acidosis: A Medical Controversy. Am J Kidney Dis. 2020 Feb;75(2):265-271.
- Abdo WF, Heunks LM. Oxygen-induced hypercapnia in COPD: myths and facts. Crit Care. 2012 Oct 29;16(5):323
- Eknoyan G. The origins of nephrology—Galen, the founding father of experimental renal physiology. Am J Nephrol. 1989;9(1):66–82. doi: 10.1159/000167939.
- Heberden W. Commentaries on the history and cure of diseases. London: Payne and Foss; 1816.
- Kidney Disease: Improving Global Outcomes (KDIGO) Acute Kidney Injury Work Group (2012) KDIGO clinical practice guideline for acute kidney injury. Kidney Int (Suppl 2):1–138
- Irving RA, Noakes TD, Raine RI, Van Zyl Smit R. Transient oliguria with renal tubular dysfunction after a 90 km running race. Med Sci Sports Exerc. 1990;22(6):756–761. doi: 10.1249/00005768-199012000-00004.

- Hultstrom M. Neurohormonal interactions on the renal oxygen delivery and consumption in haemorrhagic shock-induced acute kidney injury. Acta Physiol (Oxf) 2013;209(1):11–25. doi: 10.1111/apha.12147.
- Fani F, Regolisti G, Delsante M, Cantaluppi V, Castellano G, Gesualdo L, Villa G, Fiaccadori E. Recent advances in the pathogenetic mechanisms of sepsis-associated acute kidney injury. J Nephrol. 2018;31(3):351–359. doi: 10.1007/s40620-017-0452-4.
- Joannidis M, Druml W, Forni LG, Groeneveld ABJ, Honore PM, Hoste E, Ostermann M, Oudemans-van Straaten HM, Schetz M. Prevention of acute kidney injury and protection of renal function in the Intensive Care unit: update 2017: Expert opinion of the Working Group on Prevention, AKI section, European Society of Intensive Care Medicine. Intensive Care Med. 2017;43(6):730–749. doi: 10.1007/s00134-017-4832-y.
- Bagshaw SM, Delaney A, Jones D, Ronco C, Bellomo R. Diuretics in the management of acute kidney injury: a multinational survey. Contrib Nephrol. 2007;156:236–249. doi: 10.1159/000102089.
- Meersch M, Schmidt C, Hoffmeier A, Van Aken H, Wempe C, Gerss J, Zarbock A. Prevention of cardiac surgery-associated AKI by implementing the KDIGO guidelines in high risk patients identified by biomarkers: the PrevAKI randomized controlled trial. Intensive Care Med. 2017;43(11):1551–1561.
- Ichai C, Vinsonneau C, Souweine B, Armando F, Canet E, Clec'h C, Constantin JM, Darmon M, Duranteau J, Gaillot T, Garnier A, Jacob L, Joannes-Boyau O, Juillard L, Journois D, Lautrette A, Muller L, Legrand M, Lerolle N, Rimmele T, Rondeau E, Tamion F, Walrave Y, Velly L, Societe francaise d.'anesthesie et de r, Societe de reanimation de langue f, Groupe francophone de reanimation et urgences p, Societe francaise de n Acute kidney injury in the perioperative period and in Intensive Care units (excluding renal replacement therapies) Anaesth Crit Care Pain Med. 2016;35(2):151–165. doi: 10.1016/j.accpm.2016.03.004.
- Perner A, Prowle J, Joannidis M, Young P, Hjortrup PB, Pettila V. Fluid management in acute kidney injury. Intensive Care Med. 2017;43(6):807–815. doi: 10.1007/s00134-017-4817-x.
- Thibault R, Graf S, Clerc A, et al.. Diarrhoea in the ICU: respective contribution of feeding and antibiotics. Crit Care 2013;17:R153–8. 10.1186/cc12832
- Schiller LR, Pardi DS, Spiller R, et al.. Gastro 2013 APDW/WCOG Shanghai working party report: chronic diarrhea: definition, classification, diagnosis. J Gastroenterol Hepatol 2014;29:6–25. 10.1111/jgh.12392
- Mearin F, Lacy BE, Chang L, et al.. Bowel Disorders. Gastroenterology 2016. doi: 10.1053/j.gastro.2016.02.031 [Epub ahead of print 18 Feb 2018].

- Jack L, Coyer F, Courtney M, et al.. Probiotics and diarrhoea management in enterally tube fed critically ill patients--what is the evidence? Intensive Crit Care Nurs 2010;26:314–26. 10.1016/j.iccn.2010.07.001
- Jack L, Coyer F, Courtney M, et al.. Diarrhoea risk factors in enterally tube fed critically ill patients: a retrospective audit. Intensive Crit Care Nurs 2010;26:327–34. 10.1016/j.iccn.2010.08.001
- Tirlapur N, Puthucheary ZA, Cooper JA, et al.. Diarrhoea in the critically ill is common, associated with poor outcome, and rarely due to Clostridium difficile. Sci Rep 2016;6:24691 10.1038/srep24691
- Tirlapur, N., Puthucheary, Z. A., Cooper, J. A., Sanders, J., Coen, P. G., Moonesinghe, S. R., Wilson, A. P., Mythen, M. G., & Montgomery, H. E. (2015). Diarrhoea in the critically ill is common, associated with poor outcome, and rarely due to Clostridium difficile. *Scientific Reports*, *6*.https://doi.org/10.1038/srep24691
- de Brito-Ashurst I, Preiser JC. Diarrhea in Critically Ill Patients: The Role of Enteral Feeding. JPEN J Parenter Enteral Nutr. 2016 Sep;40(7):913-23. doi: 10.1177/0148607116651758. Epub 2016 Jun 6. PMID: 27271709.
- Girard, T. D., Pandharipande, P. P., & Ely, E. W. (2007). Delirium in the Intensive Care unit. *Critical Care*, *12*(Suppl 3), S3.https://doi.org/10.1186/cc6149
- McGuire BE, Basten CJ, Ryan CJ, Gallagher J. Intensive Care unit syndrome: a dangerous misnomer. Arch Intern Med. 2000;160:906–909. doi: 10.1001/archinte.160.7.906
- Ely EW, Gautam S, Margolin R, Francis J, May L, Speroff T, Truman B, Dittus R, Bernard R, Inouye SK. The impact of delirium in the Intensive Care unit on hospital length of stay. Intensive Care Med. 2001;27:1892–1900. doi: 10.1007/s00134-001-1132-2.
- Jackson JC, Gordon SM, Hart RP, Hopkins RO, Ely EW. The association between delirium and cognitive decline: a review of the empirical literature. Neuropsychol Rev. 2004;14:87–98. doi: 10.1023/B:NERV.0000028080.39602.17.
- Bergeron N, Dubois MJ, Dumont M, Dial S, Skrobik Y. Intensive Care Delirium Screening Checklist: evaluation of a new screening tool. Intensive Care Med. 2001;27:859–864. doi: 10.1007/s001340100909.
- Poulsen, L. M., Estrup, S., Mortensen, C. B., & Andersen-Ranberg, N. C. (2021). Delirium in Intensive Care. *Current Anesthesiology Reports*, 1–8.https://doi.org/10.1007/s40140-021-00476-z
- Siegel M. Management of agitation in the Intensive Care unit. Clin Chest Med. 2003;24:713–725. doi: 10.1016/S0272-5231(03)00104-7.

- Cohen IL, Gallagher TJ, Pohlman AS, Dasta JF, Abraham E, Papadokos PJ. Management of the agitated Intensive Care unit patient. Crit Care Med. 2002;30(1):S97–S124. doi: 10.1097/00003246-200201002-00001.
- Hirsch L. Continuous EEG monitoring in the Intensive Care unit: an overview. J Clin Neurophysiol. 2004;21:332–340.
- Mussi C, Ferrari R, Ascari S, Salvioli G. Importance of serum anticholinergic activity in the assessment of elderly patients with delirium. J Geriatr Psychiatry Neurol. 1999;12:82–86. doi: 10.1177/089198879901200208.
- Flacker J, Wei J. Endogenous anticholinergic substances may exist during acute illness in elderly medical patients. J Gerontol A Biol Sci Med Sci. 2001;56:M353–M355.
- Bourne RS, Minelli C, Mills GH, Kandler R. Clinical review: Sleep measurement in critical care patients: research and clinical implications. Crit Care. 2007;11(4):226.
- Bosma KJ, Ranieri VM. Filtering out the noise: evaluating the impact of noise and sound reduction strategies on sleep quality for ICU patients. Crit Care. 2009;13(3):151.
- Bourne RS, Mills GH. Sleep disruption in critically ill patients--pharmacological considerations. Anaesthesia. 2004;59(4):374–84.
- Drouot X, Cabello B, d'Ortho MP, Brochard L. Sleep in the Intensive Care unit. Sleep Med Rev. 2008;12(5):391–403.
- Orwelius L, Nordlund A, Nordlund P, Edell-Gustafsson U, Sjoberg F. Prevalence of sleep disturbances and long-term reduced health-related quality of life after critical care: a prospective multicenter cohort study. Crit Care. 2008;12(4):R97.
- Tembo A, Parker V, Higgins I.. : The experience of sleep deprivation in Intensive Care patients: Findings from a larger hermeneutic phenomenological study. Intensive and Critical Care Nursing. 2013;29:310–316.
- Brennan MJ, Lieberman JA. Sleep disturbances in patients with chronic pain: effectively managing opioid analgesia to improve outcomes. Curr Med Res Opin. 2009;25(5):1045–1055.
- Cooper AB, Thornley KS, Young GB, Slutsky AS, Stewart TE, Hanly PJ. Sleep in critically ill patients requiring mechanical ventilation. Chest. 2000;117(3):809–818.
- Schwarz NT, Beer-Stotz D, Bauer AJ. Pathogenesis of paralytic ileus. Ann. Surg. 2002; 235(1): 31–40.
- Vather R, O'Grady G, Bissett IP, Dinning PG. Postoperative ileus: mechanisms and future directions for research. Clin. Exp. Pharmacol. Physiol. 2014; 41(05): 358–70.

- Lubawski J, Saclarides T. Postoperative ileus: strategies for reduction. Ther. Clin. Risk Manag. 2008; 4(5): 913–7.
- Patanwala AE, Abarca J, Huckleberry Y, Erstad BL. Pharmacologic management of constipation in the critically ill patient. Pharmacotherapy. 2006 Jul;26(7):896-902. doi: 10.1592/phco.26.7.896. PMID: 16803421.
- Levi M., Opal S.M. Coagulation abnormalities in critically ill patients. Crit. Care. 2006;10:222. doi: 10.1186/cc4975.
- Eck R.J., Hulshof L., Wiersema R., Thio C.H.L., Hiemstra B., van den Oever N.C.G., Gans R.O.B., van der Horst I.C.C., Meijer K., Keus F. Incidence, prognostic factors, and outcomes of venous thromboembolism in critically ill patients: Data from two prospective cohort studies. Crit. Care. 2021;25:1–9. doi: 10.1186/s13054-021-03457-0.
- Walsh TS, Stanworth SJ, Prescott RJ, Lee RJ, Watson DM, Wyncoll D, et al. Prevalence, management, and outcomes of critically ill patients with prothrombin time prolongation in United Kingdom Intensive Care units. Crit Care Med. 2010;38((10):):1939-–1946.
- Faraoni D,, Hardy JF,, Van der Linden P. An early, multimodal, goal-directed approach of coagulopathy in the bleeding traumatized patient. Curr Opin Anaesthesiol. 2013;;26((2):):193-–195.
- Muller MC, de Jonge E, Arbous MS, Spoelstra-de Man AM, Karakus A, Vroom MB, et al. Transfusion of fresh frozen plasma in non-bleeding ICU patients–TOPIC trial: study protocol for a randomized controlled trial. Trials. 2011;12:266.
- Trappe HJ, Brandts B, Weismueller P. Arrhythmias in the Intensive Care patient. Curr Opin Crit Care. 2003 Oct;9(5):345-55. doi: 10.1097/00075198-200310000-00003. PMID: 14508146.
- Tarditi DJ, Hollenberg SM. Cardiac arrhythmias in the Intensive Care unit. Semin Respir Crit Care Med. 2006 Jun;27(3):221-9. doi: 10.1055/s-2006-945525. PMID: 16791756.
- Johnson, K., & Ghassemzadeh, S. (2022). *Chest Pain*. PubMed; StatPearls Publishing.https://www.ncbi.nlm.nih.gov/books/NBK470557/
- Asmundsson AS, Arms J, Kaila R, Roback MG, Theiler C, Davey CS, Louie JP. Hospital Course of Croup After Emergency Department Management. Hosp Pediatr. 2019 May;9(5):326-332.
- Heinonen S, Süvari L, Gissler M, Pitkänen O, Andersson S, Helve O. Transient Tachypnea of the Newborn Is Associated With an Increased Risk of Hospitalization Due to Respiratory Syncytial Virus Bronchiolitis. Pediatr Infect Dis J. 2019 Apr;38(4):419-421.

- Leisman DE, Angel C, Schneider SM, D'Amore JA, D'Angelo JK, Doerfler ME. Sepsis Presenting in Hospitals versus Emergency Departments: Demographic, Resuscitation, and Outcome Patterns in a Multicenter Retrospective Cohort. J Hosp Med. 2019 Jun 01;14(6):340-348.
- Chamorro C, Romera MA, Balandin B. Fever in critically ill patients. Crit Care Med. 2008 Nov;36(11):3129-30; author reply 3130.
- Heinz WJ, Buchheidt D, Christopeit M, von Lilienfeld-Toal M, Cornely OA, Einsele H, Karthaus M, Link H, Mahlberg R, Neumann S, Ostermann H, Penack O, Ruhnke M, Sandherr M, Schiel X, Vehreschild JJ, Weissinger F, Maschmeyer G. Diagnosis and empirical treatment of fever of unknown origin (FUO) in adult neutropenic patients: guidelines of the Infectious Diseases Working Party (AGIHO) of the German Society of Hematology and Medical Oncology (DGHO). Ann Hematol. 2017 Nov;96(11):1775-1792.
- Circiumaru B, Baldock G, Cohen J. A prospective study of fever in the Intensive Care unit. Intensive Care Med. 1999 Jul;25(7):668-73.
- Young PJ, Saxena M, Beasley R, Bellomo R, Bailey M, Pilcher D, Finfer S, Harrison D, Myburgh J, Rowan K. Early peak temperature and mortality in critically ill patients with or without infection. Intensive Care Med. 2012 Jan 31;
- Vincent JL, Baron JF, Reinhart K, Gattinoni L, Thijs L, Webb A, Meier-Hellmann A, Nollet G, Peres-Bota D; ABC (Anemia and Blood Transfusion in Critical Care) Investigators. Anemia and blood transfusion in critically ill patients. *JAMA* 2002;288:1499–1507.
- Thomas J, Jensen L, Nahirniak S, Gibney RT. Anemia and blood transfusion practices in the critically ill: a prospective cohort review. *Heart Lung* 2010;39:217–225.
- Conrad SA, Dietrich KA, Hebert CA, Romero MD. Effect of red cell transfusion on oxygen consumption following fluid resuscitation in septic shock. *Circ Shock* 1990;31:419–429
- Corwin HL. The role of erythropoietin therapy in the critically ill. Transfus Med Rev. 2006(20):27–33.
- Jahr JS, Mackenzie C, Pearce LB, Pitman A, Greenburg AG.. HBOC-201 as an alternative to blood transfusion: efficacy and safety evaluation in a multicenter phase III trial in elective orthopedic surgery. J Trauma. 2008(64):1484–97.
- Weinberg ED. Iron loading and disease surveillance. Emerg Infect Dis. 1999(5):346–52.
- Preiser, C., Chase, J. G., Hovorka, R., Joseph, J. I., Krinsley, J. S., Block, C. D., Desaive, T., Foubert, L., Kalfon, P., Pielmeier, U., Herpe, T. V., & Wernerman, J. (2016). Glucose Control in the ICU: A Continuing Story. *Journal of Diabetes Science and Technology*, *10*(6), 1372-1381.https://doi.org/10.1177/1932296816648713

- Kovalaske MA, Gandhi GY. Glycemic control in the medical Intensive Care unit. J Diabetes Sci Technol. 2009 Nov 1;3(6):1330-41. doi: 10.1177/193229680900300613. PMID: 20144387; PMCID: PMC2787033.
- Kahn JM, Le T, Angus DC, Cox CE, Hough CL, White DB, et al. The epidemiology of chronic critical illness in the United States*. Crit Care Med 2015;43: 282e7.
- Arabi YM, Casaer MP, Chapman M, Heyland DK, Ichai C, Marik PE, et al. The Intensive Care medicine research agenda in nutrition and metabolism. Intens Care Med 2017;43:1239e56.
- Ferrie S, Tsang E. Monitoring nutrition in critical illness: what can we use? Nutr Clin Pract 2017 May 1. https://doi.org/10.1177/0884533617706312. Epub.
- Kipnis E, Ramsingh D, Bhargava M, Dincer E, Cannesson M, Broccard A, et al. Monitoring in the Intensive Care. Crit Care Res Pract 2012;2012, 473507.
- Herr KA, Spratt K, Mobily PR, Richardson G: Pain intensity assessment in older adults: use of experimental pain to compare psychometric properties and usability of selected pain scales with younger adults. Clin J Pain 2004, 20:207-219.
- Cepeda MS, Africano JM, Polo R, Alcala R, Carr DB: Agreement between percentage pain reductions calculated from numeric rating scores of pain intensity and those reported by patients with acute or cancer pain. Pain 2003, 106:439-442.
- Aissaoui Y, Zeggwagh AA, Zekraoui A, et al. Validation of a behavioral pain scale in critically ill, sedated, and mechanically ventilated patients. Anesth Analg 2005;101:1470–6
- Portenoy RK, Ahmed E. Principles of opioid use in cancer pain. J Clin Oncol 2014;32:1662–70.
- Shapiro BA, Warren J, Egol AB, et al. Practice parameters for intravenous analgesia and sedation for adult patients in the Intensive Care unit: an executive summary. Society of Critical Care Medicine. Crit Care Med 1995;23:1596–600.
- Mather LE. Clinical pharmacokinetics of fentanyl and its newer derivatives. Clin Pharmacokinet 1983;8:422–46
- Hughes CG, McGrane S, Pandharipande PP. Sedation in the Intensive Care setting. Clin Pharmacol 2012;4:53–63
- Ginsberg B, Sinatra RS, Adler LJ, et al. Conversion to oral controlled-release oxycodone from intravenous opioid analgesic in the postoperative setting. Pain Med 2003;4:31–8.
- Szumita PM, Baroletti SA, Anger KE, et al. Sedation and analgesia in the Intensive Care unit: evaluating the role of dexmedetomidine. Am J Health Syst Pharm 2007;64:37–44.
- Griffiths R. Opioid-induced hyperalgesia: low-dose ketamine does work for some orthopaedic problems already. Br J Anaesth 2010;104:660–1.

- McCarthy GC, Megalla SA, Habib AS. Impact of intravenous lidocaine infusion on postoperative analgesia and recovery from surgery: a systematic review of randomized controlled trials. Drugs 2010;70:1149–63
- Kis B, Snipes JA, Busija DW. Acetaminophen and the cyclooxygenase-3 puzzle: sorting out facts, fictions, and uncertainties. J Pharmacol Exp Ther 2005;315:1–7.
- Werawatganon T, Charuluxanun S. Patient controlled intravenous opioid analgesia versus continuous epidural analgesia for pain after intra-abdominal surgery. Cochrane Database Syst Rev 2005(1): CD004088.
- Rivers E, Nguyen B, Havstad S, et al.: Early goal-directed therapy in the treatment of severe sepsis and septic shock. N Engl J Med 345:1368-1377, 2001
- Sakr Y, Vincent JL, Reinhart K, et al.: High tidal volume and positive fluid balance are associated with worse outcome in acute lung injury. Chest 128:3098-3108, 2005.
- Bondanelli M, Ambrosio MR, Zatelli MC, De Marinis L, degli Uberti EC: Hypopituitarism after traumatic brain injury. Eur J Endocrinol 152:679-691, 2005
- Buckley MS, Leblanc JM, Cawley MJ: Electrolyte disturbances associated with commonly prescribed medications in the Intensive Care unit. Crit Care Med 38(Suppl):S253-264, 2010
- Martyn JA, Richtsfeld M: Succinylcholine-induced hyperkalemia in acquired pathologic states: etiologic factors and molecular mechanisms. Anesthesiology 104:158-169, 2006
- Bugg NC, Jones JA: Hypophosphataemia. Pathophysiology, effects and management on the Intensive Care unit. Anaesthesia 53:895-902, 1998
- Spahn DR: Hypocalcemia in trauma: frequent but frequently undetected and underestimated. Crit Care Med 33:2124-2125, 2005
- Besunder JB, Smith PG: Toxic effects of electrolyte and trace mineral administration in the Intensive Care unit. Crit Care Clin 7:659-693, 1991
- Dellinger RP, Levy MM, Rhodes A, et al. Surviving sepsis campaign: international guidelines for management of severe sepsis and septic shock: 2012. Crit Care Med 2013;41:580-637.
- Osman D, Ridel C, Ray P, et al. Cardiac filling pressures are not appropriate to predict hemodynamic response to volume challenge. Crit Care Med 2007;35:64-8.
- Marik PE, Monnet X, Teboul JL. Hemodynamic parameters to guide fluid therapy. Ann Intensive Care 2011;1:1.
- Lansdorp B, Lemson J, van Putten MJ, de Keijzer A, van der Hoeven JG, Pickkers P. Dynamic indices do not predict volume responsiveness in routine clinical practice. Br J Anaesth 2012;108: 395-401.

- Cavallaro F, Sandroni C, Marano C, et al. Diagnostic accuracy of passive leg raising for prediction of fluid responsiveness in adults: systematic review and meta-analysis of clinical studies. Intensive Care Med 2010;36:1475-83.
- Kumar A, Anel R, Bunnell E, et al. Pulmonary artery occlusion pressure and central venous pressure fail to predict ventricular filling volume, cardiac performance, or the response to volume infusion in normal subjects. Crit Care Med 2004;32:691-9.
- Prekker ME, Scott NL, Hart D, Sprenkle MD, Leatherman JW. Point-of-care ultrasound to estimate central venous pressure: a comparison of three techniques. Crit Care Med 2013;41:833-41.
- Singer M, Clarke J, Bennett ED. Continuous hemodynamic monitoring by esophageal Doppler. Crit Care Med 1989;17:447-52
- Marik PE, Cavallazzi R, Vasu T, Hirani A. Dynamic changes in arterial waveform derived variables and fluid responsiveness in mechanically ventilated patients: a systematic review of the literature. Crit Care Med 2009;37:2642-7
- Guinot PG, de Broca B, Abou Arab O, et al. Ability of stroke volume variation measured by oesophageal Doppler monitoring to predict fluid responsiveness during surgery. Br J Anaesth 2013;110:28-33.
- Keller G, Cassar E, Desebbe O, Lehot JJ, Cannesson M. Ability of pleth variability index to detect hemodynamic changes induced by passive leg raising in spontaneously breathing volunteers. Crit Care 2008;12:R37.
- Squara P, Denjean D, Estagnasie P, Brusset A, Dib JC, Dubois C. Noninvasive cardiac output monitoring (NICOM): a clinical validation. Intensive Care Med 2007;33:1191-4
- Tsuruta R, Fujita M. Comparison of clinical practice guidelines for the management of pain, agitation, and delirium in critically ill adult patients. Acute Med Surg. 2018;5(3):207–12.
- Stanik-Hutt JA, Soeken KL, Belcher AE, Fontaine DK, Gift AG. Pain experiences of traumatically injured patients in a critical care setting. Am J Crit Care. 2001;10(4):252–9
- Desbiens NA, Wu AW. Pain and suffering in seriously ill hospitalized patients. J Am Geriatr Soc 2000;48(Suppl 5): S183–6.
- Stanik-Hutt JA, Soeken KL, Belcher AE, et al. Pain experiences of traumatically injured patients in a critical care setting. Am J Crit Care 2001;10(4):252–9.
- Desbiens NA, Wu AW, Broste SK, et al. Pain and satisfaction with pain control in seriously ill hospitalized adults: findings from the SUPPORT research investigations. For the SUPPORT

investigators. Study to Understand Prognoses and Preferences for Outcomes and Risks of Treatment. Crit Care Med 1996;24(12):1943–4.

- Epstein J, Breslow MJ. The stress response of critical illness. Crit Care Clin 1999; 15(1):17–33.
- Lewis KS, Whipple JK, Michael KA, et al. Effect of analgesic treatment on the physiological consequences of acute pain. Am J Hosp Pharm 1994;51(12):1539–54.
- Lindenbaum, Larry; Milia, David J. (2012). *Pain Management in the ICU. Surgical Clinics of North America, 92(6), 1621–1636.* doi:10.1016/j.suc.2012.08.013
- Merskey H, Bogduk N, editors. Classification of chronic pain. IASP task force on taxonomy. 2nd edition. Seattle (WA): IASP Press; 2011. p. 209–14.
- Merskey H, Bogduk N. Classification of chronic pain. 2nd edition. Seattle (WA): International Association for the Study of Pain; 1994. p. 3–4
- Hall-Lord ML, Larsson G, Steen B. Pain and distress among elderly Intensive Care patients: comparison of patients' experiences and nurses' assessments. Heart Lung 1998;27:123–32.
- Merskey H, Albe Fessard D, Bonica JJ, Carmon A, Dubner R, Kerr FWL, Lindblom U, Mumford JM, Nathan PW, Noordenbos W, Pagni CA, Renaer MJ, Sternbach RA, Sunderland S. Pain terms: a list with definitions and notes on usage. Recommended by the IASP subcommittee on taxonomy. Pain. 1979;6:249–52.
- Barr J, Fraser GL, Puntillo K, et al. Clinical practice guidelines for the management of pain, agitation, and delirium in adult patients in the Intensive Care unit. Crit Care Med. 2013;41(1):263–306.
- Committee for the development of Japanese guidelines for the management of pain, agitation, and delirium in Intensive Care unit, Japanese Society of Intensive Care Medicine. Japanese guidelines for the management of Pain, Agitation, and Delirium in Intensive Care unit (J-PAD). J Jpn Soc. Intensive Care Med. 2014;21:539–79.
- Chanques G, Viel E, Constantin JM, et al. The measurement of pain in Intensive Care unit: comparison of 5 self-report intensity scales. Pain. 2010;151(3):711–21.
- Sessler CN, et al. The Richmond Agitation-Sedation Scale: validity and reliability in adult Intensive Care unit patients. Am J Respir Crit Care Med. 2002;166:1338–44.
- Machata AM, Illievich UM, Gustorff B, Gonano C, Fässler K, Spiss CK. Remifentanil for tracheal tube tolerance: a case control study. Anaesthesia. 2007;62(8):796–801.
- Dahaba AA, Grabner T, Rehak PH, List WF, Metzler H. Remifentanil versus morphine analgesia and sedation for mechanically ventilated critically ill patients: a randomized double blind study. Anesthesiology. 2004;101(3):640–6.

- Memis D, Inal MT, Kavalci G, Sezer A, Sut N. Intravenous paracetamol reduced the use of opioids, extubation time, and opioid-related adverse effects after major surgery in Intensive Care unit. J Crit Care. 2010;25(3):458–62.
- DAS-Taskforce 2015, Baron R, Binder A, et al. Evidence and consensus based guideline for the management of delirium, analgesia, and sedation in Intensive Care medicine. Revision 2015 (DAS-Guideline 2015)—short version. Ger Med Sci. 2015;13:Doc19.
- Erstad BL, Puntillo K, Gilbert HC, et al. Pain management principles in the critically ill. Chest. 2009;135(4):1075–86.
- Ehieli E, Yalamuri S, Brudney CS, Pyati S. Analgesia in the surgical Intensive Care unit. Postgrad Med J. 2017;93(1095):38–45.
- Joffe AM, Hallman M, Gélinas C, Herr DL, Puntillo K. Evaluation and treatment of pain in critically ill adults. Semin Respir Crit Care Med. 2013;34(2):189–200.
- Mehta, Yatin; Gupta, Abhinav; Todi, Subhash; Myatra, SheilaNainan; Samaddar, DP; Patil, Vijaya; Bhattacharya, PradipKumar; Ramasubban, Suresh (2014). *Guidelines for prevention of hospital acquired infections. Indian Journal of Critical Care Medicine, 18(3), 149–.* doi:10.4103/0972-5229.128705
- Guideline for isolation precautions: Preventing transmission of infectious agents in healthcare settings. Available from: http://www. cdc.gov/hicpac/pdf/isolation/Isolation2007.pdf. March 10, 2014
- WHO guidelines on hand hygiene in health care: A summary. Available from: http://www.whqlibdoc.who.int/hq/2009/WHO_IER_ PSP_2009.07_eng.pdf. March 10, 2014
- Gandra, S.; Ellison, R. T. (2014). *Modern Trends in Infection Control Practices in Intensive Care Units. Journal of Intensive Care Medicine, 29(6), 311–326.* doi:10.1177/0885066613485215
- Melsen WG, Rovers MM, Koeman M, Bonten MJ. Estimating the attributable mortality of ventilator-associated pneumonia from randomized prevention studies. Crit Care Med. 2011;39(12): 2736-2742.
- Resar R, Pronovost P, Haraden C, Simmonds T, Rainey T, Nolan T. Using a bundle approach to improve ventilator care processes and reduce ventilator-associated pneumonia. Jt Comm J Qual Patient Saf. 2005;31(5):243-248.
- Niel-Weise BS, Gastmeier P, Kola A, Vonberg RP, Wille JC, van den Broek PJ. An evidence-based recommendation on bed head elevation for mechanically ventilated patients. Crit Care. 2011;15(2):R111

- Pronovost P, Needham D, Berenholtz S, et al. An intervention to decrease catheter-related bloodstream infections in the ICU. N Engl J Med. 2006;355(26):2725-2732.
- Marschall J, Mermel LA, Classen D, et al. Strategies to prevent central line-associated bloodstream infections in acute care hospitals. Infect Control Hosp Epidemiol. 2008;29(suppl 1):S22-S30
- Haley RW, Culver DH, White JW, Morgan WM, Emori TG. The nationwide nosocomial infection rate. A new need for vital statistics. Am J Epidemiol. 1985;121(2):159-167.
- Gould CV, Umscheid CA, Agarwal RK, Kuntz G, Pegues DA. Guideline for prevention of catheter-associated urinary tract infections 2009. Infect Control Hosp Epidemiol. 2010;31(4): 319-326.
- Bignardi GE. Risk factors for Clostridium difficile infection. J Hosp Infect. 1998;40(1):1-15
- Oughton MT, Loo VG, Dendukuri N, Fenn S, Libman MD. Hand hygiene with soap and water is superior to alcohol rub and antiseptic wipes for removal of Clostridium difficile. Infect Control Hosp Epidemiol. 2009;30(10):939-944.
- Gerding DN, Muto CA, Owens RC Jr. Measures to control and prevent Clostridium difficile infection. Clin Infect Dis. 2008; 46(suppl 1):S43-S49
- McCunn, Maureen; Reed, Amy J (2009). *Critical care organ support: a focus on extracorporeal systems. Current Opinion in Critical Care, 15(6), 554–559.* doi:10.1097/mcc.0b013e3283315773
- McCunn, Maureen; Reed, Amy J (2009). *Critical care organ support: a focus on extracorporeal systems. Current Opinion in Critical Care, 15(6), 554–559.* doi:10.1097/mcc.0b013e3283315773
- Vincent JL, Sakr Y, Sprung CL et al (2006) Sepsis in European Intensive Care units: results of the SOAP study. Crit Care Med 34:344–353
- Husain-Syed F, McCullough PA, Birk HW et al (2015) Cardio-pulmonary-renal interactions: a multidisciplinary approach. J Am Coll Cardiol 65:2433–2448
- Del Sorbo L, Slutsky AS (2011) Acute respiratory distress syndrome and multiple organ failure. Curr Opin Crit Care 17:1–6
- Singbartl K, Kellum JA (2012) AKI in the ICU: definition, epidemiology, risk stratification, and outcomes. Kidney Int 81:819–825
- Ranieri VM, Brodie D, Vincent JL (2017) Extracorporeal organ support: from technological tool to clinical strategy supporting severe organ failure. JAMA 318:1105–1106

- Costanzo MR, Ronco C, Abraham WT (2017) Extracorporeal ultrafiltration for fluid overload in heart failure: current status and prospects for further research. J Am Coll Cardiol 69:2428–2445
- Darmon M, Clec'h C, Adrie C et al (2014) Acute respiratory distress syndrome and risk of AKI among critically ill patients. Clin J Am Soc Nephrol 9:1347–1353
- Nishimura M. High-fl ow nasal cannula oxygen therapy in adults. J Intensive Care 2015; 3: 15.
- Spoletini G, Alotaibi M, Blasi F, Hill NS. Heated humidifi ed high-fl ow nasal oxygen in adults: mechanisms of action and clinical implications. Chest 2015; 148: 253–61.
- Nishimura M. High-fl ow nasal cannula oxygen therapy in adults: physiological benefi ts, indication, clinical benefi ts, and adverse eff ects. Respir Care 2016; 61: 529–41.
- Moller W, Celik G, Feng S, et al. Nasal high fl ow clears anatomical dead space in upper airway models. J Appl Physiol 2015; 118: 1525–32.
- Hess DR, Fink JB, Venkataraman ST, Kim IK, Myers TR, Tano BD. The history and physics of heliox. Respir Care 2006; 51: 608–12.
- Beurskens CJ, Aslami H, de Beer FM, et al. Heliox allows for lower minute volume ventilation in an animal model of ventilator-induced lung injury. PLoS One 2013; 8: e78159.
- Beurskens CJ, Brevoord D, Lagrand WK, et al. Heliox improves carbon dioxide removal during lung protective mechanical ventilation. Crit Care Res Pract 2014; 2014: 954814.
- Pepke-Zaba J, Higenbottam TW, Dinh-Xuan AT, Stone D, Wallwork J. Inhaled nitric oxide as a cause of selective pulmonary vasodilatation in pulmonary hypertension. Lancet 1991; 338: 1173–74
- Frostell C, Fratacci MD, Wain JC, Jones R, Zapol WM. Inhaled nitric oxide. A selective pulmonary vasodilator reversing hypoxic pulmonary vasoconstriction. Circulation 1991; 83: 2038–47
- Black SM, Heidersbach RS, McMullan DM, Bekker JM, Johengen MJ, Fineman JR. Inhaled nitric oxide inhibits NOS activity in lambs: potential mechanism for rebound pulmonary hypertension. Am J Physiol 1999; 277: H1849–56
- Dzierba AL, Abel EE, Buckley MS, Lat I. A review of inhaled nitric oxide and aerosolized epoprostenol in acute lung injury or acute respiratory distress syndrome. Pharmacotherapy 2014; 34: 279–90.
- Oishi P, Datar SA, Fineman JR. Advances in the management of pediatric pulmonary hypertension. Respir Care 2011; 56: 1314–39.

- Torbic H, Szumita PM, Anger KE, Nuccio P, LaGambina S, Weinhouse G. Inhaled epoprostenol vs inhaled nitric oxide for refractory hypoxemia in critically ill patients. J Crit Care 2013; 28: 844–48.
- Kollef MH, Levy NT, Ahrens TS, Schaiff R, Prentice D, Sherman G. The use of continuous i.v. sedation is associated with prolongation of mechanical ventilation. *Chest.* 1998;**114**(2):541–548.
- Pandharipande P, Shintani A, Peterson J, et al. Lorazepam is an independent risk factor for transitioning to delirium in Intensive Care unit patients. *Anesthesiology.* 2006;**104**(1):21–26.
- Jacobi J, Fraser GL, Coursin DB, et al. Clinical practice guidelines for the sustained use of sedatives and analgesics in the critically ill adult. *Crit Care Med.* 2002;**30**(1):119–141.
- Kapfhammer HP, Rothenhausler HB, Krauseneck T, Stoll C, Schelling G. Posttraumatic stress disorder and health-related quality of life in long-term survivors of acute respiratory distress syndrome. *Am J Psychiatry.* 2004;**161**(1):45–52.
- Ely EW, Truman B, Shintani A, et al. Monitoring sedation status over time in ICU patients: reliability and validity of the Richmond Agitation-Sedation Scale (RASS) *JAMA.* 2003;**289**(22):2983–2991.
- Riker RR, Picard JT, Fraser GL. Prospective evaluation of the Sedation-Agitation Scale for adult critically ill patients. *Crit Care Med.* 1999;**27**(7):1325–1329.
- Morandi A, Jackson JC. Delirium in the Intensive Care unit: a review. *Neurol Clin.* 2011;**29**(4):749–763.
- Cerejeira J, Firmino H, Vaz-Serra A, Mukaetova-Ladinska EB. The neuroinflammatory hypothesis of delirium. *Acta Neuropathol.* 2010;**119**(6):737–754.
- Brook AD, Ahrens TS, Schaiff R, et al. Effect of a nursing-implemented sedation protocol on the duration of mechanical ventilation. *Crit Care Med.* 1999;**27**(12):2609–2615
- Quenot JP, Ladoire S, Devoucoux F, et al. Effect of a nurse-implemented sedation protocol on the incidence of ventilator-associated pneumonia. *Crit Care Med.* 2007;**35**(9):2031–2036.
- Kress JP, Pohlman AS, O'Connor MF, Hall JB. Daily interruption of sedative infusions in critically ill patients undergoing mechanical ventilation. *N Engl J Med.* 2000;**342**(20):1471–1477.
- Larson MJ, Weaver LK, Hopkins RO. Cognitive sequelae in acute respiratory distress syndrome patients with and without recall of the Intensive Care unit. *J Int Neuropsychol Soc.* 2007;**13**(4):595–605.
- Beam AL, Kohane IS. Big data and machine learning in health care. *JAMA*. 2018;319:1317–1318.

- Bailly S, Meyfroidt G, Timsit JF. What's new in ICU in 2050: big data and machine learning. *Intensive Care Med*. 2018;44:1524–1527
- Zimmerman JE, Kramer AA, McNair DS, Malila FM, Shaffer VL. Intensive Care unit length of stay: benchmarking based on Acute Physiology and Chronic Health Evaluation (APACHE) IV. *Crit Care Med*. 2006;34:2517–2529.
- Scheuer ML, Wilson SB. Data analysis for continuous EEG monitoring in the ICU: seeing the forest and the trees. J Clin Neurophysiol. 2004 Sep-Oct;21(5):353-78. PMID: 15592009.
- Borowski M, Gorges M, Fried R, Such O, Wrede C, Imhoff M. Medical device alarms. *Biomed Tech (Berl)* 2011;56(2):73–83
- ERCI Institute. Top 10 technology hazards for 2012: the risks that should be at the top of your prevention list. *Health Devices*. 2011;40(11):358–373.
- Christensen M, Dodds A, Sauer J, Watts N. Alarm setting for the critically ill patient: a descriptive pilot survey of nurses' perceptions of current practice in an Australian Regional Critical Care Unit. *Intensive Crit Care Nurs*. 2014;30(4):204–210
- Bell L. Alarm fatigue linked to patient's death: interview by Laura Wallis. *Am J Nurs*. 2010;110(7):16.
- Cvach M. Monitor alarm fatigue: an integrative review. *Biomed Instrum Technol*. 2012;46(4):268–277.
- Cvach MM, Stokes JE, Manzoor SH, Brooks PO, Burger TS, Gottschalk A, Pustavoitau A. Ventilator Alarms in Intensive Care Units: Frequency, Duration, Priority, and Relationship to Ventilator Parameters. Anesth Analg. 2020 Jan;130(1):e9-e13. doi: 10.1213/ANE.0000000000003801. PMID: 30234538.
- Maday KR. The importance of nutrition in critically ill patients. *JAAPA*. 2017;30:32–7
- Yang S, Wu X, Yu W, Li J. Early enteral nutrition in critically ill patients with hemodynamic instability: An evidence-based review and practical advice. *Nutr Clin Pract*. 2014;29:90–6.
- Campos BB, Machado FS. Nutrition therapy in severe head trauma patients. *Rev Bras Ter Intensiva*. 2012;24:97–105.
- Flordelís Lasierra JL, Pérez-Vela JL, Montejo González JC. Enteral nutrition in the hemodynamically unstable critically ill patient. *Med Intensiva*. 2015;39:40–8.
- Wells DL. Provision of enteral nutrition during vasopressor therapy for hemodynamic instability: An evidence-based review. *Nutr Clin Pract*. 2012;27:521–6.

- Elke G, van Zanten AR, Lemieux M, McCall M, Jeejeebhoy KN, Kott M, et al. Enteral versus parenteral nutrition in critically ill patients: An updated systematic review and meta-analysis of randomized controlled trials. *Crit Care.* 2016;20:117.
- Gopalan S, Khanna S. Enteral nutrition delivery technique. *Curr Opin Clin Nutr Metab Care.* 2003;6:313–7.
- White H, King L. Enteral feeding pumps: Efficacy, safety, and patient acceptability. *Med Devices (Auckl)* 2014;7:291–8.
- Baniardalan M, Sabzghabaee AM, Jalali M, Badri S. Bacterial safety of commercial and handmade enteral feeds in an Iranian teaching hospital. *Int J Prev Med.* 2014;5:604–10.
- Larentis DZ, Rosa RG, Dos Santos RP, Goldani LZ. Outcomes and risk factors associated with clostridium difficile diarrhea in hospitalized adult patients. *Gastroenterol Res Pract 2015.* 2015 346341.
- Dickerson RN, Boschert KJ, Kudsk KA, Brown RO. Hypocaloric enteral tube feeding in critically ill obese patients. *Nutrition.* 2002;18:241–6.
- Manzanares W, Dhaliwal R, Jiang X, Murch L, Heyland DK. Antioxidant micronutrients in the critically ill: A systematic review and meta-analysis. *Crit Care.* 2012;16:R66.
- Bémeur C, Desjardins P, Butterworth RF. Role of nutrition in the management of hepatic encephalopathy in end-stage liver failure. *J Nutr Metab.* 2010;2010:489823.
- Horn SD, Kinikini M, Moore LW, Hammond FM, Brandstater ME, Smout RJ, et al. Enteral nutrition for patients with traumatic brain injury in the rehabilitation setting: Associations with patient preinjury and injury characteristics and outcomes. *Arch Phys Med Rehabil.* 2015;96:S245–55.
- Itoh M, Tsuji T, Nemoto K, Nakamura H, Aoshiba K. Undernutrition in patients with COPD and its treatment. *Nutrients.* 2013;5:1316–35.
- Lewington A, Kanagasundaram S. Renal association clinical practice guidelines on acute kidney injury. *Nephron Clin Pract.* 2011;118(Suppl 1):c349–90.
- Vincent JL. Give your patient a fast hug (at least) once a day. *Crit Care Med.* 2005;33(6):1225–1229. doi: 10.1097/01.CCM.0000165962.16682.46.
- Papadimos TJ, Hensley SJ, Duggan JM, Khuder SA, Borst MJ, Fath JJ, et al. Implementation of the "FASTHUG" concept decreases the incidence of ventilator-associated pneumonia in a surgical Intensive Care unit. *Patient Saf Surg.* 2008;2:3. doi: 10.1186/1754-9493-2-3.
- Vincent WR, 3rd, Hatton KW. Critically ill patients need "FAST HUGS BID" (an updated mnemonic) *Crit Care Med.* 2009;37(7):2326–2327. doi: 10.1097/CCM.0b013e3181aabc29.

- Mabasa, V. H., Malyuk, D. L., Weatherby, M., & Chan, A. (2011). A Standardized, Structured Approach to Identifying Drug-Related Problems in the Intensive Care Unit: FASTHUG-MAIDENS. *The Canadian Journal of Hospital Pharmacy*, *64*(5), 366-369. https://doi.org/10.4212/cjhp.v64i5.1073
- Kress JP, Pohlman AS, O'Connor MF, Hall JB. Daily interruption of sedative infusions in critically ill patients undergoing mechanical ventilation. *N Engl J Med.* 2000;342(20):1471–1477. doi: 10.1056/NEJM200005183422002
- Carson SS, Kress JP, Rodgers JE, Vinayak A, Campbell-Bright S, Levitt J, et al. A randomized trial of intermittent lorazepam versus propofol with daily interruption in mechanically vented patients. *Crit Care Med.* 2006;34(5):1326–1332. doi: 10.1097/01.CCM.0000215513.63207.7F.
- Geerts WH, Bergqvist D, Pineo GR, Heit JA, Samama CM, Lassen MR, et al.American College of Chest Physicians Prevention of venous thromboembolism: American College of Chest Physicians evidence-based clinical practice guidelines (8th edition) *Chest.* 2008;133(6 Suppl):381S–453S. doi: 10.1378/chest.08-0656.
- Pun BT, Ely EW. The importance of diagnosing and managing ICU delirium. *Chest.* 2007;132(2):624–636. doi: 10.1378/chest.06-1795.
- Daley RJ, Rebuck JA, Welage LS, Rogers FB. Prevention of stress ulceration: current trends in critical care. *Crit Care Med.* 2004;32(10):2008–2013. doi: 10.1097/01.CCM.0000142398.73762.20.
- Anger KE, Szumita PM. Barriers to glucose control in the Intensive Care unit. *Pharmacotherapy.* 2006;26(2):214–228. doi: 10.1592/phco.26.2.214.
- Pronovost P, Weast B, Schwarz M, Wyskiel RM, Prow D, Milanovich SN, et al. Medication reconciliation: a practical tool to reduce the risk of medication errors. *J Crit Care.* 2003;18(4):201–205. doi: 10.1016/j.jcrc.2003.10.001.
- Wilcox, L., Lu, J., Lai, J., Feiner, S., & Jordan, D. (2010). Physician-Driven Management of Patient Progress Notes in an Intensive Care Unit. *Proceedings of the SIGCHI conference on human factors in computing systems . CHI Conference*, *2010*, 1879. https://doi.org/10.1145/1753326.1753609
- Bade R, Schlechtweg S, Miksch S. Connecting time-oriented data and information to a coherent interactive visualization. *Proc. CHI.* 2004:105–12.
- Malhotra S, Jordan D, Shortliffe E, Patel V. Workflow modeling in critical care: Piecing together your own puzzle. *J Biomed Info.* 2007;40(2):81–92.
- Sbickland RA. Hill TR. Zaloga GE Bedside analysis of arterial blood gases and electrolytes during and after cardiac surge~ JCoo Anesth 1989; 1:248-52

- Zaloga GE Bedside reagent testing: blood. CSF. and bacterial cultures. J Crit Illness 1988; 3:85-94
- Trundle OS. Weizenecker RA. Capillary glucose testing: a cost... saving bedside system. Lab Management 1986 (May): 59-62
- Zaloga G~ Hill TR. Strickland RA. Kennedy 0. Visser M. Ford K. et ale Bedside blood gas and el~lyte monitoring in critically ill patients. Crit Care Med 1989; 17:920-25
- Brown M. ~nderJS. Noninvasive oxygen monitoring. Crit Care Clin 1988; 4:493-509.
- King l: Simon RH. Pulse oximetry for tapering supplemental oxygen in hospitalized patients. Chest 1987; 92:713-16
- Chernow B. Diaz M. Cruess 0, Balestrieri F. Uddin D. Rainey TG. et ale Bedside blood glucose detenninations iIi critical care medicine: a comparison analysis of two techniques. Crit Care Med 1982; 10:463-65
- Zaloga G~ Chernow B. Cook D. Snyder R. Clapper M. O·Brian)T. Assessment ofcalcium homeostasis in the critically illsurgical patient. Ann SUrg 1985; 202:587...94
- Zaloga GE Interpretation ofthe serum magnesium level. chest 1989; 95:257...58.
- Zaloga GE Bedside reagent testing: urine and GI tract speci'" mens. J Crit Illness 1987; 2:68-79.
- Andrews, F. J., & Nolan, J. P. (2006). Critical care in the emergency department: Monitoring the critically ill patient. *Emergency Medicine Journal : EMJ*, *23*(7), 561-564. https://doi.org/10.1136/emj.2005.029926
- Holland R, Webb R K, Runciman W B. Oesophageal intubation: an analysis of 2000 incident reports. *Anaesth Intensive Care* 199321608–610.
- Salem M R. Verification of endotracheal tube position. *Anesthesiol Clin North America* 200119813–839.
- Wouters P F, Gehring H, Meyfroidt G.*et al* Accuracy of pulse oximeters: the European Multi-Center Trial. *Anesth Analg* 200294S13–S16.
- National Institute for Clinical Excellence Guidance on the use of ultrasound locating devices for placing central venous catheters. Technology appraisal guidance No. 49, September 2002. www.nice.org.uk
- Rivers E, Nguyen B, Havstad S.*et al* Early goal directed therapy in the treatment of severe sepsis and septic shock. *N Engl J Med* 20013451368–1377.
- Staven K, Saxholm H, Smith-Erichsen N. Accuracy of infrared ear thermometry in adult patients. *Intensive Care Med* 199723100–105.

- Jackson, M., & Cairns, T. (2021). Care of the critically ill patient. *Surgery (Oxford, Oxfordshire)*, *39*(1), 29-36. https://doi.org/10.1016/j.mpsur.2020.11.002
- McDermid Robert C., Stelfox Henry T., Bagshaw Sean M. Frailty in the critically ill: a novel concept. *Crit Care.* 2011;15:301.
- Malbrain M.L., Marik P.E., Witters I. Fluid overload, de-resuscitation, and outcomes in critically ill or injured patients: a systematic review with suggestions for clinical practice. *Anaesthesiol Intensive Ther.* 2014;46:361–380.
- Finfer S., Bellomo R., Boyce N. For the SAFE Study Investigators. A comparison of albumin and saline for fluid resuscitation in the Intensive Care unit. *N Engl J Med.* 2004;350:2247–2256
- Nielsen N., Wetterslev J., Cronberg T. Targeted temperature management at 33 degrees C versus 36 degrees C after cardiac arrest. *N Engl J Med.* 2013;369:2197–2206
- Casaer M.P., Mesotten D., Hermans G. Early versus late parenteral nutrition in critically ill adults. *N Engl J Med.* 2011;365:506–517.
- Investigators N-SS. Finfer S., Chittock D.R. Intensive versus conventional glucose control in critically ill patients. *N Engl J Med.* 2009;360:1283–1297.
- Steiner L.A. Postoperative delirium. Part 1: pathophysiology and risk factors. *Eur J Anaesthesiol.* 2011;28:628–636.
- Bion J., Richardson A., Hibbert P., The Matching Michigan Collaboration & Writing Committee 'Matching Michigan': a 2-year stepped interventional programme to minimise central venous catheter-blood stream infections in Intensive Care units in England. *BMJ Qual Saf.* 2013;22:110–123.

Part I

EXTRA EDGE

How to interpret ABG and ECG

ABG: Analyzing arterial blood gas (ABG) is crucial for identifying and treating patients' acid-base balance and oxygenation status. The effectiveness of this screening tool depends on one's ability to read the data accurately. Alkaline balance issues can complicate a variety of medical situations, and on rare occasions, the anomaly could be so severe that it poses a risk to one's life. Doctor dealing with the patients must have basic understanding of acid-base balance and basic management. The senior consultant should be an intensivist and should be responsible for the overall strategy of the treatment [1].

The standard base excess (SBE), the strong ion difference (SID), and the HCO3 - (in the setting of pCO2) are the three most frequently employed approaches to acid-base physiology. SID, which is defined as the absolute difference between totally dissociated anions and cations, was first proposed. The weak acids and CO2 balance this discrepancy in accordance with the electrical neutrality concept. When weak acids are used to determine SID, CO2 has been renamed as effective SID (SIDe), which is the same as "buffer base". According to this, the dissociated (A-) plus undissociated (AH) weak acid forms are currently used to define Stewart's original word for total weak acid concentration (ATOT). Anion gap (AG) is the term used to describe this situation where normal concentration is actually produced by A- In order to quantify the acid-base status of a specific blood sample, all three approaches essentially produce the same findings[2].

Why is it Necessary to Order an ABG Analysis?

Because of the following benefits, using an ABG analysis becomes essential:

- Assists in making a diagnosis.
- Directs treatment strategy.
- Assists in managing the ventilator.
- The control of acid and bases has improved, enabling drugs to work at their best.
- Acid/base balance may change electrolyte levels that are crucial to a patient's condition.

The right method to gather, handle, and analyse the specimen is essential for producing accurate results for an ABG. Each of the aforementioned stages could experience clinically significant mistakes, but ABG values are particularly susceptible to preanalytic errors. Nonarterial samples, air bubbles in the sample, insufficient or insufficient anticoagulation in the specimen, and delayed examination of a noncooled sample are the most frequent issues[3].

Obtain a relevant clinical history

Not analyze an ABG first before getting the patient's pertinent clinical history, which can provide insight into the cause of the specific acid-base illness. For instance, a patient who has a history of hypotension, renal failure, uncontrolled diabetes, or treatment with medications like metformin is likely to have metabolic acidosis; a patient who has a history of using diuretics, taking bicarbonate, having high nasogastric aspiration, or vomiting is likely to have metabolic alkalosis. Respiratory alkalosis is more likely to happen in sepsis, hepatic coma, and pregnancy, while respiratory acidosis is more likely to occur in COPD, muscle weakness, postoperative patients, and opioid overdose[4].

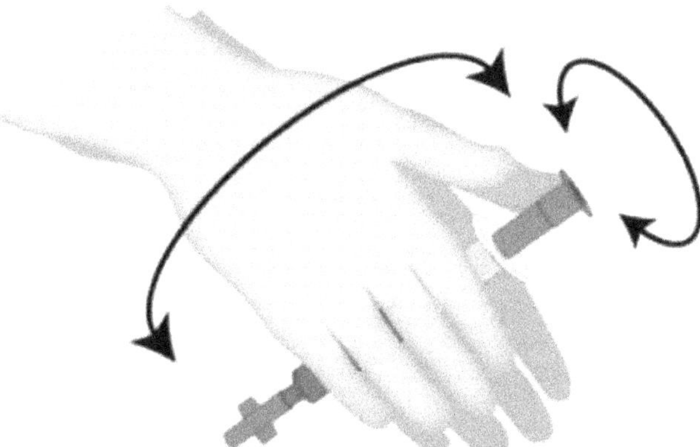

Fig E1: Correct method of mixing of the arterial sample with the anticoagulant in two dimensions of red blood cells

Look at the oxygenation status of the patient

The patient's oxygenation state is assessed using the paO2, but you should not speak on it without first knowing the matching FiO2. Determine the expectedpaO2, which is typically five times the FiO2.

Classify the hypoxia as low, moderate, or serious based on the predicted paO2.

If the pattern of change in HCO3 - (whether raised in alkalosis or lowered in acidosis) reflects the change in pH, then it is a metabolic disorder. If paCO2, a respiratory acid, is increased, i.e., >40 (acidosis) or decreased, i.e., 40 (alkalosis), then it is a respiratory disorder[5].

Clinical Significance

The gold standard for determining a patient's oxygenation, ventilation, and acid-base status is blood gas arterial monitoring. Although non-invasive monitoring has mostly taken the place of ABG monitoring, the latter is still helpful for validating and adjusting non-invasive evaluation methods[6].

Monitoring of oxygenation is routinely carried out in the context of severe sepsis, acute respiratory failure, and ARDS in the Intensive Care unit (ICU) and emergency room settings. To help identify the source of hypoxemia, an alveolar-arterial (A-a) oxygen gradient can be calculated. The existence or lack of a gradient, for instance, can assist in identifying if an aberration in oxygenation may be brought on by hypoventilation, a shunt, a V/Q mismatch, or hindered diffusion. The A-a gradient is less accurate at greater percentages of inspired oxygen because the equation for the predicted A-a gradient assumes the patient is breathing room air.The most accurate way to gauge respiratory status is to calculate the intrapulmonary shunt fraction, or the percentage of cardiac output going into pulmonary units that are not involved in gas exchange. The shunt fraction is typically calculated with 1.0 supplied FiO2, however venous admixture would be a more accurate word if performed at a lower FiO2.Calculating the PaO2/FiO2 or P/F ratio, which is a ratio of PaO2 and the proportion of inspired oxygen, makes oxygenation assessment more straightforward. The P/F ratio has limits, though, because the difference between venous admixture and the P/F ratio at a particular shunt fraction depends on the supplied FiO2. The P/F ratio was additionally employed to classify ARDS disease severity for scientific purposes.The oxygenation index is a further statistic frequently utilised in ICUs to measure oxygenation (OI). Compared to the P/F ratio, this index is thought to be a stronger predictor of lung injury, especially in the newborn and paediatric population. Included in it is the degree of intrusive ventilators necessary to keep oxygenation levels high. The mean airway pressure (Paw) in cm H2O, as recorded by the ventilator, and the FiO2, which is calculated as the percentage divided by the PaO2, are combined to form the OI. The OI is frequently used to direct management, including starting inhaled nitric oxide, giving out surfactants, and determining whether extracorporeal membrane oxygenation could be require[7].

Even in the presence of supplemental oxygen, respiratory failure cannot be ruled out by a normal PaO2 measurement. The PaCO2 measures both cellular and pulmonary CO2 production. It has a close association with the depth and rate of breathing, making it a more sensitive indicator of ventilatory failure than PaO2, especially when additional oxygen is present[8]. The pulmonary empty space calculation is a reliable measure of overall lung function. Physical dead space, or end-tidal PCO2 divided by PaCO2, is the difference between the PaCO2 and mixed expired PCO2 levels.Shunting and increased ventilation of the pulmonary units compared to their perfusion both result in an increase in pulmonary dead space. Hence, pulmonary empty space is one of the best predictive indicators of lung function at the bedside in ARDS patients. The diagnosis of many other illnesses like pulmonary embolism may also be aided by the pulmonary dead space fraction[9].

The aforementioned respiratory system disorders can impact acid-base balance. For instance, acidemia and alkalemia are the outcomes of acute respiratory acidosis, respectively. Hypoxemic hypoxia also triggers anaerobic metabolism, which results in metabolic acidosis and acidemia. Acute metabolic acidosis and alkalosis lead to acidemia and alkalemia, respectively, therefore anomalies in the metabolic system also affect the acid-balance. Patients with diabetic ketoacidosis, septic shock, renal failure, medication or toxin use, and gastrointestinal or renal HCO3 loss exhibit metabolic acidosis. Kidney disease, electrolyte imbalances, protracted vomiting, hypovolemia, diuretic use, and hypokalemia are a few factors that can lead to metabolic alkalosis[10].

ECG: When administering anaesthesia, dynamic electrocardiographic (ECG) monitoring is normal procedure, however views on its application during moderate (conscious) and severe sedation are divided. Under its 1991 guidelines, the American Dental Society of Anesthesiology recommended pulse oximetry for patient monitoring. When under profound sedation, the recommendations at the time also recommended ECG monitoring, but not when under moderate (aware) sedation. The American Dental Association recently updated its monitoring recommendations to incorporate ECG monitoring for all patients who are under heavy sedation as well as for patients who are consciously relaxed but have poor cardiovascular health[11].

General Principles Of Cardiac Function

Cardiovascular output, or heart rate, is the most important cardiovascular event needed to maintain blood flow throughout the body. The heart must maintain a regular cycle of relaxation and contraction in addition to blood volume and contractile strength if it is to achieve its goal. This regularity is the result of a number of intricate electrophysiological processes that take place within the heart tissues and may be observed to use an instrument called an electrocardiogram.

The rhythmic contraction and relaxation of the atria and ventricles are fundamental actions needed for a healthy cardiac cycle. The working cells and the specialised neural-like conducting cells make up the two main cell kinds of the heart. The muscle, or myocardium, of the atria and ventricles is made up of the working cells. The sinuatrial (SA) node, the atrioventricular (AV) node, the bundle of His, and the Purkinje fibres are examples of specialised cells. These cells produce and carry electrical impulses, which control the rhythm of a cardiac cycle throughout the myocardium. Specialized cells have a characteristic known as automaticity, which reflects an ability to start electrical impulses on demand. This is unrelated to any hormones or nerves, however autonomic nerves can affect the actual pace at which they fire, with sympathetic nerves speeding up and parasympathetic nerves slowing down[12].

Each cardiac cycle begins with an impulse that the SA node spontaneously produces. This impulse then spreads across the remaining neural-like conducting tissues and onto the muscle (myocardial) cells. Arrhythmias and dysrhythmias were terms used interchangeably to describe abnormalities in this conduction system that affect cardiac function.

The ECG Tracing

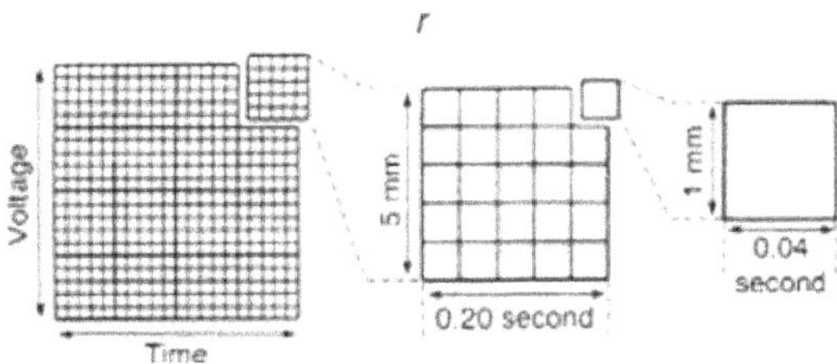

Fig E2: Standard ECG paperD

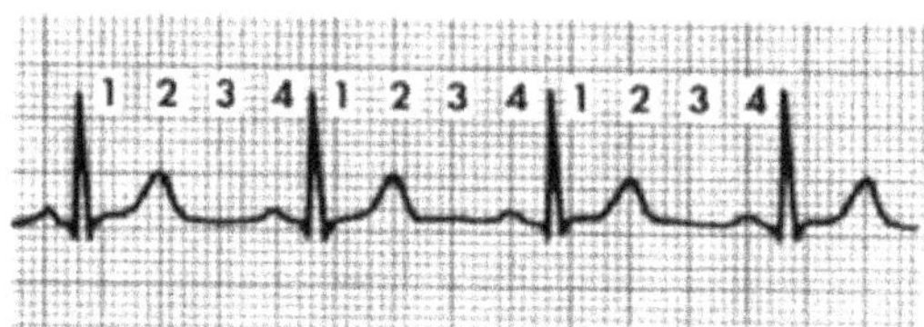

Fig E3: The normal ECG tracing

The sinoatrial node, often known as the heart's pacemaker, starts the electrical sequence of a cardiac cycle. This is due to the fact that the SA node spontaneously fires more frequently compared to what the other specialised tissues do. If this rate were to drop, however, other parts of this specialised system may take over, a condition known as escape.

The isoelectric line, which represents the resting membrane potentials, is the baseline of an ECG trace. The trace often returns to the isoelectric point after each of the deflections from this point, which are labelled with letters in alphabetical sequence. The P wave, which is the initial deflection, shows that the atrial muscle cells have depolarized. Neither the firing of the SA node nor the contraction of this muscle are represented by it. Based on the P waves' consistency and shape, these occurrences are inferred. One assumes the contraction starts at the apex of the P wave and that the SA node fires at the beginning of the P wave. Although atrial repolarization occurs after depolarization, the ECG doesn't show this to have happened. It's a common misperception that the succeeding QRS complex hides repolarization signs. It's a common misperception that the succeeding QRS complex hides repolarization signs. Yet, if this were the case, repolarization would be seen in situations when the QRS complex is absent or delayed, such as in AV blocks. The proper answer is that atrial repolarization has an amplitude that is too small for surface electrodes to detect[13].

The depolarization of ventricular muscle cells is represented by the QRS complex. The first down deflection is represented by the Q component, the first upward deflection by the R portion, and the return to the baseline, or so-called isoelectric point, by the S portion.Frequently, the Q component is not visible, and the depolarization only appears as a "RS" complex. The complex, in any case, does not signify ventricular contraction. One anticipates that contraction will start at the complex's apex in the R part. Contrary to the atria, ventricular contraction can be medically verified by palpating a pulse or observing the wave form of a pulse oximeter.A patient in cardiac arrest may have normal QRS complexes on his or her ECG; ventricular muscle cells are depolarizing, but there is no contraction. This phenomenon is called pulseless electrical activity. Following depolarization, ventricular muscle repolarizes, and this event is great enough in amplitude to generate the T wave on the ECG tracing.

The PR interval is the distance between the start of the P wave and the start of the R component of the QRS complex. (This is standard so because complex's Q component is typically undetectable.) One can presume that an electrical impulse enters the ventricle during in the PR interval because it begins with atrial muscle depolarization and concludes with the beginning of ventricular depolarization. One may conclude that an AV block is present if the PR interval is prolonged. An ECG's electrical events are depicted and outlined.

Technical Considerations

Willem Einthoven, a Dutch scientist, created a galvanometer in 1901 that could capture the electrical activity of the heart. He discovered that the spreading of action potentials across both positively and negatively charged electrode can result in a tracing. (The current is grounded using a third electrode.) He discovered that tracings changed depending on where the positive and negative electrodes were placed, and he then defined three directions or leads that formed a triangular with the heart in the centre.The three electrode configurations are referred to as the principal limb leads I, II, and III. This is known as Einthoven's triangle in modern times. As the 20th century's study progressed, new configurations were found that allow medical professionals to examine electrical impulses as they propagate all through the heart in numerous directions, much like how an apple slicer divides an apple into several portions. A 12-lead ECG is now analysed by a cardiologist to help in the diagnosis of infarctions, hypertrophy, and complicated arrhythmias[14].

ECG Paper

An ECG monitor shows a trace without a backdrop matrix. However, the majority of these displays come with additional printer that, upon request, can provide a printout with gridlines. The record paper is moving at a speed of 25 mm/s as the stylus of the recording device is pushed by electric impulses. As a result, an ECG trace is produced whose elements can be measured.

An ECG's vertical axis represents voltage and the angle at which waveforms depart from the baseline.Such factors play a role in the diagnosis of ischemia and infarction but are typically irrelevant for routine monitoring. The horizontal axis represents time and the order of occurrences, both of which are critical for identifying arrhythmias. Little and large squares are used to split up the standard ECG recording material. The former stand for intervals of 0.04 seconds. A large square, or 0.20 seconds, is made up of five little squares.

ECG Analysis

Heart rate is shown on dynamic ECG monitors, but can also be determined from a written trace using one of two techniques:

1. Calculate the number of big (0.2-second) boxes between the next two QRS complexes when the heart rate is steady, then multiply that amount by 300. Since heart rate is measured in beats per minute, or 60 seconds, the number of large time boxes is divided into 300 by the fact that 300 is equal to 60. For instance, the heart rate is 100 beats per minute if there are 3 huge boxes between QRS complexes, thus 300 3 100. The heart rate is 75 beats per minute if 4 big time boxes are recorded between QRS complexes.

2. So because time intervals between QRS complexes change from beat to beat, the first approach will not be reliable if the heart rate is erratic. ECG graph paper is typically graded with marks spaced every three seconds. Simply count the number of QRS complexes every three or six seconds in certain circumstances and increase this figure by twenty or ten, as appropriate.

Never forget that activities occurring during the PR interval are related to supraventricular activity. Try to determine if an incident is ventricular or supraventricular in origin when anomalies are detected. One recommendation for how to analyse an ECG tracing is as follows.

It's what I refer to as a 5-step analysis.

Step 1: Is the Rhythm Regular or Irregular?

Ventricular rhythm is normal if the times between QRS complexes (R-R intervals) are constant. Atrial rhythm is normal if the time between P waves (P-P intervals) is constant.

Step 2: Are All QRS Complexes Similar, and Are They Narrow?

The QRS complex shouldn't last longer than 0.10 seconds (212 tiny squares). A widening complicated indicates ventricular hypertrophy or the beginning of ventricular depolarization by pacemaker tissue below the AV node, such as in ventricular-paced rhythm. As a result, the current must flow into the second ventricle after the first ventricle depolarizes. When the current spreads down the bundle into both ventricles simultaneously, it takes less time.A supraventricular rhythm is one in which the QRS complexes are narrow and which is started by a pacemaker at the AV node or higher. The pacemaker is in the ventricles and is referred to be a ventricular rhythm if the complexes are broad. If the appearance of complexes varies, and over one pacemaker is producing impulses. Ectopy is the term used to describe the rhythm, and ectopic pacemakers are the phenomena.

Step 3: Are All P Waves Similar and Are PR Intervals Normal?

If the P waves are all uniform and of an original condition, the SA node is likely the main pacemaker. The rhythm in this instance has a sinus nature. If P waves are irregular in shape or nonexistent, another tissue or tissues are acting as pacemakers.

The PR interval typically lasts between 0.10 and 0.20 seconds (3-5 tiny squares). The situation known as AV block is characterised by longer intervals, which show that the impulse is being delayed from accessing the ventricles.

Step 4: Is the Rate Normal?

Calculate the large squares between QRS complexes and divide the total by 300 if the rhythm is regular. Instead, increase the number of QRS complexes in a 6-second period by 10 if the rhythm is erratic. Rates under 60 show bradycardia, whereas those over 100 show tachycardia. Between QRS complexes, there are around four huge boxes, therefore the rate is 75.

Step 5: Do Waves and Complexes Proceed in Normal Sequence?

A QRS complex should be followed by a T wave after every P wave. This guarantees that each cardiac cycle will proceed normally[15].

2. X-Ray:

Interpreting chest radiographs of severely unwell patients in Intensive Care units (ICUs) is difficult for both the radiologist and the Intensive Care doctors. These difficulties result from a number of reasons, including: ICU patients are susceptible to a number of cardiac conditions, which when combined with the underlying illness that caused admission result in a complex radiological appearance that can be challenging to interpret solely based on image results.In the case of an ICU patient, the inferior anteroposterior (AP) radiograph is used in place of the normal posteroanterior (PA) radiograph. Additional abnormalities on the ICU chest radiograph are obscured by instruments, mechanical ventilation, cardiac and other vital sign monitors, tube feeding, etc. While managing critically ill patients, radiologists and Intensive Care doctors are under pressure to quickly interpret chest x-rays, frequently with insufficient patient data, in part because things may shift quickly in the critically ill[16]. The ICU patient's wide variety of line placement, where erroneous placement is widespread and could not be visible to the spectator without clinical input, makes radiological interpretation difficult. In the ICU patient, air space shadowing may look the same in a number of cardiopulmonary diseases.While chest radiography is still the preferred imaging technique for ICU patients, computed tomography is frequently used in conjunction with a suspected pulmonary embolism as computed tomographic pulmonary angiography (CTPA). Whenever scheduled pleural treatment is being considered, ultrasound is utilised to confirm pleural and pericardial effusions[17].

The Normal Chest X-ray

An antroposterior (AP) radiograph is typically used in place of the normal PA chest radiograph in ICU patients. The optimal patient-to-x-ray plate spacing for these radiographs is 72 inches when the patient is upright and at maximal intake; however, due to the limited movement of ICU patients, a range of 40 inches is more frequently employed when the patient is prostrate or seated.The mediastinum and heart are enlarged on a radiograph taken in this fashion due to gravitational and geometrical forces[18].

Moreover, the reclined posture affects the physiology of the pulmonary vasculature, causing blood to be directed to the lung apices, which appears healthy on an AP supine radiograph but incorrect on a PA radiograph. Supine radiographs have additional drawbacks, such as difficulty distinguishing pleural effusions from air space shadowing and difficulty spotting a pneumothorax. Other difficulties arise while presenting a radiograph in full inspiration in an ICU patient since these patients are frequently resistant or in discomfort following surgery. A less-than-perfect inspiratory effort produces aberrations that alter the appearance of the heart and mediastinum and make it hard to diagnose basilar atelectasis and pulmonary edoema[19].

3. How to do bedside point of care test

Point of care testing, otherwise referred to as near patient, bedside, or additional laboratory testing, isn't really new. Many of the early "diagnostic tests" were first done at urine tests, for instance, just at bedside. So over past few years, however, analytical methods have already been developed which enable a wide range of tests to really be done quickly and simply without requiring sophisticated laboratory equipment[20].

End of meant to ensure should be performed by laboratory staff and adhere to the instructions given in the directions box. Wherever practical, points of care testing equipment should be connected to the laboratory information system to enable real time monitoring of performance and integration of data into the patient's electronic record.

This method must satisfy all the standards associated to clinical risk management and clinical governance furthermore, it recognises all of the stakeholders in point of care testing. All potential buyers must be represented on the multidisciplinary team which directs point-of-care testing[21].

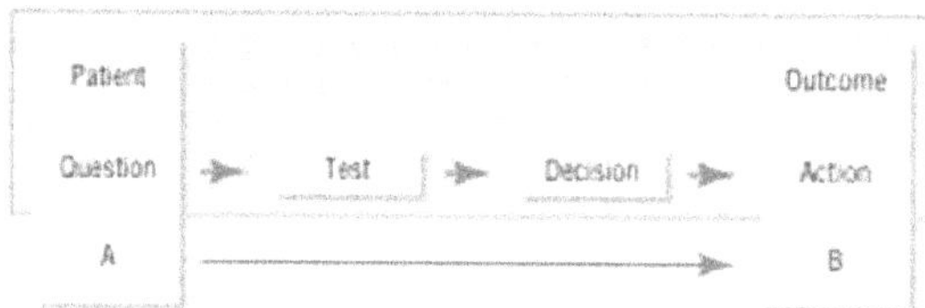

Figure E4: Objective of point of care testing

PoCT devices are typically categorised into two groups: those that are larger bench-top devices with more complex built-in fluidics, frequently variations of those found in normal laboratories, as well as smaller handheld devices, containing quantitative and qualitative strips. All devices share a number of essential design features that work together to achieve, to the greatest extent feasible. Although if not all are featured in the more basic gadgets, such dipsticks. It is growing more possible to create smaller and smaller devices that contain each of these essential design features thanks to the trend of growing device miniaturisation and the use of technology developed in relation to consumer electronics[22].

Small Handheld PoCT Devices

There are numerous small devices for PoCT, ranging from basic "dipstick" to the highly developed small cartridge devices used in blood gas analysis. The client or a health professional will often use such portable devices in close proximity to the patient, such as at the bedside, at the clinic, or at home. Because of their mobility, these devices are typically operated in a different manner than bigger or bench-top devices, which is frequently referred to as the operating workflow[23]. Small, portable devices, for instance, frequently use fingerstick, capillary samples that are applied directly to the PoCT instrument without the need for sample containers, labelling, or transport that are necessary for evaluation by a larger bench-top PoCT instrument some distances from the patient. Even if skipping these extra processes is very handy, there are dangers involved with such operations, so the testing method must be developed to reduce those risks with the help of the proper training and documentation[24].

Larger Bench-Top PoCT Devices

This type of instrument's design is similar to several of those utilised in the main laboratory. In order to provide services like diabetes management, laboratory equipment first occasionally moved to outpatient clinics. These devices are currently employed in a variety of point of care venues as a greater amount of this care is provided in settings other than hospitals. Yet, as space is frequently at a premium in such places, equipment must be made to be less complicated and larger so that non-laboratory employees may use them. The creation of solutions to address these objectives is made easier by the overall trend of miniaturisation and rising computer processing capacity[25].

4. Culture report how to analyse

For roles in antimicrobial therapy in the United States, there is presently a shortage of pharmacists with infectious diseases training. To increase effective antibiotic prescribing, pharmacists in a range of other disciplines must assume these responsibilities. 1 According to research conducted in hospital environments, 50% of inpatients are thought to get at least one antibiotic, 30% of which are broad-spectrum antibiotics, during their stay. 2-5 Although numbers can vary by institution and how "suitable" is defined, it has been estimated that the inappropriate usage of antibiotics can reach 50%. 6–9 When drugs are used improperly, they can have more negative side effects, secondary infections, drug interactions, higher expenses, longer durations of stay, and readmission rates.Moreover, bacterial resistance could emerge, that might result in treatment failure. The scheduling of cultures, typical culture sites, interpreting the Gram stain, the use of fast diagnostic tests, traditional antibiotic susceptibility testing, and automated testing are all covered in this essay. We refer to antibiotics throughout the article rather than antimicrobials because we did not discuss testing for viruses or fungus [26].

Obtaining Cultures

In order to direct therapy, medical providers must immediately get cultures while also emphasising the significance of early antibiotic delivery. The 2016 Surviving Sepsis Campaign recommendations state that antibiotics must be given within an hour of a sepsis diagnosis and that cultures shouldn't cause more than a 45-minute lag in giving antibiotics. Giving the right medications to septic patients within an hour can lower mortality. Collecting cultures prior to the administration of antibiotics can help clinicians discover the offending bacterium, potentially enabling de-escalation via effective therapy. If blood cultures are taken after taking antibiotics, the quality of such samples may decline, which could raise the patient's costs and the duration of their stay.Areas which are either sterile or bacterially populated can be used to produce cultures. Those with bacterial colonisation run the danger of being contaminated by natural flora and could produce erroneous results. Places like blood, pericardial fluid, and cerebral spinal fluid are usually considered of that as sterile. Sputum and nasal passageways are two locations that are recognisedfor infection. The risk of contamination may also grow with improper culturing. Here are some things to keep in mind while evaluating the results of stool, blood, respiratory, urine, skin and soft tissue, bone, and joint cultures[27].

Blood Cultures

Differentiating between bacteremia and contamination is crucial when assessing blood cultures. When bacteria from an external entity are added to a sample that was obtained, contamination occurs. When a single needle venipuncture is carried out, for instance, typical skin germs might be injected. Medical equipment like central venous catheters also may contain bacteria. Contrary to venipuncture, central venous catheters are linked to increased rates of contamination. While more recent testing techniques enable the identification of bacteria, even in minute quantities, contamination rates are rising. The physician must evaluate the detailed medical appearance and establish if the patient exhibits bacteremia-related signs and symptoms while assessing probable contamination. For instance, if a patient has hypotension, a tachycardia, and a fever, bacteremia might be present. One study that looked at 500 blood cultures discovered that Corynebacterium species and Staphylococcus epidermidis were contaminated 94% and 79% of the time, respectively. Yet, these two bacteria may actually indicate an infection in populations like immunosuppressed individuals. Staphylococcus aureus and Streptococcus pneumoniae are two gram-positive bacteria that are connected to real infection. To ensure that bacteremia has resolved, further cultures must be taken[28].

Respiratory Cultures

Sputum cultures, endotracheal aspirates, and, less commonly, broncho alveolar lavage are frequently requested by physicians to identify pneumonia. They are carried out in addition to chest radiography and the assessment of signs and symptoms (cough, fever, sputum production, and pleuritic chest pain). So because upper respiratory tract is bacterially populated as opposed to the lower respiratory tract, which is usually painless, sputum cultures can be challenging to interpret. There are many different reports on the sensitivity and specificity of sputum cultures.The appearance of epithelial in a sputum culture, which can indicate culture infection, must be noted. Less than 10 epithelial cells per low-powered field should be present in sputum cultures. Sputum cultures ought to be avoided in some patient populations, such as individuals with chronic obstructive pulmonary disease (COPD) who are going through an exacerbation. The 2017 Global Initiative for Chronic Obstructive Lung Disease guidelines advise assessing clinical symptoms such sputum production, purulence, and dyspnea rather than utilising such cultures to identify whether an infection is present. Endotracheal aspiration or bronchoalveolar lavage are commonly used to acquire cultures from patients who are continuously maintained. Despite having lesser risk and a smaller price tag, endotracheal aspiration has a worse specificity than bronchoalveolar lavage for the diagnosis of pneumonia. A larger use of antibiotics may arise from this decreased selectivity. Recommendations disagree about the selection for bronchoalveolar lavage or endotracheal aspiration, depending on whether the decision is founded on antibiotic de-escalation or the expenses and drawbacks of these procedures. Before proposing bronchoalveolar lavage or endotracheal aspiration, physicians must adhere to the institutional guidelines at their respective setting[29].

Urine Cultures

Despite having lesser risk and a smaller price tag, endotracheal aspiration has a worse accuracy than bronchoalveolar lavage for the diagnosis of pneumonia. A larger use of antibiotics may arise from this decreased selectivity. Recommendations disagree about the selection for bronchoalveolar lavage or endotracheal aspiration, depending on whether the decision is founded on antibiotic de-escalation or the expenses and drawbacks of these procedures. Before proposing bronchoalveolar lavage or endotracheal aspiration, physicians must adhere to the institutional guidelines at their respective setting.UTIs are diagnosed when there are ten or more leukocytes per microliter in the urine, however this shouldn't be the only factor used to determine the condition. It is recommended to obtain cultures midstream in patients without urinary catheters to prevent contamination. The amount of colony-forming units (CFUs) per millilitre (ml) in the urine culture serves as a proxy for the sample's bacterial content. Infection is indicated by a urine culture with more than 103 CFUs per millilitre. Nonetheless, patients with lower CFUs still may develop a genuine infection if they also have symptom and urine leukocytes. Lower CFUs are also seen in patients with catheter-associated UTI. On the other hand, when pollutants are present and following a specimen that was improperly obtained, greater CFU counts can happen. Unless such patient has health risks for those other types of bacteria and the test is properly obtained, infection may be the cause of bacteria that are normally not observed in UTIs. Escherichia coli, Klebsiella species, Proteus species, and Staphylococcus saprophyticus are typical bacteria found in simple UTIs[30].

Skin and Soft Tissue Infections

The Infectious Diseases Society of America (IDSA) advises getting cultures for carbuncles and abscesses, while they also add that empiric care without the need for a culture is permissible. The IDSA advises just taking blood cultures for sepsis when certain conditions apply to the patient. Immunosuppression, cancer, animal bites, and/or immersion injuries are some of these risk factors. 34 Cultures of the skin's surface should only be acquired in cases of purulent discharge. When skin cultures are obtained for infections without discharge, it frequently results in the discovery of polymicrobial organisms that are not the infection's aetiology and an overly broad course of treatment. The patient's medical history and physical exam are crucial for making the diagnosis, just like with UTIs.Individuals with non-purulent cellulitis are more likely to have group A streptococci infection while those with purulent discharge are much more probable to have S. aureus infection[31].

Bone and Joint Infections

Bacteria from blood, prosthetics, trauma, or the spread of a skin infection can cause bacterial joint and bone infections. Understanding the origin can aid in identifying the germs that might be responsible. Fever, painful and swollen joints, soreness, and a reduced motion range are typical signs of joint infections. Joint infections are more prevalent in patients who have joint prosthesis or have recently had joint surgery (often within three months). Synovial fluid cultures, when the fluid is obtained after surgery or through aspiration, are used to identify joint infections. Increased white blood cell (WBC) counts can assist rule in (90% specificity) but not rule out (56% sensitivity) joint infections, particularly when the level surpasses 50,000 cells/mm3. The Gram stain's accuracy (45-71%) for identifying joint infections is also poor.Last but not least, determining the quantity of protein or glucose in the synovial fluid is useless for diagnosis. Osteomyelitis patients frequently exhibit signs of fever, sluggishness, inflammation, erythema, and edoema. Osteomyelitis is mostly diagnosed by using radiographs and bone biopsy cultures to pinpoint the causative organism. In order to identify the organism causing hematogenous osteomyelitis, blood cultures might also be taken. Last but not least, although these can't be utilized in diagnosis without the need for culture, patients often have high WBC counts, a raised erythrocyte sedimentation rate, and elevated C-reactive protein values[32].

Cerebrospinal Fluid cultures

Meningitis is typically diagnosed using cultures of the cerebrospinal fluid (CSF). While lower WBC counts could be found, CSF cultures linked to untreated bacterial meningitis often exhibit an increased WBC count (> 1,000 cells/mm3). A traumatic lumbar puncture might also result in increases in WBC count. The WBC CSF count rises by one for every 1,000 red blood cells in the CSF as a basic guideline. Neutrophils are often > 80%, however, lymphocytes > 50% can be found in 10% of patients. Gram stain is helpful in making a diagnosis of bacterial meningitis in patients, particularly when there is a higher bacterial burden. The Gram stain's specificity has been estimated to be as high as 97% in various circumstances. Last but not least, if the CSF Gram stain and culture are negative, polymerase chain reaction (PCR), which has great sensitivity and specificity, may be employed to check out bacterial meningitis[33].

Stool Cultures

Patients who appear with severe or recurrent diarrhea or who have traveled to regions with subpar public sanitation systems may want to consider bringing stool samples. It is enough to get one stool culture, and it can identify the pathogen 87-94% of the time. Stool cultures are often examined in laboratories for germs including Salmonella, Shigella, E. coli, and Campylobacter. In patients who have health risks for the infection, such as those who have taken antibiotics within the previous two months, have experienced more than two unformed bowel movements in a 24-hour period, have increased WBC counts, have deteriorated renal function, or have decreased albumin levels, Clostridium difficile checking may also be taken into account. For the detection of C. difficile, there are numerous assays available. Such tests are usually performed using the molecular assay, glutamate dehydrogenase (GDH) immunoassay, and toxin A and B enzyme immunoassay. The toxin A and B immunoassay is typically run first in labs, together with the GDH assay. Although the sensitive of the tests is lower (41-92%), the combination of these two tests offers a high specificity (97% or above). 48,49 When the GDH and the toxin A and B enzyme assays are both positive, C. difficile is probably the cause. Further testing with molecular tests should be conducted because it can increase sensitivity and specificity if one is positive and the other is negative. Testing after remission is useless since positive stool cultures might last for weeks after infection[34].

Early bacterial Identification

Antibiotic susceptibility evaluation is essential since it helps clinicians decide on the best treatment option for an infection. Gram staining, matrix-assisted laser desorption/ionization-time of flight mass spectrometry (MALDI-TOF), PCR, nanoparticle probe technology, and peptide nucleic acid fluorescence in situ hybridization are a few different methods for identifying bacteria early (PNA-FISH).

Gram Staining

Gram staining is a diagnostic procedure that, by making the bacteria visible, provides an early indicator of possible bacteria. Whether an organism is gram-positive or gram-negative can be determined using the Gram stain. Gram-negative bacteria are pink in hue, and gram-positive bacteria are purple in color. The size, layout, and shape of the organism can also offer additional details that can aid in identifying it. Cocci, that like spheres, bacilli, which resemble rods, and coccobacilli, which combine the two, are typical shapes detected on the Gram stain. Cocci can be grouped in clusters or chains, for instance; gram-positive Staphylococcus species can be found in clusters. A microbiologist may use size to distinguish between various bacilli, albeit the doctor is rarely informed of this. The operator places bacteria on a slide before passing it through a flame to guarantee the bacteria remain on the slide for the Gram stain. After that, crystal violet dye is used to stain the bacteria, which turns them all purple. The dye is then washed away with acetone after being injected with iodine, which helped it adhere to the peptidoglycan layer of the cell wall. Because gram-positive bacteria have a tight relationship with a thick peptidoglycan layer, the purple dye adheres to them while washing off gram-negative bacteria, which have a thin peptidoglycan coating. Finally, gram-negative bacteria are stained pink by a dye such safranin. To better distinguish between bacteria, additional tests might be run. Gram-negative bacteria that are lactose-fermenting and those that are not could be distinguished using MacConkey agar plates. To distinguish between Staphylococcus aureus and other Staphylococcus species, perform the coagulase test. If the coagulase test is positive, Staphylococcus aureus is probably the bacteria; if it is negative, Staphylococcus epidermis or Staphylococcus saprophyticus is probably the bacteria[35].

Rapid Diagnostic Test

Faster diagnosis and de-escalation of antibiotic medication are made possible by rapid diagnostic testing. When making suggestions to physicians depending on such tests, pharmacists have been crucial. The MALDI-TOF, PCR, PNA-FISH, and nanoparticle probe technology are some of these quick medical diagnostics. It is possible to comprehend MALDI-TOF by breaking down the acronym. A sample is grown on an agar plate, transferred to a MALDI plate, and then a matrix is introduced to perform MALDI-TOF. The sample desorbs from the plate and forms ionized molecules as a result of the laser being converted into heat with the aid of the matrix. The molecules transform to gas, which, according to its size and charge, then flies into the Time-Of-Flight tube. A spectrum depending on the size and charge of the molecules is produced because molecules with a smaller size-to-charge ratio move more quickly. This spectrum has been compared to the libraries of known organism spectra, like Escherichia coli. The MALDI-TOF machine's score value, which represents the likelihood of recognizing the genus and/or species under test, also correlates with the spectra. The primary benefit of MALDI-TOF is the bacteria can be identified in much less than five hours. The test presently does not offer susceptibility data and is unable to identify heteroresistance. Whenever a subgroup of bacterial cells exhibits higher levels of antibiotic resistance than the rest of the culture, this is known as heteroresistance.PCR is a different, quick identification technique that functions by producing several copies of the DNA segments used in order to identify bacteria. A DNA segment, nucleotides, polymerase, and a primer are required for PCR. Heat triggers DNA to separate into two single strands[36]. The polymerase then uses the nucleotides to create new DNA strands from these primed strands. To create numerous copies of DNA fragments that may be examined to determine the bacterium, the process must be repeated. The benefits of PCR include the capacity to detect germs while a patient is receiving antibiotic therapy and the quick identification of bacteria (less than an hour). However, the method has certain drawbacks because PCR may identify bacteria that are no longer alive after an infection has been cured in a patient.PNA-FISH uses probes to recognize ribosomal RNA to identify bacteria as opposed to PCR and nanoprobe-particle technologies, which identify bacteria by the detection of DNA. Another way to understand PNA-FISH is to break down the acronym. In this process, microorganisms that have been glued to a slide are probed with fluorescent peptide-nucleic acid (PNA). These probes hybridize (bond) to ribosomal RNA, which allows for real-time visualization under a fluorescence microscope (In Situ). Rapid detection (less than an hour) and the capacity to identify bacteria that are more difficult to grow using conventional techniques (anaerobes, Mycoplasma species) are three benefits of PNAFISH. It is also less expensive than PCR. As various bacteria use various packages, PNA-biggest FISH's drawback is the fact that the researcher must predict what the prospective bacteria are. Making the right kit selection may be aided by understanding the Gram stain. Hence, the scientist would choose the kit to be used with E. Coli/P. Aeruginosa if lactose-positive gram-negative bacilli were developing. In addition, PNA-FISH could only identify medication resistance in cases when ribosomal RNA changes take place[37].

5. How to manage DKA And interpret

Diabetes patients with both type 1 and type 2 diabetes mellitus can develop diabetic ketoacidosis (DKA), an uncommon but highly dangerous hyperglycemic crisis. Proper management and treatment are essential due to its rising prevalence, economic burden from treatment, and related complications[38].

Introduction

As a result of water loss, a rise in insulin counter-regulatory hormones, and rapidly deteriorating peripheral insulin resistance, infections, acute illnesses of the cardiovascular system (myocardial infarction, stroke), gastrointestinal tract (bleeding, pancreatitis), diseases of the endocrine axis (acromegaly, Cushing's syndrome), and stress from latest surgical procedures can all contribute to the development of DKA. Drugs including diuretics, beta-blockers, corticosteroids, antipsychotics, and/or anticonvulsants may impair volume status and carbohydrate metabolism, which could lead to DKA. DKA may also be caused by psychological issues, food issues, complications with the insulin pump, and illegal drug usage. It is now understood that DKA can occur alongside newly diagnosed type 2 diabetes mellitus. Now of their presentation, such individuals are obese, primarily African Americans or Hispanics, and very insulin resistant[39].

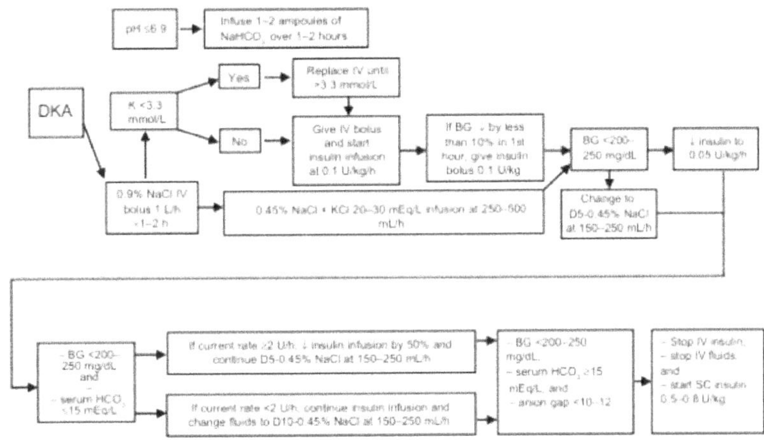

Figure E5: Workflow of management of adult DKA

Diagnosis

Blood glucose levels are one of the diagnostic criteria for DKA. 250 mg/dL, a bicarbonate concentration of 18 mEq/L, an arterial pH of 7, as well as a corrected albumin anion gap of. Positive urine and serum ketones may help to confirm the DKA diagnosis. Acetoacetate concentration is low in early DKA, yet many laboratories use it as a main substrate for measuring ketone levels in serum, hence this method has a high specificity but a low sensitivity for the diagnosis of DKA. In contrast, -OHB is a prevalent and early ketoacid that may be the first to indicate the onset of DKA; nonetheless, its detection calls for the use of a unique assay that is distinct from all those employed for the regular measurement of ketone bodies. It has been demonstrated that the $3.8 mmol/L levels of -OHB determined by a particular assay are both extremely sensitive and specific for the diagnosis of DKA. Due to the coexisting underlying chronic metabolic acidosis or combined acid-base problems in patients with chronic renal disease stage 4-5, the diagnosis of DKA may be difficult. In these patients, an anion gap of.20 typically indicates the presence of DKA[40].

Treatment

Optimization of 1) volume status, 2) hyperglycemia and ketoacidosis, 3) electrolyte abnormalities, and 4) probable precipitating causes are among the therapeutic objectives of DKA therapy. The vast majority of DKA patients visit the emergency department. Hence, while a screening test is being conducted, fundamental metabolic data are being acquired, and a diagnosis is being made, emergency physicians should begin the care of hyperglycemic crises[41].

Early DKA management ought to involve a number of crucial steps, including:

1. obtain blood samples for a metabolic profile prior to starting intravenous fluids;

2. infuse 1 L of 0.9% sodium chloride more than a period of an hour following the initial blood samples;

3. verify a potassium level of.3.3 mEq/L prior to starting insulin therapy (supplement potassium intravenously if necessary);

4. start insulin therapy only after steps 1-3 have been completed.

Fluid Therapy:

With DKA, fluid loss is often 6–9 L. Between 24 to 36 hours, it is intended to replenish the entire volume lost, with the initial 8 to 12 hours seeing the administration of 50% of the resuscitation fluid. The initial fluid of preference is a crystalloid fluid. Depending on the patient's hemodynamic condition, current guidelines call for starting the process of volume restoration with intravenous boluses of isotonic saline (0.9% NaCl).

After that, an intravenous infusion of 0.45% NaCl solution will only further reduce plasma osmolality and aid water in entering the intracellular compartment based on corrected serum sodium concentration. A common laboratory finding in DKA is hyperosmolar hyponatremia caused by hyperglycemia, which is typically accompanied by dehydration and increased adjusted sodium values. Fluids can be supplied at a reduced rate of 4–14 mL/kg/h after the first hydration. To prevent hypoglycemia when blood sugar levels drop below 200-250 mg/dL, intravenous fluids must be changed to a dextrose-containing 0.45% NaCl solution, or the rate of insulin infusion must be reduced[42].

Insulin Therapy:

Treatment of DKA with intravenous insulin:

The infusion of insulin is crucial in the therapy of DKA since it increases peripheral tissues' ability to utilise glucose, reduces gluconeogenesis and glycogenolysis, and inhibits ketogenesis. In individuals with DKA, intravenous infusion is the recommended method of delivering insulin. Low-dose insulin administered at doses of 5–10 U/h has replaced high-dose insulin administered at rates up to 100 U/h by various methods of delivery. 14 We advise administering a 0.1 U/kg first dose of normal insulin followed by continuous insulin infusion. 0.1 U/kg of insulin can be administered once again with maintaining insulin infusion if plasma glucose doesn't really decrease by at least 10% in the first hour of insulin infusion rate[43].

Treatment of DKA with subcutaneous insulin:

Initial research evaluating the best insulin doses and routes of distribution for treating DKA showed that subcutaneous continuous insulin therapy is efficient but not as efficient as intravenous insulin infusion.

Potassium, bi-carbonate and phosphate therapy:

When treating DKA, serum potassium should be regularly watched. When insulin is administered, acidemia and has that are corrected, and potassium is driven cytosolic. This causes hypokalemia, which can cause arrhythmias and cardiac collapse. During treating DKA, if serum potassium falls to 3.3 mEq/L, insulin must be halted, and potassium must be given orally.Since metabolic acidosis would be resolved by insulin therapy, bicarbonate medication is not recommended for moderate to severe cases of DKA. Because there aren't enough prospective, randomised research, the use of bicarbonate in severe DKA is debatable. Bicarbonate treatment is suspected to cause intracellular acidosis to rise, as well as paradoxical central nervous system acidosis, increasing hypokalemia, cerebral edoema in young people and kids, and peripheral hypoxemia. Bicarbonate therapy may be recommended if the pH is 6.9 or lower because severe acidosis is linked to even worse health outcomes, can damage the sensorium, and can worsen cardiac contractility.

In DKA, the median whole-body phosphate shortage is 1 mmol/kg. 90% of patients were reported to have had hypophosphatemia while receiving insulin infusions and fluids, and this will further lower the serum phosphate content while on insulin therapy for DKA[44].

Treatment of DKA in dialysis patients:

In the US, diabetes is a major contributor to the final analysis kidney disease (ESKD). DKA is uncommon in dialysis patients, although it is becoming more common as diabetic ESKD is becoming more common.

Metabolic Treatment targets:

Metabolic markers must be measured often (every 2-4 hours) to track treatment progress and verify DKA remission. Whenever plasma glucose is 200-250 mg/dL, serum bicarbonate is 15 mEq/L, venous blood pH is.7.3, and the anion gap is #12, DKA is cured.

- Key DKA management points
- Before beginning insulin therapy, the potassium level must be.3.3 mEq/L (if necessary, potassium supplementation must be administered intravenously).
- Start a continuous insulin infusion at 0.1 U/kg/h after administering a priming insulin dose at 0.1 U/kg. Each hour, check the blood sugar at the bedside to alter the insulin infusion rate.
- Reduce the pace of the insulin infusion till the DKA has been treated in order to prevent hypoglycemia while the insulin is being administered.
- Only switch to subcutaneous insulin when DKA has been resolved.

DKA management protocols in clinical care:

There is an increasing request to successfully transmit modern knowledge to the bedside with a number of DKA recommendations and technical research on the subject released by several associations. The creation of inpatient standardized protocols for the care of DKA is one strategy for delivering optimal clinical practices[45].

6. How to evaluate shock, Respiratory failure, neuro examination

Shock: Urgent situations like shock call for constant examination, resuscitation, and re-evaluation at the bedside. The first bedside examination enables the physician to ascertain if the patient displays a clinical presentation that is compatible with cardiogenic, vasodilatory, or hypovolemic shock. The prompt first resuscitation recommended by the survey method typically includes intubation, ventilation, and volume support. Vasoactive therapy, which includes inotropic support for cardiogenic shock and pressor therapy for vasodilatory shock, is initiated once the patient has been adequately volume-resuscitated. The secondary survey is essential for establishing early definite therapy and is useful in identifying the shock's underlying cause. There is a hemodynamic component to early shock, which is frequently quickly reversible. Multiple-system organ failure (MSOF) and mortality are caused by an inflammatory condition that is present in septic shock as well as chronic shock from any cause. Early diagnosis of shock and a quick pace of hemodynamic resuscitation to stop or reduce the inflammatory component is essential to treating shock successfully[46].

Respiratory failure: Aerobic metabolism is facilitated by the respiratory system, which permits gas exchange between both the environment and the body. The respiratory system particularly delivers oxygen and expels carbon dioxide from the body. Respiratory failure occurs when the respiratory system is unable to carry out any of these functions. Whenever the respiratory system is unable to sufficiently oxygenate the body, type 1 respiratory failure—which results in hypoxemia—occurs. When the respiratory system is unable to sufficiently expel carbon dioxide from the body, type 2 respiratory failure—which results in hypercapnia—occurs. Chronicity is a factor that can classify respiratory failure (i.e., acute, chronic, and acute on chronic). The management of respiratory failure requires a thorough understanding of the condition. Both types of respiratory failure could become life-threatening and result in respiratory arrest, coma, and death if they aren't recognized and treated right away[47].

Evaluation:

A variety of medical conditions can result in the syndrome of respiratory failure. As a result, there isn't a single method for determining respiratory failure. Laboratory tests (such as a complete blood count with differential, a comprehensive metabolic panel with magnesium/phosphorous, procalcitonin, troponin, and thyroid-stimulating hormone), an infectious workup (such as blood and sputum cultures, respiratory pathogen panel tests, and urinary antigen tests), and 12-lead electrocardiography could all be appropriate diagnostic studies.

Arterial Blood gas:

The criterion for identifying respiratory failure is arterial blood gas (ABG). An ABG gives data on pH, arterial carbon dioxide partial pressure, arterial oxygen partial pressure, and serum bicarbonate, at the very least (HCO3). Remember that the HCO3 received from an ABG is a computed number and could not be correct. Instead, a determined HCO3 from a fundamental metabolic panel ought to be utilized to analyse an ABG.

By interpreting the PaO2, oxygenation is evaluated. PaO2 less than 60 mmHg is considered hypoxemia. By interpreting the PaCO2, ventilation is evaluated. A PaCO2 level over 45 mmHg is considered to be hypercapnic.

By assessing the renal reaction to PaCO2, data from the ABG can also be utilised to distinguish between acute and chronic respiratory failure. The kidneys' response to respiratory acidosis is to increase HCO3 absorption in the proximal convoluted tube. The magnitude of HCO3 absorption in acute respiratory acidosis is lower than that of the magnitude of HCO3 absorption in chronic respiratory acidosis since this is a slow process. This feature makes it possible to distinguish between acute and chronic respiratory failure[48].

Capnometry:

It is possible to quantify carbon dioxide in exhaled gas qualitatively or quantitatively using capnometry. A qualitative measurement of carbon dioxide in exhaled gas called colorimetric capnometry depends just on colour change of a pH-sensitive indicator. A method for detecting the amount of carbon dioxide in exhaled gas that depends on relative pressure measurements is known as infrared capnometry (pCO2). Comparative to qualitative capnometry, quantitative capnometry offers greater information.

End-tidal pCO2 (PETCO2), a measure of the partial pressure of carbon dioxide at the end of expiration, is close to the carbon dioxide partial pressure in arterial blood in the non-pathological state (PaCO2). Usually, the PaCO2 is 2 to 3 mmHg higher than that of the PETCO2. The difference between PaCO2 and PETCO2 rises to more than 3 mmHg in the medical problem, where gas exchange is compromised, as a result of increased dead space ventilation.

Quantitative capnometry results can be visually plotted and shown as waveform capnography. These waveforms can be analyzed to identify pathological conditions (i.e., apnea, bronchospasm, hyperventilation, and hypoventilation).

Radiography:

There are numerous imaging modalities available to assess respiratory insufficiency. The plain film, computed tomography, magnetic resonance, nuclear medicine, angiography, and ultrasound are a few examples of these possibilities[49].

Pulse Oximetry:

Spectrophotometry, which determines a substance's content by determining the absorption of particular light wavelengths passed through the substance in question, is the foundation of pulse oximetry. Molecular oxygen is necessary for hemoglobin's structure and chemical make-up. Oxygenated hemoglobin has a reduced affinity for oxygen in tense conditions. Deoxygenated hemoglobin has a larger affinity for oxygen while you're calm. Because deoxygenated hemoglobin absorbs light at wavelengths of 660 nm and oxygenated hemoglobin at wavelengths of 940 nm, pulse oximetry makes use of these hemoglobin structural states. Pulsatile blood analysis ensures accurate measurement of arterial oxygenation. Using proprietary algorithms, it is possible to translate light absorption into the percentage of oxygen-saturated hemoglobin (SpO2). The diagnosis and treatment of respiratory failure can both be considerably aided by this non-invasive technique.

Ultrasonography:

The bedside gold standard for the quick identification of acute respiratory failure is the bedside lung ultrasonography in an emergency (BLUE)-protocol. The methodology, which enables reproducible analysis, is based on ten ultrasonographic signals or profiles and defined thoracic locations (BLUE points). By examining the ultrasonographic profiles acquired from all three BLUE locations on either side of the body, the BLUE protocol is carried out. The postero-lateral alveolar and/or pleural syndrome (PLAPS)-point and the Lower BLUE point are the three standardized BLUE points. There are a total of six BLUE points. The 10 ultrasonographic characteristics are listed here with their associated clinical states, however, the theory and practise of the BLUE protocol are outside the scope of this page.

- A typical lung surface A-lines, the bat sign, and lung sliding
- Inflammatory syndrome Rocket lungs
- Consolidating lungs Tissue-like and fractal indications
- Poumonary effusions: Sinusoid and quadral signs
- Pneumothorax: the lung point and the spherical sign.

Evaluation of respiratory failure also may involve bronchoscopy, echocardiography, nocturnal polysomnography, and pulmonary function tests. If the aforementioned diagnostic tests are needed, pulmonary consulting is advised[50].

7. Acute abdomen, acute liver failure, and oliguria

Acute abdomen: Abdominal acuteness is a disorder that needs to be treated right away. An infection, inflammation, vascular blockage, or blockage are all potential causes of acute abdomen. Usually, the patient will experience an abrupt onset of stomach pain along with accompanying nausea or vomiting. The majority of people with just an acute abdomen seem sick.

An extensive history and physical examination must be part of the treatment plan for a patient with an acute abdomen. The source of the discomfort is important because it could indicate a confined disease. Nonetheless, it may manifest as broad stomach pain in people with free air. The absence of bowel sounds may be audible during auscultation, and rebound discomfort and guarding during palpation may be indicative of peritonitis. Appendicitis, perforated peptic ulcer, acute pancreatitis, ruptured sigmoid diverticulum, ovarian torsion, volvulus, ruptured aortic aneurysm, lacerated spleen or liver, and ischemic bowel are among the illnesses that may trigger an acute abdomen[51].

Etiology: Acute appendicitis, cholecystitis, pancreatitis, and diverticulitis are a frequent cause of acute abdomen. An acute abdomen is caused by acute peritonitis, which can develop as a side effect of inflammatory bowel illness, cancer, or the rupture of a hollow viscus. Mesenteric ischemia and ruptured abdominal aortic aneurysm are two vascular conditions that result in an acute abdomen. Ovarian torsion and ruptured ectopic pregnancy are two obstetric and gynecologic causes. In addition to ureteral colic and pyelonephritis, urologic diseases also can cause sudden abdominal pain. Acute abdomen is frequently attributed to small intestinal blockage by authors. Necrotizing enterocolitis in newborns is a possibility[52].

Evaluation: Once more, it's critical to identify and manage the acute abdomen as soon as possible. The two must be evaluated and treated together. Imaging and blood testing are examples of diagnostic interventions. A 12-lead ECG can aid in ruling out myocardial infarction as the source of acute severe stomach pain in persons older than 40. If a patient has mesenteric ischemia and is experiencing atrial fibrillation, this information is crucial. Typically, a full metabolic profile, lipase, and a complete blood count (CBC) are collected. A glucose must be requested if there is sepsis or mesenteric ischemia. In order to diagnose an ectopic pregnancy, a urine or serum pregnancy test is required. In the last three decades, diagnostic imaging has made significant advancements. In less than 5 minutes, a bedside ultrasound in the emergency room can identify cholecystitis, hydronephrosis, hemoperitoneum, and the existence of an abdominal aortic aneurysm. For cases of cholecystitis, pediatric appendicitis, ruptured ectopic pregnancy, and ovarian torsion, diagnostic ultrasonography is the treatment of choice. The diagnosis of an acute abdomen is now much simpler because of multislice helical CT scanning. Intravenous (IV) contrast is sufficient in most situations. Oral contrast takes time and is typically unnecessary. Given the length of time necessary in a patient who may be unsteady, MRI is typically not used[53].

Treatment: Tachycardia and hypotension indicate sepsis, hypovolemia, or blood loss and call for swift, vigorous fluid resuscitation with suitable large-bore IV access. When sepsis, peritoneal soiling, or infection are possibilities, broad-spectrum antibiotics that cover gram-negative enteric pathogens should be given promptly. Those who are ill need constant vital sign monitoring and resuscitation. Opioids are a recommended treatment for providing adequate pain relief. Anti-emetics are also crucial to utilize. Urgent consultation with a surgeon should be made if it is believed that there is a surgical emergency as a result of the presentation or physical findings. Before performing possibly time-consuming diagnostics, the surgeon must be contacted.

In conclusion, the acute abdomen is made up of a number of intrabdominal processes that demand quick action both for diagnosis and treatment. The symptoms of an acute abdomen might be overt or covert, but they must constantly be detected. Resuscitative therapy must be administered together with prompt, suitable testing. Immediate contact with a specialist is also required if the problem might perhaps require surgery[54].

Acute liver failure

In patients who do not otherwise have liver disease, acute liver failure (ALF) is a rare and frequently diverse presentation of severe liver dysfunction. Despite having a high complication and death rate, emergency liver transplantation and advances in Intensive Care treatment have increased overall survival. The cornerstones for the care of ALF continue to be a strong degree of suspicion, early referral to a specialized liver transplantation hospital, and proper supportive management. The therapy of multi-organ failure and a greater understanding of the mechanism of liver injury can aid outcomes in the future[55].

Treatment: Supportive care, the avoidance, and control of problems, specialized treatment when the precise etiology is recognized, and the assessment of the prognosis and the requirement for liver support, including potential liver transplantation, comprise the management of ALF. Every patient needs to be hospitalized, ideally at a facility with the resources and training needed for a liver transplant[56].

- Access blood pressure control, the requirement for intravenous fluids, and the preservation of normal electrolyte and acid-base balances. For order to guarantee sufficient renal and cerebral perfusion, vasopressors are suggested for keeping a mean arterial pressure of 75 mm Hg or above.
- Because the patients have coagulopathy and weak platelet functioning, monitor the hematocrit for any hemorrhage. Only patients with active bleeding or just prior to an invasive operation should receive blood products containing platelets and fresh frozen plasma for coagulopathy. Proton pump inhibitors must be empirically begun in patients for the prevention of gastrointestinal bleeding.
- Consider performing a fever workup that includes blood and urine cultures, and so when necessary, begin experimental antibiotics.
- If the patient exhibits symptoms of deteriorating encephalopathy, evaluate hepatic encephalopathy and safeguard the airway (aspiration risk). Such patients ought to follow a strategy to prevent cerebral edoema and must be intubated.
- It is recommended to provide sufficient nourishment, ranging from 1.0 to 1.5 g of protein per kilogram each day.
- Keep an eye out for hypoglycemia and keep your blood sugar levels between 160 and 200.
- With the exception of those we determine to be absolutely necessary, stop taking any home medications.

Management and complications:

- Renal failure: It can be brought on by hepatorenal syndrome, acute tubular necrosis, or hypovolemia. In cases of severe hypotension, vasopressor medication using norepinephrine or dopamine is recommended. Transplantation of the kidneys might be used as a stopgap before a potential liver transplant. In severely ill patients, continuous renal replacement therapy is recommended to hemodialysis.
- Broad-spectrum antibiotics ought to be employed to treat sepsis, particularly aspiration pneumonia and fever. In all patients with ALF, monitoring cultures of the blood, sputum, and urine should be taken.

- Metabolic disorders: Hypoglycemia is caused by poor gluconeogenesis and glycogen synthesis, and it requires ongoing 10% to 20% glucose infusions. Aggressive repletion is necessary to treat hypophosphatemia brought on by ATP consumption in the presence of hepatocyte necrosis. If the patient doesn't really receive a liver transplant, acidosis with a pH of less than 7.3 predicts 95% mortality in acetaminophen overdose. Alkalosis in ALF is caused by hyperventilation.
- Most common causes of mortality in ALF is cerebral edoema, which also causes ischemic brain damage, intracranial pressure, and herniation. Individuals who have arterial ammonia concentrations over 200 micromoles/liter are more likely to develop intracranial hypertension. Hypoxia, systemic hypotension, decreased cerebral perfusion pressure (CPP), and astrocyte swelling, which happens as a result of elevated ammonia levels and glutamine synthesis in the brain, are causes of cerebral edoema. If present, abnormal pupillary reflexes, muscle stiffness, and decerebrate posture signal the beginning of intracranial hypertension. If an ICP monitoring device is implanted, precautions should be made to keep the intracranial pressure (ICP) below 25 mm Hg and the cerebral perfusion pressure (CPP) above 50 mm Hg.
- Encephalopathy: A major characteristic of ALF is encephalopathy. Patients with grade 3 encephalopathy and higher must undergo a head CT scan to check for cerebral edoema and intracranial haemorrhage.

Similar to encephalopathy, coagulopathy is a characteristic of ALF. Despite the existence of significant coagulopathy, bleeding episodes are uncommon. Hence, routine coagulopathy correction also isn't advised until there is overt bleeding or before invasive treatments. If necessary, transfusions of platelets, plasma, and cryoprecipitate can be administered. Recombinant factor VII can lead to thrombus; in cases of persistent cholestasis or if a nutritional shortage is detected, parenteral vitamin K therapy (slow intravenous infusion) may be an option[57].

Oliguria: Oliguria is a common symptom of major illness and was one of the earliest "biomarkers" of acute kidney injury (AKI), documented by Ephesus and Galen between 100 and 200 AD, with Galen suggesting a possible differential diagnosis for the treatment of an oliguric patient. Heberden, an English physician, later coined the term "ischuria renal" to characterize renal failure accompanied by oliguria[58].

In fact, all categorization systems for AKI (RIFLE (Risk, Injury, Failure, Loss of kidney function, and End-stage kidney disease), AKIN (Acute Kidney Injury Network), and the KDIGO (Kidney Disease: Improving Global Outcomes) AKI criteria) include urine output (UO) as part of the diagnostic criteria for AKI even though many new AKI biomarkers have really been discovered. The most prevalent definition of oliguria is a urine output of less than 0.5 ml/kg during a period of 6 hours, while other time frames and cut-offs have really been recorded that range from 1 to 24 hours[59].

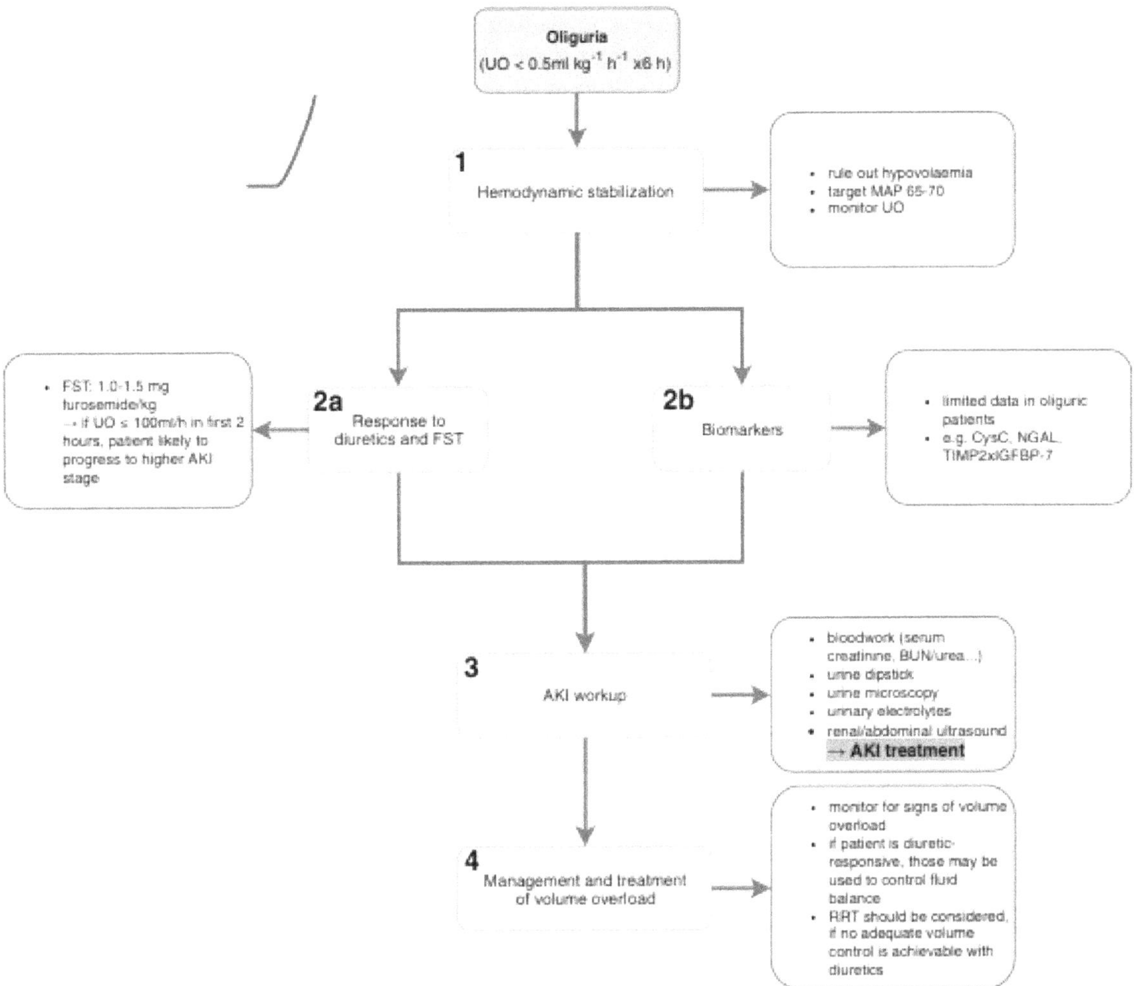

Figure E6: illustrates a 4-step approach to the clinical management of oliguric patients (UO urine output, step 1: hemodynamic stabilisation, step 2a: response to diuretics and FST, step 2b: biomarkers [steps 2a and 2b may be considered as alternative approaches], step 3: AKI workup, and step 4: management and treatment of volume overload).FST furosemide stress test, AKI acute kidney damage, MAP mean arterial pressure, BUN (blood urea nitrogen), CysC (cystatin C), NGAL (neutrophil gelatinase-associated lipocalin), TIMP-2 x IGFBP-7 (tissue inhibitor of metalloproteinase 2 insulin-like growth factor binding protein 7), and RRT (renal replacement therapy)) are all examples of blood markers[60].

8. critical care communication

Be truthful, keep it short, and take a seat. Communication is both an institutional medical activity and a cultural resource of immense significance. Information exchange is one means of describing communication, but it can additionally refer to the entire network of connections between both the parties engaged as well as their surrounding environment. Both verbal and nonverbal forms of communication are possible; in fact, up to 65% of human conversation takes place nonverbally. Whereas verbal communication utilizes a digital code, nonverbal communication employs an analogic code and frequently conveys more information than we would like to hear by using visuals, gestures, and attitudes[61].

Because it incorporates individual rights and expectations for a high quality of life, "communication" has gained importance in the healthcare system ever since the introduction of the informed consent procedure. The reality that roughly 95% of patients dying in Intensive Care units (ICU) cannot voice their willingness regarding intrusive therapies adds another conundrum to this procedure. Patients' wishes and opinions regarding end-of-life decisions could be translated by doctors by asking the patient's family when it's not possible to communicate directly with the patient, such as when the patient is unconscious or unable to comply, in order to reach shared decisions with them.

Elderly family members had a greater understanding of issues, according to research by Mathew et al. They theorized that this might be because they had less access to online resources. Clarity of explanation is necessary for effective communication since the message must be linear and compatible with the cultural background of the audience. Facts must be presented clearly.

We should recall that doctors invest the majority of their lives in the Intensive Care unit (ICU), which is a completely separate world full of strange experiences and technical equipment (such as mechanical ventilators and vital sign monitors) that simply have no place in "normal" life, to excuse them from using technical language too frequently. Additionally, communication skills are rarely taught to medical students[62].

According to Curtis et al., physicians must plan visits with families in the same way they plan any other invasive medical procedure, checking the most crucial information and making sure their own emotions don't get in the way of the patient's family relationships.

The doctor must begin by discussing issues that really are pertinent to each and every family while keeping in mind that his or her patients' family members may have very different ideas about sickness and viewpoints from their own. The doctor must also be informed of and comprehend the patient's expectations, which are things that families likely grasp better. Doctors have a responsibility to confirm that the exchange of information had a place and was accurately supplied and received, especially when a critical and final decision needs to be made based on that communication.

Developing good communication clearly has ethical implications. Since the ethical component is linked to a social and affective dimension, communication quality also exists behind its contents. The doctors in critical care should take into account the emotions of the people they are informing because communication involves both intellectual and emotional components that are active at the same time. Even when information is misunderstood, the emotional component of communication can remain preserved. The patient's relative should be accorded dignity and given consideration for their difficulties. Even though the families were unable to completely comprehend the patient's situation, Mathew reported a high level of family satisfaction[63].

9. Resources in Critical care

Critical care in poor nations has the same difficulties as other facets of healthcare. Yet, critical care confronts an extra difficulty because it is sometimes thought to be too expensive or sophisticated for settings with limited resources. This disregard for the hierarchy is unacceptable. Overall death is influenced by hospital care for the sickest patients, and community trust in healthcare is essential for involvement and adherence to public health initiatives. Rapid fluid resuscitation, early antibiotic administration, and health care are some of the most cost-effective critical care procedures. Even resource-intensive interventions may be cost-effective when compared to immunizations and treatment for human immunodeficiency virus, according to evidence from the surgical literature, despite the fact that cost-effectiveness studies on critical care in resource-poor settings haven't been conducted. Critical care gives a remarkable chance to provide large incremental benefits, probably much more so than in the industrialized world, where many critically ill patients are younger and have fewer comorbidities[64].

Essential considerations: The following are important factors to take into account while establishing critical care in situations with limited resources: personnel and training, tools and support services, ethics, and research. Creating rules even for complex procedures and linking education to service commitment are two strategies for training and keeping skilled employees. The use of economical and sustainable technology must be the main focus of equipment and support services. Where possible, ethical decision-making must be supported by facts, and it must always be founded on clearly stated policies. Research ought to take place in areas with limited resources and should concentrate on cost-effectiveness, needs analysis, and prognostication.

Future directions: The gradual introduction of service enhancements, the use of human resources via training, a focus on sustainable technology, continual cost-effectiveness analysis, and the sharing of context-specific best practices are all key to the growth of critical care in resource-limited contexts. The right moment has arrived for the development of critical care, despite the fact that many contemporary discussions in global health are dominated by prevention, public health, and disease-specific agendas. Leaders in global health funding want to increase life expectancy and quality. A critical component of the continuum of care required to make that possible is critical care[65].

9. Post ICU care syndrome and outpatient clinics For ICU patients

Post-Intensive Care syndrome (PICS) is the name given to the incapacity that persists after a severe illness. This includes the Intensive Care unit (ICU) survivor's cognitive impairment, psychological wellness, and physical function. As a result, the psychological well-being of the survivor's family members—known as PICS-Family—may also be negatively impacted (PICS-F).

PICS is described as a new or worsening impairment in physical, cognitive, or behavioral general health that develops after a critical illness and persists after discharge from the acute care setting. An example of this would be ICU-acquired neuromuscular weakness[66].

PICS-F is a term used to describe the acute and long-term psychological effects of critical illness on the patient's family. It covers both the symptoms that family members may go through while a loved one is critically ill as well as those that may appear after the person passes away or is released from the Intensive Care unit. Up to 30% of family members or carers have been seen to endure stress, anxiety, sadness, and difficult sorrow.

Clinical manifestation

PICS can appear in a variety of ways (a combination of cognitive, psychological, and physical signs and symptoms), with the major characteristics being that these are just becoming apparent or getting worse after overcoming a serious disease. After healing, the symptoms may last for a few months to several years. General weakness, exhaustion, decreased mobility, worried or sad mood, sexual dysfunction, sleep disorders, and cognitive problems (memory loss, sluggish brain processing, poor concentration, etc.) are some of the prevalent symptoms[67].

Prevention and management

Every patient entering an Intensive Care unit (ICU) ought to undergo a psychological examination, that should cover the following topics: (a) pre-admission history; (b) historical stress tolerance; (c) medication history; (d) present mental and clinical status; and (e) environmental and familial factors.

Treatment for the ICU syndrome entails (a) removing or correcting the causes, (b) administering sedatives (anxiolytic and antipsychotic drugs) as needed, (c) reducing or removing sources of environmental stress, and (d) maintaining regular patient and family communication.

The adage "Prevention is better than cure" applies equally to PICS management.

PICS has employed the ABCDE bundle with good preventative rates. This includes monitoring, assessing, and managing delirium; awakening (using light or minimum sedation); breathing (spontaneous breathing trials); coordination of care and communication among many specialties; and early ambulation in the ICU[68].

The quality and quantity of life experienced by patients who recover from acute critical illness are currently of interest to intensivists and government officials in some parts of the world. The traditional and historical focus of Intensive Care has been on reducing short-term death rates, but survivors present significant mortality in the medium and long term as well as expertise in a number of physical illnesses, cognitive dysfunction, depression, and sexual dysfunction after leaving the Intensive Care unit (ICU)[69].

Outpatient clinics for ICU:

ORGANIZATION OF POST-INTENSIVE CARE OUTPATIENT CLINIC

The requirement for experts, patient and/or family eligibility for participation, time and duration of patient and family follow-up, choice of instruments for measuring results, and criteria for which patients will be sent to reference services vary greatly among post-ICU outpatient clinics.

The following follow-up strategies for ICU patients have been tested over the years: (1) ICU team integration with primary public health; (2) peer support (i.e., formation of patient groups that exchange experiences in face-to-face meetings or through online forums); (3) frequent phone calls from the ICU staff to clear up any questions[70].

Eligibility of the professional

ICU survivors and their families may receive assistance from outpatient clinics in the form of clinical or informational services, depending on the model chosen and the resources at their disposal. Functional evaluation, physical therapy evaluation, medical evaluation, pharmaceutical evaluation, medical consultation, psychosocial assistance, and rehabilitation therapy, among others, may be provided according to the amenities supplied. The cost of the operation increases with the number of professionals involved.

Eligibility of the patient

The patients who are invited or referred to the post-ICU outpatient clinics vary. The majority of authors advise against post-ICU outpatient follow-up except for patients who need mechanical breathing for less than 48 hours or ICU care for two to five days. The cost-effectiveness of continuing all cases that have been discharged does not seem to exist[71].

Family member eligibility

Due to the high prevalence of psychiatric illnesses seen in ambulatory patients, several specialists advise carers and family members to undergo evaluations as well.

When to start and for how long to keep outpatient follow-up?

The first visit to the outpatient clinic must take place between the sixth and twelfth week following discharge, according to Van der Schaaf et al. It appears important at this point for patients, families, and carers to realize that motor sequelae might not recover as rapidly as anticipated and that long-term adjustments to household organization and structure will be required. Our opinion is that a very late start to outpatient follow-up (> 6 months after hospital discharge) serves only to diagnose the functional and cognitive sequelae of patients and to confirm any organizational and psychological issues that have already developed within the family as a result of the lack of prior guidance from the medical team[72].

10. Reading material journals and recent research articles

It is a requirement for researchers and physicians to read scientific literature. The development of a system to select and read the appropriate articles is crucial because of the large number of medical and dental publications.

to describe how to read a scientific publication in a logical and systematic manner. A person ought to be able to develop the abilities to read a scientific article with ease by dividing the process down into smaller, step-by-step components.

The article's main points can be thoroughly and effectively read if the individual decides to read it from beginning to end. It is suggested how to read articles that have been published in scholarly journals in a clear and structured way[73].

Scientific literature can often be classified as primary or secondary. Both "main literature" and "core" of scientific publications are summaries of original research. These are all the papers published to convey findings about new scientific discoveries and discuss past work to recognize this and set new findings inside the correct perspective. "Secondary literature" comprises review articles, books, editorials, practise guidelines, and other forms of publication wherein original research information was examined. An paper that has been peer-reviewed is worth more than one that has not.

Not that all research publications published were outstanding, so it is pragmatic to evaluate if indeed the level of the study deserves reading of the manuscript. The very first step for just a reader is to pick the best article to read, taking into account their specific needs. The next step is understanding the selected article carefully and effectively[74].

11. Upto date Ovid and clinical keys

An "information paradox" has resulted from the explosion of biological information, making it more and more challenging to locate pertinent data when required. Therefore, this is becoming more and more essential that physicians learn the basics of biomedical informatics.

Using Google, Ovid, PubMed, or UpToDate, medical students, residents, and seeing physicians at the authors' institution were required to respond within five minutes to a series of four clinical tests depending on anesthesia and/or critical care between December 2008 and June 2009. (only one search tool per question). Participants were asked to rate the findings on a four-point confidence scale after every search. Users were randomly assigned to one of the four search tools & instructed to complete eight questions, four of which had to be repeated, one to three weeks after responding to the initial four questions. A correct response with the maximum amount of trust was the outcome.The search engine that had the greatest number of users was Google. Visitors of Google and UpToDate were more likely to provide accurate answers than users of PubMed. UpToDate garnered the highest support from the subjects. Searches on Google and UpToDate were completed more quickly than those on PubMed or Ovid[75].

12. How to search in PubMed

A website called PubMed indexes journal articles and more going all the way back to 1947. It covers preclinical sciences, health care systems, nursing, dentistry, veterinary medicine, and other relevant fields. The National Library of Medicine (NLM) and the National Center for Biotechnology Information (NCBI), both located just at the National Institutes of Health (NIH) in Bethesda, Maryland, established and manage PubMed. At the end of 2020, PubMed had more than 30 million records. MEDLINE, PubMed Central, and other PubMed records are available on the platform known as PubMed.

Pubmed tools

Clinical Queries

To allow pre-made filters to apply to various clinical research fields, use Clinical Queries. Clinical research, review articles, and medical genetics are separated out of the results. Just as you would in the PubMed search box, enter your search here.

See: for further details.

Journals in NCBI databases:

To focus your search on a particular journal or to learn more about journals listed in MEDLINE, see Journals in NCBI Databases.

Single citation matcher:

To locate citations in PubMed, use the Single Citation Matcher. Any field is open to entry or omission[76].

Special queries:

The National Library of Medicine's searchers has developed search filters for numerous popular subjects. In the PubMed Special Queries page, you may view and activate them.

How to use MeSH : Medical Subject Heading

MeSH, or medical subject headings, is an acronym. To make records searchable, a controlled vocabulary of terms has been allocated to them.

To maintain continuity throughout the search process, this list of terms is standardised. There are about 29,000 MeSH words in total, and they are updated yearly to reflect terminological modifications.

Find Medical Subject Headings (MeSH) in the MeSH database to locate material that is indexed with the selected MeSH word.

MeSH words can be used to accommodate for language differences, acronyms, and British vs. American English.

How to use Keywords:

Automatic Term Mapping

When you type phrases into the search box in PubMed, Automatic Term Mapping (ATM) is utilised.

The search terms you provide in the search field are automatically mapped to MeSH terms according to the term "automatic term mapping."

Click on the Details arrow in your Advanced > History and Search Details box to witness Automatic Term Mapping in action.

Automatic Term Mapping is disabled when a phrase is surrounded by quotations or is truncated. Instead, no mapping is used; the terms are searched exactly as they are entered.

Using Keywords

All words used to describe your thought or idea might be used as keywords.

Single words or phrases can be used as keywords.

To assure that the term gets searched as a whole, surround all phrases with quotations.

Visit the MeSH database and browse the entry terms provided in the MeSH record for additional suggestions[77].

13. Critical care courses fellowship program and national and international

Professionals in the fields of pulmonary, critical care, and sleep medicine act as mentors for students at any and all academic levels for both clinical care and scientific research. Quality in teaching necessitates training on adult learning principles, the acquisition & application of critical professional skills, such as assessment & feedback methods, and curriculum building, including tactics of effective teaching across settings ranging from lecture hall to the bedside.

Individuals who are interested in making teaching a center of an academic career, as well as the foundation of promotion, must invest in professional growth as teachers and educators. Opportunities for professional development involve becoming more skilled as just a teacher through fellowships specifically devoted to medical education, acting as just a peer observer, or even being observed by another teacher. Resource repositories, CME classes, and online training modules are just a few of the additional possibilities for training as a teacher and educator that are now accessible. Enrolling in master's or even other advanced degree courses that emphasize both quantitative and qualitative methods in addition to other important research skills can be beneficial to people who have an interest in medical education research. A network of medical educators exists locally, regionally, nationally &

worldwide. Prospective clinician-educators must look for chances to get involved in this network. There really are chances to help with the creation, design & evaluation of courses and programs for all of these levels. Last but not least, there have been growing demands for academic clinician-educators engaged in advancement must create academic literature, ranging from curricular materials to journal articles centred on learning and instruction[78].

The numerous facets of being a doctor and other healthcare practitioner are closely related to teaching. Modern pulmonary, critical care & sleep medicine offers teaching opportunities in a wide range of environments, such as the outpatient medical centre, the Intensive Care unit, and also the ambulatory clinic. These opportunities also provide exposure to a variety of learners, such as trainees (from medical students to fellows), attending physicians, interprofessional teams (from nurses to respiratory therapists and other allied health practitioners), and the general public, including patients and family members[79].

The development of a career as a medical educator calls for careful preparation to ensure the acquisition of the variety of skills, to learn the same fundamentals of education research, and also to navigate this same promotion maze, despite the fact that many health care professionals are naturally gifted teachers and can unknowingly incorporate techniques those who notice as learners of skilled teachers. The route calls again for the development of a wide range in teaching abilities, the creation of a creative curriculum, as well as the consideration of methods for enhancing both instruction and evaluation of difficult concepts and competencies. Also, to succeed as a medical educator, research activities must be centered around the development of enduring teaching materials and new understanding regarding educational processes and outcomes.

For those individuals thinking about making teaching & education the focus of their professions, the article outlines possibilities & career paths. The goal is to provide advice on how to create a lucrative profession as just a medical educator[80].

14. Leadership in critical care

A multidisciplinary group of healthcare professionals provides treatment for seriously ill patients in the ICU. A group of professionals from different specialities, including critical care specialists, doctors, nurses, and others that are entirely involved in Intensive Care, work as a unit to offer coordinated patient care. It's a challenging managerial task to manage so many healthcare providers & guarantee the rapid and effective treatment of critically ill patients.

Leadership

Task behavior and relationship behaviour are really the two categories in situational leadership, according to Hersey and Blanchard. Task behaviour indicates that leader is focused on the important duties. They organises a group, clarifies its positions, and outlines all tasks that must be completed. Standard operating procedures should be created in order to accomplish this. Relational behaviour refers to the leader's emphasis on building strong bonds among the team. By conversing, listening, offering emotional support, and acting in a moderating & supportive manner, one keeps the personal connection that has with the group[81].

Delegating leadership

The leader can transition to delegating leadership even as team becomes competent as well as "mature." Always stimulating the team, building confidence & fostering teamwork is delegation. Due to their knowledge and skills, people who really are competent at accomplishing activities typically have a strong commitment to completing such duties and are eager to assume responsibility. A monitoring system must be built to ensure the leader is always informed of what is happening in order to manage the assigned activities. This formal, final responsibility of the ICU director is not lessened or diminished by delegation. Unexpected occurrences may frequently cause the leader to quickly transition between work delegation to task ownership[82].

Personal qualities

The leader possesses two faces: an exterior face as well as an inward face. In other words, both internal as well as external leadership have certain features.

External leadership

The field of Intensive Care medicine is really very collaborative & interdisciplinary. The respect & confidence shown by all specialties & its experts must preferably become the foundation of a director of the ICU's position. Both of the hospital management and the other directors ought to warmly welcome him. He will undoubtedly benefit from having a good reputation in his country's society.

A complicated hospital service network includes the ICU. Effective and considerate collaboration among all the services is required for this. A unique awareness for such cross-disciplinary interactions must be instilled inside the ICU staff by the ICU manager[83].

Internal leadership

The ICU manager has oversight of a team's atmosphere &"mental state" because they are "the boss" of the ICU. Working well with other people is a human skill known as "emotional intelligence," which really is crucial for management work. This is amazing how much a team's "psychological" depends just on team leader. The Seven Habits of Highly Effective People by Steven R. Covey offers the following advice: "Seek first to understand, followed by being understood." Only if we're listening can we truly comprehend. It is evident that we're not interested in understanding when we do not listen. Speaking is not as effective as listening for learning[84].

15. Administration role and responsibilities

Discover key success characteristics for such roles as we examine the duties of physician executives that have titles like chief medical officer (CMO), vice president of clinical activities, or vice dean of clinical affairs in Association of American Medical Colleges (AAMC) partner institutions.

340 physician leaders in 281 AAMC member institutions completed an online survey. With addition to certain other inquiries, the poll asked about respondents' demographics, job titles, report structures, time commitments, level of responsibility, accomplishments, and difficulties in their jobs.

154 doctors from 139 institutions responded, with response times of 45% and 49%, respectively. 49 percent of these jobs were in place for ten years or less. CMO (48%) was the most popular administrative title. Eighty-five percent of these workers directly answered to the organization's dean or CEO. Quality and safety accounted for 31% of administrative work, clinical care coordinating for 21%, and graduate medical education for 9%. The remaining 39% covered a wide range of duties, from nursing services (2% to 6% in information technology). Personal stature and relationships, a clear definition of duties, and the senior administration's dedication to the post were all important factors in job performance[85].

Physician leaders—often referred to as CMOs—have new or strengthened positions at teaching hospitals and medical schools. This role of CMOs extends much beyond the conventional spheres of safety and quality. For these positions to be successful, the job must be clearly defined through the business, and senior executives must clearly demonstrate their commitment.

Inquiries to deans and CEOs of AAMC member organizations (i.e., medical schools, hospitals, or health systems) someone that we were looking for physician leader(s) who were recognized as responsible for clinical care integration and coordination in their organizations led to an identification of the survey pool. In order to provide questions or unsupported claims in different formats, such as multiple-choice questions, questions that require or allow free-text answers, and responses to assertions using a four-point rating scale, we created a web-based survey using Survey Monkey (www.SurveyMonkey.com, Portland, Oregon) (i.e., strongly agree, agree, disagree, strongly disagree).37 questions were included in with us survey about the demographics of CMOs, one‘s job descriptions, how long they have held one‘s positions and whether they are qualified for them, reporting structures, time commitments, levels of responsibility, accomplishments, and challenges they have faced in those roles, in addition to success and job satisfaction-related factors. They told survey respondents all the responses would be kept private while only the group findings would be made public absent their express permission. The American Institutes for Human Research Institutional Review Board, which offers IRB review services to the AAMC, approved the survey[86].

16. ICU at remote locations, ICU in the sky, and air ambulance transfer

Introduction

Throughout the past 20 years, there has been an increase in the usage of air medical transportation. Air medical transportation has advanced through the First World War's usage of balloons through current large-scale rescue operations by Indian forces in Kashmir and Uttarakhand. Every day, many more patients are moved around the world to various point that require specialised medical care. Critical patients are now being transferred between hospitals that use the existing air infrastructure[87].

Equipment

Airway management tools (laryngoscopes, endotracheal tubes, tracheostomy tubes, etc.), patient monitors, vascular access tools, as well as a sufficient quantity of oxygen cylinders all are standard equipment for all medical transport. Critical patients, especially trauma victims, were transported using vacuum stabilising mattresses (Ferno (UK) Limited, West Yorkshire, UK) loaded with tiny polyvinyl granules that conform to a shape of the supine patient to avoid unwanted & harmful movement of the patient. Based on what is required, a intra-aortic balloon pump (IABP), cardiac pacing device, and fracture stabilisers (cervical collar, Thomas splint, etc.) are included. Because there could not be a charging station on board, spare dry, non-spilling batteries were transported.

All of the equipment complies to aviation standards for portability, compactnes& radio interference immunity. Equipment safety & integrity checks were performed more regularly because of their increased susceptibility towards wear & damage[88].

Staffing

According to how serious the situation was, there were one to two doctors and a nurse just on medical team. In addition to managing emergency situations, some 50 doctors of various specialities, including anaesthesia and critical care, cardiology, cardiac surgery, emergency medicine, and paediatrics, had received training in handling both logistical and administrative aspects of air medical transfer. Each particular case will determine which doctor should accompany the patient. Most air ambulances have difficulties with limited space, a moving cabin & demanding working conditions. The selection of highly motivated employees & their training in stress management in the aircraft's cramped cabin with scarce resources are thus of utmost importance[89].

Procedure of air medical transport

The Chairman, Critical Care & Trauma of our Institute is in charge of all medical transportation. The hospital call centre typically receives requests about patient transport, and those are forwarded to a operations manager, which serves as that of the liaison between all parties. He gathers information about the situation from of the doctor who did admit the patient, notifies our hospital's admitting specialty, looks into the availability of aircraft, requests clearance from the airport authorities, but then assembles the team of flight medical staff to make the necessary preparations. The group is sent to the airport following approval from across all parties.

Stretchers are available on request to a concerned airline and thus are contingent upon on the availability of the required number of seats for regularly scheduled commercial flights, including international flights. Usually standard method would be to obtain consent from airline's designated physician on the "Medif form" issued by the physician, which is provided just at airline office at least 2-3 days beforehand. A fixed stretcher must be assembled in various aeroplanes, typically near the back of the aircraft with such a curtain surrounding it as well as an oxygen cylinder underneath. One doctor and one nurse often make up the supporting personnel.

The accompanying physician is responsible for any and all supplies and patient care. The medical team might make a request to the relevant embassy for an emergency visa during overseas transfers.

Up till the patient is turned over to the admitting team, the transport team, the patient's family, as well as the operations manager stay in touch & keep each other updated on the patient's status as well as additional needs.

Patients are welcomed at the hospital serving as the transferee, after which the initial assessment is completed as well as any interventions required for just a secure travel were carried out. The patient provides informed consent, as well as the condition is disclosed to the patient's family.

The patient's transfer to a admitting specialist as well as the family's briefing mark that end of a medical transport[90].

17. Tele ICU

"Telemedicine" and "telehealth" are frequently used interchangeably in population in general contexts. However, telehealth applications are more specialized and focused on telemedicine, particularly Tele-ICU. Telehealth is defined as "the application of telecommunications technology to offer health-related services and information that support patient care, administrative activities, and health education" by the Agency for Healthcare Research and Quantity. Telemedicine is described as "the utilization of medical information, exchanged from one site to another via electronic communications, to enhance patients' health status" by the American Telemedicine Association.

Technologies that aren't just utilized for telemedicine can be included in telehealth services. Telehealth services generally include web-based patient e-health services such as consumer medical and health information resources and health/patient Internet portals. Other forms of communication, including audio-only (telephone) or textual (e-mail, messengers, fax), are, however, typically not regarded as telemedicine[91].

Tele ICU technology

The shift from specialized optic cable networks to virtual private networks over the open Internet has allowed the technologies needed for Tele-ICU programs to become more cost-effective in recent decades. 12 Interaction between the Tele-ICU team (hub) and the distant ICU must be trustworthy for a program to be successful.

The technology employed in ICUs is a reflection of the distinct process and patient features present there. The sorts of care delivery models and organizational traits that should be taken into consideration will assist define the technical requirements for Tele-ICU systems[92].

Tele-ICU services have two different sorts of administrative structures from an organizational standpoint:

- Networked applications. Hence, a single hub center that offers Tele-ICU services to numerous sites is the key feature. For instance, big academic hospitals in cities help out nearby tiny rural hospitals.
- A program that is point-to-point. The primary distinguishing feature is that smaller or understaffed hospitals contract out medical services to specialists at a sizable central hospital, typically within a single health system.

Physician intensivists, advanced practice providers (APP), registered nurses (RNs), administrative and technological support staff, and other healthcare professionals work in and operate the monitoring system (hub)[93].

Technology is developed in response to the types of care delivery methods used in Tele-ICU. Care delivery methods could be categorized into 4 basic categories, however, the majority of current Tele-ICU systems are built on a structure with a centralized support center and continuous care model:

- Model of continuous care. remote ICU monitoring on a round-the-clock basis. Under this concept, a group of ICU doctors, APPs, and RNs work in an operational center. High readability links to backup and IT support are present.
- Model of episodic care. Remote treatment that involves simply provider-to-provider communication, irregular scheduling (daily rounds, shift changes), or both.
- Model of responsive care. When an alarm or phone call triggers a remote consultation, reactive, episodic care takes place.
- Technology for Tele-ICU 3
- Monitoring of a patient remotely. Telemetry devices are used by remote healthcare practitioners to gather and transfer data to their monitoring stations for analysis.

The gear and software setup may vary depending on the specific Tele-ICU program, however, the following are the common delivery modes for Tele-ICU:

- A two-way audiovisual link in real-time or live (synchronous) between a patient and a distant doctor
- Transfer of a documented health history to a health professional, typically a doctor or APP, via the store-and-forward (asynchronous) method. Using CPOE may potentially be a part of this.
- Remote patient monitoring is the process of sending real-time data from the patient's location to a telemedicine provider in a different location, typically by an RN, using connected electronic gadgets like bedside monitors.

18. Digital ICU

Electronic Intensive Care Unit

Electronic ICUs (e-ICU), which relieve the pressure on traditional ICUs, are likely the best course of action. All patient information, clinical profiles, tests, and therapies can be saved on the e-ICU platform and viewed and remotely monitored. It establishes an electronic connection between patients in Intensive Care units and high-dependency units and their physicians, nurses, support workers, and even relatives. Smart alarm systems with quick troubleshooting procedures, teleconsultations with specialists, and automated real-time patient parameter monitoring are all made possible. Patients can be remotely monitored continuously (24/7) using e-monitoring[94].

It will be extremely difficult to set up an e-ICU in India because electronic ICU data capture is not yet commonplace there. But the COVID-19 outbreak has raised awareness of its pressing need. By bringing the ICUs of the COVID-19 hospitals together on a single platform, Karnataka became the first state in India to build a dedicated command center for critical care assistance. A central group of doctors kept an eye on the entire group. Experts continuously tracked and examined cumulative data. There have been references to neuroIntensive Care models for a number of years, therefore the field is not new. As a result, the current demand mandates the development of such electronic hubs, with experts from around the world connected by electronic means for better patient care[95].

Advantages and Benefits of Electonic Intensive Care Unit

The COVID-19 era's urgent demand for e-ICU is justified by its numerous benefits. Professionals continuously monitor and evaluate cumulative data. In addition to enabling the current medical personnel to work in rotation to assure ongoing accessibility, this can decrease the workforce of HCWs needed. It allows a comfortable face-to-face interaction with physical separation. This will conserve priceless PPE, which is also scarce in underdeveloped nations, and lessen the professional transfer of COVID-19 to doctors.

The risk of disease transmission to patients or other HCWs is eliminated for doctors who are quarantined or home-isolated and may continue to monitor their patients. Saving money on doctor travel, PPE requirements, and the necessary number of HCW can reduce costs. It is simple to perform efficient triage and risk classification.

Internists, intensivists, anesthetists, infection control, microbiologists, pulmonologists, and other medical specialists can all benefit from peer mentoring, shared choices, and scholarly debates to better patient care and outcomes. Large-scale research and data analysis may be stimulated and promoted by this. The system can eventually develop to also include teaching and resident training, which will once more be patient-focused and real-time with less bedside teaching[96].

19. ICU at home

Although quick admission and discharge of ICU patients are necessary for effective hospital and Intensive Care unit (ICU) throughput, healthcare systems face ethical challenges when caring for complex patients with multimorbidity. The great majority of patients require ICU hospitalization, and timely discharge of ICU patients to ward beds may not be possible when hospital attendance is close to maximum capacity.

The national coalition for health care estimates that the medical expenses in 2009 were almost 2.5 trillion USD or 17.6% of the US gross domestic product. According to estimates, the expense of patient care in ICUs in the US accounts for 15% to 25% of all hospital expenses there as well as 1% to 2% of the GDP. By 2019, these expenses are projected to rise to 6% of the nation's GDP, or an astounding 38% of all US healthcare expenditures. 33 billion USD is spent each year on ICU hospitalization because of extended hospital stays.

There are patients who are no more in the acute stage of their illness but are not totally ready for ICU discharge. However, patients who are nearing the end of their life may benefit from being released to their homes and receiving ongoing critical care there. In addition to artificially raising ICU occupancy rates, length of stay (LOS), and expenses for patients and the healthcare system, the resulting delay in ICU discharge could also make it more difficult to admit new ICU patients, raise the likelihood of getting nosocomial infections, and delay the start of rehabilitation therapies[97].

Although professional society recommendations for ICU discharge were written more than 10 years ago, they do not directly address the problems associated with ICU-to-home discharges. In this context, earlier research has demonstrated that a large number of patients have a prolonged length of stay (LOS), with up to 30% of LOS being regarded as unnecessary.

Continuing Intensive Care at home has a number of benefits, including a setting with less noise and especially at night light that supports the come back to more physiological circadian rhythms and better sleep, open visiting hours that permit unrestricted visits by family and friends, and simpler access to personal belongings, such as books, computers, tablets, TVs, music players, and so on. The management of these patients typically entails a multidisciplinary team's integrative view with harmonized techniques rather than only mechanical breathing skills. In addition, providing ongoing critical care services at home should be a financially sensible substitute for the ICU in the management of patients in need.

It would additionally assist private healthcare organizations in making sound plans and providing the necessary resources, such as people and equipment. The care previously provided by the hospital is now being supplied by support services and/or, most crucially, by family members of the patient.

Finally, we argue that providing Intensive Care services at home to patients, their families, and healthcare professionals represents more of a possibility than a risk; this requires in-depth original research and systematic reviews[98].

20. Homecare

The majority of patients in Intensive Care units have serious illnesses or injuries & require life-saving medical care. These illnesses or injuries can take a long time to cure from. Nothing is understood on how elderly patients perceive their own level of recovery after Intensive Care. One purpose of this research was to examine and report the experiences of older individuals who had been treated in an Intensive Care unit and needed care after two months of someone being released from the hospital.Two months after being discharged, telephone interviews with 15 patients 65 years of age or older who had received care inside an Intensive Care unit are conducted. A qualitative content analysis was used to examine the interview texts [99]. There have been six themes that have been found: "Discharge - a matter of physicians' & nurses' decisions,""Wanted to go home,""Feeling well enough and feeling better, but...", "Recovered or not, that's the question,""In need of aid from others," and "In need of care."Patients expressed strong confidence in the medical professionals' evaluation of overall condition because it related to hospital discharge, yet they additionally expressed a desire to return to their homes as soon as possible to their own private and familiar surroundings. The hospital wasn't really perceived by the patients as just a place of healing. In accordance to their strength and energy levels, patients reported that are accustomed to having to take care of themselves. They first turn to family or close friends for assistance. Individuals who disclosed comorbidity weren't convinced themselves to be recovered, whereas others claimed that they had recovered but still experienced a variety of unpleasant symptoms[100].

21. COVID management, Isolation policy

Coronavirus disease 2019 (COVID-19) is a highly contagious viral infection brought on by coronavirus 2 that causes serious acute respiratory syndrome (SARS-CoV-2). More than 6 million people have died as a result of its terrible effects on the planet. SARS-CoV-2 spread quickly and widely throughout the world when the first instances of this mostly respiratory viral infection were initially discovered in

Wuhan, Hubei Province, China, in late December 2019. The World Health Organization (WHO) was forced to declare it a worldwide pandemic on March 11, 2020, as a result of this[101].

Even while significant advancements in clinical research have improved our knowledge of SARS-CoV-2, outbreaks of this viral disease persist in several nations, which are linked to the emergence of mutant versions of the virus.

SARS-CoV-2, like some other RNA viruses, is susceptible to genetic evolution with the emergence of mutations over time, resulting in mutant forms that may have distinct properties from its ancestral strains. This is true even when SARS-CoV-2 adapts to its new human hosts. Many SARS-CoV-2 variations have already been identified throughout this epidemic, however only a small number are deemed to be variants of concern (VOCs) by the WHO due to its effects on public health around the world [102].

Patients eligible for home isolation

- The treating Medical Officer should clinically classify the patient as a mild or asymptomatic condition. The family will also be given a designated control room contact number at the district and subdistrict levels so they can receive appropriate advice for undergoing testing, clinical management-related guidance, and, if necessary, allocation of a hospital bed.
- These individuals ought to have the necessary equipment at the home for both self-isolation and quarantining family contacts.
- A carer must be present to provide care around the clock, preferably a person who has finished the COVID-19 vaccination program. The length of home isolation requires a line of communication between both the carer and a medical officer.
- Only after a thorough review by the treating medical officer are elderly patients older than 60 and those who have co-morbid diseases such as Hypertension, Diabetes, Heart disease, Chronic lung, liver, or renal disease, Cerebrovascular disease, etc. permitted to be isolated at home.
- Home isolation is not advised for patients with immunity impaired status (HIV, transplant recipients, cancer patients, etc.), and it should only be permitted after just a thorough review by the attending medical officer.

Treatment for patients with mild /asymptomatic disease in home isolation

- Patients are required to communicate with a medical officer who is treating them and to notify them right away if their condition worsens.
- Upon consultation with the treating Medical Officer, the patient should continually take drugs for additional co-morbidities or illnesses.
- Patients should follow symptomatic care for fever, a runny nose, and a cough, as necessary.

- Patients can take steam inhalations three times per day or gargle with warm water.
- See the treating physician if a fever cannot be managed with the highest dose of Tab. Paracetamol 650 mg four times per day.
- Do not rush for self-medication, blood investigation, or radiological imaging like chest X-ray or chest CT scan without consulting you're treating Medical Officer.
- Steroids should not be self-administered and are not recommended for mild illness. Steroid abuse and improper use could result in extra difficulties.
- Generic prescription sharing must be avoided because each patient's treatment must be monitored closely separately based on their unique condition.
- If the individual experiences shortness of breath or a drop in oxygen saturation, they may need to be admitted to the hospital and should contact their treating medical officer, the surveillance team, or the control room as away.

When to seek medical attention

The patient's or caregiver's health will continue to be monitored. If serious signs or symptoms appear, prompt medical assistance should be sought. These could include.

- Unresolved High-grade fever (greater than 100° F for further than 3 days)
- breathing difficulty, a drop in oxygen saturation ($SpO2$ 93% on room air at least three times within an hour), or a respiratory rate of more than 24 breaths per minute.
- Mental disorientation or difficulty to awaken,
- Persistent chest discomfort or pressure
- Extreme weariness and myalgia.

22. Super specialty services onco ICU, gastro ICU, nephron ICU, ECMO ICU, transplant icu

Onco ICU

We have witnessed a rapid specialisation to numerous sorts of ICUs since the late 1950s, when critical care was first established as just a formal field, in the interest of developing life support systems & novel therapies. In the 1920s, Walter Dandy created the one of the earliest known specialty units at the Johns Hopkins Hospital, that had three beds for patients recovering from neurosurgery operations. Early ICUs was designed for close observation of medical professionals who stayed nearby the patient so they could respond swiftly and give care.The focus of ICU care as it progressed has been on delivering newly created supportive measures, such as improvements in mechanical ventilation, renal replacement therapy, constant hemodynamic monitoring, and extracorporeal support. The ICU's expansion led to a rise in the demand for critical care physicians. Then, intensivists brought about change by realising how high-intensity staffing provided the most effective treatment for patients and so by emphasising better patient-centered care.Specialized ICUs were started with intention of improving results. Have there historically been separate Intensive Care units for the clinical specialties of cardiology and neurology. There are additionally additional specialist ICUs available for cardiothoracic surgery, burns, trauma, and organ transplants [103].

Due to their underlying disease, the stage of their treatment plan, as well as the toxicities associated with their treatment that really can cause organ dysfunction, hemodynamic compromise, and infection, cancer patients admitted to an Intensive Care unit (ICU) have specific critical care necessities. Up to 20% of patients admitted to ICUs are thought to have a cancer diagnosis. According to estimates, there will be 1.7 million new cases of cancer in the United States in 2016. All cancers currently have a six-year survival rate of 67%, as well as recent research, shows that ICU survival rates for solid tumor and hematologic malignancies had also increased from an average of 15% to about 50% over the past two decades. The understanding of potential complications leading to critical illness must extend from of the oncology floor to an ICU as cancer treatments advance as well as options change. For instance, two recent therapies—anti-PD-1 inhibitor therapy & chimeric antigen receptor T-cell therapy—have severe side effect profiles, such as pneumonitis and cytokine storm, which could raise the frequency of ICU admissions. Additionally, as the prevalence of cancer is now only predicted to increase, we think it's vital to create efficient models of care for critically ill cancer patients. There are now a number of models, and yet no published research studies comparing their efficacy. For established patients, an ICU could be available at sizable freestanding cancer hospitals. In addition to having medical and surgical ICUs, some hospitals offer separate oncological ICUs. Yet, other hospitals include general medical or surgical Intensive Care units (ICUs) where patients with cancer are treated alongside others who are severely ill. Does the layout of the ICU or its location have an impact on how well patients with cancer do? Are dedicated oncological ICUs necessary?[104].

Nephro ICU

One frequent location for high-acuity nephrology consults is really the critical care unit (ICU). The prognosis of acute kidney injury (AKI) needing renal replacement treatment was worse, with short-term mortality rates that frequently reach 50%. Advanced chronic kidney disease is associated with increased ICU mortality. As a result, it's crucial for nephrologists within practice to feel at ease caring for seriously unwell patients. We concentrate on a few of the most frequent AKI factors that cause inside the critical care setting and employ these AKI causes to explore a few of the most important critical care nephrology-related subjects, such as acute respiratory distress syndrome, extracorporeal membrane oxygenation, developing concepts through fluid management & shock [105].

Transplant ICU

The practise of medicine has already been altered by knowledge and technology, and both, together with the desire to improve results, are the primary forces behind the emergence of subspecialties in almost every area of clinical medicine. The development of sub-specialized units inside the fields of pediatrics and neonatology, cardiology and cardiac surgery, and neurology and neurosurgery constitutes an exception in critical care medicine. End-stage organ failure (ESOF) patients are a special patient population, especially some who require or even have received solid-organ transplantation (SOT). The healthcare team faces difficulties at each and every level as a result of the complexity of SOT patient management. It really is crucial to provide SOT patients with critical care prior to and following transplantation. It affects their likelihood of being an organ donor candidate, which in turn affects their post-transplant morbidity, mortality, and allograft survival. Given this same pre-transplant ESOF, a lengthy, intricate surgical procedure, special post-operative management of a recipient (including allograft) & careful immunosuppression management, it is essential that critical care provided to a transplant patient be provided by a multidisciplinary team consisting of transplant doctors & experienced intensivists[106].

ECMO ICU

Extracorporeal membrane oxygenation (ECMO) use increased substantially in the last ten years, and it is currently regarded as just a standard form for life-saving care within critical care medicine. Medical education, training & experience are still absolutely necessary, nevertheless. ECMO had historically been employed to treat end-stage lung illness as well as circulatory collapse, but it is currently also being employed to treat right heart failure, as just a stopgap measure before heart and lung transplantation, and as a rescue therapy both sepsis and post-organ transplantation[107].

23. Resources in critical care

It can be difficult to tell patients in Intensive Care units and their relatives. Patients frequently face worry and anxiety when they are unexpectedly admitted. Stress has been linked to confusing, disorganized, or inconsistent information and communication. Despite the demand for knowledge, there isn't any strategically located, simple-to-access, standardized Intensive Care unit education curriculum.

A gap analysis was done after educational materials for patients in the Intensive Care units of the four participating hospitals were gathered.

Important content types and formats are noted. Three steps of the information pathway were used to structure the educational content: arriving at the Intensive Care unit; comprehending the Intensive Care unit and cooperating with care; and Intensive Care unit transitions. Significant differences in content structure and classifications were found by the gap analysis.

Coordination of education for such patients and their families, as well as the creation of a consistent communication framework for clinicians, can be facilitated by structuring a digital learning centre using various stages of the patient's stay in the Intensive Care unit and placing resources in the context of an information pathway. When constructing the learning centre, this should take into account the ideal digital format[108].

24. critical care communication

Communication is both an institutional medical activity and a cultural resource of immense significance. Information exchange is one means of describing communication, but it may also refer to the entire network of connections between both the parties engaged as well as the surrounding environment. All verbal and nonverbal forms of communication are possible; in fact, up to 65% of human conversation takes place nonverbally. Whereas verbal communication uses a digital code, nonverbal communication employs an analogic code and frequently conveys more information than we would like to by using visuals, gestures, and attitudes.

Because it incorporates individual rights and expectations for just a high quality of life, "communication" has gained importance in the healthcare system since the introduction of the informed consent procedure. As approximately 95% of patients dying in Intensive Care units (ICU) cannot communicate the desire for intrusive therapy, this procedure is complicated significantly.When it's hard to interact with patients directly, like if they are unconscious or unable of cooperating, doctors may ask their families to understand their wishes and thoughts on end-of-life options in order to arrive at joint decisions with them. This method calls for the ability to explain to the family the implications of each and every choice and the knowledge that all are working to respect and carry out the patients' desires[109].

To ensure independence for making choices that correspond to patients' preferences, a dialogue between patients' friends and family and doctors is required. However, this dialogue is really only probable when communication is effective, which means that messages and news are transmitted in a comprehensive way and family can further elaborate the received information.When delivering the data, the doctor should talk clearly and simply, and the person hearing (the relative) must provide feedback to the latter. A communication that doesn't feedback is ineffective. In the most recent issue of JOACP, Mathew et al. revealed that 71% of those who had received formal information about the clinical history of a loved one had questions about the diagnosis, prognosis, or therapy. Azoulay et al. reported in 2000 that 50% of relatives had insufficient connection with doctors. Lack of interaction may occur for a number of causes, including language use, cultural differences, an improper venue, and the intense stress endured by the relatives of patients sent to the Intensive Care unit (ICU)[110].

Senior family members had more understanding issues, according to study by Mathew et al. They theorised that this could have been because they had less access to online resources. Clarity of explanation is necessary for effective communication since the information must be linear and compatible with the cultural background of the audience. Facts must be presented clearly.

People must recall that doctors spend the majority of their lives in the Intensive Care unit (ICU), a completely seperate world full of strange experiences and technical equipment (such as mechanical ventilators and vital sign monitors) that simply have no place in "normal" life, to excuse them from using technical language too frequently. Moreover, medical students are rarely trained how to communicate effectively.

Curtis et al. proposed that doctors must arrange sessions with families as would organise any other intrusive medical duty, checking most critical information and providing care that their own feelings don't really disrupt the interaction with patient's family[111].

The doctor must begin by discussing issues that really are pertinent to each and every family while keeping in mind the fact that his or her patients' family members might have entirely different ideas about sickness and viewpoints from their own. The doctor must also be informed of and comprehend the patient's expectations, which are things that families likely grasp more well. Doctors have a responsibility to confirm that the information exchange had place and was accurately supplied and received, particularly when a critical and final decision needs to be made based on that communication.

There's a clear ethical implication in creating successful communication. Since the ethical component is linked to a social and affective dimension, communication quality also exists behind the contents. The doctors in critical care must take into account the emotions of the people they are educating because communication involves both intellectual and emotional components that are active at the same time. Even when information is misunderstood, the emotional component of communication may still be preserved. The patient's relative should be treated with respect and given consideration for the difficulties. Even though the families were unable to completely comprehend the patient's situation, Mathew reported a high level of family satisfaction.

In our ICUs, the rescue culture and the seriousness of sickness coexist; small, congested spaces are the surroundings of quick, challenging dialogues; we now need to learn how and where to eliminate barriers to effective communication for the benefit of patients and our professionals[112].

References

1. Kellum JA. Making Strong Ion Difference the "Euro" for Bedside AcidBase Analysis. Yearbook of Intensive Care and Emergency Medicine. Spr Ber Heid Publ 2005;5:675.
2. Phillips B, Peretz DI. Blood Gas Pre-analytical considerations. Specimen collection, Calibration, and Controls (proposed guidelines). In: National Committee for Clinical Laboratory Standards. NCCLS publication. villanova PA, NCCLS; 1985.
3. Börner U, Müller H, Höge R, Hempelmann G. The influence of anticoagulation on acid-base status and blood-gas analysis. Acta Anaesthesiol Scand 1984;28:277-9.
4. Hutchison AS, Ralston SH, Dryburgh FJ, Small M, Fogelman I. Too much heparin: possible source of error in blood gas analysis. Br Med J 1983;287:1131-2.
5. Toffaletti J, Ernst P, Hunt P, Abrams B. Dry electrolyte-balanced heparinized syringes evaluated for determining ionized calcium and other electrolytes in whole blood. Clin Chem 1991;37:1730-3.
6. Gattinoni L, Pesenti A, Matthay M. Understanding blood gas analysis. Intensive Care Med. 2018 Jan;44(1):91-93.
7. Kim Y, Massie L, Murata GH, Tzamaloukas AH. Discrepancy between Measured Serum Total Carbon Dioxide Content and Bicarbonate Concentration Calculated from Arterial Blood Gases. Cureus. 2015 Dec 07;7(12):e398.
8. Kumar V, Karon BS. Comparison of measured and calculated bicarbonate values. Clin Chem. 2008 Sep;54(9):1586-7.
9. Dev SP, Hillmer MD, Ferri M. Videos in clinical medicine. Arterial puncture for blood gas analysis. N Engl J Med. 2011 Feb 03;364(5):e7.
10. Toffaletti J, Ernst P, Hunt P, Abrams B. Dry electrolyte-balanced heparinized syringes evaluated for determining ionized calcium and other electrolytes in whole blood. Clin Chem 1991;37:1730-3.
11. Rosenberg MB, Campbell RL. Guidelines for intraoperative monitoring of dental patients undergoing conscious sedation, deep sedation, and general anesthesia. Oral Surg Oral Med Oral Pathol. 1991;71:2–8.

12. American Dental Association. Guidelines for the Use of Conscious Sedation, Deep Sedation and General Anesthesia for Dentists. Adopted by the House of Delegates, American Dental Association, October 2005.

13. Eichhorn JH, Cooper JB, Cullen DJ, et al. Standards for patient monitoring during anesthesia at Harvard Medical School. JAMA. 1986;256:1017–1020.

14. Guyton AC, Hall JE. Textbook of Medical Physiology. 10th ed. Philadelphia, Pa: WB Saunders Co; 2000.

15. Brunwald E, Zipes DP, Libby P. Heart Disease: A Textbook of Cardiovascular Medicine. 6th ed. Philadelphia, Pa: WB Saunders Co; 2001.

16. Brainsky A, Fletcher RH, Glick HA, Lanken PN, Williams SV, Kundel HL. Routine portable chest radiographs in the medical Intensive Care unit: Effects and costs. Crit Care Med 1997;25:801-5.

17. Chahine-Malus N, Stewart T, Lapinsky SE, Marras T, Dancey D, Leung R, et al. Utility of routine chest radiographs in a medicalsurgical Intensive Care unit: A quality assurance survey. Crit Care 2001;5:271-5.

18. Graat ME, Kr^ner A, Spronk PE, Korevaar JC, Stoker J, Vroom MB, et al. Elimination of daily routine chest radiographs in a mixed medical-surgical Intensive Care unit. Intensive Care Med 2007;33:639-44. 4. Bhagwanjee S. Muckart DJ. Routine daily chest radiography is not indicated for ventilated patients in a surgical ICU. Intensive Care Med 1996;22:1335-8.

19. Henschke CI, Yankelevitz DF, Wand A, Davis SD, Shiau M. Accuracy and efficacy of chest radiography in the Intensive Care unit. Radiol Clin North Am 1996;34:21-31.

20.Price CP, Hicks JM, eds. Point-of-care testing. Washington: AACC Press, 1999. 2 England JM, Hyde K, Lewis SM, Mackie IJ, Rowan RM, et al.

21.Guidelines for near-patient testing: haematology. Clin Lab Haem 1995;17:300-9.

22. Price C, St John A. Point-of-Care Testing Making innovation work for patient-centred care. Washington, USA: AACC Press; 2012.

23. Tideman PA, Tirimacco R, Senior DP, Setchell JJ, Huynh LT, Tavella R, et al. Impact of a regionalised clinical cardiac support network on mortality among rural patients with myocardial infarction. Med J Aust. 2014;200:157–60.

24. National Health Service Whole system demonstrator programme: an overview of telecare and telehealth. http://webarchive.nationalarchives.gov.uk/20130107105354/http://www.dh.gov.uk/en/Publicationsandstatistics/Publications/PublicationsPolicyAndGuidance/DH_100946 (Accessed 10 May 2014)

25. Olansky L, Kennedy L. Finger-stick glucose monitoring: issues of accuracy and specificity. Diabetes Care. 2010;33:948–9.

26. Heil EL, Kuti JL, Bearden DT, Gallagher JC. The essential role of pharmacists in antimicrobial stewardship [published online April 13, 2016] *Infect Control Hosp Epidemiol.* 2016;37(7):753–754. doi: 10.1017/ice.2016.82.

27. Baggs J, Fridkin SK, Pollack LA, et al. Estimating national trends in inpatient antibiotic use among US hospitals from 2006 to 2012. *JAMA Intern Med.* 2016;176(11):1639–1648. doi: 10.1001/jamainternmed.2016.5651.

28. Ashraf MS, Cook PP. Antibiotic misuse in hospital, outpatient, and long-term care settings. *N C Med J.* 2016;77(5):346–349. doi: 10.18043/ncm.77.5.346.

29. Kunin CM, Johansen KS, Woming AM, Daschner FD. Report of a symposium on use and abuse of antibiotics worldwide. *Rev Infect Dis.* 1990;12(1):12–19.

30. Maki DG, Schuna AA. A study of antimicrobial misuse in a university hospital. *Am J Med Sci.* 1978;275(3):271–282.

31. Malani AN, Richards PG, Kapila S, et al. Clinical and economic outcomes from a community hospital's antimicrobial stewardship program [published online May 10, 2012] *Am J Infect Control.* 2013;41(2):145–148. doi: 10.1016/j.ajic.2012.02.021.

32. Shehab N, Patel PR, Srinivasan A, Budnitz DS. Emergency department visits for antibiotic-associated adverse events. *Clin Infect Dis.* 2008;47(6):735–743. doi: 10.1086/591126.

33. Mauldin PD, Salgado CD, Hansen IS, et al. Attributable hospital cost and length of stay associated with health care-associated infections caused by antibiotic-resistant gram-negative bacteria [published online October 19, 2009] *Antimicrob Agents Chemother.* 2010;54(1):109–115. doi: 10.1128/AAC.01041-09.

34. Llor C, Bjerrum L. Antimicrobial resistance: risk associated with antibiotic overuse and initiatives to reduce the problem. *Ther Adv Drug Saf.* 2014;5(6):229–241. doi: 10.1177/2042098614554919.

35. Fridkin S, Baggs J, Fagan R, et al. Vital signs: improving antibiotic use among hospitalized patients. *MMWR Morb Mortal Wkly Rep.* 2014;63(9):194–200.

36. Bailey AM, Stephan M, Weant KA, Justice SB. Dosing of appropriate antibiotics and time to administration of first doses in the pediatric emergency department. *J PediatrPharmacol Ther.* 2015;20(4):309–315. doi: 10.5863/1551-6776-20.4.309.

37. Rhodes A, Evans LE, Alhazzani W, et al. Surviving sepsis campaign: international guidelines for management of sepsis and septic shock: 2016 [published online January 18, 2017] *Intensive Care Med.* 2017;43(3):304–377. doi: 10.1007/s00134-017-4683-6.

38. 2011 National Diabetes Fact Sheet. Atlanta, GA: Centers for Disease Control and Prevention; 2011. Available from: http://www.cdc.gov/ diabetes/pubs/factsheet11.htm. Accessed April 7, 2014.

39. Gosmanov AR, Wall BM. Diabetic ketoacidosis. In: Bope ET, Kellerman RD, editors. Conn's Current Therapy 2014. Philadelphia, PA: Elsevier Saunders; 2014:710–713.

40. Kitabchi AE, Umpierrez GE, Miles JM, Fisher JN. Hyperglycemic crises in adult patients with diabetes. Diabetes Care. 2009;32(7): 1335–1343.

41. Kitabchi AE, Nyenwe EA. Hyperglycemic crises in diabetes mellitus: diabetic ketoacidosis and hyperglycemic hyperosmolar state. Endocrinol Metab Clin North Am. 2006;35(4):725–751, viii.

42. Randall L, Begovic J, Hudson M, et al. Recurrent diabetic ketoacidosis in inner-city minority patients: behavioral, socioeconomic, and psychosocial factors. Diabetes Care. 2011;34(9):1891–1896.

43. Umpierrez GE, Smiley D, Kitabchi AE. Narrative review: ketosisprone type 2 diabetes mellitus. Ann Intern Med. 2006;144(5): 350–357.

44. Gosmanov AR, Umpierrez GE, Karabell AH, Cuervo R, Thomason DB. Impaired expression and insulin-stimulated phosphorylation of Akt-2 in muscle of obese patients with atypical diabetes. Am J Physiol Endocrinol Metab. 2004;287(1):E8–E15.

45. Kitabchi AE, Umpierrez GE, Murphy MB, Kreisberg RA. Hyperglycemic crises in adult patients with diabetes: a consensus statement from the American Diabetes Association. Diabetes Care. 2006;29(12): 2739–2748.

46. Haddad M, Sharma S. StatPearls [Internet]. StatPearls Publishing; Treasure Island (FL): Jul 18, 2022. Physiology, Lung.

47. Kempker JA, Abril MK, Chen Y, Kramer MR, Waller LA, Martin GS. The Epidemiology of Respiratory Failure in the United States 2002-2017: A Serial Cross-Sectional Study. Crit Care Explor. 2020 Jun;2(6):e0128.

48. Vallabhajosyula S, Kashani K, Dunlay SM, Vallabhajosyula S, Vallabhajosyula S, Sundaragiri PR, Gersh BJ, Jaffe AS, Barsness GW. Acute respiratory failure and mechanical ventilation in cardiogenic shock complicating acute myocardial infarction in the USA, 2000-2014. Ann Intensive Care. 2019 Aug 28;9(1):96.

49..Hendrickson KW, Peltan ID, Brown SM. The Epidemiology of Acute Respiratory Distress Syndrome Before and After Coronavirus Disease 2019. Crit Care Clin. 2021 Oct;37(4):703-716.

50. Cummings MJ, Baldwin MR, Abrams D, Jacobson SD, Meyer BJ, Balough EM, Aaron JG, Claassen J, Rabbani LE, Hastie J, Hochman BR, Salazar-Schicchi J, Yip NH, Brodie D, O'Donnell

MR. Epidemiology, clinical course, and outcomes of critically ill adults with COVID-19 in New York City: a prospective cohort study. Lancet. 2020 Jun 06;395(10239):1763-1770.

.51.Elhardello OA, MacFie J. Digital rectal examination in patients with acute abdominal pain. Emerg Med J. 2018 Sep;35(9):579-580.

52. Maleki Verki M, Motamed H. Rectus Muscle Hematoma as a Rare Differential Diagnosis of Acute Abdomen; a Case Report. Emerg (Tehran). 2018;6(1):e28.

53. Kaushal-Deep SM, Anees A, Khan S, Khan MA, Lodhi M. Primary cecal pathologies presenting as acute abdomen and critical appraisal of their current management strategies in emergency settings with review of literature. Int J Crit IllnInj Sci. 2018 Apr-Jun;8(2):90-99.

54. Li PH, Tee YS, Fu CY, Liao CH, Wang SY, Hsu YP, Yeh CN, Wu EH. The Role of Noncontrast CT in the Evaluation of Surgical Abdomen Patients. Am Surg. 2018 Jun 01;84(6):1015-1021.

55. Ramachandran A, Jaeschke H. Acetaminophen Hepatotoxicity. Semin Liver Dis. 2019 May;39(2):221-234.

56. Lima LCD, Miranda AS, Ferreira RN, Rachid MA, Simões E Silva AC. Hepatic encephalopathy: Lessons from preclinical studies. World J Hepatol. 2019 Feb 27;11(2):173-185.

57. Chauhan A, Webb G, Ferguson J. Clinical presentations of Hepatitis E: A clinical review with representative case histories. Clin Res Hepatol Gastroenterol. 2019 Nov;43(6):649-657.

58. Heberden W (1816) Commentaries on the history and cure of diseases. Payne and Foss, London

59. Eknoyan G (1989) The origins of nephrology—Galen, the founding father of experimental renal physiology. Am J Nephrol 9(1):66–82. https://doi.org/10.1159/000167939

60. Eknoyan G (2002) Rufus of ephesus and his "diseases of the kidneys". Nephron 91(3):383–390. https://doi.org/10.1159/00006 4277.

61. Roosevelt FD. 32nd President of the United States, Advice to His son James on How to Make a Public Speech. As Quoted in Basic Public Speaking, by Soper PL; 1963. :12. 62. Piazza O, Pellegrini C, Rossano F, Servillo G, Tufano R, Piazza T. Individual perception of stress in the ICU. *Eur J Anaesthesiol.* 2004;21:749–51.

63. Cohen S, Sprung C, Sjokvist P, Lippert A, Ricou B, Baras M, et al. Communication of end-of-life decisions in European Intensive Care units. *Intensive Care Med.* 2005;31:1215–21.

64. Curtis JR, Patrick DL, Shannon SE, Treece PD, Engelberg RA, Rubenfeld GD. The family conference as a focus to improve communication about end-of-life care in the Intensive Care unit: Opportunities for improvement. *Crit Care Med.* 2001;29:N26–33.

65. Watzalawick P. W. W. Norton & Company; 2011. Pragmatics of Human Communication: A Study of Interactional Patterns, Pathologies, and Paradoxes.

66. Needham DM, Davidson J, Cohen H, Hopkins RO, Weinert C, Wunsch H, et al. Improving long-term outcomes after discharge from Intensive Care unit: Report from a stakeholders' conference. Crit Care Med 2012;40:502–9.

67. Medicine SoCC. Post-Intensive Care Syndrome Patients and Families 2013; Available from URL: http://www.myicucare.org/Adult-Support/Pages/ Post-intensive-Care-Syndrome.aspx. Last accessed 2016 January 10.

68. Davidson JE, Jones C, Bienvenu OJ. Family response to critical illness: postIntensive Care syndrome-family. Critical Care Med 2012;40:618-24.

69. Schmidt M, Azoulay E. Having a loved one in the ICU: the forgotten family. CurrOpin Crit Care 2012;18:540-7.

70. Winters BD, Eberlein M, Leung J, Needham DM, Pronovost PJ, Sevransky JE. Long-term mortality and quality of life in sepsis: a systematic review. Crit Care Med. 2010;38(5):1276-83.

71. Wong LY, Bellomo R, Robbins R, Martensson J, Kanaan R, Newton R, et al. Long-term outcomes after severe drug overdose. Crit Care Resusc. 2016;18(4):247-54.

72. Normilio-Silva K, de Figueiredo AC, Pedroso-de-Lima AC, Tunes-da-Silva G, Nunes da Silva A, Delgado Dias Levites A, et al. Long-term survival, quality of life, and quality-adjusted survival in critically ill patients with cancer. Crit Care Med. 2016;44(7):1327-37.

73. How to read clinical journals: I. Why to read them and how to start reading them critically. *Can Med Assoc J.* 1981;124:555–8.

74. Durbin CG., Jr How to read a scientific research paper. *Respir Care.* 2009;54:1366–71.

75. Druss BG, Marcus SC. Growth and decentralization of the medical literature: Implications for evidence-based medicine. *J Med Libr Assoc.* 2005;93:499–501.

76. How to read a scientific paper. [Last accessed on 2011 Oct 9]. Available from: http://www.sciencebuddies.org/science-fair-projects/top_science-fair_how_to_read_a_scientific_paper.shtml .

77. Hudson-Barr D. How to read a research article. *J Spec PediatrNurs.* 2004;9:70–2.

78. Bannard-Smith J, Bishop S, Gawne S, Halder N. Twelve tips for junior doctors interested in a career in medical education. Med Teach 2012;34:1012–1016.

79. Castiglioni A, Aagaard E, Spencer A, Nicholson L, Karani R, Bates CK, Willett LL, Chheda SG. Succeeding as a clinician educator: useful tips and resources. J Gen Intern Med 2013;28:136–140.

80. Hatem CJ, Searle NS, Gunderman R, Krane NK, Perkowski L, Schutze GE, Steinert Y. The educational attributes and responsibilities of effective medical educators. Acad Med 2011;86:474–480.

81..Shortell SM, Zimmerman JE, Rousseau DM, Gillies RR, Wagner DP, Draper EA, Knaus WA, Duffy J. The performance of Intensive Care units: does good management make a difference? *Med Care.* 1994;**32**:508–525. doi: 10.1097/00005650-199405000-00009.

82.Hersey P, Blanchard KH. *Management of Organizational Behavior: Utilizing Human Resources.* Englewood Cliffs, NJ: Prentice-Hall, Inc; 1977.

83.Kakabadse A, Bank J, Vinnicombe S. *Working in Organisations.* 2. Burlington, USA: Gower; 2004.

84.Covey SR. *The Seven Habits of Highly Effective People.* New York: Franklin Covey Co. Fireside; 1990.

85. Chappell RW Jr. Secrets of a chief medical officer. What they didn't teach you in medical school but you wish they had. Physician Exec. 2005;30:30–32.

86. Myerson DE. Radical change, the quiet way. Harv Bus Rev. 2001;79:92–100.

87. Phillips M, Arthur AO, Chandwaney R, Hatfield J, Brown B, Pogue K, et al. Helicopter transport effectiveness of patients for primary percutaneous coronary intervention. *Air Med J.* 2013;32:144–52.

88. Gearhart PA, Wuerz R, Localio AR. Cost-effectiveness analysis of helicopter EMS for trauma patients. *Ann Emerg Med.* 1997;30:500–6.

89. Silbergleit R, Scott PA, Lowell MJ, Silbergleit R. Cost-effectiveness of helicopter transport of stroke patients for thrombolysis. *Acad Emerg Med.* 2003;10:966–72.

90. Mehra A. Air ambulance services in India. *J Postgrad Med.* 2000;46:314–7.

91. Telehealth. Available at: https://healthit.ahrq.gov/key-topics/telehealth. Accessed March 31, 2019.

92. Telemedicine Glossary. Available at: https://thesource.americantelemed.org/ resources/telemedicine-glossary. Accessed March 31, 2019.

93. Margolis SA, Ypinazar VA. Tele-pharmacy in remote medical practice: the Royal Flying Doctor Service Medical Chest Program. Rural Remote Health 2008;8(2):937.

94. Celi LA, Hassan E, Marquardt C, Breslow M, Rosenfeld B. The eICU: It's not just telemedicine. *Crit Care Med.* 2001;29(Suppl 8):N183–9.

95. Karnataka Sets up Critical Care Support Unit by Linking COVID Hospitals Across State. Press Trust of India. [Last accessed on 2020 Jun 05]. Available from: https://www.businessstandard.com/article/ptistories/karnatakasetsupcriticalcare-supportunitbylinkingcovidhospitalsacrossstate120041500931_1.html .

96. Ganapathy K. Telemedicine and neurosciences. *Neurol India.* 2018;66:642–51.

97. Lau VI, Priestap FA, Lam JNH, et al.: Factors associated with the increasing rates of discharges directly home from Intensive Care units—a direct from ICU sent home study. J Intensive Care Med. 2016; 33:121–127

98. Stelfox HT, Soo A, Niven DJ, et al.: Assessment of the safety of discharging select patients directly home from the Intensive Care unit: A multicenter population-based cohort study. JAMA Intern Med. 2018; 178:1390–1399.

99. Telemedicine Practice Guidelines Enabling Registered Medical Practitioners to Provide Healthcare Using Telemedicine. Board of governors, in Supersession with Medical Council of India. [Last accessed on 2020 Mar 26]. Available from: https://www.mohfw.gov.in/pdf/Telemedicine.pdf .

100. Becker CD, Fusaro MV, Scurlock C. Telemedicine in the ICU: Clinical outcomes, economic aspects, and trainee education. *CurrOpinAnaesthesiol.* 2019;32:129–35.

101. Ajzen, I. (2002). Perceived behavioral control, self-efficacy, locus of control, and the theory of planned behavior 1. *J. Appl. Soc. Psychol.* 32, 665–683. doi: 10.1111/j.1559-1816.2002.tb00236.x

102. Bolton, D., O'Ryan, D., Udwin, O., Boyle, S., and Yule, W. (2000). The long-term psychological effects of a disaster experienced in adolescence: II: general psychopathology. *J. Child Psychol. Psychiatr. Allied Discipl.* 41, 513–523. doi: 10.1111/1469-7610.00636

103. Soares M, Bozza FA, Angus D, et al. Organizational characteristics, outcomes, and resource use in 78 Brazilian Intensive Care units: The ORCHESTRA study. *Intensive Care Med* 2015;41:2149-60. 10.1007/s00134-015-4076-7

104. Encina B, Lagunes L, Morales-Codina M. The Immunocompromised oncohematologial critically ill patient: considerations in severe infections. *Ann Transl Med* 2016;4: 327-30. 10.21037/atm.2016.09.12

105. SEER Stat Fact Sheet: Cancer of Any Site. Seer.cancer.gov. Accessed 12/24/2016.

106. Niemann CU, Kramer DJ. Transplant critical care: standards for the Intensive Care of the patient with liver failure before and after transplantation. *Liver Transpl.* 2011;17:485–7.

107. 1. Rubenfeld GD, Caldwell E, Peabody E, . et al. Incidence and outcomes of acute lung injury. *N Engl J Med.* 2005. October 20; 353 16: 1685– 93.

108. Brower RG, Matthay MA, Morris A, . et al .; Acute Respiratory Distress Syndrome Network Ventilation with lower tidal volumes as compared with traditional tidal volumes for acute lung injury and the acute respiratory distress syndrome. *N Engl J Med.* 2000. May 4; 342 18: 1301– 8.

109. Makdisi G, Wang IW. Extra Corporeal Membrane Oxygenation (ECMO) review of a lifesaving technology. *J Thorac Dis.* 2015. July; 7 7: E166– 76.

110. Knezevic I, Poglajen G, Ksela J, . et al. ECMO as a Bridge-to-Transplant in Patients With Cardiogenic Shock. *J Heart Lung Transplant*. 2015. April; 34 4: S314– 5.

111. Hannawi B, Estep J, Nguyen D, . et al. Extra Corporeal Membrane Oxygenation (ECMO) as a Bridge to Adult Heart Transplantation: Bridge to Bridge Strategy vs Direct ECMO Bridge Strategy (UNOS Analysis). *J Heart Lung Transplant*. 2017. April; 36 4: S137.

112. Thompson JT, Molnar JA, Hines MH, Chang MC, Pranikoff T.. Successful management of adult smoke inhalation with extracorporeal membrane oxygenation. *J Burn Care Rehabil*. 2005 Jan–Feb; 26 1: 62– 6.

Part II

Cardiac Intensive Care

Chapter 7:

Cardiac Intensive Care unit

Since the first coronary care unit emerged in the early 1960s, critical care cardiology has been gradually and quickly evolving as a sub-specialization within cardiovascullar medicine [1]. A hospital ward known as the Cardiovascular Intensive Care Unit (CICU) is dedicated to the treatment of patients with severe Cardiovascular Diseases (CVD), including those with Acute Coronary Syndrome (ACS), lethal arrhythmia, and acute heart failure. Multisystem organ dysfunction and non - cardiovascular comorbidities are becoming more common in modern cardiac ICUs [3]. It follows that patients admitted to modern CICUs would likely be vulnerable to comparable avoidable consequences related to both their multisystem severe illness and the resources needed to treat their complicated diseases. The need for CICU doctors to comprehend the issues most relevant to critically ill cardiovascular patients—who might not be well represented in the general ICU—occurs concurrently [4].

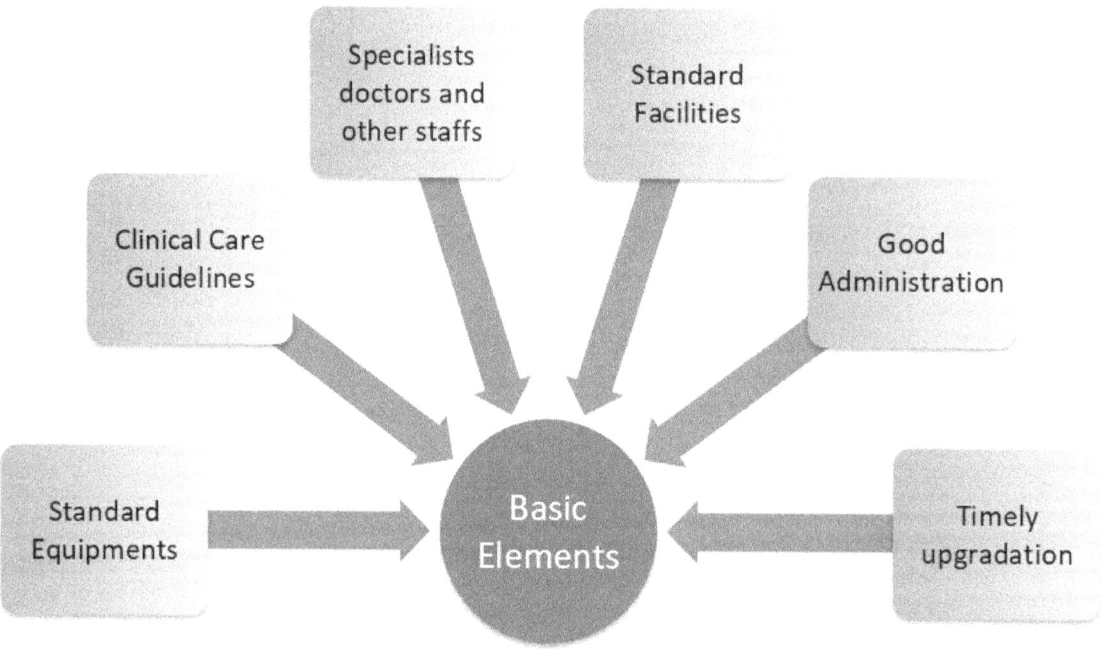

Figure7.1: Basic Elements required for building up a successful Cardiovascular Intensive Care Unit

Acute Myocardial Infarction (AMI) patients were typically treated with bed rest and sedation prior to the development of the coronary care unit (CCU) in the 1960s; in-hospital mortality was 31%, and 1-year all-cause mortality was 46%. The first CCUs worked on the basis of 4 fundamental principles.

First principle: assigning patients to a single physical location according to their diagnoses (geographic grouping);

Second principle: providing emergency Cardiopulmonary Resuscitation (CPR)/defibrillation.

Third principle: using telemetry monitoring to detect arrhythmias

Fourth principle: empowering healthcare workers other than doctors by teaching them practical guidelines to conduct resuscitative measures. These divisions concentrated not only on which therapies to use but also on how to utilize them (the provision of healthcare) [6].

Patients with AMI were the ones in whom the initial CCU's effects could be seen the most clearly. The cardiovascular Intensive Care unit (CICU) now manages a much wider range of conditions. The CICU management is the final one for patients with hemodynamically significant heart failure, patients with cardiac arrest, perioperative management of patients needing cardiac surgery or advanced intervention, decompensated valvular heart disease, unstable arrhythmias, and mechanical circulatory support, according to integrated health care systems. The modern CICU comes with a lot of resuscitative management features along with the presence of routine ICU facilities [6,7].

A complex patient community with a heavy incidence of critical cardiovascular and non-cardiovascular disorders is served by modern cardiac Intensive Care units (CICU). A multidisciplinary strategy is necessary for the treatment of these patients, combining highly specialized knowledge and abilities in cardiovascular disorders with those in an emergency, critical care, and internal medicine. One of the most challenging training phases, the CICU has traditionally presented unique challenges to both seasoned intensivists and fellows-in-training (FIT) [1].

For patients with severe cardiovascular disease (CVD), which includes vascular and heart disease, special systemic management is referred to as cardiovascular Intensive Care. Coronary artery diseases like myocardial infarction and angina, myocarditis, hypertensive heart disease, cardiomyopathy, heart arrhythmia, and valvular disease. Aortic dissection, peripheral artery disease, aortic aneurysm, etc. are examples of vascular illnesses. Cardiovascular disease is the second leading cause of death in the world. An intense care unit for severe CVD patients, known as a cardiovascular Intensive Care unit (CICU), has been constructed in several general hospitals to prevent death from CVDs [2].

Different cardiac and vascular illnesses are included in CVDs. Each CVD's onset etiology is unique. Age, obesity, smoking, hypertension, hyperlipidemia, and diabetes mellitus are only a few of the risk factors for heart disease. Numerous significant cardiovascular risk factors are treatable with medication and lifestyle changes, such as the control of diabetes, hypertension, and hyperlipidemia. According to estimates, 90% of CVD can be avoided [5].

A significant proportion of the geriatric population has CVDs. According to reports, 11.3% of Americans aged 20 to 40 had cardiovascular disease (CVD), compared to 37.5% of those aged 40 to 60, 71.2% of those aged 60 to 80, and 85.6% of those over the age of 80 [13].

The coronary care unit (CCU) was founded as a facility accountable for critical care in the acute stage in order to enhance the outcome of CVDs because they include a number of terminal emergency disorders [5].

The coronary care unit (CCU) was founded as a facility accountable for Intensive Care in the acute stage in order to enhance the outcome of CVDs because they include a number of lethal emergency disorders. A hospital ward with a focus on treating patients with serious heart conditions like AMI, arrhythmias, and cardiomyopathy is known as the CICU. These individuals frequently express heart failure and cardiogenic shock complaints. Therefore, individuals with severe CVD require constant observation as well as acute care.

Acute myocardial infarction individuals were the primary target population during the time CICU was not used to being there. Defibrillation and Percutaneous Coronary Intervention (PCI) were crucial therapies that used to be reserved for preventing the death of a patient. The demand for cardiovascular Intensive Care, including respiratory maintenance and blood purifying therapy, grew as the target patients progressed to failure of heart, out-of-hospital cardiac arrest, shock, etc [6].

The provision of continuous electrocardiographic monitoring of the heart rhythm is the primary characteristic of the CICU (ECG). This enhances the prognosis of patients with severe CVD by enabling early intervention with medicine, cardioversion, or defibrillation. In the CICU, systemic treatment is necessary for conjunction with circulation management. A ventilator, a blood purifying system, supplementary circulation equipment such as an intra-aortic balloon pump (IABP), and a percutaneous cardiopulmonary support system (PCPS) must therefore be prepared in the CICU. The need for technology to undertake targeted temperature monitoring for patients undergoing resuscitation following cardiogenic out-of-hospital cardiac arrest has recently become essential (OHCA) [7].

The monitoring systems on the bedside like respiratory rate, ECG, blood pressure; thermometer, cardiac ultrasound, blood gas analyzer, portable X-ray, doppler blood flow, pulse oximeter, and echocardiography are the diagnostic equipment that is necessary for the cardiac Intensive Care unit. Cardiac pacemakers, a managing system for temperature, a defibrillator, an intra-aortic balloon pump, a noninvasive ventilation system, a blood purifier, mechanical ventilation system are the therapeutics equipment required in the cardiac Intensive Care unit [7].

Cardiovascular Intensive Care requires committed medical personnel in order to provide the finest patient care. Additionally, technicians and nurses who have received training in providing CVD patients with specialized treatment are assigned. In the CICU, team medical care provided through the cooperation of the medical personnel is essential for optimal patient management. The CICU medical team must be able to assess echocardiographic electrocardiograms and cardiac functions [8].

Cardiologists are now required to supervise systemic Intensive Care procedures like respiratory and infusion management in addition to circulation control. Collaboration between cardiologists and critical care experts is essential to managing CVD patients with a variety of consequences, including sepsis, renal failure, and respiratory failure. The CICU is a high-risk setting where complex patients are admitted who have acute illnesses that may turn life-threatening at any time. According to reports, simulation-based training programs for cardiac critical care units have many advantages, enabling clinicians to gain not just practice-specific procedural skills but also competence and confidence as members of an effective and trained resuscitation team [8].

An ECG, which assesses a patient with cardiovascular disease's heart rhythm, is the most crucial monitoring device in this setting. In addition, individuals with CVD worsened by cardiogenic shock or abrupt heart failure may need monitoring of hemodynamic variables of invasive arterial blood pressure and pulmonary artery pressure. In determining the severity of such patients, hemodynamic testing is crucial [9].

Cardiogenic shock is defined as despite adequate fling status (systolic blood pressure 90 mmHg) there is heart failure associated with hypotension, with clinical signs of hypoperfusion like mental confusion, narrow pulse pressure, dizziness, oliguria, cold extremities, metabolic acidosis, increased serum lactate, and increased serum creatinine levels. It is frequently accompanied by increased LV end-diastolic pressure (LVEDP), and a decrease in LV contractility and stroke volume [10].

The severity of cardiogenic shock has been divided into five stages by the Society for Cardiovascular Angiography and Interventions (SCAI), with stage A denoting a chance of developing the condition, stage B denoting the onset of shock (missing hypoperfusion), stage C denoting classic cardiogenic shock (hypoperfusion that requires timely intervention, such as inotrope, pressor, or mechanical support, beyond volume resuscitation to restore perfusion), and stage D denoting deterioration (failure in responding to initial intervention set), and E denoting extremis (collapse of the circulatory system) [13].

The most common cause of shock in CICUs is a cardiogenic shock from an acute myocardial infarction, which has been affecting more than 50% of the patients. In addition to coronary revascularization, intravenous volumetric therapy and the injection of positive inotropes such as vasopressor noradrenalin and dobutamine are the cornerstones of treatment for these individuals. Despite these guidelines in therapy mortality of patients is seen so, the surgeons have developed temporary circulatory support [11,12].

Standard of care for unconscious victims of out-of-hospital heart attack, therapeutic hypothermia has been shown to enhance neurologic outcomes. Targeted-temperature maintenance was used to treat patients who had been revived due to non-shockable rhythms, such as asystole and pulseless electrical activity, in the most recent large randomized trial, Therapeutic Hypothermia After Cardiac Arrest in Non-Shockable Rhythm (HYPERION). Patients in the targeted-temperature group had significantly better neurological outcomes [13, 14].

In the past ten years, there has been a significant increase in the use of veno - arterial extracorporeal membrane oxygenation (VA-ECMO) purpose of providing provisional circulatory assistance for critically ill patients. VA-ECMO is now one of the most frequently used devices in the management of severe cardiogenic shock stages D and E. (according to SCAI). VA-ECMO is meant to act as a stopgap measure before myocardial healing, transplantation, durable mechanical circulatory support, or a choice based on an assessment of the end-organ damage's reversibility as well as the patient's general prognosis [15,16].

The invention of CPR, which included the quick use of external defibrillation for ventricular arrhythmias, was crucial to the CCU's success [16].

Sudden cardiac arrest (SCA) has become one of the major causes of death. According to an initial heart-rhythm examination, ventricular fibrillation (VF), which has decreased over the past 20 years, is present in between 25 and 50 percent of SCA sufferers. There are occurrences of collapses and episodes of unconsciousness in individuals with Ventricular Fibrillation or rapid ventricular tachycardia (VT), but by the time emergency medical workers record the initial electrocardiogram (ECG), their rhythms have degraded to asystole. If onlookers take prompt action while VF is still present, SCA sufferers can live. Once the rhythm has degenerated to asystole, the likelihood of successful resuscitation decreases. VF cardiac arrest is advised to be treated with immediate bystanders CPR and early electric defibrillation [17,18].

It can be hard to spot cardiac arrest. To start the chain of survival, both bystanders and emergency call takers (emergency medical dispatchers) must accurately diagnose cardiac arrest. The carotid pulse (or any other pulse) cannot be reliably used to determine whether circulation is present or not [18].

The crucial connections required for a successful resuscitation are enumerated in The Chain of Survival. Most of these links are relevant to people who have had primary cardiac and asphyxial arrest [19]. The chain of survical may be summarized as **"4 Early"** principle which is as followed:

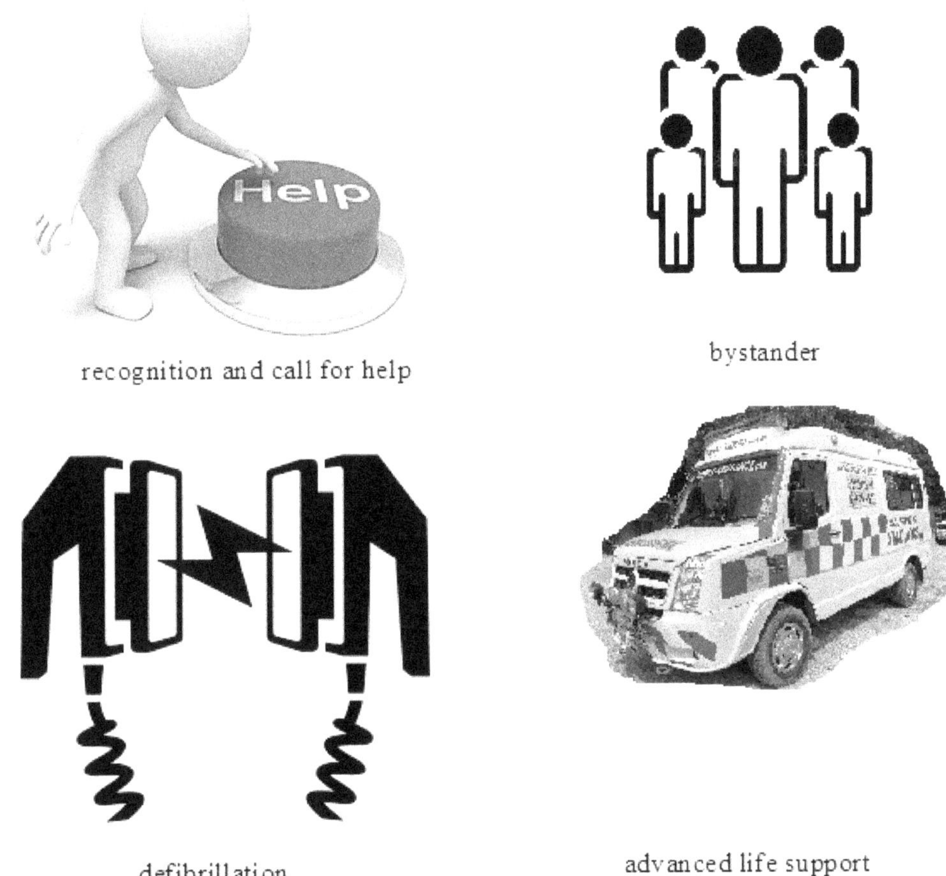

Figure 7.2: The "4 Early" elements are (Top-left) Early recognition and call for help; (Top-right) Early bystander; (Bottom-left) Early defibrillation;(Bottom-right) Early advanced life support and standardized post-resuscitation care

Chapter 8:

Hemodynamic Monitoring and ECG

In general, patients who are admitted to the Intensive Care Unit (ICU) have organ damage (single or multiple) or are in danger of having such organ failure, including those who have undergone significant surgery or been severely injured. One of the main contributing factors to organ damage is hemodynamic instability, which results in an imbalance between oxygen demand and delivery [20]. Hemodynamic instability is caused by changes in effective circulation volume (e.g., hypovolemia), cardiovascular function, and/or vascular tone (e.g., vasoplegic shock in sepsis) which can be managed with regular monitoring and clinical examination of some of the basic vitals like blood pressure, heart rate, respiratory rate, central venous pressure, saturation levels of oxygen, and urinary output but when monitoring of these vitals is not achieved there is an increase in demand for hemodynamic monitoring like cardiac output, mixed venous oxygen saturation, pulmonary arterial pressure, stroke volume variation that helps in guiding management of fluid and inotropic/ vasopressor support [21].

Hemodynamic monitoring has advanced from simple CO monitoring to complex equipment during the past few decades. These methods and tools can be categorized in one of two ways: 1) calibrated versus non-calibrated methods, or 2) by how invasive they are (invasive, less invasive, or non-invasive).

Knowing the Fick principle, which Adolf Fick first introduced in 1870, is the first step in calculating the CO. In short, it says that by utilizing an indicator and monitoring the quantity of indicator which is taken up by the organs as well as its concentration in venous and arterial blood, the flow of blood to an organ may be determined.

CO is measured using the formula:

$$CO = VO_2 / CaO_2 - Cvo_2$$

In this formula, CvO 2 and CaO2 are the mixed and arterial-venous oxygen contents, respectively, and VO 2 is the oxygen consumption. In a closed rebreathing circuit, the VO 2 can be monitored with a spirometer. Blood samples from a pulmonary artery catheter (PAC) (deoxygenated blood) and a peripheral arterial line (oxygenated blood) are used to quantify arterial and mixed venous oxygen, respectively [21,22].

Constant measurements' bias is eliminated or reduced through repeated calibration. It speaks of the process of assessing and modifying the tool's accuracy and precision. By using correction factors based on the patient's demographics (patient age, weight, gender, etc.) or computations, non-calibrated procedures attempt to eliminate bias. However, calibration will frequently be required in circumstances where aortic compliance, afterload, preload, and contractility might all fluctuate significantly (such as in critical illness) [23].

Invasive techniques:

Pulmonary artery catheter (PAC): PAC is the gold standard technique, it is a flow-directed catheter that passes from the right atrium via the right ventricle until it reaches the pulmonary artery. It is inserted through an introduction into the subclavian, jugular, or less frequently, the femoral vein. It enables direct, simultaneous monitoring of the right atrium's PAOP and PAP, CO, or wedge pressures, which are a good indicator of the left atrium's filling pressures. Given since no other monitoring system can directly assess the pressure levels, the best predictor for the PAC is still pulmonary hypertension or right ventricular heart failure [24,25].

Low-invasive techniques:

Transpulmonary thermodilution: the PICCO system, the PiCCO system measures CO intermittently (for calibration) and continuously using an arterial line with a thermistor and a central vein catheter. Compared to PAC, this method has a number of benefits, including the ability to examine fluid response, a real continuous CO, and promptly available readings. Its disadvantages include the requirement for a specific arterial line, which is commonly implanted in the femoral artery, a central venous line, which is implanted in the jugular or subclavian vein, and routine calibration, which must be done three to four times daily with cold fluid boluses (extra fluid load). The volume assessment is not constant or automatic [26,27].

Transpulmonary thermodilution: the VolumeView ®/EV1000 ® system (calibrated):It is comparable to the PiCCO method but different in that it uses a formula to estimate the maximum upslope and downslope times of the thermodilution curve, whereas the PiCCO system uses the time constant obtained from the mean presentation, mean passage, and downward slope of the thermodilution curve [28,29]

Transpulmonary dye dilution: the LiDCO ® system (calibrated): the LiDCO process utilizes lithium as an intravascular indicator instead of thermal dilution, which is administered into a central or peripheral vein and detected in a peripheral artery using a customized sensor probe connected to the pressure line. It is connected to a system for measuring pulse contours [30].

Ultrasound flow dilution: the COstatus ® system (calibrated): the COstatus ® system uses transpulmonary ultrasound dilution technology to evaluate changes in blood flow and ultrasound velocity after saline injection in order to determine CO [31].

Pulse contour and pulse pressure analysis (non-calibrated): The method of pulse pressure monitoring is used by a number of devices to calculate CO. The challenge is that in order to calculate CO from pulse pressure measurement, one would have to make an educated guess on the pressure-volume relationship of the aorta in addition to data about the heart rate and blood pressure. A three-element model that integrates arterial compliance, aortic characteristic impedance, and systemic vascular resistance serves as the foundation for the majority of the procedures in use today. These models function rather well in individuals who are stable but are inaccurate in patients who are unstable or when vasoactive medications are used [32].

System for measuring cardiac output produced from inhaling partial CO2 (NiCO®) (non-calibrated): The CO is measured by NiCO® using a partial rebreathing technique. The system comprises a pulse oximeter coupled with a CO 2 and airflow sensor. By dividing the respiratory minute capacity by the exhaled CO2 content, we may calculate CO2 generation [33].

Transesophageal echocardiography: In perioperative and critical care medicine, transesophageal echocardiography (TEE) is a vital cardiovascular diagnostic technique. Real-time views of the heart architecture and blood flow are provided using ultrasound. In combination with other invasive or less invasive monitoring, it may aid in defining pathophysiological anomalies in patients such as valvulopathy, pulmonary hypertension, pericardial effusions, and abnormalities of wall motion [34].

Esophageal doppler: To calculate the stroke volume and CO, the blood circulation in the descending aorta is monitored using a pliable ultrasound probe. With the exception of dislocation, this probe can be left in place for extended periods of time and can interpret afterload and real-time CO data. It offers numerous other measures in addition to a preload estimation using the adjusted flow time [35].

Non-invasive techniques:

Transthoracic echocardiography: Pulsed wave Doppler velocities in the left ventricular outflow route (LVOT) can be used by TTE to quantify CO. The right ventricular outflow tract (RVOT), ascending aorta, pulmonary artery, and mitral valve annulus are additional locations where it can be measured, however, these have received less validation [36].

Non-invasive pulse contour systems: Depending on an arterial pulse pressure curve that is determined using a completely non-invasive technique, these devices aim to calculate CO [36].

Bioimpedance: A modest current of electricity is applied via skin electrodes. The impedance and/or amount of the conducting tissues then fluctuate, resulting in variations in voltage over the circuit.

Because blood has a low resistance, variations in the intrathoracic volume of blood have a significant effect on impedance [37].

Estimated continuous cardiac output: With the help of an algorithm based on the characteristics of patients and measurements of the patient's pulse rate, non-invasive blood pressure, and oxygen saturation in the periphery, this non-invasive gadget estimates the CO. These measures are used to calculate the pulse wave transit time, which is then used along with the heart rate to calculate the CO [38].

Ultrasonic cardiac output monitoring (USCOM ®): USCOM® calculates the pre-calculated valve areas and the rate of flow inside the pulmonary and aortic outflow tracts to determine a CO. It has a low procedural risk and a quick learning curve [39].

Indications of hemodynamic monitoring:

Although the level of monitoring for each patient transferred to the ICU should be consistent, it might vary. Perhaps all that is needed for hemodynamically stable patients is constant electrocardiographic (ECG) monitoring, routine non-invasive blood pressure checks, and peripheral pulse oximetry. An arterial line should be inserted for constant invasive blood pressure monitoring and routine investigation of arterial blood gases in patients who are unstable or at risk of becoming unstable. A central venous line is necessary for administering medications to patients undergoing vasopressors or inotropic as well as, when necessary, for measuring central venous pressure (CVP) and central venous saturation of oxygen (ScvO 2). Advanced hemodynamic monitoring will be necessary to direct medical therapy once initial resuscitation is unable to improve the patient's hemodynamic and/or respiratory state. We can determine whether vasopressors, inotropic, or fluid resuscitation, medications are still necessary by monitoring CO and its constituents (contractility, afterload, and preload). According to the hemodynamic profile, it may be used as a diagnostic tool to identify the kind of shock (obstructive, hypovolemic, distributive, or cardiogenic) [40-43].

Echocardiography (ECG):

The powerful technology of echocardiography (also known as echo) enables at-the-bedside evaluation of the patient's hemodynamic status as well as direct viewing and evaluation of all cardiac structures. In addition to detecting intracardiac/intrapulmonary shunts, echo allows for the diagnosis of valvular disease, the assessment of ventricular function as well as the pericardium, the calculation of flows, and the determination of relative pressures between both cardiac chambers [45]. It serves as a primary instrument for a thorough assessment of patients hospitalized in the Intensive Care unit (ICU). It is non-invasive, secure, reasonably priced, widely accessible, and enables an evaluation of the heart's hemodynamic, functional, and anatomical properties [46].

Focused cardiac echocardiography has developed into a vital diagnostic tool for the emergency room doctor and the Intensive Care physician caring for patients who are in shock, have had chest trauma, are experiencing shortness of breath and chest pain, as well as those who are presenting with these symptoms. Cardiac echocardiography enables the rapid diagnosis of cardiac tamponade and pericardial effusions, as well as the assessment of cardiac volume and contractility status. It also enables the identification of right ventricular strain, which may be present in the presence of a sizable pulmonary embolism [44].

Although traditionally thought of as the purview of cardiologists, the use of echo has grown in recent years to include other disciplines, including anesthesia. A sizable portion of patients can receive satisfactory results using transthoracic echocardiography (TTE). Transesophageal echocardiography (TEE), on the other hand, may offer a clearer assessment when the ultrasound signal quality is low or in specific clinical situations, such as acute aortic illnesses and valvular diseases [47,48].

A general practitioner is sufficient to operate an echocardiogram, real-time results are acquired, and information is provided prior to invasive monitoring are some of its benefits. Despite the potential applications, most intensivists still find it difficult to receive echocardiography training. The Intensive Care unit (ICU) imaging poses significant technical challenges, such as poor lighting, difficulty positioning patients, weight gain due to edema and/or surgical emphysema, chest drainages, positive pressure ventilation, abdominal/chest dressings, and changing rapidly hemodynamic assistance and ventilatory settings [47].

In the Intensive Care unit, unstable patients frequently have hypotension. The last stage of various cardiovascular illnesses, "cardiogenic shock" can develop from sustained hypotension. Severe left ventricular (LV) systolic dysfunction, any condition that results in the heart's underfilling due to hypovolemia (such as dehydration, hemorrhage, allergy, or sepsis), and increased LV filling pressure (eg: significant LV remodeling, cardiac tamponade, valvular disease) are the clinical circumstances that define hypotension most frequently [49].

In a number of the clinical situations already covered, hypotension is frequently accompanied by dyspnea, but an acute pulmonary embolism is a condition in which this association is most prominent. TTE can only offer hazy indicators of pulmonary embolism, however, TEE should help with the diagnosis because it is highly accurate at spotting thrombi in the pulmonary arteries [50]. Other prevalent main causes of breathlessness in patients who are admitted to the ICU include myocardial infarction and acute heart failure. TTE is a highly helpful technique for diagnosing these conditions, determining LV diastolic and systolic function, and directing patient care [51].

Chest pain, which can be present in different clinical scenarios and is linked to LV systolic failure, is typically the initial symptom of acute coronary syndrome and its consequences. Aortic dissection, on the other hand, is a significant additional potential cause of chest pain that need to constantly be taken into account in the ICU [51]. TTE can accurately rule out type B aortic dissection because it can assess the ascending aorta, aortic root, and proximal region of the aortic arch well, but it cannot evaluate the distal portion of the arch and the descending thoracic aorta. TEE can help with the diagnosis because it makes the descending aorta more visible [52].

Because it enables a thorough assessment of cardiac anatomy, function, and hemodynamics and provides important information for the treatment and diagnosis of the pathological processes most frequently encountered in ICU patients, an echocardiogram is an essential tool in the management of patients in the Intensive Care unit [53]

For the purpose of preparing Intensive Care clinicians for Level 1 competence in echocardiogram and chest ultrasonography, Fast assessment diagnostic echocardiography (FADE) is a formative program. Over the course of two days, a variety of blended learning strategies are used, including practical instruction on live models, ICU study performances, theoretical presentations, and clinical case presentations of recorded exams [54,55].

Chapter 9:

Catheter insertion: arterial and venous

In Intensive Care units and operating rooms, arterial catheterization is a routine technique. It entails inserting a catheter into the luminal of an artery in order to enable constant access to arterial blood samples and at least a continual display of blood pressure. For arterial blood gas sampling and invasive blood pressure monitoring, a vascular access device known as the arterial catheter is introduced into an artery. Arterial catheter use is typically limited to critical care settings [56,57].

Different places of insertion are attainable with an understanding of anatomy. Carl Ludwig, a German physiologist, discovered the existence of the arterial waveform in 1847 by inserting a catheter into an artery. The well-known Seldinger technique has lately been used, which involves directing a catheter into a vessel over a wire that has already been placed into the lumen or the artery [56].

Indications: Physicians can keep an eye on intra-arterial blood pressure on a real-time basis thanks to arterial catheters. This is crucial for the administration of vasodilators and inotropes, two vasoactive infusions, but it's also crucial for individuals with uncontrolled blood pressure. Clinical staff can titrate vasoactive drugs to meet predetermined clinical status thanks to the availability of reliable, real-time hemodynamic information. Since the arterial waveform is utilized to time the intra-aortic balloon pump (IABP) with the cardiac cycle, arterial monitoring is crucial for patients who need an IABP. Numerous clinical circumstances in Intensive Care units necessitate continuous arterial blood pressure monitoring in addition to routine arterial blood sampling for carbon dioxide, partial pressure oxygen, and pH determination analyses. This is crucial when administering vasoactive drugs since the clinician must make decisions about the dosage of these medications based on minute-by-minute assessments. Sometimes, life-saving methods call for perfusing an extracorporeal circuit under the force of arterial blood flow. Inserting an arterial catheter for constant arterio-venous hemoperfusion, often known as dialysis, is a routine procedure [58,59].

Contraindications: clinicians must be careful while inserting the arterial catheter to avoid serious complications. Anatomical variations where there could be an absence of collateral circulation (absence of the ulnar artery), distal or peripheral arterial vascular inadequacies, peripheral arterial vascular diseases (medium to small vessel arteritis), and infection there at site of insertion are examples of contraindications. Coagulation disorders, medication anticoagulation, burns, and surgical treatments at the point of insertion should all receive special attention [56, 60].

Arterial catheter insertion sites:

Due to its low complication risk and convenience of access, the radial artery is the most often used location to implant an arterial catheter. The ulnar and radial arteries give blood to the hand. If the ulnar artery is patent and supplies sufficient collateral blood flow, catheterization of the radial artery shouldn't impair hand perfusion. Prior to catheterization, Allen's test is generally carried out to evaluate the safety of radial artery catheterization. The patient is requested to clench and unclench their fist until the hand turns white in order to do an Allen test, which involves blocking the radial and ulnar arteries with digital pressure. The ulnar artery is then freed, and the perfusion of the limb is checked. Collateral circulation is deemed adequate if color returned to the entire hand despite the radial artery being blocked. The ulnar artery perfusion is deemed to be inadequate if the hand is blanched for 15 seconds or more; arterial catheterization should not be continued [61,57].

A modified Allen's test may be used in Intensive Care since many critically sick patients are unconscious or drugged and are unable to comply with the conventional Allen's test. A modified Allen's test involves occluding the radial artery and monitoring the limb's perfusion. The collateral circulation from the ulnar artery is deemed adequate if the limb maintains its pink color [60].

The second site of preference for an arterial catheter is frequently the femoral artery. Both palpation and catheterization are relatively simple procedures. Since there is no collateral supply for the femoral artery, there is a significant clinical risk of limb ischemia. There is debate over whether there is a higher chance of infection at the femoral location [60,61]

Long-term use of the brachial artery is not advised because it has no collateral circulation and is simple to palpate in the antecubital fossa [60].

Collateral circulation benefits the posterior tibial and dorsalis pedis arteries. Despite reports of beneficial use, the dorsalis pedis is rarely used in therapeutic settings because of the potential risk of dislodgment. In children and newborns, successful tibial artery catheterization has been documented. A child case report of severe ischemic damage that required amputation does exist. Although the axillary artery has received much attention in research, it is rarely chosen for arterial catheterization in clinical practice [62].

Technique:

Palpation: The operator needs to be aware of the arterial vessel's anatomical position before inserting the arterial catheter. Finding the right spot for the process is demonstrated by the direct examination of the arterial pulse. The position of arterial insertion will affect the angle of insertion, and the depth of the artery present in the subcutaneous tissue will also affect the degree of difficulty [62].

Allen test: Prior to inserting a radial arterial catheter, this is a well-known, traditional method. This test is intended to confirm that there is adequate collateral ulnar artery blood flow to prevent distal ischemic damage [62].

Doppler auditory assistance: An auditory doppler instrument can help the operator fine-tune the entry point for accessing the needle in conjunction with palpating the arterial pulse. When the arterial pulse is hard to localize due to weak pulsations caused by low blood pressure, this gadget may be especially useful [61,62].

Ultrasound guidance: A high success rate has been linked to the use of ultrasound guidance during the radial, arterial-line placement technique. Due to the varied artery caliber that is anticipated in newborns, young infants, and older children, this measurement may be especially significant in pediatric patients. The norm of care today is artery cannulation guided by ultrasound [63].

Seldinger technique: With the aid of a guidewire, the operator is able to access the artery lumen using this technique [60].

Catheter over the needle: Peripheral arteries which run more superficially and are easily perceptible can also be accessed using the standard procedure for introducing a peripheral venous catheter [61].

Securing the arterial catheter: This operation is helpful to extend the catheter's lifespan and prevent the need for additional procedures. The best dressings for direct visualization of the site of insertion are transparent adhesive dressings [61].

Arterial catheter monitoring: Once the catheter has been successfully inserted, it is critical to be aware of any potential traps when interpreting the data while taking into consideration the correct transducer location and system dampening. For instance, the data will provide an unnaturally high-pressure value if the transducer is positioned too low in relation to the catheter, whereas the data will produce an abnormally low-pressure value if the transducers are positioned too high in relation to the catheter [60,61].

Care and management of arterial catheter: Comparatively speaking to other vascular access devices, arterial catheters have a higher risk of bleeding. Making ensuring the vascular catheter is always visible is a good idea for this reason. This is quite simple if the device is in the hand or foot, but more challenging for femoral devices. In order to prevent hemorrhage from going undetected, the device must be checked properly and frequently if it is not visible. Blood may collect beneath the patient if bleeding is coming from the femoral site, tracking down to the groin and making blood loss difficult to notice [64].

To avoid accidentally administering IV drugs, arterial catheters should indeed be clearly marked as such. Labels should be put at any stopcocks in the hemodynamic monitoring system and where the catheter will be inserted. An arterial catheter used to administer medication has the potential to cause amputation, gangrene, compartment syndrome, discomfort, and motor impairment. Similar to a venous cannula, the arterial catheter insertion site needs to be checked regularly for any signs of infection, edema, bleeding, irritation, or leakage. The gadget should be taken out if any of these warning indicators are present [64,65].

Blood flow may be hampered by arterial catheters, hence perfusion studies are crucial. It is important to check the distal limb for capillary filling, movement, temperature, color, and feeling. When using wide-bore femoral IABP catheters, which have the potential to significantly reduce distal blood flow, foot pulses should be monitored [65].

Central venous catheter*:*

The terminal lumen of a central venous catheter (CVC) is located within the superior vena cava, inferior vena cava, or right atrium after being advanced into a major, central vein (most frequently the subclavian, internal jugular, or femoral). These components and the methods used to install them are referred to as "central lines" or "central venous access." The first description of a CVC location dates back to 1929 [66].

Insertion sites:

The common femoral, internal jugular and subclavian veins are the three main access points for the implantation of central venous catheters. For the temporary implantation of conspicuous venous catheters, certain locations are favored. The internal jugular vein (IJ) is frequently used for procedures because of its dependable structure, accessibility, low risk of complications, and capacity for ultrasound guiding. The right IJ creates a more direct path to the right atrium and superior vena cava (SVC) as compared to the left. Additionally, it is wider and more superficial, making cannulation likely simpler. The IJ site can be reached anteriorly, posteriorly, or centrally at the sternocleidomastoid muscle (SCM) bifurcation when anatomic landmarks are applied [66].

The subclavian vein location benefits from having low rates of thrombotic and infectious complications. Furthermore, the SC site is reachable in trauma situations where a cervical collar precludes the use of the IJ. The non-compressible site posterior to the clavicle and a significantly increased risk of pneumothorax is drawbacks, as is the limited availability of ultrasound during CVC installation [67].

In severely ill patients, the femoral site is occasionally preferred since it is free of various resuscitation tools and gadgets that could be needed for observing and airway access. The common femoral vein has the advantage of being a readily compressible location, which may be beneficial in individuals with trauma as well as other coagulopathic conditions. Iatrogenic pneumothorax is not a problem, unlike the IJ and SC locations. Because it allows for more arm and leg mobility than other locations, a femoral CVC may make patients feel more at ease [68]

Indications: There are many different and frequently contextual indications for central venous access. They are, in no particular order: [69]

Multiple infusions may not be possible with peripheral intravenous access for treatments like chemotherapy, total parenteral nutrition, vasopressors, and other acidic drugs administered to peripheral veins. Unable to get venous access in an emergency. The starts of extracorporeal treatments such as continuous renal replacement therapy, plasmapheresis, and hemodialysis. Monitoring of the hemodynamics, such as central venous pressures. For venous procedures such as intravenous stenting, the installation of an inferior vena cava filter, thrombolytic treatment, and transvenous cardiac pacing.

Contraindications: Central venous catheter placement has both relative and absolute contraindications, some of which may be site-specific.

Relative contraindications: Coagulopathy, despite the fact that only 0.8% of cases involve clinically severe bleeding. The risk of adverse outcomes appears to be higher in people who have thrombocytopenia. An uncooperative patient who is awake. landmark distortion caused by birth defects or trauma. morbidly obese [69].

Absolute contraindications: At the prospective location of the central line, there is an active skin or soft tissue infection. Implantable/indwelling devices at the site, such as pacemakers and hemodialysis catheters, might cause anatomical deformation. Vascular injuries close to or far from the catheter insertion site, such as those caused by trauma [69].

Patients who have significant coagulopathy and a higher risk of bleeding typically have an international normalized ratio (INR) of greater than 3.0. Based on the emergency of the clinical situation, it may be justified to think about delivering fresh frozen platelets and plasma prior to the treatment or shortly thereafter. Site-specific contraindications need to be evaluated case by case. Due to the SC site's physical proximity to numerous other important veins and the proceduralist's difficulty to maintain pressure in the case of an unintentional arterial puncture or rupture of the vein itself, the procedure is contraindicated in coagulopathic patients. If a cervical collar is in situ or if the IJ site will be needed for another invasive surgery during the same hospitalization, the IJ site may be somewhat contraindicated. Similarly, if it is expected that femoral access would be required for a procedure like cardiac catheterization, the femoral site should be avoided [70,71]

The central venous catheter kit contains: (Large Bore Single-lumen, Dual-lumen, or triple-lumen) Central venous catheter. a syringe and an introducer needle of 18 gauge. #11 blade Scalpel. Guidewire. Vasodilator. Suture material, is usually made of 3-0 silk suture and used with a straight needle or a needle driver. Saline lock (number varies according to the device's kind). tiny gauge needle (25 or 27 gauge), syringe, with 1% lidocaine [71].

Complications: There are many potential issues that could arise not just from the indwelling equipment but also from the procedure of placing a central venous catheter.

Procedural: Due to guidewire discomfort of the atria or ventricles, arrhythmias frequently manifest as bundle branch blockages or ventricular irregularities. arterial laceration. Pulmonary puncture that results in a pneumothorax or not. Hematoma development from bleeding can restrict the airway. Tracheal damage. During venous puncture or catheter removal, air emboli occur [72].

Postprocedural complications: Bacterial or fungal bloodstream infections caused by catheters. Stenosis of the central vein. Thrombosis. Multiple efforts at delayed bleeding in a coagulopathic patient [72].

Chapter 10:

Cardiac pacing and DC cardioversion

Cardiac pacing: With Hyman's "artificial pacemaker" (his term), which used a hand crank to generate an electric current that drove a DC generator from where electrical impulses were sent to the patient's right atrium through a needle electrode positioned intercostally, cardiac pacing, or by stimulatinf electricity to modify or create cardiac mechanical activity, got its start in the 1930s [73].

The development of permanent cardiac pacing is among the most significant medical breakthroughs of the 20th century. Sick sinus syndrome is presently the most typical reason for permanent pacemaker placement, despite the fact that it was initially created to treat Stokes-Adams episodes (in patients with total heart block) [74].

The sinus node, which acts as the heart's pacemaker, is where normal cardiac activity starts. After crossing the atria to reach the atrioventricular (AV) node, electrical wavefronts quickly spread to and depolarized the ventricles by entering the His-Purkinje system. When intrinsic cardiac automatic processing or integrity of conduction starts to fail, the electrical increased activity of cardiac tissue enables an external, small electrical stimulus to start driving myocytes to the threshold, resulting in the depolarization of nearby myocytes through biological processes that consume energy and the subsequent transmission of an electrical wave front, with nearly instantaneous muscle contractions via excitation-contraction coupling [77]. Pacemakers deliver this outside stimulus. In order to administer depolarizing pulses and detect intrinsic cardiac activity, pacemakers have leads that extend from a pulse generator or container that houses the batteries and electronics into the myocardium. Whenever a voltage difference (potential difference) is supplied between both the two electrodes, pacing happens. In bipolar pacing, the cathode of the lead tip and a proximal ring (anode) have a different potential. Current is transmitted between both the lead point and the pulse generator can during unipolar pacing. The stimulation threshold is the lowest amount of energy needed in depolarizing the myocardium. The amplitude (which is measured in volts) and duration (that is measured in milliseconds) of the delivered stimulus serve as two descriptors [75,76].

Indications of cardiac pacing: Cardiac electrical signalling is disrupted by illnesses of the sinoatrial node, Atrioventricular (AV) node, or His-Purkinje system brought on by ageing, inflammation, fibrosis, infarction, or other disorders. Pacing is typically recommended when symptomatic bradycardias occur.

A temporary pacemaker is preferable if the bradyarrhythmia is reproducible, which is a crucial factor to take into account. Examples include inferior myocardial ischemia or Lyme disease, which can both present with worrisome bradycardia but frequently heal spontaneously within a week [78]. Beta-blockers, calcium-channel blockers, the majority of antiarrhythmic medications, ivabradine, as well as other medications, as well as obstructive sleep disorder (especially during apnea), infectious diseases (Lyme disease, psittacosis, Legionnaires' disease, Chagas disease, typhoid fever, Q fever, typhus, among others), and metabolic conditions (hypothyroidism, hypothermia, hypoxia, and anorexia nervosa). Heart rates may slow in younger people with hyper-vagotonia associated with exercise or vasovagal episodes. The kind of conduction system defect (sinus node, AV node, or intraventricular conduction delay, such as a left bundle branch block) that warrants pacing will dictate the type of pacemaker (atrial, dual-chamber, ventricular, or biventricular) [79,80].

DC cardioversion:

In the 1950s, external electrical cardioversion (EEC) was initially used. This initial experience showed that the heart might be stimulated by electrical energy that was externally applied to the thorax. Either direct current (DC) energy or alternating current (AC) energy can be used to provide electrical counter shocks. Sinusoidal energy waveforms called alternating currents alternate among negative and positive polarity. Once discharged, the energetic pulse lasts for about 200 ms. Due to the larger energy flux and duration, alternating current defibrillation can seriously harm the myocardium. DC cardioversions, whether urgent or elective, provide several benefits, including the cessation of ventricular and atrial tachycardia and restoration of sinus rhythm [81,82].

It is unclear exactly how defibrillation works. According to Zipes et al., the primary contributor to the process of electrical defibrillation is the failure of the remaining cardiac tissue to sustain the reentrant tachycardia following depolarization of a critical threshold. Another study team contends that defibrillation shock waves can stop ventricular fibrillation by prolonging refractoriness in a sufficient amount of myocardial tissue (VF). 3 It is unknown whether the mechanisms proposed for the cessation of VF are comparable to those used for atrial fibrillation (AF) [83].

Indications:

Atrial fibrillation and atrial flutter: The majority of electrical cardioversion procedures are currently used to change atrial flutter and AF into sinus rhythm. Since it is paroxysmal, AF that occurs in Intensive Care units following cardiac surgery is not a candidate for electrical cardioversion [81].

Ventricular and supraventricular tachycardia: When ventricular tachycardia becomes unstable and worsens hemodynamically, emergency electrical cardioversion is done. Treatment for ventricular tachycardia is to end this impairment as soon as possible. In the event that vagotonic maneuvers, such as carotid sinus massaging for persistent supraventricular tachycardia, and antiarrhythmic medication are ineffective, electrical cardioversion should be the next course of action. Typically, 95% of ventricular tachycardia cardioversion attempts are successful [84].

Other rhythm disorders: Treatment with electrical shocks fails to stop automaticity-related tachycardias. This type of multifocal atrial tachycardia is frequently mistaken for AF, which could result in the incorrect administration of direct current (DC) shocks [85].

For recurring (within hours or even days) paroxysms (self-terminating episodes) of AF, serial DC shocks are inappropriate. This scenario occurs quite frequently in cardiac surgery recovery rooms or in Intensive Care units [86].

Inability of DC cardioversion to stop automatic tachycardias Multifocal atrial tachycardia may appear to be atrial fibrillation on the surface. The 12-lead electrocardiogram should be carefully examined to prevent the delivery of an unnecessary shock. In cases of digitalis poisoning, electrical cardioversion is also not advised [82].

The presence of anticoagulation is typically not a problem when cardioverting ventricular arrhythmias. The objective is the quick eradication of (or prevention against) hemodynamic deterioration that poses a hazard to life. In order to reduce the risk of emboli and strokes while elective cardioversion of atrial fibrillation, anticoagulation is crucial [82].

Complications: Minimal complications arise. Inadequate anticoagulant therapy can cause thromboembolism, atrial arrhythmia, non-sustained VT, bradycardia, heart block, necrosis of the myocardium, transient left bundle branch block, transient hypotension, myocardial dysfunction, pulmonary edoema, and skin burn. These are just a few of the potential side effects. The quantity of applications is correlated with pain at the site of application. In stable individuals with left atrial thrombosis and inadequate anesthetic, EEC is contraindicated [81].

According to several researchers, electrical cardioversion is secure during pregnancy. Cardioversion performed at different stages of pregnancy with energies between 50 J and 300 J showed no effects on the fetus, indicating that a potentially dangerous electrical charge may not reach the fetus [81].

Patients who undergo electrical cardioversion while wearing a pacemaker or an ICD risk developing malfunction, such as acute or long-term alterations in the pacing or sensitive thresholds. If a person with a pacemaker needs to have cardioversion, the device's leads should be tested for functionality, and high-voltage programming should also be done. The defibrillator paddles should be positioned at least 15 cm away from the pacemaker during cardioversion. They ought to be placed perpendicular to the endocardial, anterolateral, or anterior leads. Patients with pacemakers or ICDs may be at risk for burns in the cardiac tissue in which the pacemaker lead is connected during cardioversion if the electrical charge is administered through it [81].

Chapter 11:

Cardiopulmonary Resuscitation

When a person experiences cardiac arrest, a series of procedures known as cardiopulmonary resuscitation (CPR) are used to revive them. The efforts of a few doctors in the 1950s led to the development of our present modern method for handling this process, which will be covered in more detail here. The American Heart Association's recommendations are the ones that are most frequently recognized in North America (AHA). Ventricular fibrillation is the most typical cause of sudden cardiac arrest in adults. Even though improvements in emergency cardiac treatment have increased survival rates, sudden cardiac arrest continues to be a major cause of death in many regions of the world [87].

Electrical defibrillation is the only effective therapy for ventricular fibrillation. Most frequently, an automatic external defibrillator (AED) is used for this. Brain death is most likely to happen in even less than 10 minutes if an AED is not easily accessible for defibrillation. In order to maintain artificial breathing and circulation till defibrillation can be done, CPR is used. When performed correctly, traditional manual CPR, which combines chest compressions and emergency breathing, can restore up to 33% of a person's normal cardiac output and oxygenation [87].

In Europe, sudden cardiac arrest (SCA) is among the major causes of death. If onlookers take prompt action while VF remains present, more SCA sufferers will survive. Once the rhythm has degenerated to asystole, the likelihood of successful resuscitation decreases [94].

VF cardiac arrest is advised to be treated with quick bystander CPR & quick electrical defibrillation. The majority of non-cardiac cardiac arrests are caused by respiratory conditions including hypoxia and drowning, which affect many youngsters. Chest compressions and rescue breathing are essential for the effective resuscitation of these individuals [94].

The chain of survival: The crucial connections required for an effective resuscitation are enumerated in The Chain of Survival [94].

Earlier recognition and call for emergency help: Recognizing chest pain as a sign of myocardial ischaemia is important. Within the initial hour of the development of chest pain, cardiac arrest happens in 25 to 30 percent of myocardial ischaemic patients. Recognizing the cardiac origin of chest pain and contacting emergency personnel prior to a victim passing out allows the emergency services to arrive earlier, perhaps before a cardiac arrest has happened, which improves survival. Early detection of cardiac arrest is essential to permit immediately activating the EMS and the beginning of bystander CPR. Unresponsiveness and irregular respiration are the main findings.

Early bystander CPR: CPR should be started right away to increase survival rates after cardiac arrest by two to four times. If possible, onlookers who have received CPR training should perform both ventilations and chest compressions [94].

Early defribillation: When defibrillation occurs within three to five minutes of collapse, survival rates can reach 50 to 70%. Public access and on-site AEDs can help with this. Delaying defibrillation for even one minute lowers the likelihood of surviving to discharge by 10-12%.

Standardized post-resuscitation care and early advanced life care: If early efforts at resuscitation are unsuccessful, advanced life support may be required, including airway control, medications, and correcting causative causes [94].

The reader is guided through the process of recognising cardiac arrest, dialling EMS, beginning CPR, and utilising an AED. To concentrate on the important actions, the number of steps taken has been decreased. The method is described as a linear series of stages for clarity's sake. It is acknowledged that the initial stages of assessing reaction, opening the airway, confirming breathing, and dialling an ambulance dispatcher may be carried out simultaneously or quickly.

Opening the airway and checking for breathing: The skilled caretaker needs to quickly check the sufferer who has collapsed to see if they are breathing regularly and responsive [94].

While determining whether the patient is breathing normally, open the airways by using a head tilt and chin lift approach.

Emergency services are alerted: Early communication with emergency personnel will help the dispatcher recognize cardiac arrest, give CPR instructions over the telephone, dispatch emergency services and first responders, and help find and dispatch an AED [94].

Chest compressions: To activate the emergency medical services (EMS) response and start CPR as soon as possible, the cardiac arrest must be recognized as soon as possible. Call for assistance after making sure the area is secure. Start CPR simultaneously by conducting chest compressions (C), then clearing the airway (A), and finally giving rescue breaths (B) (the sequence of CAB compared to the formerly done ABC sequence). Chest compressions are started at a frequency of 100 to 120 per minute with the hands placed on the lower side of the sternum. While avoiding excessive depths of compression, the objective is to depress the sternum to a minimum depth of two inches [88].

To keep the pressure in the coronary arteries perfusing, the walls of the chest should be permitted to fully recoil on the upstroke. After completing 30 compressions, there is a short pause for 2 rescue breaths. Chest compressions must continue as much as feasible with as little interruption as feasible when necessary because of the crucial role they play in coronary artery perfusion.

The rescuer conducts a head tilt/chin lift procedure to free the airway after 30 chest compressions (considering that there is no suspicion of injury to the cervical spine). If cervical spine trauma is thought to have occurred, the jaw-thrust maneuver is used to clear the airway without elevating the head. Two rescuing breaths are given: the rescuer takes a "normal" breath (not one that is deep or prolonged) and gives a second-long rescue breath that should be long enough to start allowing the chest to rise. Before starting again with chest compressions, the procedure is repeated again for a second rescue breath [88].

An ideal barrier device, like that of a rescue mask, should be readily available to a healthcare worker who is willing to act as an outside rescuer. This isn't always the case, though. The alternative to this is mouth-to-mouth rescue breaths, which many unskilled rescuers are reluctant to carry out, especially on an unidentified victim. Healthcare professionals must decide for themselves on this. For unskilled lay rescuers, compression-only CPR has been acknowledged as adequate. Compression-only CPR should indeed be administered until EMS arrived if extenuating circumstances prevent a health professional in and out setting from doing rescue breathing without the need for a barrier device [89].

Until an AED is available or until more assistance arrives, the sequence of 30 chest compressions accompanied by two rescue breaths is continued. If an AED is present, the pads should be placed on the patient's front and back while being careful to repeat chest compressions as soon as possible. The majority of contemporary devices speak further instructions; after being hooked to the patient, AEDs will determine the patient's present cardiac rhythm and recommend whether defibrillation is necessary. Stop compressions of the chest and keep away from the person till defibrillation is complete if the AED recommends a shock. Restart cycles of rescue breaths and chest compressions immediately after defibrillation are finished, or if no shock is recommended until more assistance is available [90].

Complications: The prognosis for cardiac arrest is grim; the majority of individuals do not survive. Those who do survive may experience varied degrees of neurologic impairment from hypoxia encephalopathy, which might complicate their hospital stay. Any organ system can be injured by an ischemic stroke. When done appropriately, chest compressions can result in fractured ribs, which can be compounded by pneumothorax [91,92].

Chapter 12:

Unique Bedside Tips CICU

Due to the high volume of operations carried out in operating rooms (OR) and interventional radiology (IR), bedside interventions may relieve the pressure on those services and be completed more quickly by the personnel that is nearest to the patient. Additionally, it was shown that it could stop major negative effects from occurring when transporting patients to the OR or IR. Ultrasound guidance may be required for some patient-bed operations. The ICU team should have access to ultrasound, and portable equipment can be used to guide procedures like paracentesis, pericardial puncture, thoracocentesis, abscess drainage, venous central line placement, or arterial line placement [93].

Since they can be utilized for the monitoring of vascular access or the evacuation of fluid from the pleura, pericardium, abdomen, cystostomy, etc., handheld ultrasound equipment has improved the operations' ease of use in recent years. In individuals with deep vein thrombosis who are contraindicated to anticoagulants or who experience recurrent thromboembolism despite effective anticoagulation, inferior vena cava filters are implanted. The patient's bed can be used for intravascular echography, which is available as rotating or sectorial ultrasonography, to implant filters. At the patient's bedside, transesophageal echocardiography can also be utilized to direct the placement of chemotherapeutic chambers or compartments for continuous high doses of diuretics [94].

The insertion of central venous catheters, arterial lines, pulmonary artery catheterization, percutaneous tracheostomies, pericardiocentesis, port-a-cath lumbar punctures, temporary pacemaker insertion, and suprapubic cystostomies are just a few procedures that make use of special kits that are readily available. These kits contain betadine, catheters, drainage catheters, needles, blades, syringes, bags, and tubes, as well as lidocaine with and without adrenaline for the procedure itself. They also include drapes, gloves, caps, gowns, and masks for the doctor. The package offers the greatest amount of barrier protection and also reduces the likelihood of iatrogenic infection [95].

The way bedside assessment is utilized in the modern ICU varies among institutions and even between different ICUs within the same institution, in particular, understanding this unclear and subpar evidence base. The difficulty of repositioning patients, clinical instability, the existence of ECG monitors, lines and tubes, bulky dressings, and elevated amounts of ambient ICU noise represent common challenges to physical diagnosis. Performing a thorough physical exam in the modern ICU also presents a unique challenge. Although a systematic strategy for PE in the ICU has been promoted, little information exists to describe actual practice [96].

Intensive-care unit (ICU) construction and renovation projects frequently include the formation of multidisciplinary design teams by hospitals. However, experts in infection control are infrequently included on these teams. This exclusion appears shortsighted given that nosocomial infections are frequent in Intensive Care units, architectural elements can influence the risk of transmission of infectious agents, and outbreaks can happen while construction is taking place. Professionals in infection control are knowledgeable about the pertinent research as well as the rules and recommendations pertaining to ICU layout and infection control procedures. In addition to being crucial to the construction and design of safe and efficient units, their participation in the design team can potentially enable the gathering of comparison data, turning the construction project into a research endeavor [97].

Performing bedside procedures: Before deciding to execute a process at the request of the patient in the ICU, we should restrict visitors' access to the area around the patient or possibly the entire unit while the treatment is being performed. This guarantees sterility and offers some degree of seclusion. During the treatment, nurses should be present, and they ought to be knowledgeable about the procedure. Most of the time, propofol, midazolam, and pethidine are required to achieve sufficient sedation. The nurse must be aware of the vial volume and dilution, however, the doctor must prescribe the doses for analgesia and sedation [96]

Adequate planning is essential for the procedure's security, including pre-sedation, intravenous access, first kit preparation, and sufficient surveillance. Depending on the bedside operation being done, specific locations for venous access are preferred. When doing bedside operations on an unstable patient, airway management equipment should be accessible. Before starting a procedure, it is best to get the patient's informed consent whenever possible. If the patient is unstable, consent should be acquired from a member of the family or tutor. The risk of nosocomial pathogens should be understood by every member of the team [98].

Nosocomial device-related infections have been demonstrated to decrease with good hand cleanliness, site selection that is appropriate, the use of proper skin preparatory agents, as well as an aseptic procedure with a complete body drape during device installation [99].

Chapter 13:

Important Topics and Some Conditions That are Managed in CICU

Medical

End-stage Heart failure: Heart failure affects at least 10 million people in Europe and about 5 million in North America, making it a significant public health issue. Heart failure is one of the primary causes of death and hospitalization among the elderly due to its age-dependent increase in prevalence and incidence [100]. The percentage of individuals who progress to an advanced form of the disease, also known as end-stage, refractory, or fatal heart failure, is rapidly increasing due to the rise in life expectancy around the world and advancements in the treatment of heart failure in recent times [101].

Pharmacological management: Unless there are contraindications, angiotensin-converting enzyme (ACE) inhibitors are advised as first-line therapy for all patients with decreased left ventricular (LV) systolic function regardless of clinical symptoms. ACE medications have been proven to improve survival, decrease reinfarctions, and increase hospital stays in people who suffer from heart failure after the acute phase of myocardial infarction [102]. Renal function, serum electrolytes, especially potassium, and blood pressure (lying down and standing) should all be carefully monitored throughout the course of treatment. Angiotensin II type I receptor blockers (ARBs) may be used as an alternative to ACE inhibitors in patients with symptomatic chronic heart failure who cannot take ACE medications to reduce morbidity and mortality [103].

Inhibitors of the renin-angiotensin system should be co-administered with diuretics, which helps improve dyspnea and exercise intolerance because individuals with end-stage heart failure frequently exhibit indications of fluid retention or have a history of doing so. Due to their synergistic method of action, thiazides and loop diuretics can be utilized successfully in the event of a fluid overload that is resistant to treatment in end-stage heart failure. Patients with symptomatic stable systolic heart failure should get further treatment with adrenergic receptor blockers in the absence of contraindications, in addition to the conventional regimen of ACE inhibitors and diuretics [104,105].

Aldosterone receptor antagonists are advised in addition to adrenergic receptor blockers, ACE inhibitors, and diuretics in patients with advanced heart failure unless contraindicated because they are known to increase survival and morbidity. In symptomatic patients with heart failure with tachyarrhythmia caused by atrial fibrillation (AF) who have already received appropriate doses of beta-blockers, cardiac glycosides are recommended for heart rate management. The class III antiarrhythmic amiodarone may restore and maintain sinus rhythm or increase the achievement of electrical cardioversion in heart failure patients with atrial fibrillation (AF). Amiodarone is an effective treatment for the majority of supraventricular and ventricular arrhythmias in patients with heart failure [103, 104].

Surgical management: Cardiovascular resynchronization therapy (CRT) using biventricular pacing improves symptoms and exercise tolerance while lowering hospitalizations and mortality in patients with reduced LV function (ejaculation fraction (EF) 35%), left bundle branch block, sinus rhythm, or echocardiographic signs of ventricular dyssynchrony and QRS width 120 ms [108]. Patients with heart failure in NYHA classes III-IV with LVEF 35% and QRS width 120 ms were randomly assigned to receive the best pharmacological treatment alone, in combination with CRT, or in combination with implantable cardioverter-defibrillator (ICD). Importantly, although mortality was lower in both device arms, there was no discernible difference between CRT and CRT/ICD in terms of mortality [106, 107].

ICD implantation has been found to decrease mortality in cardiac arrest survivors and patients with persistent symptomatic ventricular tachyarrhythmias for secondary prevention of sudden cardiac death (SCD). ICD therapy is recommended for some patients with LVEF 30% after myocardial infarction (>40 days) and in patients with ischaemic and non-ischaemic heart failure (NYHA class II–III) with LVEF 35% to lower mortality for the primary prevention of SCD in heart failure patients receiving optimal pharmacological treatment [109, 110,111].

Cardiogenic shock: The complex disorder known as a cardiogenic shock (CS) is defined by end-organ hypoperfusion brought on by a decrease in cardiac output brought on by a primary cardiac disease. The clinical manifestations of CS might range widely in terms of hemodynamic characteristics [112]. The common factor, though, is insufficient cardiac output necessitating medication and/or artificial circulatory support. A thorough examination of the etiology of CS is necessary for best-practice management in the CICU. Acute myocardial infarction and either acute or chronic heart failure continue to be the most frequent causes of CS. CS is typically compounded by multiorgan system dysfunction, regardless of the etiology, necessitating a multidisciplinary approach to management in an Intensive Care setting [113].

Pulmonary artery catheterization: The pathophysiology of CS is predisposed to metabolic disturbances and hemodynamic instability. Therefore, it's crucial to invasively monitor end-organ perfusion measurements in addition to systemic arterial pressures in order to accurately pinpoint the cause of the shock state. In a critical care situation, the pulmonary artery (PA) catheter is a crucial diagnostic tool that is frequently used to help determine the existence and type of CS as well as to direct treatment [114,115].

Pharmacological management: Inotropes boost cardiac output and contractility in CS. Vasopressors boost systemic vascular resistance by raising vascular tone, which raises blood pressure. Dobutamine, milrinone, norepinephrine, epinephrine, vasopressin, and dopamine are examples of frequently used vasotropes and inotropes. The two main inotropes utilized in a modern CICU are dobutamine and milrinone, and both promote myocardial contractility, albeit in distinct ways. In CS patients with hypotension, vasopressors such as norepinephrine, epinephrine, dopamine, and vasopressin are frequently utilized [116-118]

Non-pharmacological management:

Ultrafiltration: The critical care management of CS includes adjunct nonpharmacologic therapy. Elevated intracardiac filling pressures brought on by fluid and sodium retention by the kidneys as a consequence of neurohormonal activation are frequently seen in acute heart failure and CS [119]. The cornerstone of therapy to relieve congestion is diuretics. However, diuretic resistance can be brought on by proteinuria, reduced renal blood flow, and poor absorption. This vicious cycle is then exacerbated by increased congestion, which can then result in multiorgan dysfunction, including acute renal failure. Acute right ventricular failure may also enhance shock and end-organ failure, decrease left ventricular filling, increase ventricular interdependence, and worsen congestion linked to right ventricular distention [120,121].

Mechanical ventilation: In cases, of necessitating airway protection, or general hemodynamic instability, mechanical ventilation may be necessary. Physiologic objectives for oxygenation or ventilation in CS are not well CS caused by acute hypoxemia, increased labor of breathing, and decreased state of consciousness supported by evidence, despite the significant rate of respiratory failure needing mechanical ventilation. Clinicians need to be aware of how positive pressure ventilation affects the hemodynamics of the left and right ventricles as well as the best analgesics and sedatives to use in CS [122-124].

Acute coronary syndrome: Unstable angina (UA), non-ST elevated myocardial infarction (NSTEMI), and ST-elevated myocardial infarction (STEMI) are all cardiac ischemia conditions that fall under the umbrella term of acute coronary syndrome (ACS). A thorough evaluation of clinical characteristics, such as electrocardiogram (ECG) abnormalities and biochemical indicators of myocardial necrosis, is the foundation for the diagnosis and classification of ACS.

Initial management:

Early: To avoid potentially catastrophic clinical effects and alleviate persistent ischemia, it is critical to assess individuals with suspected ACS right away. It is important to do early risk stratification that takes into account a physical exam, patient's demographics, ECG, medical history, and cardiac biomarker measures.

Pharmacological management:

Antithrombotic agents: A key component of the care of ACS is antiplatelet medication, which lowers the risk of thrombosis by preventing platelet release and aggregation [125].

Clopidogrel- Clopidogrel was a routine treatment for individuals presenting with ACS prior to the release of additional therapeutic medicines. A 2001 experiment that randomly allocated patients who presented with UA or NSTEMI to receive either clopidogrel or a placebo in addition to aspirin for a duration of 3–12 months was the first to show the efficacy of doing so. The primary endpoint of cardiovascular death, nonfatal MI, or stroke was observed to be decreased in the group given dual antiplatelet treatment (DAPT) [125].

Prasugrel- Prasugrel was associated with a substantial 2.2% absolute decrease in a nonfatal MI, a composite endpoint of cardiovascular death, or nonfatal stroke as compared to clopidogrel, according to a 2007 landmark trial comparing the two medications [126].

Ticagrelor- Comparing ticagrelor to clopidogrel, there was a 1.9% absolute reduction in the composite endpoint of vascular mortality, MI, or stroke [127].

Anticoagulants: Parenteral anticoagulants and antiplatelet medications are utilized during the initial therapy of ACS. During this time, parenteral anticoagulants such as fondaparinux, unfractionated heparin (UFH), low-molecular-weight heparin, or bivalirudin may be administered [128].

Adjuvant therapies: For patients presenting with NSTEMI, UA, or STEMI, oral β-blocker medication should be started within 24 hours of the event's beginning. By preventing the actions of catecholamines on β-receptors found in the heart, β-blockers lower myocardial contractility, sinus node rate, and AV node conduction velocity [129].

Valvular heart disease: In the etiology of acute decompensated heart failure, valvular dysfunction occurs as frequently as acute coronary syndromes. Over 10% of people over the age of 75 have significant valvular dysfunction, which is a prevalence that rises with age. Despite solid guidelines for treating valvular heart disease in the general population, there are few studies and guidelines on the treatment of these individuals, particularly in an Intensive Care unit (ICU) setting. When normal inotrope and vasopressor therapy fails to stabilize patients, a number of therapeutic alternatives have become accessible in the last ten years. These include mitral clipping, extracorporeal membrane oxygenation (ECMO), and balloon valvuloplasty in patients with severe aortic valve stenosis and assist devices. In cases of shock brought on by valvular dysfunction, these therapeutic options should be viewed as a bridge to surgical procedures because hemodynamic and stabilization of organ function are crucial for enabling valve repair or replacement, which is still the preferred course of action in this circumstance but is not always feasible in the acute setting [131].

Pericarditis: Clinical manifestations of pericardial disorders include cardiac tamponade, pericardial effusion, acute pericarditis, and constrictive pericarditis [132].

Acute pericarditis: Inflammation of the pericardium causes the common disorder known as acute pericarditis, which can happen on its own or as a symptom of another systemic illness. Three main medications—NSAIDs, colchicine, and corticosteroids—have been the focus of medical treatment for viral or idiopathic acute pericarditis. Patients with myopericarditis have comparable treatment options and prognoses as those with acute pericarditis [132,133].

Constrictive pericarditis: The symptoms and constrictive characteristics of patients with temporary constrictive pericarditis brought on by pericardial inflammation may disappear with medical treatment alone. Surgery is considered the gold standard for treating chronic constrictive pericarditis [137,138].

Cardiac tamponade: Pericardial fluid builds up under pressure, which is a symptom of cardiac tamponade. The parietal pericardium moves less when the pericardial effusion enlarges. Tamponade happens when systemic venous return to the right atrium is compromised due to compression of all heart chambers brought on by elevated intrapericardial pressure [134,135]. A pericardiocentesis or surgical evacuation of pericardial fluid is urgently needed in cases of acute cardiac tamponade with hemodynamic compromise. Although meticulous hemodynamic surveillance with serial echocardiography and therapy of the underlying reason for tamponade may be appropriate in patients with hemodynamically stable individuals. Percutaneous catheter pericardiocentesis or surgical pericardiectomy can be used to drain the pericardial fluid from a patient with cardiac tamponade [136].

Myocarditis: Myocarditis is an inflammatory disease of the myocardium that can be developed as a result of an infection, which may be immune-mediated, or result from exposure to toxins. Acute, subacute, fulminant, and chronic types of myocarditis can occur. A month or less must pass between the onset of symptoms and the diagnosis to be considered acute myocarditis. A severe, fast-progressing form of acute myocarditis called fulminant myocarditis causes cardiogenic shock and necessitates the use of inotropes or mechanical circulatory support. Subacute myocarditis can also be referred to as resolving myocarditis whenever there is evidence of prior active myocarditis. It is characterized by continuous myocardial injury brought on by a chronic or recurring stimulus for myocardial inflammation. when symptoms last for a long time (more than a month) the condition is called chronic inflammatory myocardiopathy [139].

In cases of suspected myocarditis, the etiology and therapy may necessitate the participation of multiple specialists. If a particular cause is found, treatment is focused on the underlying aetiological process or condition, such as corticosteroids or other immunosuppressants in the event of immune-mediated disease or anti-infective medicines in the case of a curable infection [140]. Non-steroidal anti-inflammatory medicines (NSAIDs), which are a cornerstone of pericarditis therapy, are not advised in myocarditis, in part because of their inefficiency and risk for myocarditis exacerbation [141,142]. A temporary mechanical circulatory support device, such as venoarterial extracorporeal membrane oxygenation (VA-ECMO) and rotary blood pumps, may be used to temporarily sustain patients with considerable hemodynamic impairment or fulminant myocarditis. Patients with myocarditis whose heart failure or arrhythmias are resistant to these short-term treatments may be candidates for cardiac transplantation or the implantation of a left ventricular assist device. Such patients need to be discussed right away with a heart transplant facility [143].

Aortic dissection: the most common life-threatening disorder that affects the aorta is acute aortic dissection. The intima is torn, occasionally spreading to the media (entry tear), and the layers are divided during an acute aortic dissection. The deepest layer typically sheds in the direction of blood flow. As a result, a dissection membrane creates a false lumen that is isolated from the genuine lumen. The two lumina and dissection membranes frequently follow the blood flow in the aorta's craniocaudal direction in a spiral pattern [144].

The ascending aorta is not affected by type B aortic dissection, which has the entry tear distal to the outflow of the left subclavian artery. This is in contrast to type A aortic dissection, which affects the ascending aorta, according to the Stanford classification [144].

Pharmacotherapy: Delivery of morphine plus beta-blockers along with vasodilators or ACE inhibitors can result in pain alleviation and systolic blood pressure of 100 to 120 mm Hg. Massive hypertension typically necessitates the conjunction of many antihypertensives; monotherapy rarely works [145].

Surgery: It is imperative to do surgery on type A aortic dissection as soon as possible in order to stop a rupture or the onset of pericardial tamponade. Surgery on the aortic arch and ascending aorta is carried out to treat type A aortic dissection. In the Intensive Care unit, individuals with uncomplicated acute type B aortic dissection must be closely watched. Blood pressure management is crucial. In the event of immediate problems from type B aortic dissection, quick interventional or, rarely, surgical treatment may be taken into consideration. In cases of acute type B aortic dissection with complications, endovascular implantation of stent grafts is now the recommended method for treating distal mal perfusion or impending aortic rupture [146,147].

Vascular diseases: Despite a reduction in cardiovascular disease (CVD)-related mortality over the past three decades, CVD prevalence is still significant. Acute heart failure (AHF) accounts for 5.6% of all emergency hospitalizations in people over the age of 65 and has an inpatient death rate of 11%. 2. In the USA, one in five heart failure patients is hospitalized and admitted to an Intensive Care unit (ICU), and multiorgan failure complicated 31.7% of hospitalizations for cardiogenic shock (CS) brought on by acute myocardial infarction [148]. Therefore, the modern ICU must possess the knowledge and skills necessary to treat acute cardiovascular care across an expanding range and complexity of cardiovascular disorders, either as a presenting disease or as a comorbid illness in critically ill patients hospitalized for other reasons [149].

In order to prevent the development of permanent or irreparable non-cardiac organ dysfunction, general and specialized therapies should be carried out during the first 60–120 minutes of presentation in cardiovascular instability of any etiology [150].

Management of Airway and respiratory- Both as a cause of ICU admission and as a result of worsening cardiac failure in the ICU, associated respiratory impairment is frequent. To enable appropriate tissue oxygenation, arterial oxygen saturation must be restored to normal. Cardiogenic pulmonary edema prevents gas from passing through alveolar membranes, which contributes to hypoxia and hypercarbia and can negatively affect coronary perfusion and pulmonary vascular resistance (PVR). Through the recruitment of alveoli, redistribution of extravascular lung water, improvement of compliance, and surfactant synthesis, non-invasive positive pressure ventilation (NIPPV) lowers shunt and work of breathing [151].

Circulatory management- Myocardial depression can be made worse by the hypoxia and lactic acidosis brought on by CS, both directly and by reducing the response to vasopressors. Treatment for hypotension despite overt fluid excess is the first-line fluid challenge using a balanced solution. In the most severe cases, this frequently calls for the inclusion of vasoactive medications and consideration of suitability for MCS [152].

By optimizing CO and blood pressure, inotropes and vasopressors try to restore organ perfusion. The action of most vasoactive medications on the release and use of intracellular calcium is typical. The word "MCS" refers to a variety of apparatuses, such as extracorporeal membrane oxygenation, intra-aortic balloon pump, ventricular assist devices, and complete artificial hearts [153].

Refractory patients:

Heart transplantation- Heart transplantation is still the only effective treatment for eligible individuals with refractory heart failure, despite being the gold standard technique. Due to the quick advancement of underlying cardiac disease or the acute, irreversible signs of de novo illness, ICU admission is frequently the defining event that initiates an urgent examination. Organ failures and pulmonary hypertension may be stabilized and even returned to normal with the help of temporary or long-lasting ventricular assist devices [148].

Arrhythmias: Arrhythmias are a common problem that intensivists deal with. They are a significant cause of morbidity and prolonged hospital stays. The majority of patients with structural cardiac disease are at risk for arrhythmias. An insult such as infection, hypoxia, cardiac ischemia, an excess of catecholamines (endogenous or exogenous), or an electrolyte disturbance may be the cause of an arrhythmia in a particular patient. Correction of these abnormalities is part of management, along with medical treatment aimed at the arrhythmia itself [218].

Cardiac arrhythmias, which may be the main cause of ICU admission or a contingency in critically ill patients, put patients hospitalized in the Intensive Care unit (ICU) at a higher risk for developing them. Atrial fibrillation, atrial flutter, ventricular arrhythmias, and other supraventricular tachycardias (SVTs) are examples of tachyarrhythmias, and bradyarrhythmias (eg, junctional rhythm, sinus bradycardia, and atrioventricular [AV] conduction block) which make up the majority of arrhythmias in the Intensive Care unit (ICU).

Atrial fibrillation: AF, which can occur in up to 31% of ICU patients, is the most prevalent persistent arrhythmia in the general population. Hypotension, septic shock, the use of vasopressors or inotropes, electrolyte imbalance, fluid overload, heart failure, and postoperative status are some of the risk factors for AF in the ICU setting. Three techniques are used in the acute therapy of AF: rhythm control (cardioversion), anticoagulation, and rate control.

Cardioversion: Electrical cardioversion or pharmaceutical cardioversion are both options. In patients with AF who have a severe hemodynamic impairment (such as decompensated heart failure, hypotension), presumed to be connected to the arrhythmia, immediate electrical direct current (DC) cardioversion is recommended. Amiodarone and Ibutilide are the antiarrhythmic medications most frequently chosen in the Intensive Care unit (ICU). The choice of medication will depend on the underlying cardiac function. Although especially evaluated in ICU patients, intravenous ibutilide is said to have a 50% success rate [219].

Anticoagulation: The risk of embolization in each patient is the basis for the general anticoagulant strategy. Warfarin, apixiban, dabigitran, and rivaroxiban are a few different types of oral anticoagulants. Any patient's anticoagulation choice must be considered against the possibility of bleeding.

Surgical

CABG: Cardiopulmonary bypass is commonly used during CABG procedures, which has a distinctive impact on the physiology of patients and might cause certain postoperative issues in some patients. By cycling the patient's venous blood through a mechanical oxygenator, cardiopulmonary bypass enables a motionless and bloodless surgical field while preserving tissue perfusion and blood oxygenation [149,150]. However, when blood comes into touch with the nonendothelialized surface of the bypass circuit, the body experiences a severe form of systemic inflammatory response syndrome (SIRS), which activates the coagulation system [151]. Heparin is frequently administered to prevent clotting, however, SIRS also causes significant fluid changes, abnormal capillary bed control, and tissue hypoperfusion despite water retention. Microemboli and SIRS-related hypoperfusion can harm organ systems and increase postoperative morbidity. In the weeks following surgery, patients may experience chest discomfort, shortness of breath, or dysregulation of blood pressure due to SIRS (fig 1) [152,153].

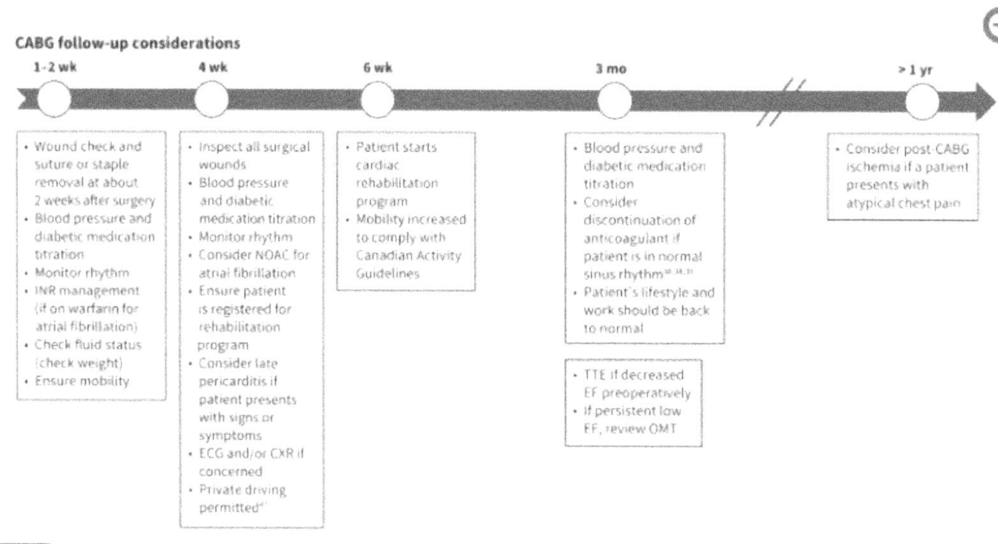

Figure 13.1: management of patients after CABG.

Vascular disease: It can be very difficult to manage critical care for people who have had vascular surgery (fig 1). There is a considerable risk of serious postoperative consequences since this patient population has significant comorbidities combined with the extensive surgical insult brought on by vascular surgery. The successful treatment of patients undergoing massive vascular surgery depends on accurate preoperative medical risk classification and optimization, great surgical skill and anesthetic management, and attentive ICU care. In order to restore and maintain physiologic homeostasis while keeping a high index of suspicion for procedure-specific complications, the intensivist, and critical care team must be proactive [154].

Post angioplasty: Patients with coronary stents who are admitted to the Intensive Care unit (ICU) may be more susceptible to stent thrombosis, a serious complication with a high morbidity and death rate. P2Y12 receptor antagonist and aspirin used together as dual antiplatelet medication considerably lower the risk of stent thrombosis, however, it might occasionally need to be stopped if bleeding occurs or invasive procedures with a high bleeding risk are required. If aspirin can be used in certain circumstances, it may offer some protection from problems. A short-acting antiplatelet drug, such as a small molecule glycoprotein IIb/IIIa inhibitor, may be beneficial if all antiplatelet therapy needs to be stopped. Close observation of patients with coronary stents may enable early detection and ICU-based therapy of any cardiac problems.

Postoperative critical care of surgical vascular patients by major systems

Neurologic
- Multimodal pain management
- Monitoring for early signs of CVA and SCI
- Maintain appropriate CSF pressure
- Ensure adequate SCPP

Respiratory
- Early extubation when possible
- Postextubation incentive spirometry and deep-breathing maneuvers
- Lung protective ventilation strategy for ALI
- Inspiratory muscle strength training to expedite ventilator weaning process
- VAP-prevention bundle

Cardiovascular
- Monitoring for symptoms/signs of myocardial ischemia
- Check myocardial biomarkers
- Early resumption and/or starting aspirin, beta-blocker, statins
- Avoid hypertension/hypotension
- Acute limb ischemia (check peripheral pulses hourly by palpation or Doppler)
- Monitoring for limb compartment syndrome
- Daily surgical inspection of vascular surgery wounds

Renal
- Maintain euvolemia and adequate renal perfusion pressure
- Avoid nephrotoxins

Hematologic
- Monitor for bleeding complications and retroperitoneal hematoma
- Conservative blood transfusion strategy unless evidence of organ ischemia
- Thromboembolic prophylaxis

Gastrointestinal
- Monitoring for early signs of mesenteric ischemia
- Monitoring for abdominal compartment syndrome
- Early resumption of oral feeding or early starting of enteral feeding
- Stress gastritis prophylaxis

Figure 13.2: postoperative critical care of surgical vascular patients by major systems.

ECMO VA: Extracorporeal membrane oxygenation (ECMO) use has grown significantly over the past ten years, and it is now regarded as a standard form of life-saving care in critical care medicine. Medical education, training, and experience are still absolutely necessary, nevertheless [155]. ECMO has historically been used to treat end-stage lung illness and circulatory collapse, but it is now also being used to treat right heart failure, as a stopgap measure before lung and heart transplantation, and as a rescue therapy for sepsis and post-organ transplantation [156]. Two of the most challenging conditions that can occur in the Intensive Care unit (ICU) which put patients at high risk for ICU mortality are hypoxic respiratory failure and/or cardiogenic shock. Cardiopulmonary bypass techniques, like ECMO, enable the provision of more aggressive lung rest methods and cardiovascular support than would otherwise be possible [157]. ECMO can provide different levels of assistance, including respiratory support only, respiratory support along with right ventricular support, and full cardiopulmonary support.

Today, with careful patient selection, ECMO is utilized as a preventive treatment for hypoxic respiratory failure and severe refractory cardiogenic shock to allow for recovery or serve as a bridge to transplant [158]. By sustaining systemic circulation until cardiac recovery, ECMO is used to assist the individual as a bridge to recovery, surgery, or another destination. ECMO is viewed as a bridge to LVAD therapy in individuals with end-stage heart failure or failure to improve. E-CPR, which helps to reestablish circulation following cardiac arrest, is another application of VA-ECMO [159,160].

Patients requiring VAD: Patients with end-stage heart failure survive longer thanks to left ventricular assist devices, whose use is on the rise. First-generation pulsatile devices have been replaced by continuous-flow left ventricular assist devices. Unique management issues are raised by these patients. Care must be made to sustain the right ventricle without assistance during the first few days after installation. To achieve the best left ventricular assist device settings and cardiac function, invasive blood pressure monitoring, echocardiography, and pulmonary artery catheterization are required. Anticoagulation is required to stop life-threatening thrombotic and embolic consequences, however, due to inherited bleeding disorders and prescribed anticoagulants, bleeding is a primary cause of morbidity. The device can be infected, which poses a life-threatening risk. In order to prevent seeding the device, all infections must be aggressively treated [161].

Monitoring: Since improving a patient's hemodynamics, temperature, ventilation, metabolism, and nutrition is the key to improving a patient's survival, monitoring is crucial to the daily treatment of ICU patients in critical care. The provision of oxygen to tissues in accordance with their metabolic requirements, in order to support mitochondrial respiration and, by extension, life, is the crucial endpoint. In this way, monitoring oxygenation and perfusion is necessary while putting any resuscitation plan into action. In an approach that was suitably named "goal-guided therapy," the growing idea has been to improve macrocirculation by first optimizing cardiac function in stages and then assessing the sufficiency of perfusion and oxygenation on specified parameters. On the other hand, maintaining a normal temperature is important and needs to be checked frequently. It involves serial evaluations of respiratory system mechanics, gas exchange, and the preparedness of patients for release from invasive positive pressure ventilation when it comes to respiratory surveillance of ventilated ICU patients. Additionally, the assessment of metabolic and nutritional care should enable control over blood glucose, blood sugar levels, and the supply of nutrients [162].

ECG interpretation: The Joint European Society of Cardiology/American College of Cardiology (ESC/ACC) updated the diagnostic standards for myocardial infarction (MI) in 2000. This was based on developments in the specific and sensitive biochemical marker cardiac troponin, which was used to diagnose myocardial injury [163]. The discovery of ischemia alterations on an electrocardiogram (ECG), pathologic findings, a rise and decline in biochemical markers like troponin, one of the classic ischemic symptoms, or a coronary artery intervention are used to make the diagnosis of MI. This definition presents various difficulties in the identification of MI in the Intensive Care unit (ICU). Because critically sick patients are commonly sedated, endotracheally intubated, or unconscious, ischemia symptoms are typically concealed by analgesia and are difficult to communicate. Second, many critically ill individuals with increased troponin levels have no signs of coronary thrombosis [164].

The ECG has become a more important diagnostic tool for identifying myocardial ischemia as a result of the limitations of MI in the ICU. When clinicians encounter a critically ill individual who simultaneously has an increased troponin level, the validity of ECG interpretation becomes a crucial factor [165]. An important feature of diagnostic testing is reliability, which is the degree to which measurement equipment gives reliable, stable, and uniform results during observational data under the same circumstances. Furthermore, accurate diagnostic test interpretation is required; in other words, an ECG is only effective in clinical practice if the interpretation of an ECG, performed on many occasions and by various observers, yields the same outcomes [166].

ECG basics and wave interpretation:

The electrocardiogram, often known as an ECG or EKG, is a non-invasive test that records an electrical trace of the heart from the body's surface. An important clinical application of the non-invasive diagnostic technique known as the electrocardiogram (ECG) is determining the severity of cardiovascular illnesses. ECG is being used more frequently to check on patients on antiarrhythmics and other medications, to evaluate patients before non-cardiac surgery, to screen people working in high-risk occupations, and to check on athletes. Given that cardiovascular illness is the leading cause of mortality, it is crucial for medical professionals to gain the skills and knowledge necessary to read ECGs in order to give the best care as soon as possible.

The purpose of electrocardiogram interpretation is to establish the normality or pathology of the ECG waves and intervals. The analysis of electrical signals provides a good estimate of heart pathology [167].

P-wave: On the ECG, it shows atrial depolarization. Right atrial and left atrial depolarization are represented by the first and second halves of the P wave, respectively. Atrial hypertrophy may be indicated by an aberrant P wave [168].

PR- interval: It comprises the lag at the AV node and measures the interval between the start of atrial depolarization and the commencement of ventricular depolarization. Various illnesses can result from variations in the PR interval. A first-degree AV block may be indicated by a long PR interval, whereas an enhanced AV conduction abnormality, such as a bypass tract, Wolf-Parkinson-White syndrome, or Lown-Ganong-Levine syndrome, may be indicated by a short PR interval [169].

R-wave: The electrical impulse that travels down the ventricles during depolarization is represented by this wave, which is the tallest in the QRS complex. R-wave progression refers to the R-gradual wave's amplitude increase as it progresses from right to left in the precordial leads. Numerous factors, such as anteroseptal MI in the past, left ventricular hypertrophy, improper lead placement, etc., might result in a decreased R-wave progression [176].

T-wave: This is ventricular repolarization in action. The effects of both cardiac and noncardiac factors, such as (hormonal and neurological). In leads with large R waves, it is typically positive [170].

ST segment: It shows when ventricular depolarization ends and ventricular repolarization starts. When observed in two or even more contiguous leads during an acute myocardial infarction, ST-elevation is extremely specific. In addition to these conditions, Prinzmetal angina, acute myocarditis, acute pericarditis, hyperkalemia, pulmonary embolism, and subarachnoid hemorrhage are also linked to ST elevation. An ST depression of more than 1 mm is frequently indicative of angina or myocardial ischemia [171].

QT interval: It signifies the beginning of ventricle depolarization and the conclusion of ventricle repolarization. Medications, congenital long QT syndrome, and electrolyte imbalances like hypomagnesemia and hypocalcemia are all prevalent causes of QT prolongation. Short QT syndrome, acidosis, hyperkalemia, hyperthermia, and hypercalcemia are all possible causes of a short QT interval (less than 360 milliseconds) [172].

U wave: The T wave is followed by a tiny wave. It stands for the papillary muscles' or Purkinje fibers' delayed repolarization. It frequently goes hand in hand with hypokalemia [173]

J wave: It is an aberrant ECG finding in hypothermia and is additionally known as the Osborn wave. At the junction of the QRS complex and ST segment, it appears as an additional deflection on the ECG [174].

Epsilon wave: It is a little positive deflection that is typically hidden near the end of the QRS complex and is a hallmark of arrhythmogenic right ventricular dysplasia [175].

Hemodynamic monitoring: Although the level of monitoring for each patient admitted to the ICU should be consistent, it might vary. Perhaps all that is needed for hemodynamically stable patients is continuous electrocardiographic (ECG) monitoring, routine non-invasive blood pressure checks, and peripheral pulse oximetry (peripheral oxygen saturation or SpO 2). An arterial line should be inserted for continuous invasive blood pressure monitoring and routine investigation of arterial blood gases in patients who are unstable or at risk of becoming unstable. Advanced hemodynamic assessment will be necessary to direct medical care if the patient's hemodynamic and/or respiratory state does not improve after the first resuscitation. We can determine whether vasopressors, fluid resuscitation, or inotropic medications are still necessary by monitoring CO and its constituents (preload, afterload, and contractility) [177].

Chapter 14:

Parameters Used In CICU

CVP:

The right atrium or superior vena cava pressure is measured by central venous pressure (CVP) monitoring, typically with the help of a central venous catheter (CVC), also referred to as a central line. The effectiveness of cardiac preload and circulating blood volume can be assessed by CVP monitoring. In critical care situations, inserting a CVC to test CVP is an invasive approach to determining the fluid status of patients [178,179].

A CVC is a catheter whose tip is positioned within the right atrium, inferior vena cava, or the proximal third of the superior vena cava. Both proximal central veins and peripheral veins can be used to place these catheters [180]. The CVC can then be electronically connected to a cardiac monitor, permitting a transduced waveform and a continuously updated numerical value to be displayed together. As patients in all of these settings typically have a CVC already in place, which can readily be attached to a cardiac monitor to detect CVP, this is frequently feasible in critical care [181].

CVP is a measure of right ventricular and, to a lesser degree, left ventricular preload and is used to determine whether blood volume is adequate [182].

Additionally, CVP shows the venous return threshold and provides information on right ventricular function. CVP measures could therefore be useful in assisting with and directing fluid management [183].

Limitations: Critical care professionals frequently use CVP to help them decide whether to deliver intravenous (IV) fluid treatment. A systematic study found insufficient evidence for CVP monitoring in critical care and came to the conclusion that it was not a reliable indicator of fluid responsiveness. Accurate CVP measurement might be hampered by abnormal right atrial pressure in conditions such as atrial fibrillation, tricuspid regurgitation, atrioventricular block, chronic obstructive pulmonary disease, cardiac tamponade, and mechanical ventilation [181].

Complications: Since CVP screening is an invasive hemodynamic procedure, it necessitates stringent asepsis compliance and high-level competence. According to recent research, 5–19% of all patients experience mechanical difficulties, and 5-26.5% of those patients also experience catheter-associated infections and 2-26.3% thrombotic complications [183].

It is advised that the nurse keep an eye out for mechanical issues like dysrhythmias during catheter insertion, recognize patients who are at risk for pulmonary artery injury (like rupture) and infarction, and put preventive measures in place to lessen the potential dangers of catheter-induced pulmonary artery injury [184].

Arterial lines: the indwelling artery catheter (AC), a technique that is often and widely utilized in Intensive Care units (ICUs) but for which there is no proof of its impact on pertinent outcomes. In the US, an AC is administered to about one-third of all ICU patients, with even higher usage in select subgroups [185]. This translates to about 2 million patients obtaining ACs per year and the exact number of AC therapies and catheters is probably substantially greater due to replacements and reinsertions. The main purposes of ACs are to monitor blood pressure and to assist in diagnostic blood tests, such as arterial blood gas analysis. These objectives don't, however, call for an AC [186]. Monitoring blood pressure is non-invasive. Phlebotomy or intermittent arterial puncture are two ways to acquire blood that will be used for laboratory testing [187].

Infections and arterial thrombosis are just two examples of the direct side effects of ACs. While AC devices resemble peripheral IV catheters in appearance, they are 2.5 times more likely to cause bloodstream infections. The lack of awareness of this risk may be due to both the observation that infected ACs hardly ever show symptoms of infection to the naked eye and the poor concordance between AC tip cultures and blood cultures obtained through the AC. Although the majority of the ischemia that results is transient, thrombosis due to ACs is not uncommon [188,189].

PA catheter: Through central venous access, a pulmonary artery catheter (PAC) is placed into the right portion of the heart and carried into the pulmonary artery. To aid in diagnosis and therapy, PAC measures cardiac output, stroke volume, intracardiac pressures, mixed venous oxygen saturation, and a number of other computed factors. The insertion of the line is mostly responsible for procedure complications. Cardiac arrhythmia, pulmonary hemorrhage and infarction, and related death from balloon tip rupture are rather infrequent consequences [190].

The catheter is not a kind of treatment, but rather a monitoring device that aids in diagnosis. After receiving proper training in the interpretation of data, specialists in the field should insert PACs to assist in treatment decisions for ICU patients. Critical hemodynamic information from a PAC includes cardiac output, intracardiac pressures, intrapulmonary pressures, and mixed venous oxygen saturation [191]. These variables, along with other derived variables derived from these measurements, are used to direct treatment for critically ill patients. These derived variables include right and left ventricular stroke work indices, pulmonary and systemic vascular resistance, right and left ventricular end-systolic and diastolic indices, arterial and venous oxygen content, right ventricular ejection fraction, oxygen delivery, oxygen consumption, and oxygen extraction ratio [190].

A PAC is a tool for both diagnosis and hemodynamic monitoring. Clinicians in cardiac catheterization labs, adult medical ICUs, and coronary care units (CCUs) employ the PAC. It is used to guide therapy and distinguish between distinct types of shock states in patients undergoing cardiothoracic surgery, including those undergoing coronary artery bypass graft (CABG, or bypass surgery), valvular surgery, and postoperative monitoring of critically ill patients [192].

Advantages: Many doctors still look for hemodynamic data throughout current clinical practice to treat critically ill patients. The effectiveness of the test has therefore been assessed by comparing a number of non-invasive monitoring equipment to PAC as the reference standard. Less invasive monitoring technologies are unable to reliably or continuously measure several hemodynamic variables, while PACs do. In addition to being used as a monitoring and data-gathering device, the PAC also offers the advantage of being a multi-lumen infusion port. Multiple drips are necessary for critically ill patients, and the standard of care nowadays is to establish central venous access using a CVC [193].

In addition to intracardiac screening, a PAC can also be implanted through central access and shares the same short-term difficulties as line insertion. The central venous oxygen saturation test (ScVO2) is another crucial procedure that heavily relies on the PAC. The treatment of patients experiencing septic shock and sepsis depends heavily on the measurement of ScVO2 [194].

Complications:

- those resulting from central venous access, including pneumothorax, air embolism, post-operative neuropathy (pain and feeling deficiency), and arterial puncture (air outside the lungs).
- those that result from using a catheter (right bundle branch block, complete heart block, and severe dysrhythmias).
- pulmonary infarction, pulmonary artery rupture, and venous thrombosis (clots in veins), which are caused by prolonged catheter occupancy [194].

CO monitoring: When a patient is severely unwell and at high risk for bleeding, hemodynamic instability, and significant fluid changes, cardiac output (CO) monitoring is a crucial tool. When a monitor is utilized in conjunction with the delivery of fluids and vasopressors to reach predetermined therapeutic objectives, thereby enhancing patient care and outcome, it is a crucial part of goal-directed therapy (GDT). Clinical evaluation and regular assessment are not reliable ways to evaluate CO. The Ficks principle, Doppler, thermodilution, bioimpedance, and pulse contour analysis are some of the techniques used for CO monitoring. Each approach has benefits and drawbacks of its own. An ideal CO monitoring should have a quick response time, be continuously operational, cost-effective, reproducible, and be slightly or completely non-invasive [195].

The following categories roughly classify CO monitoring techniques: There are three types of cardiac imaging: (1) invasive (intermittent bolus pulmonary artery thermodilution and continuous pulmonary artery thermodilution); (2) minimally invasive (lithium dilution CO (LiDCO), pulse contour analysis CO (PiCCO and FloTrac), transesophageal echocardiography (TEE); and (3) non-invasive (partial gas rebreathing, thoracic bioimpedance, and bioreactance, Photoelectric plethysmography, Doppler method, and endotracheal cardiac output monitor (ECOM) [195].

Invasive methods:

PAC- Dexter invented the pulmonary artery catheter (PAC), which Swan et al later adapted to evaluate central filling pressure and carbon monoxide (CO) levels. However, using it has been linked to a number of side effects, including pneumothorax, infection, arrhythmia, damage to the valve, rupture of the pulmonary artery, thrombosis resulting in embolism, and knotting [196].

Continuous measurement of CO by PAC- Continuous CO (CCO) is a variation of PAC that uses a catheter with a copper filament that stays in the right ventricle. The right heart's blood is intermittently heated by the filament, and a thermistor located close to the catheter's tip detects the resulting signal. On the monitor, the average CO measurement over time is shown. The main benefits of CCO over traditional PAC include the avoidance of repeated boluses, which lowers the risk of infection and operator error. Additionally, this catheter can be used to continuously evaluate systemic vascular resistance (SVR), stroke volume (SV), and mixed venous saturation [197].

Minimally invasive methods:

Pulse power analysis- This approach is predicated on the idea that changes in blood pressure relative to the mean have a direct impact on SV. Every eight hours and when significant hemodynamic changes call for calibration [198].

For continuous monitoring of SV and SV changes, the LiDCO system where pulse contour analysis combined with lithium indicator dilution (SVV). It is a minimally invasive procedure that was initially introduced in 1993 and calls for both an arterial catheter and a venous (central or peripheral) line. The arterial concentration is determined by drawing blood through a disposable lithium-sensitive sensor that has an ionophore that is only permeable to Li after a bolus of lithium chloride has been injected into the vein. Li dosage and area are used to determine CO in accordance with the concentration-time circulation. As quaternary ammonium residue produces electrode drift, it is not recommended for patients receiving Li treatment, and calibration is also impacted by neuromuscular blockers [198].

Pulse contour analysis- It is based on the idea that the SV is proportional to the area under the systolic component of the arterial pressure waveform. Erlanger and Hooker proposed that CO was proportional to arterial pulse pressure in their initial description of it in 1904 This technique divides the area from post-diastole to the conclusion of the ejection phase by the aortic impedance, which assesses stroke volume (SV). Additionally, it monitors pulse pressure change and stroke volume variation, both of which are helpful in predicting fluid responsiveness [199].

Non-invasive:

Partial gas rebreathing- The partial gas rebreathing monitor, also referred to as the NICO system, determines CO via the indirect Fick's principle. It is applied to individuals receiving mechanical ventilation who are intubated. At a steady state, the ratio of CO2 entering the airways through the pulmonary artery to CO is constant and equals the ratio of CO2 leaving the lungs by exhalation and the pulmonary veins [200].

The requirement for tracheal intubation with a fixed ventilator setting is a significant drawback. In patients with severe chest injuries, high CO situations,, large intrapulmonary shunt, and low minute ventilation, it is also not very accurate [200].

Thoracic bioimpedance- A non-invasive technique for measuring CO is thoracic bioimpedance (TEB). It was first used by astronauts in the 1960s. It is founded on the premise that the thorax functions as a cylinder that is perfused with fluid that has a particular resistance. The thorax's electrical resistance to a high frequency, low amplitude current is measured [201].

Thoracic bioreactance- Thoracic bioreactance is a variation of TEB that eliminates noise and outside sources of interference. It examines modifications in the electrical voltage signal's phase in relation to the current placed across the thorax. Electrical inductive and capacitive characteristics fluctuate as a result of intrathoracic volume changes [201]

Doppler- A probe is placed suprasternal to measure flow via the aorta or on the left chest to measure transpulmonary flow in portable, non-invasive Ultrasonic Cardiac Output Monitors. It makes use of the Doppler effect. The device's portability makes it ideal for usage in ERs, operating rooms, Intensive Care units, and even wards. It is a non-invasive gadget that may be utilized by skilled nursing personnel and serves as a crucial screening tool for cardiac surgery patients after surgery [202].

Thermodilution: It has been created a new thermodilution technique to monitor CO automatically and constantly. In order to identify a lo-cm thermal filament in the right ventricle (RV) while being used, pulmonary artery catheters (PACs) have been modified [203].

The thermal filament continuously delivers a safe amount of heat into the blood using a pseudorandom binary sequence without the use of any fluid injectate. A thermodilution "washout" curve is created by cross-correlating the temperature change that results with the input sequence in the pulmonary artery (PA) and detecting it downstream from there [203].

There is no need for an additional catheter positioning methodology because the PAC is inserted using the normal approach. The measurement process begins after the catheter is linked to the monitor. The initial CO measurement is generated and shown after a few minutes. The displayed CO is refreshed every 30 seconds to reflect the average flow over the past 3 to 6 minutes. There is no need for special user calibrating or catheter placement. The method for calculating volumetric fluid flow described here is based on stochastic system identification methods and conservation of mass, or thermodilution. This approach requires little user calibration, is simple to use, measures actual volumetric flow, and is not depending on vascular geometry [203].

Transpulmonary thermodilution: Many questions about a patient's hemodynamic treatment in the operating room or Intensive Care unit cannot be answered by a straightforward clinical examination. Particularly, arterial pressure only permits an approximation of cardiac output. Through cardiac output and other parameters, transpulmonary thermodilution is a technique that offers a complete hemodynamic examination.

Transpulmonary thermodilution periodically monitors cardiac output by analyzing the thermodilution curve that is obtained at the tip of an arterial catheter following the injection of a cold bolus into the venous circulation. The calibration of pulse contour analysis is made possible by this measure. This allows for continuous and real-time cardiac output monitoring, something the pulmonary artery catheter does not provide for. Beyond cardiac output, transpulmonary thermodilution offers a number of other factors. It calculates the four ventricular cavities' end-diastolic volume, which is a measure of cardiac preload. It provides an estimate of the united ventricles' systolic performance. Compared to the pulmonary artery catheter, it is more direct, but it does not allow for an accurate estimate of right and left heart performance.

Although it is quicker and easier to do than an echocardiogram, it does not give a complete assessment of the anatomy and functioning of the heart. The ability to measure extravascular lung water at the bedside, which quantifies the amount of pulmonary vascular permeability, and pulmonary edema which quantifies the severity of a pulmonary capillary leak, is a unique benefit of transpulmonary thermodilution [204].

Chapter 15:

Management of certain cases

Heart transplantation

Advanced heart failure is still only successfully treated with heart transplantation (HTx), and the survival and quality of life rates are quite good. The amount of organs accessible may be increased by using expanded donor criteria, obtaining hearts through donation after circulatory death, and transplanting patients using cutting-edge methods for organ preservation. After HTx, vigilant hemodynamic parameter monitoring is required since even little alterations in preload and afterload can have a negative impact on heart function and be challenging to cure. In addition to the usual monitoring, it is advised to perform continuous perioperative monitoring of systemic, pulmonary artery, and central venous pressure (CVP), as well as mixed venous oxygen saturation (SvO2), intermittent measurements of pulmonary capillary wedge pressure (PCWP), cardiac output, and left atrial pressure (LAP) [205].

Graft failure- Early primary graft dysfunction (PGD), which is defined as PGD identified within 24 hours following HTx, is linked to noticeably higher 30-day and 1-year mortality. In early PGD, the number of inotropes and mechanical assistance are utilized to classify the various types of dysfunction into left ventricular (LV), right ventricular (RV), and biventricular dysfunction. After HTx, LV failure is less frequent than RV failure, and LV systolic dysfunction might be an indication of subpar graft quality or acute rejection. One of the most serious side effects of HTx is isolated RV failure, which is a risk factor for mortality on its own. For chronotropic and inotropic stimulation of the denervated heart, inotropes are typically administered to patients. We frequently infuse isoproterenol for a minimum of twenty-four hours to decrease PVR and promote myocardial contraction and HR in order to prevent RV failure. Isoproterenol, milrinone, dobutamine, and dopamine are common ingredients in inotropic drugs [205].

Renal function- Acute kidney injury (AKI) after HTx is a frequent consequence, occurring at a rate of 25.6–50.2% and at a rate of 12.1-22.3% when dialysis is required. Post-HTx AKI is linked to decreased renal oxygen transport during CPB, bleeding/tamponade, venous congestion, postoperative RV failure, and the use of calcineurin inhibitors (CNI). Low-dose (50 ng/kg/min) atrial natriuretic peptide (ANP) infusion in early AKI post-HTx enhances renal blood flow and glomerular filtration rate and lowers the risk of dialysis in AKI following heart surgery [205].

Immunosuppression- Successful HTx requires effective immunosuppression, which has feared negative effects such as increased susceptibility to infections and cancer. It also protects against acute and chronic transplant rejection. Initiation therapy with anti-lymphocyte globulins or anti-thymocyte or interleukin-2 receptor antagonists, which is associated with greater long-term survival, is given to 51% of HTx recipients for severe immunosuppression immediately post-HTx [205].

Left ventricular failure: The pericardium, myocardium, and endocardium make up the heart. Heart failure can result from pathology in any of those structures. Left ventricular dysfunction results in inadequate blood flow to important body organs, which is known as left ventricular failure [206].

Management: Patients should be informed about the value of changing their lifestyles to better manage their disease. This includes limiting one's intake of salt and abstaining from narcotics, alcohol, and tobacco. It is crucial to treat the underlying cause of heart failure since certain disorders, such as alcohol-induced cardiomyopathies, tachycardia, or ischemia-induced cardiomyopathies, may be treatable by addressing the precipitating factors. Blood pressure must be tightly under control to stop further worsening. In addition to loop diuretics for volume overload, the pharmaceutical approach to treating HFrEF and HFpEF differs. Angiotensin-converting enzyme (ACE) inhibitors or angiotensin II receptor blockers (ARBs) combined with a beta blocker is the majority of treatment for HFrEF (carvedilol, metoprolol, or bisoprolol) [206,207].

Other drugs include hydralazine, nitrates, and inhibitors of the mineralocorticoid receptor, like ivabradine, spironolactone, and digoxin (as a last resort). In patients of African American descent, nitrates and hydralazine may be very effective. The mortality benefits of digoxin, diuretics, and ivabradine have not been demonstrated [207].

After receiving appropriate medical treatment, patients with severe symptoms and an ejection fraction under 35% should be referred for cardiac resynchronization therapy (CRT) or an implantable cardioverter-defibrillator (ICD), depending on the QRS width and the type of intraventricular conduction delay. Options for advanced cases include heart transplantation, continuous infusion of inotropic drugs like milrinone or dobutamine, and mechanical circulatory aid devices like LVAD [208].

Refractory arrhythmias

Rapid diagnosis and action are frequently necessary for the disciplines of emergency medicine and critical care for particular conditions. It is good knowledge that assessment of the underlying cause and level of left ventricular function (dysfunction) is crucial in all individuals with tachyarrhythmias. Understanding the process that brought about the issue is essential for administering the proper medication for arrhythmias in Intensive Care patients. Antiarrhythmic medications may or may not be used therapeutically to treat cardiac arrest or atrial fibrillation. Any patient with atrial fibrillation has rhythm control as an alternative to sinus rhythm restoration as their main objective.(rhythm or rate control)? The preventative use of antiarrhythmic medications in cardiac arrest victims has never been fully explored. There is currently no consensus on the appropriate time to administer antiarrhythmic medications—whether it is before or only after numerous defibrillation shocks have failed to restart circulation. One of the most crucial things is to employ automated external defibrillators to lower the rate of sudden cardiac death, both outside and within hospitals. However, it is now widely acknowledged that even when AEDs are installed in homes and used by family members, this therapy is unable to stop sudden death. To increase survival, more cardiac resuscitation techniques are necessary [210].

AICD:

Short-term management: ICD failure that manifests as unwarranted shocks necessitates immediate device investigation and reprogramming for short-term control. The patient's clinical state and underlying rhythm are taken into account while determining the short-term therapy of ICD lead failure. The magnet should be adhered to the skin with adhesive and put immediately over the device. Most of the time, the ICD emits an audible tone to signal adequate magnet placement. An ICD will lose its ability to detect when a magnet is attached to it (as long as the magnet remains applied). The application of a magnet won't change the device's pacing (bradycardia) settings [211].

Long-term management: First, the lead architecture and suspected lead failure mechanism need to be taken into account. This also applies to integrated bipolar leads with conductor fractures that involve the distal coil as well as leads with DF-4 connector pins. If there is a single fracture in the conductor of the ring electrode, only a new pace/sense lead needs to be installed. It might also be suitable to switch sensing electrodes utilizing still-functioning or abandoned lead components. Both methods might be more advantageous than inserting a fresh defibrillation lead. There is a theoretical worry about the current being shunted to the abandoned lead if there is an additional defibrillation coil placed in the heart [211].

Aortic dissection and repair: Patients undergoing vascular surgery have a number of comorbid conditions and are at significant risk for perioperative complications. Recent years have seen significant advancement in aortic repair surgery, with an increasing preponderance of endovascular procedures (EVAR). Endovascular treatment considerably lowers the likelihood of cardiac problems, but high-risk patients need postoperative ST-segment monitoring. The open aortic repair might herald an unacceptably high risk of respiratory problems, which might rule out surgery. An endovascular method considerably reduces this risk, thus whenever possible, endovascular repair should be performed without general anesthesia. Preoperative risk classification and secondary prevention are essential activities because preoperative renal function and postoperative kidney injury are significant predictors of short- and long-term outcomes. Open repair requires selective renal and distal aortic perfusion for intraoperative renal preservation. When compared to open repair, EVAR has reduced rates of postoperative renal failure, with a risk of acute kidney injury (AKI) that is about half as high and a demand for hemodialysis that is about one-third as high. Historically, the most notable and terrifying consequence of aortic surgery was spinal cord ischemia. Endovascular repair often results in less blood loss and less coagulopathy because it avoids significant aortic dissection and aortic cross-clamping [212].

Acute limb ischemia: Acute limb ischemia (ALI) is characterized by a sudden drop in limb perfusion that endangers limb viability and is a serious vascular emergency. If the clinical presentation happens within 14 days of the onset of symptoms, it is deemed acute. While collateral blood supply is frequently present in critical limb ischemia (CLI), also known as chronic limb-threatening ischemia (CLTI), ALI threatens limb viability in a relatively short amount of time because there is not enough time for new blood vessel formation to make up for the loss of perfusion [213].

Management: Vascular surgery, vascular medicine, and/or interventional therapy must be available around the clock due to the high amputation and fatality rates in ALI. Unfractionated heparin (UFH) is used as an immediate anticoagulant to stop thrombus growth and maintain microcirculation. Often, analgesic therapy is required. The various therapeutic approaches are discussed, including pharmacological (thrombolysis), interventional (thromboaspiration, mechanical thrombectomy, and stent implantation), established surgical (Fogarty thrombembolectomy, by-pass, endarterectomy, patch angioplasty, or combinations), and minor or major amputation when necessary. Additionally updated are postoperative management, reperfusion injury, compartment syndrome, and long-term care [213].

TAVR: As a method to medically treat aortic stenosis (AS) in high-risk patients, transcatheter aortic valve replacement (TAVR) is quickly gaining favor. TAVR is far less invasive than the conventional method of replacing an aortic valve with a median sternotomy. Patients having TAVR frequently have many comorbidities, and a specific set of problems that may become apparent in the Intensive Care unit may exacerbate their postoperative course (ICU) [214].

A sternotomy is not performed, cardiopulmonary bypass (CPB) is not required, and patients may be extubated in the operating room (OR) during TAVR, making it less invasive than classic aortic valve replacement (AVR). Despite being less invasive, TAVR has a distinct set of postoperative events and problems that have been documented over the past few years as the number of procedures has grown. While patients receiving TAVR share some ICU management concerns with patients undergoing classic AVR, TAVR patients have additional ICU problems that the intensivist must be aware of and appropriately address [214].

WATCHMAN procedure: The inter-atrial septum is bridged using a transseptal cannula that is placed through the femoral vein and guided by a fluoroscope. The WATCHMAN Access Sheath and dilator are moved across the wire into the left atrium once access to the left atrium has been gained. A guidewire is then inserted into the upper pulmonary vein. The access sheath is gently inserted over a pigtail catheter into the distal section of the LAA after the guidewire is withdrawn. The entry sheath is prepared, the WATCHMAN Delivery System is inserted, and the device is gradually progressed. After then, the WATCHMAN gadget is introduced into the LAA. Transesophageal echocardiography (TEE) and fluoroscopy are used to check the device release criteria, and the device is then made available for use [215].

Left atrial appendage closure (LAAC) with Watchman seems to be a promising, secure, and efficient replacement for OAC. Current and upcoming studies should concentrate on comparing the safety and effectiveness of various LAAC devices, patient selection, different post-procedural antithrombotic regimens, head-to-head comparisons with NOAC, a better understanding of device-related thrombus, and the role of the LAA in the spread of non-valvular AF in order to solidify the position of Watchman [216].

ABG analysis: ABG analysis is one of the most frequently requested diagnostics in the ICU. When the results are likely to affect patient management, it is ideal to get an ABG sample. The evaluation of patient breathing, the necessity to quantify the response to therapeutic or diagnostic interventions, the monitoring of the severity and progression of a known disease process, and the assessment of acid-base balance are common indications for the ABG sample. ABG measurements that are repeated are linked to higher costs, blood loss, the spread of infection, and patient discomfort. In patients without an intra-arterial catheter, the requirement for numerous unpleasant punctures may result in significant blood loss. The arterial blood gas analysis is frequently requested as a routine test, and the ABG results typically do not alter patient management, which increases expense and resource usage. Since the majority of routine ABGs are performed without intervention, a tailored strategy might lower the incidence of incorrect ABGs [217].

References

- Lüsebrink, E., Kellnar, A., Scherer, C., Krieg, K., Orban, M., Petzold, T., Peterss, S., Kääb, S., Brunner, S., Braun, D., Hagl, C., Hausleiter, J., Massberg, S., & Orban, M. (2021). New challenges in cardiac Intensive Care units. Clinical Research in Cardiology: Official Journal of the German Cardiac Society, 110(9), 1369–1379. https://doi.org/10.1007/s00392-021-01869-0
- Kasaoka, S. (2017). Evolved role of the cardiovascular Intensive Care unit (CICU). *Journal of Intensive Care*, *5*(1). https://doi.org/10.1186/s40560-017-0271-7
- Cardiovascular Intensive Care. (n.d.). Www.biomedcentral.com. Retrieved December 28, 2022, from https://www.biomedcentral.com/collections/cic
- Fordyce, C. B., Katz, J. N., Alviar, C. L., Arslanian-Engoren, C., Bohula, E. A., Geller, B. J., Hollenberg, S. M., Jentzer, J. C., Sims, D. B., Washam, J. B., & van Diepen, S. (2020). Prevention of Complications in the Cardiac Intensive Care Unit: A Scientific Statement From the American Heart Association. *Circulation*, *142*(22). https://doi.org/10.1161/cir.0000000000000909
- McGill, H. C., McMahan, C. A., & Gidding, S. S. (2008). Preventing Heart Disease in the 21st Century. *Circulation*, *117*(9), 1216–1227. https://doi.org/10.1161/circulationaha.107.717033
- Loughran, J., Puthawala, T., Sutton, B. S., Brown, L. E., Pronovost, P. J., & DeFilippis, A. P. (2016). The Cardiovascular Intensive Care Unit—An Evolving Model for Health Care Delivery. *Journal of Intensive Care Medicine*, *32*(2), 116–123. https://doi.org/10.1177/0885066615624664
- Fukuda, T. (2016). Targeted temperature management for adult out-of-hospital cardiac arrest: current concepts and clinical applications. *Journal of Intensive Care*, *4*(1). https://doi.org/10.1186/s40560-016-0139-2
- Katz, J. N., Shah, B. R., Volz, E. M., Horton, J. R., Shaw, L. K., Newby, L. K., Granger, C. B., Mark, D. B., Califf, R. M., & Becker, R. C. (2010). Evolution of the coronary care unit: clinical characteristics and temporal trends in healthcare delivery and outcomes. *Critical Care Medicine*, *38*(2), 375–381. https://doi.org/10.1097/CCM.0b013e3181cb0a63
- Hollenberg, S. M. (2013). Hemodynamic Monitoring. *Chest*, *143*(5), 1480–1488. https://doi.org/10.1378/chest.12-1901

- Thiele H, Ohman EM, de Waha-Thiele S, Zeymer U, Desch S (2019) Management of cardiogenic shock complicating myocardial infarction: an update 2019. Eur Heart J 40:2671–2683. https://doi.org/10.1093/eurheartj/ehz363
- . Werdan K, Boeken U, Briegel MJ, Buerke M, Geppert A, Janssens U, Kelm M, Michels G, Pilarczyk K, Schlitt A, Thiele H, Willems S, Zeymer U, Zwißler B, Delle-Karth G, Ferrari M, Figulla H, Heller A, Hindricks G, Pichler-Cetin E, Pieske BM, Prondzinsky R, Thielmann M, Bauersachs J, Kopp I, Ruß M (2021) Kurzversion der 2. Aufage der deutsch-österreichischen S3-Leitlinie "Infarkt-bedingter Kardiogener Schock—diagnose, monitoring und therapie." Anaesthesist. 70:42–70. https://doi. org/10.1007/s00101-020-00868-6
- . Orban M, Mayer K, Morath T, Bernlochner I, Hadamitzky M, Braun S, Schulz S, Hoppmann P, Hausleiter J, Tiroch K, Mehilli J, Schunkert H, Massberg S, Laugwitz KL, Sibbing D, Kastrati A (2014) Prasugrel vs clopidogrel in cardiogenic shock patients undergoing primary PCI for acute myocardial infarction. Results of the ISAR-SHOCK registry. Thromb Haemost 112:1190–1197. https://doi.org/10.1160/TH14-06-0489
- Go, A. S., Mozaffarian, D., Roger, V. L., Benjamin, E. J., Berry, J. D., Borden, W. B., Bravata, D. M., & Dai, S. (2012). Heart Disease and Stroke Statistics--2013 Update: A Report From the American Heart Association. *Circulation*, *127*(1), e6–e245. https://doi.org/10.1161/cir.0b013e31828124ad
- Scherer C, Lüsebrink E, Kupka D, Stocker TJ, Stark K, Stremmel C, Orban M, Petzold T, Germayer A, Mauthe K, Kääb S, Mehilli J, Braun D, Theiss H, Brunner S, Hausleiter J, Massberg S, Orban M (2020) Long-term clinical outcome of cardiogenic shock patients undergoing Impella CP treatment vs. standard of care. J Clin Med. 9:3803. https://doi.org/10.3390/jcm9123803
- Baran DA, Grines CL, Bailey S, Burkhof D, Hall SA, Henry TD, Hollenberg SM, Kapur NK, O'Neill W, Ornato JP, Stelling K, Thiele H, van Diepen S, Naidu SS (2019) SCAI clinical expert consensus statement on the classifcation of cardiogenic shock: this document was endorsed by the American College of Cardiology (ACC), the American Heart Association (AHA), the Society of Critical Care Medicine (SCCM), and the Society of Thoracic Surgeons (STS) in April 2019. Catheter Cardiovasc Interv 94:29–37. https://doi.org/10.1002/ccd.28329
- Lascarrou JB, Merdji H, Le Gouge A, Colin G, Grillet G, Girardie P, Coupez E, Dequin PF, Cariou A, Boulain T, Brule N, Frat JP, Asfar P, Pichon N, Landais M, Plantefeve G, Quenot JP, Chakarian JC, Sirodot M, Legriel S, Letheulle J, Thevenin D, Desachy A, Delahaye A, Botoc V, Vimeux S, Martino F, Giraudeau B, Reignier J, CRICS-TRIGGERSEP Group (2019) Targeted temperature management for cardiac arrest with nonshockable rhythm. N Engl J Med. 381:2327–2337. https://doi.org/10.1056/NEJMo a1906661

- Berdowski J, Berg RA, Tijssen JG, Koster RW. Global incidences of out-ofhospital cardiac arrest and survival rates: systematic review of 67 prospective studies. Resuscitation 2010;81:1479–87.
- Grasner JT, Herlitz J, Koster RW, Rosell-Ortiz F, Stamatakis L, Bossaert L. Quality management in resuscitation – towards a European cardiac arrest registry (EuReCa). Resuscitation 2011;82:989–94.
- Grasner JT, Bossaert L. Epidemiology and management of cardiac arrest: what registries are revealing. Best Pract Res Clin Anaesthesiol 2013;27:293–306
- Teboul JL, Saugel B, Cecconi M, De Backer D, Hofer CK, Monnet X, Perel A, Pinsky MR, Reuter DA, Rhodes A, Squara P, Vincent JL, Scheeren TW. Less invasive hemodynamic monitoring in critically ill patients. Intensive Care Med. 2016 Sep;42(9):1350-9. doi: 10.1007/s00134-016-4375-7. Epub 2016 May 7. PMID: 27155605.
- Malbrain ML, Marik PE, Witters I, et al.: Fluid overload, de-resuscitation, and outcomes in critically ill or injured patients: a systematic review with suggestions for clinical practice. *Anaesthesiol Intensive Ther.* 2014;46(5):361–80. 10.5603/AIT.2014.0060
- Fick A: Uber die messing des Blutquantums in den Hertzvent rikeln.Sitzber Physik Med Ges Wurzburg.1870;36.
- Swan HJ, Ganz W, Forrester J, et al.: Catheterization of the heart in man with use of a flow-directed balloon-tipped catheter. *N Engl J Med.* 1970;283(9):447–51. 10.1056/NEJM197008272830902
- Sandham JD, Hull RD, Brant RF, et al.: A randomized, controlled trial of the use of pulmonary-artery catheters in high risk surgical patients. *N Engl J Med.* 2003;348(1):5–14. 10.1056/NEJMoa021108
- Squara P, Bennett D, Perret C: Pulmonary artery catheter: does the problem lie in the users? *Chest.* 2002;121(6):2009–15. 10.1378/chest.121.6.2009
- Goedje O, Hoeke K, Lichtwarck-Aschoff M, et al.: Continuous cardiac output by femoral arterial thermodilution calibrated pulse contour analysis: comparison with pulmonary arterial thermodilution. *Crit Care Med.* 1999;27(11):2407–12.
- Michard F, Teboul JL: Predicting fluid responsiveness in ICU patients: a critical analysis of the evidence. *Chest.* 2002;121(6):2000–8. 10.1378/chest.121.6.2000
- Michard F, Chemla D, Teboul JL: Applicability of pulse pressure variation: how many shades of grey? *Crit Care.* 2015;19:144. 10.1186/s13054-015-0869-x

- Kiefer N, Hofer CK, Marx G, et al.: Clinical validation of a new thermodilution system for the assessment of cardiac output and nd volumetric parameters. *Crit Care.* 2012;16(3):R98. 10.1186/cc11366
- Jonas MM, Tanser SJ. Lithium dilution measurement of cardiac output and arterial pulse waveform analysis: an indicator dilution calibrated beat-by-beat system for continuous estimation of cardiac output. Curr Opin Crit Care. 2002 Jun;8(3):257-61. doi: 10.1097/00075198-200206000-00010. PMID: 12386506.
- Galstyan G, Bychinin M, Alexanyan M, Gorodetsky V. Comparison of cardiac output and blood volumes in intrathoracic compartments measured by ultrasound dilution and transpulmonary thermodilution methods. Intensive Care Med. 2010 Dec;36(12):2140-4. doi: 10.1007/s00134-010-2003-5. Epub 2010 Aug 6. PMID: 20689918.
- Cecconi M, Malbrain ML. Cardiac output obtained by pulse pressure analysis: to calibrate or not to calibrate may not be the only question when used properly. Intensive Care Med. 2013 Apr;39(4):787-9. doi: 10.1007/s00134-012-2802-y. Epub 2013 Jan 4. PMID: 23287877.
- Scolletta S, Romano SM, Biagioli B, Capannini G, Giomarelli P. Pressure recording analytical method (PRAM) for measurement of cardiac output during various haemodynamic states. Br J Anaesth. 2005 Aug;95(2):159-65. doi: 10.1093/bja/aei154. Epub 2005 May 13. PMID: 15894561.
- American Society of Anesthesiologists and Society of Cardiovascular Anesthesiologists Task Force on Transesophageal Echocardiography. Practice guidelines for perioperative transesophageal echocardiography. An updated report by the American Society of Anesthesiologists and the Society of Cardiovascular Anesthesiologists Task Force on Transesophageal Echocardiography. Anesthesiology. 2010 May;112(5):1084-96. doi: 10.1097/ALN.0b013e3181c51e90. PMID: 20418689.
- McKendry M, McGloin H, Saberi D, Caudwell L, Brady AR, Singer M. Randomised controlled trial assessing the impact of a nurse delivered, flow monitored protocol for optimisation of circulatory status after cardiac surgery. BMJ. 2004 Jul 31;329(7460):258. doi: 10.1136/bmj.38156.767118.7C. Epub 2004 Jul 8. Erratum in: BMJ. 2004 Aug 21;329(7463):438. PMID: 15242867; PMCID: PMC498021.
- Saugel B, Meidert AS, Langwieser N, Wagner JY, Fassio F, Hapfelmeier A, Prechtl LM, Huber W, Schmid RM, Gödje O. An autocalibrating algorithm for non-invasive cardiac output determination based on the analysis of an arterial pressure waveform recorded with radial artery applanation tonometry: a proof of concept pilot analysis. J Clin Monit Comput. 2014 Aug;28(4):357-62. doi: 10.1007/s10877-013-9540-8. Epub 2013 Dec 10. PMID: 24322474.

- Summers RL, Shoemaker WC, Peacock WF, Ander DS, Coleman TG. Bench to bedside: electrophysiologic and clinical principles of noninvasive hemodynamic monitoring using impedance cardiography. Acad Emerg Med. 2003 Jun;10(6):669-80. doi: 10.1111/j.1553-2712.2003.tb00054.x. PMID: 12782531.
- Ball TR, Tricinella AP, Kimbrough BA, Luna S, Gloyna DF, Villamaria FJ, Culp WC Jr. Accuracy of noninvasive estimated continuous cardiac output (esCCO) compared to thermodilution cardiac output: a pilot study in cardiac patients. J Cardiothorac Vasc Anesth. 2013 Dec;27(6):1128-32. doi: 10.1053/j.jvca.2013.02.019. Epub 2013 Aug 29. PMID: 23992653.
- Van den Oever HL, Murphy EJ, Christie-Taylor GA. USCOM (Ultrasonic Cardiac Output Monitors) lacks agreement with thermodilution cardiac output and transoesophageal echocardiography valve measurements. Anaesth Intensive Care. 2007 Dec;35(6):903-10. doi: 10.1177/0310057X0703500608. PMID: 18084981.
- Vincent JL, Sakr Y, Sprung CL, et al.: Sepsis in European Intensive Care units: results of the SOAP study. *Crit Care Med* 2006;34(2):344–53. 10.1097/01.CCM.0000194725.48928.3A.
- ProCESS Investigators, . Yealy DM, Kellum JA, et al.: A randomized trial of protocol-based care for early septic shock. *N Engl J Med.* 2014;370(18):1683–93. 10.1056/NEJMoa1401602
- ARISE Investigators, . ANZICS Clinical Trials Group, . Peake SL, et al.: Goal-directed resuscitation for patients with early septic shock. *N Engl J Med.* 2014;371(16):1496–506. 10.1056/NEJMoa1404380
- Mouncey PR, Osborn TM, Power GS, et al.: Trial of early, goal-directed resuscitation for septic shock. *N Engl J Med.* 2015;372(14):1301–11. 10.1056/NEJMoa1500896
- Perera P, Lobo V, Williams SR, Gharahbaghian L. Cardiac echocardiography. Crit Care Clin. 2014 Jan;30(1):47-92, v. doi: 10.1016/j.ccc.2013.08.003. PMID: 24295841
- Joseph MX, Disney PJ, Da Costa R, Hutchison SJ. Transthoracic echocardiography to identify or exclude cardiac cause of shock. Chest. 2004;126:1592–7. doi: 10.1378/chest.126.5.1592.
- Levitov A, Frankel HL, Blaivas M, et al. Guidelines for the appropriate use of bedside general and cardiac ultrasonography in the evaluation of critically ill patients–part II: cardiac ultrasonography. Crit Care Med. 2016;44:1206–27. doi: 10.1097/CCM.0000000000001847.
- Parker MM, Shelhamer JH, Bacharach SL, et al. Profound but reversible myocardial depression in patients with septic shock. Ann Intern Med. 1984;100:483–90. doi: 10.7326/0003-4819-100-4-483.
- Treiber SC, Khandheria BK. The value of contrast echocardiography. J Patient Cent Res Rev. 2016;3:40–7. doi: 10.17294/2330-0698.1215.

- McConnell MV, Solomon SD, Rayan ME, Come PC, Goldhaber SZ, Lee RT. Regional right ventricular dysfunction detected by echocardiography in acute pulmonary embolism. Am J Cardiol. 1996;78:469–73. doi: 10.1016/S0002-9149(96)00339-6.
- Quiñones M, et al. ACC/AHA Clinical Competence Statement on Echocardiography. A Report of the American College of Cardiology/American Heart Association/American College of PhysiciansAmerican Society of Internal Medicine Task Force on Clinical Competence. JACC. 2003;41:87–708.
- Marcelino PA, Marum SM, Fernandes AP, Germano N, Lopes MG. Routine transthoracic echocardiography in a general Intensive Care Unit: an 18 month survey in 704 patients. Eur J Intern Med. 2009;20(3):e37–42.
- Lichtenstein D, Mezière GA. Relevance of Lung Ultrasound in the Diagnosis of Acute Respiratory Failure: The BLUE Protocol. Chest. 2008;134:117–125.
- Cholley B, Vieillard-Baron A, Mebazaa A. Echocardiography in the ICU: time for widespread use. Intensive Care Med. 2005;32:9–10.
- Vignon P, Dugard A, Abraham J, et al. Focused training for goal-oriented hand-held echocardiography performed by non-cardiologist residents in the Intensive Care unit. Intensive Care Med. 2007;33:1795–99.
- Adler Y, Charron P, Imazio M, et al. 2015 ESC Guidelines for the diagnosis and management of pericardial diseases: the Task Force for the Diagnosis and Management of Pericardial Diseases of the European Society of Cardiology (ESC) Eur Heart J. 2015;36:2921–64. doi: 10.1093/eurheartj/ehv318.
- Greer MR, Carney S, McPheeters RA, Aguiniga P, Rubio S, Lee J. Radial Arterial Lines Have a Higher Failure Rate than Femoral. West J Emerg Med. 2018 Mar;19(2):364-371.
- Kaki A, Blank N, Alraies MC, Kajy M, Grines CL, Hasan R, Htun WW, Glazier J, Mohamad T, Elder M, Schreiber T. Access and closure management of large bore femoral arterial access. J Interv Cardiol. 2018 Dec;31(6):969-977.
- Saugel B, Kouz K, Meidert AS, Schulte-Uentrop L, Romagnoli S. How to measure blood pressure using an arterial catheter: a systematic 5-step approach. Crit Care. 2020 Apr 24;24(1):172.
- Chim H, Bakri K, Moran SL. Complications related to radial artery occlusion, radial artery harvest, and arterial lines. Hand Clin. 2015 Feb;31(1):93-100.
- Nguyen Y, Bora V. StatPearls [Internet]. StatPearls Publishing; Treasure Island (FL): Sep 18, 2022. Arterial Pressure Monitoring.

- López-Briz E, Ruiz Garcia V, Cabello JB, Bort-Martí S, Carbonell Sanchis R, Burls A. Heparin versus 0.9% sodium chloride locking for prevention of occlusion in central venous catheters in adults. Cochrane Database Syst Rev. 2018 Jul 30;7(7):CD008462.
- Nuttall G, Burckhardt J, Hadley A, Kane S, Kor D, Marienau MS, Schroeder DR, Handlogten K, Wilson G, Oliver WC. Surgical and Patient Risk Factors for Severe Arterial Line Complications in Adults. Anesthesiology. 2016 Mar;124(3):590-7.
- Scales K. Arterial catheters: indications, insertion and use in critical care. Br J Nurs. 2010 Oct 28-Nov 10;19(19):S16-21. doi: 10.12968/bjon.2010.19.Sup9.79306. PMID: 21042242.
- Chee BC, Baldwin IC, Shahwan-Akl L, Fealy NG, Heland MJ, Rogan JJ. Evaluation of a radial artery cannulation training program for Intensive Care nurses: a descriptive, explorative study. Aust Crit Care. 2011 May;24(2):117-25.
- Saugel B, Kouz K, Meidert AS, Schulte-Uentrop L, Romagnoli S. How to measure blood pressure using an arterial catheter: a systematic 5-step approach. Crit Care. 2020 Apr 24;24(1):172.
- Beheshti MV. A concise history of central venous access. Tech Vasc Interv Radiol. 2011 Dec;14(4):184-5.
- Konner K. History of vascular access for haemodialysis. Nephrol Dial Transplant. 2005 Dec;20(12):2629-35.
- American Society of Anesthesiologists Task Force on Central Venous Access. Rupp SM, Apfelbaum JL, Blitt C, Caplan RA, Connis RT, Domino KB, Fleisher LA, Grant S, Mark JB, Morray JP, Nickinovich DG, Tung A. Practice guidelines for central venous access: a report by the American Society of Anesthesiologists Task Force on Central Venous Access. Anesthesiology. 2012 Mar;116(3):539-73.
- Konner K. History of vascular access for haemodialysis. Nephrol Dial Transplant. 2005 Dec;20(12):2629-35.
- Suess EM, Pinsky MR. Hemodynamic Monitoring for the Evaluation and Treatment of Shock: What Is the Current State of the Art? Semin Respir Crit Care Med. 2015 Dec;36(6):890-8.
- Lamperti M, Bodenham AR, Pittiruti M, Blaivas M, Augoustides JG, Elbarbary M, Pirotte T, Karakitsos D, Ledonne J, Doniger S, Scoppettuolo G, Feller-Kopman D, Schummer W, Biffi R, Desruennes E, Melniker LA, Verghese ST. International evidence-based recommendations on ultrasound-guided vascular access. Intensive Care Med. 2012 Jul;38(7):1105-17.
- Dietrich CF, Horn R, Morf S, Chiorean L, Dong Y, Cui XW, Atkinson NS, Jenssen C. Ultrasound-guided central vascular interventions, comments on the European Federation of

Societies for Ultrasound in Medicine and Biology guidelines on interventional ultrasound. J Thorac Dis. 2016 Sep;8(9):E851-E868.

- Pinski SL. Marcapasos permanentes. In: Doval HC, Tajer CD, Schwartzman RA, eds. Evidencias en cardiologia: de los ensayos clinicos a las conductas terapeuticas. Buenos Aires: Editorial GEDIC, 2001: 366–40
- Kusumoto FM, Goldschlager N. Cardiac pacing. N Engl J Med 1996; 334: 89–97.
- Kaushik V, Leon AR, Forrester JS Jr, Trohman RG. Bradyarrhythmias, temporary and permanent pacing. Crit Care Med 2000: 28 (suppl 10): N121–28.
- Bernstein AD, Daubert JC, Fletcher RD, et al. The revised NASPE/BPEG generic code for antibradycardia, adaptive-rate, and multisite pacing. North American Society of Pacing and Electrophysiology/British Pacing and Electrophysiology Group. Pacing Clin Electrophysiol 2002; 25: 260–64.
- Andersen HR, Nielsen JC, Thomsen PE, et al. Atrioventricular conduction during long-term follow-up of patients with sick-sinus syndrome. Circulation 1998; 98: 1315–21.
- Gregoratos G, Abrams J, Epstein AE, et al. ACC/AHA/NASPE 2002 guideline update for implantation of cardiac pacemakers and antiarrhythmia devices. www.acc.org/clinical/guidelines/ pacemaker/pacemaker.pdf (accessed Oct 3, 2004).
- Brandt J, Anderson H, Fahraeus T, Schuller H. Natural history of sinus-node disease treated with atrial pacing in 213 patients: implications for selection of stimulation mode. J Am Coll Cardiol 1992; 20: 633–39.
- Haywood GA, Ward J, Ward DE, Camm AJ. Atrioventricular Wenckebach point and progression to atrioventricular block in sinoatrial disease. Pacing Clin Electrophysiol 1990; 13: 2054–58.
- Sucu, M., Davutoglu, V., & Ozer, O. (2009). Electrical cardioversion. *Annals of Saudi Medicine, 29*(3), 201-206. https://doi.org/10.4103/0256-4947.51775
- Trohman RG, Parrillo JE. Direct current cardioversion: indications, techniques, and recent advances. Crit Care Med. 2000 Oct;28(10 Suppl):N170-3. doi: 10.1097/00003246-200010001-00010. PMID: 11055687.
- Zoll PM, Linenthal AJ, Gibson W, Paul MH, Norman LR. Termination of ventricular fibrillation in man by externally applied electric counter shock. N Engl J Med. 1956;254:727–732.

- Jones JL. Waveforms for implantable cardioverter defibrillators (ICDs) and transchest defibrillation. In: Tacker WA, editor. Defibrillation of the heart. St. Louis: Mosby-Year Book; 1994. pp. 46–81.
- Arnold AZ, Mick MJ, Mazurek RP, Loop FD, Trohman RG. Role of prophylactic anticoagulation for direct current cardioversion in patients with atrial fibrillation or atrial flutter. J Am Coll Caridiol. 1992;19:851–855.
- Trohman RG, Parrillo JE. Direct current cardioversion: indications, techniques, and recent advances. Crit Care Med. 2000;28:170–173.
- Truong HT, Low LS, Kern KB. Current Approaches to Cardiopulmonary Resuscitation. Curr Probl Cardiol. 2015 Jul;40(7):275-313.
- Giacoppo D. Impact of bystander-initiated cardiopulmonary resuscitation for out-of-hospital cardiac arrest: where would you be happy to have a cardiac arrest? Eur Heart J. 2019 Jan 14;40(3):319-321.
- Marsch S, Tschan F, Semmer NK, Zobrist R, Hunziker PR, Hunziker S. ABC versus CAB for cardiopulmonary resuscitation: a prospective, randomized simulator-based trial. Swiss Med Wkly. 2013;143:w13856.
- Liao X, Chen B, Tang H, Wang Y, Wang M, Zhou M. [Effects between chest-compression-only cardiopulmonary resuscitation and standard cardiopulmonary resuscitation for patients with out-of-hospital cardiac arrest: a Meta-analysis]. Zhonghua Wei Zhong Bing Ji Jiu Yi Xue. 2018 Nov;30(11):1017-1023.
- Bobrow BJ, Clark LL, Ewy GA, Chikani V, Sanders AB, Berg RA, Richman PB, Kern KB. Minimally interrupted cardiac resuscitation by emergency medical services for out-of-hospital cardiac arrest. JAMA. 2008 Mar 12;299(10):1158-65.
- Svensson L, Bohm K, Castrèn M, Pettersson H, Engerström L, Herlitz J, Rosenqvist M. Compression-only CPR or standard CPR in out-of-hospital cardiac arrest. N Engl J Med. 2010 Jul 29;363(5):434-42.
- Maconochie IK, de Caen AR, Aickin R, Atkins DL, Biarent D, Guerguerian AM, Kleinman ME, Kloeck DA, Meaney PA, Nadkarni VM, Ng KC, Nuthall G, Reis AG, Shimizu N, Tibballs J, Pintos RV., Pediatric Basic Life Support and Pediatric Advanced Life Support Chapter Collaborators. Part 6: Pediatric basic life support and pediatric advanced life support: 2015 International Consensus on Cardiopulmonary Resuscitation and Emergency Cardiovascular Care Science with Treatment Recommendations. Resuscitation. 2015 Oct;95:e147-68.
- Perkins, Gavin D.; Handley, Anthony J.; Koster, Rudolph W.; Castrén, Maaret; Smyth, Michael A.; Olasveengen, Theresa; Monsieurs, Koenraad G.; Raffay, Violetta; Gräsner, Jan-Thorsten;

Wenzel, Volker; Ristagno, Giuseppe; Soar, Jasmeet (2015). European Resuscitation Council Guidelines for Resuscitation 2015. Resuscitation, 95(), 81–99. doi:10.1016/j.resuscitation.2015.07.015

- Barsuk JH, Cohen ER, Feinglass J, et al. Clinical outcomes after bedside and interventional radiology paracentesis procedures. The American Journal of Medicine. 2013;126:349-356
- Brown SM, Kasal J. Bedside ultrasound in the Intensive Care unit: Where is the evidence? Seminars in Respiratory and Critical Care Medicine. 2015 Dec;36(6):878-889
- Thakkar R, Wright SM, Alguire P, et al. Procedures performed by hospitalist and non-hospitalist general internists. Journal of General Internal Medicine. 2010;25:448-452
- Metkus TS, Kim BS. Bedside Diagnosis in the Intensive Care Unit. Is Looking Overlooked? Ann Am Thorac Soc. 2015 Oct;12(10):1447-50. doi: 10.1513/AnnalsATS.201505-271OI. PMID: 26389653; PMCID: PMC4627420.
- Harvey MA. Critical-care-unit bedside design and furnishing: impact on nosocomial infections. Infect Control Hosp Epidemiol. 1998 Aug;19(8):597-601. doi: 10.1086/647881. PMID: 9758063.
- Hoppe U C, Böhm M, Dietz R.*et al* Leitlinien zur Therapie der chronischen Herzinsuffizienz. *Z Kardiol* 200594488–509.Current recommendations of the German Cardiac Society for the treatment of chronic heart failure.
- Ewersdfs
- Swedberg K, Cleland J, Dargie H.*et al* Guidelines for the diagnosis and treatment of chronic heart failure: executive summary (update 2005): The Task Force for the Diagnosis and Treatment of Chronic Heart Failure of the European Society of Cardiology. *Eur Heart J* 2005261115–1140.Current ESC practice guidelines; compare with reference 1.
- Hunt S A. ACC/AHA 2005 guideline update for the diagnosis and management of chronic heart failure in the adult: a report of the American College of Cardiology/American Heart Association Task Force on Practice Guidelines (Writing Committee to Update the 2001 Guidelines for the Evaluation and Management of Heart Failure). *J Am Coll Cardiol* 200546e1–82.Current ACC/AHA practice guidelines including comprehensive overview of the literature until 2005, together with references 1 and 2.
- 104. Cleland J G, Gemmell I, Khand A.*et al* Is the prognosis of heart failure improving? *Eur J Heart Fail* 19991229–241.
- 105. Böhm M, Werner N, Kindermann M. Drug treatment for chronic heart failure. *Clin Res Cardiol* 200695(suppl 4)36–56.

- 106. Flather M, Yusuf S, Kober L.*et al* Long-term ACE-inhibitor therapy in patients with heart failure or left-ventricular dysfunction: a systematic overview of data from individual patients. ACE-Inhibitor Myocardial infarction Collaborative Group. *Lancet* 20003551575–1581.Meta-analysis of clinical trials on the use of ACE inhibitors in heart failure.
- 107. Taylor A L, Ziesche S, Yancy C.*et al* Combination of isosorbide dinitrate and hydralazine in blacks with heart failure. *N Engl J Med* 20043512049–2057
- 108. Bristow M R, Saxon L A, Boehmer J.*et al* Comparison of Medical Therapy, Pacing and Defibrillation in Heart Failure (COMPANION) Investigators. Cardiac resynchronization therapy with or without implantable defibrillator in advanced chronic heart failure. *N Engl J Med* 20043502140–2150.First study to show that CRT improves mortality in heart failure.
- 109. Cleland J G, Daubert J C, Erdmann E.*et al* The effect of cardiac resynchronization on morbidity and mortality in heart failure. *N Engl J Med* 20053521539–1549.
- 110. Götze S, Butter C, Fleck E. Cardiac resynchronization therapy for heart failure—from experimental pacing to evidence-based therapy. *Clin Res Cardiol* 200695(suppl 4)18–35.
- 111. Lee D S, Green L D, Liu P P.*et al* Effectiveness of implantable defibrillators for preventing arrhythmic events and death. *J Am Coll Cardiol* 2003411573–1582.Meta-analysis of trials on secondary prevention of SCD.
- 112. Bohula EA, Katz JN, van Diepen S et al. Demographics, Care Patterns, and Outcomes of Patients Admitted to Cardiac Intensive Care Units: The Critical Care Cardiology Trials Network Prospective North American Multicenter Registry of Cardiac Critical Illness. JAMA Cardiol. 2019 Jul 24;
- 113. Holland EM, Moss TJ. Acute Noncardiovascular Illness in the Cardiac Intensive Care Unit. J Am Coll Cardiol. 2017 Apr 25;69(16):1999–2007.
- 114. Vallabhajosyula S, Dunlay SM, Prasad A et al. Acute Noncardiac Organ Failure in Acute Myocardial Infarction With Cardiogenic Shock. J Am Coll Cardiol. 2019 Apr 6;73(14):1781–91.
- 115. van Diepen S, Reynolds HR, Stebbins A et al. Incidence and outcomes associated with early heart failure pharmacotherapy in patients with ongoing cardiogenic shock. *Crit Care Med.* 2014 Feb;42(2):281–8.
- 116. Schumann J, Henrich EC, Strobl H et al. Inotropic agents and vasodilator strategies for the treatment of cardiogenic shock or low cardiac output syndrome. *Cochrane Database Syst Rev.* 2018 Jan 29;1 CD009669.
- 117. van Diepen S, Katz JN, Albert NM et al. Contemporary Management of Cardiogenic Shock: A Scientific Statement From the American Heart Association. *Circulation.* 2017 Oct 17;136(16):e232–e268.

- 118. Jentzer JC, Coons JC, Link CB, Schmidhofer M. Pharmacotherapy update on the use of vasopressors and inotropes in the Intensive Care unit. *J Cardiovasc Pharmacol Ther.* 2015 May;20(3):249–60.
- 119. Costanzo MR. Ultrafiltration in Acute Heart Failure. *Card Fail Rev.* 2019 Feb;5(1):9–18.
- 120. Zochios V, Jones N. Acute right heart syndrome in the critically ill patient. *Heart Lung Vessel.* 2014;6(3):157-70
- 121. Neri M, Villa G, Garzotto F et al. Nomenclature for renal replacement therapy in acute kidney injury: basic principles. *Crit Care.* 2016 Oct 10;20(1):318.
- 122. Costanzo MR, Guglin ME, Saltzberg MT et al. Ultrafiltration versus intravenous diuretics for patients hospitalized for acute decompensated heart failure. *J Am Coll Cardiol.* 2007 Feb 13;49(6):675–83.
- 123. Giglioli C, Landi D, Cecchi E et al. Effects of ULTRAfiltration vs. DIureticS on clinical, biohumoral and haemodynamic variables in patients with deCOmpensated heart failure: the ULTRADISCO study. *Eur J Heart Fail.* 2011 Mar;13(3):337–46.
- 124. Bart BA, Goldsmith SR, Lee KL et al. Ultrafiltration in decompensated heart failure with cardiorenal syndrome. *N Engl J Med.* 2012 Dec 13;367(24):2296–304. Heart Failure Clinical Research Network.
- 125. Sanofi Aventis. Clopidogrel (Plavix) package insert. Bridgewater NJ; 2013.
- 126. Eli Lilly and Company. Prasugrel (Effient) package insert. Indianapolis, IN; 2009.
- 127. Astra Zeneca LP. Ticagrelor (Brilinta) package insert. Wilmington, DE; 2011.
- 128. Yusuf S, Zhao F, Mehta SR, et al. Effects of clopidogrel in addition to aspirin in patients with acute coronary syndromes without ST-segment elevation. N Engl J Med 2001;345:494 – 502.
- 129. Kezerashvili A, Marzo K, De Leon J. Beta blocker use after acute myocardial infarction in the patient with normal systolic function: When is it “ok” to discontinue? Curr Cardiol Rev. 2012;8:77– 84.
- 130. Køber L, Torp-Pedersen C, Carlsen JE, et al. A clinical trial of the angiotensin-converting-enzyme inhibitor trandolapril in patients with left ventricular dysfunction after myocardial infarction. Trandolapril Cardiac Evaluation (TRACE) Study Group. N Engl J Med 1995;333:1670 –1676.
- 131. Geppert A. Patienten mit Klappenvitium auf der Intensivstation [Patients in the Intensive Care unit with valvular diseases]. Med Klin Intensivmed Notfmed. 2013 Oct;108(7):555-60. German. doi: 10.1007/s00063-012-0140-z. Epub 2013 Sep 15. PMID: 24037458.

- 132. Spodick DH. Acute cardiac tamponade. *N Engl J Med.* 2003;349(7):684-690
- 133. Imazio M, Cecchi E, Demichelis B, et al. Myopericarditis versus viral or idiopathic acute pericarditis. *Heart* 2008;94(4):498-501
- 134. Troughton RW, Asher CR, Klein AL. Pericarditis. *Lancet* 2004;363(9410):717-727
- 135. Reddy PS, Curtiss EI, O'Toole JD, Shaver JA. Cardiac tamponade: hemodynamic observations in man. *Circulation* 1978;58(2):265-272
- 136. Kerber RE, Gascho JA, Litchfield R, Wolfson P, Ott D, Pandian NG. Hemodynamic effects of volume expansion and nitroprusside compared with pericardiocentesis in patients with acute cardiac tamponade. *N Engl J Med.* 1982;307(15):929-931.
- 137. Sagrista-Sauleda J, Permanyer-Miralda G, Candell-Riera J, Angel J, Soler-Soler J. Transient cardiac constriction: an unrecognized pattern of evolution in effusive acute idiopathic pericarditis. *Am J Cardiol.* 1987;59(9):961-966
- 138. Haley JH, Tajik AJ, Danielson GK, Schaff HV, Mulvagh SL, Oh JK. Transient constrictive pericarditis: causes and natural history. *J Am Coll Cardiol.* 2004;43(2):271-275.
- 139. Global Burden of Disease Study 2013 Collaborators . Global, regional, and national incidence, prevalence, and years lived with disability for 301 acute and chronic diseases and injuries in 188 countries, 1990-2013: a systematic analysis for the Global Burden of Disease Study 2013. *Lancet* 2015;386:743–800
- 140. Schultheiss HP, Khl U, Cooper LT. The management of myocarditis. *Eur Heart J* 2011;32:2616–25.
- 141. Cooper LT, Hare JM, Tazelaar HD. et al. Usefulness of immunosuppression for giant cell myocarditis. *Am J Cardiol* 2008;102:1535–9.
- 142. Khatib R, Reyes MP, Smith F, Khatib G, Rezkalla S. Enhancement of coxsackievirus B4 virulence by indomethacin. *J Lab Clin Med* 1990;116:116–20
- Ammirati E, Frigerio M, Adler ED. et al. Management of acute myocarditis and chronic inflammatory cardiomyopathy: an expert consensus document. *Circ Heart Fail* 2020;663–87
- Weigang, E., Nienaber, C. A., Rehders, T. C., Ince, H., Vahl, F., & Beyersdorf, F. (2008). Management of Patients With Aortic Dissection. *Deutsches Ärzteblatt International*, *105*(38), 639-645. https://doi.org/10.3238/arztebl.2008.0639
- Borst HG. Aneurysma und Dissektion der Aorta ascendens und des Aortenbogens. In: Borst HG, Klinner W, Oelert H, editors. *Herzchirurgie: Die Eingriffe am Herzen und an den herznahen Gefäßen.* Berlin, Heidelberg, New York: Springer; 1991. pp. 434–463

- Nienaber CA, Fattori R, Lund G, et al. Nonsurgical reconstruction of thoracic aortic dissection by stent-graft placement. *N Engl J Med.* 1999;340:1539–1545
- Eggebrecht H, Nienaber CA, Neuhäuser M, et al. Endovascular stent-graft placement in aortic dissection: a meta-analysis. *Eur Heart J.* 2006;27:489–498.
- Cook, D. J., Webb, S., & Proudfoot, A. (2022). Assessment and management of cardiovascular disease in the Intensive Care unit. *Heart*, *108*(5), 397-405. https://doi.org/10.1136/heartjnl-2019-315568
- Bhatnagar P, Wickramasinghe K, Wilkins E, et al.. Trends in the epidemiology of cardiovascular disease in the UK. *Heart* 2016;102:1945–52. 10.1136/heartjnl-2016-309573
- Adams KF, Fonarow GC, Emerman CL, et al.. Characteristics and outcomes of patients hospitalized for heart failure in the United States: rationale, design, and preliminary observations from the first 100,000 cases in the acute decompensated heart failure national registry (ADHERE). *Am Heart J* 2005;149:209–16. 10.1016/j.ahj.2004.08.005
- Yancy CW, Jessup M, Bozkurt B. ACCF/AHA guideline for the management of heart failure: a report of the American College of Cardiology Foundation/American Heart Association Task Force on practice guidelines. *Circulation* 2013;2013:e240–327.
- Ponikowski P, Voors AA, Anker SD, et al.. 2016 ESC Guidelines for the diagnosis and treatment of acute and chronic heart failure: The Task Force for the diagnosis and treatment of acute and chronic heart failure of the European Society of Cardiology (ESC)Developed with the special contribution of the Heart Failure Association (HFA) of the ESC. *Eur Heart J* 2016;37:2129–200. 10.1093/eurheartj/ehw128
- Doll JA, Ohman EM, Patel MR, et al.. A team-based approach to patients in cardiogenic shock. *Catheter Cardiovasc Interv* 2016;88:424–33. 10.1002/ccd.26297.
- Crimi, Ettore; Hill, Charles C. (2014). *Postoperative ICU Management of Vascular Surgery Patients. Anesthesiology Clinics, 32(3), 735–757.* doi:10.1016/j.anclin.2014.05.001
- Rubenfeld GD, Caldwell E, Peabody E, . et al. Incidence and outcomes of acute lung injury. *N Engl J Med*. 2005. October 20; 353 16: 1685– 93.
- Brower RG, Matthay MA, Morris A, . et al .; Acute Respiratory Distress Syndrome Network Ventilation with lower tidal volumes as compared with traditional tidal volumes for acute lung injury and the acute respiratory distress syndrome. *N Engl J Med*. 2000. May 4; 342 18: 1301– 8.
- Brogan TV, Thiagarajan RR, Rycus PT, Bartlett RH, Bratton SL.. Extracorporeal membrane oxygenation in adults with severe respiratory failure: a multi-center database. *Intensive Care Med*. 2009. December; 35 12: 2105– 14.

- Makdisi G, Wang IW. Extra Corporeal Membrane Oxygenation (ECMO) review of a lifesaving technology. *J Thorac Dis*. 2015. July; 7 7: E166– 76.
- Napp LC, Kühn C, Hoeper MM, . et al. Cannulation strategies for percutaneous extracorporeal membrane oxygenation in adults. *Clin Res Cardiol*. 2016. April; 105 4: 283– 96.
- Scherer M, Moritz A, Martens S.. The use of extracorporeal membrane oxygenation in patients with therapy refractory cardiogenic shock as a bridge to implantable left ventricular assist device and perioperative right heart support. *J Artif Organs*. 2009; 12 3: 160– 5.
- Pratt AK, Shah NS, Boyce SW. Left ventricular assist device management in the ICU. Crit Care Med. 2014 Jan;42(1):158-68. doi: 10.1097/01.ccm.0000435675.91305.76. PMID: 24240731.
- Kipnis, E., Ramsingh, D., Bhargava, M., Dincer, E., Cannesson, M., Broccard, A., Vallet, B., Bendjelid, K., & Thibault, R. (2011). Monitoring in the Intensive Care. *Critical Care Research and Practice, 2012*. https://doi.org/10.1155/2012/473507
- Lim, Wendy; Qushmaq, Ismael; Cook, Deborah J.; Devereaux, P J.; Heels-Ansdell, Diane; Crowther, Mark A.; Tkaczyk, Andrea; Meade, Maureen O.; Cook, Richard J. (2006). *Reliability of electrocardiogram interpretation in critically ill patients*. Critical Care Medicine, 34(5), 1338–1343.* doi:10.1097/01.ccm.0000214679.23957.90
- Myocardial infarction redefined: A consensus document of the Joint European Society of Cardiology/American College of Cardiology Committee for the Redefinition of Myocardial Infarction. J Am Coll Cardiol 2000; 36: 959 –969
- Ammann P, Maggiorini M, Bertel O, et al: Troponin as a risk factor for mortality in critically ill patients without acute coronary syndromes. J Am Coll Cardiol 2003; 41: 2004 –2009
- Ammann P, Fehr T, Minder EI, et al: Elevation of troponin I in sepsis and septic shock. Intensive Care Med 2001; 27:965–969
- Fye WB. A history of the origin, evolution, and impact of electrocardiography. Am J Cardiol. 1994 May 15;73(13):937-49.
- Baranchuk A, Bayés de Luna A. The P-wave morphology: what does it tell us? Herzschrittmacherther Elektrophysiol. 2015 Sep;26(3):192-9.
- PIPBERGER HV, TANENBAUM HL. [The P wave, P-R interval, and Q-T ratio of the normal orthogonal electrocardiogram]. Circulation. 1958 Dec;18(6):1175-80.
- Zema MJ, Kligfield P. ECG poor R-wave progression: review and synthesis. Arch Intern Med. 1982 Jun;142(6):1145-8.
- Channer K, Morris F. ABC of clinical electrocardiography: Myocardial ischaemia. BMJ. 2002 Apr 27;324(7344):1023-6.

- de Bliek EC. ST elevation: Differential diagnosis and caveats. A comprehensive review to help distinguish ST elevation myocardial infarction from nonischemic etiologies of ST elevation. Turk J Emerg Med. 2018 Mar;18(1):1-10.
- Tse G, Chan YW, Keung W, Yan BP. Electrophysiological mechanisms of long and short QT syndromes. Int J Cardiol Heart Vasc. 2017 Mar;14:8-13.
- Levis JT. ECG Diagnosis: Hypothermia. Perm J. 2010 Fall;14(3):73.
- Wang J, Yang B, Chen H, Ju W, Chen K, Zhang F, Cao K, Chen M. Epsilon waves detected by various electrocardiographic recording methods: in patients with arrhythmogenic right ventricular cardiomyopathy. Tex Heart Inst J. 2010;37(4):405-11.
- Sattar, Y., & Chhabra, L. (2021). *Electrocardiogram*. PubMed; StatPearls Publishing. https://www.ncbi.nlm.nih.gov/books/NBK549803/
- Huygh, J., Peeters, Y., Bernards, J., & G. Malbrain, L. N. (2015). Hemodynamic monitoring in the critically ill: An overview of current cardiac output monitoring methods. *F1000Research*, *5*. https://doi.org/10.12688/f1000research.899
- Adam SA, Osborne S, Welch J (eds). Critical care nursing: science and practice. 3rd edn. Oxford: Oxford University Press; 2017. https://doi.org/10.1093/ med/9780199696260.001.0001
- American Association of Critical Care Nurses. AACN practice alert: pulmonary artery/central venous pressure monitoring in adults. AACN Adv Crit Care. 2020;31(1):41–48. https://doi.org/10.4037/aacnacc202032
- Bannon M, Heller SF, Rivera M. Anatomic considerations for central venous cannulation. Risk Manag Healthc Policy. 2011;4:27–39.
- Bennett SR. Sepsis in the Intensive Care unit. Surgery (Oxf). 2015;33(11):565– 571. https://doi.org/10.1016/j.mpsur.2015.08.0024
- Berlin DA, Bakker J. Starling curves and central venous pressure. Crit Care. 2015;19(1):55. https://doi.org/10.1186/s13054-015-0776-1
- Chlabicz M, Kazimierczyk R, Lopatowska P et al. Fluid therapy in non-septic, refractory acute decompensated heart failure patients—the cautious role of central venous pressure. Adv Med Sci. 2019;64(1):37–43. https://doi. org/10.1016/j.advms.2018.11.001
- Barry Hill;Catherine Smith; (2021). *Central venous pressure monitoring in critical care settings . British Journal of Nursing, (), –.* doi:10.12968/bjon.2021.30.4.230
- Angus DC, Carlet J; 2002 Brussels Roundtable Participants. Surviving Intensive Care: a report from the 2002 Brussels Roundtable. Intensive Care Med . 2003; 29 (3): 368 - 377.

- Zazzle t-shirts. Zazzle website. http://www.zazzle.ca/the_plural_of_ anecdote_is_not_data_tee_shirts-235279170565465750 . Accessed May 15, 2014.
- Topol EJ. Nesiritide - not verifi ed . N Engl J Med . 2005; 353 (2): 113 - 116 .188. The EC/IC Bypass Study Group. Failure of extracranial-intracranial arterial bypass to reduce the risk of ischemic stroke. Results of an international randomized trial. N Engl J Med . 1985 ; 313 (19): 1191 - 1200.
- Garland, Allan (2014). *Arterial Lines in the ICU. Chest, 146(5), 1155–1158.* doi:10.1378/chest.14-1212
- Pulmonary Artery Catheter Consensus Conference Participants. Pulmonary Artery Catheter Consensus Statement. *Critical Care Medicine* 1997;25:910-25.
- Shah MR, Hasselblad V, Stevenson LW, Binanay C, O'Connor CM, Sopko G, et al. Impact of pulmonary artery catheter in critically ill patients. Meta-analysis of randomized clinical trials. *JAMA* 2005;294:1664-70.
- Wiener RS, Welch HG. Trends in the use of the pulmonary artery catheter in the United States, 1993-2004. *JAMA* 2007;298(4):423-9.
- Zion MM, Balkin J, Rosenmann D, Goldbourt U, Reicher-Reiss H, Kaplinsky E, et al. Use of pulmonary artery catheters in patients with acute myocardial infarction. Analysis of experience in 5,841 patients in the SPRINT Registry. SPRINT Study Group. *Chest* 1990;98(6):1331-5.
- Rajaram, S. S., Desai, N. K., Kalra, A., Gajera, M., Cavanaugh, S. K., Brampton, W., Young, D., Harvey, S., & Rowan, K. (2013). Pulmonary artery catheters for adult patients in Intensive Care. *The Cochrane Database of Systematic Reviews*, *2013*(2). https://doi.org/10.1002/14651858.CD003408.pub3
- Mehta Y, Sharma KK. Double knot with formation of a double loop of pulmonary artery catheter. J Cardiothorac Anesth. 1990;4:149–150.
- Linton RA, Band DM, Haire KM. A new method of measuring cardiac output in man using lithium dilution. Br J Anaesth. 1993;71:262–266.
- Hofer CK, Cecconi M, Marx G, della Rocca G. Minimally invasive haemodynamic monitoring. Eur J Anaesthesiol. 2009;26:996–1002.
- Funk DJ, Moretti EW, Gan TJ. Minimally invasive cardiac output monitoring in the perioperative setting. Anesth Analg. 2009;108:887–897.
- Kubicek WG, Karnegis JN, Patterson RP, Witsoe DA, Mattson RH. Development and evaluation of an impedance cardiac output system. Aerosp Med. 1966;37:1208–1212.

- Keren H, Burkhoff D, Squara P. Evaluation of a noninvasive continuous cardiac output monitoring system based on thoracic bioreactance. Am J Physiol Heart Circ Physiol. 2007;293:H583–H589.
- CONMED Corporation. ECOM endotracheal cardiac output monitor. 2010.
- Meyer S, Todd D, Wright I, Gortner L, Reynolds G. Review article: Non-invasive assessment of cardiac output with portable continuous-wave Doppler ultrasound. Emerg Med Australas. 2008;20:201–208.
- Yelderman, Mark L.; Ramsay, Mike A.; Quinn, Michael D.; Paulsen, A.W.; McKown, Russel C.; Gillman, Paula H. (1992). *Continuous thermodilution cardiac output measurement in Intensive Care unit patients. , 6(3), 270–274.* doi:10.1016/1053-0770(92)90137-V
- Monnet X, Teboul JL. Transpulmonary thermodilution: advantages and limits. Crit Care. 2017 Jun 19;21(1):147. doi: 10.1186/s13054-017-1739-5. PMID: 28625165; PMCID: PMC5474867.
- Møller-Sørensen, H., Norum, H. M., & Ricksten, S.-E. (2019). 10 tips for Intensive Care management of transplanted heart patients. *Intensive Care Medicine*, *45*(3), 374–376. https://doi.org/10.1007/s00134-019-05545-w
- Chahine, J., & Alvey, H. (2021, July 25). *Left Ventricular Failure.* PubMed; StatPearls Publishing. https://www.ncbi.nlm.nih.gov/books/NBK537098/
- Yancy CW, Jessup M, Bozkurt B, Butler J, Casey DE, Drazner MH, Fonarow GC, Geraci SA, Horwich T, Januzzi JL, Johnson MR, Kasper EK, Levy WC, Masoudi FA, McBride PE, McMurray JJ, Mitchell JE, Peterson PN, Riegel B, Sam F, Stevenson LW, Tang WH, Tsai EJ, Wilkoff BL. 2013 ACCF/AHA guideline for the management of heart failure: executive summary: a report of the American College of Cardiology Foundation/American Heart Association Task Force on practice guidelines. Circulation. 2013 Oct 15;128(16):1810-52.
- Yancy CW, Jessup M, Bozkurt B, Butler J, Casey DE, Colvin MM, Drazner MH, Filippatos GS, Fonarow GC, Givertz MM, Hollenberg SM, Lindenfeld J, Masoudi FA, McBride PE, Peterson PN, Stevenson LW, Westlake C. 2017 ACC/AHA/HFSA Focused Update of the 2013 ACCF/AHA Guideline for the Management of Heart Failure: A Report of the American College of Cardiology/American Heart Association Task Force on Clinical Practice Guidelines and the Heart Failure Society of America. Circulation. 2017 Aug 08;136(6):e137-e161.
- Trappe, J. (2010). Treating critical supraventricular and ventricular arrhythmias. *Journal of Emergencies, Trauma and Shock*, *3*(2), 143-152. https://doi.org/10.4103/0974-2700.62114.
- Kalahasty, G., & Ellenbogen, K. A. (2011). Management of the Patient With Implantable Cardioverter-Defibrillator Lead Failure. *Circulation*, *123*(12), 1352–1354. https://doi.org/10.1161/circulationaha.110.986828

- Bradfield JS, Ajijola OA, Vaseghi M, Shivkumar K. Mechanisms and management of refractory ventricular arrhythmias in the age of autonomic modulation. Heart Rhythm. 2018 Aug;15(8):1252-1260. doi: 10.1016/j.hrthm.2018.02.015. Epub 2018 Feb 14. PMID: 29454137.
- Paulis, S. D., Arlotta, G., Calabrese, M., Corsi, F., Taccheri, T., Antoniucci, M. E., Martinelli, L., Bevilacqua, F., Tinelli, G., & Cavaliere, F. (2022). Postoperative Intensive Care Management of Aortic Repair. *Journal of Personalized Medicine*, *12*(8). https://doi.org/10.3390/jpm12081351
- Olinic, M., Stanek, A., Tătaru, A., Homorodean, C., & Olinic, M. (2019). Acute Limb Ischemia: An Update on Diagnosis and Management. *Journal of Clinical Medicine*, *8*(8). https://doi.org/10.3390/jcm8081215
- Raiten, J. M., Gutsche, J. T., Horak, J., & Augoustides, J. G. (2012). Critical care management of patients following transcatheter aortic valve replacement. *F1000Research*, *2*. https://doi.org/10.12688/f1000research.2-62.v1
- Möbius-Winkler S, Sandri M, Mangner N, Lurz P, Dähnert I, Schuler G. The WATCHMAN left atrial appendage closure device for atrial fibrillation. J Vis Exp. 2012 Feb 28;(60):3671. doi: 10.3791/3671. PMID: 22395336; PMCID: PMC3399494.
- Wintgens LIS, Maarse M, Swaans MJ, Rensing BJWM, Van Dijk VF, Boersma LVA. The WATCHMAN left atrial appendage closure device for patients with atrial fibrillation: current status and future perspectives. Expert Rev Med Devices. 2020 Jul;17(7):615-626. doi: 10.1080/17434440.2020.1781615. Epub 2020 Jul 27. PMID: 32543911.
- Chandran, J., Sriram, S., & Krishna, B. (2021). Clinical Utility of Arterial Blood Gas Test in an Intensive Care Unit: An Observational Study. *Indian Journal of Critical Care Medicine : Peer-reviewed, Official Publication of Indian Society of Critical Care Medicine*, *25*(2), 172-175. https://doi.org/10.5005/jp-journals-10071-23719.
- Tracy C, Boushahri A. Managing arrhythmias in the Intensive Care unit. Crit Care Clin. 2014 Jul;30(3):365-90. doi: 10.1016/j.ccc.2014.03.009. PMID: 24996602.
- Tarditi DJ, Hollenberg SM. Cardiac arrhythmias in the Intensive Care unit. Semin Respir Crit Care Med. 2006 Jun;27(3):221-9. doi: 10.1055/s-2006-945525. PMID: 16791756.

Part II

EXTRA EDGE

Important topics and Some Conditions that are Managed in CICU

Medical

End-stage Heart failure: Heart failure affects at least 10 million people in Europe and about 5 million in North America, making it a significant public health issue. a9 (global data) Heart failure is one of the primary causes of death and hospitalization among the elderly due to its age-dependent increase in prevalence and incidence [100]. The percentage of individuals who progress to an advanced form of the disease, also known as end-stage, refractory, or fatal heart failure, is rapidly increasing due to the rise in life expectancy around the world and advancements in the treatment of heart failure in recent times [101].

Pharmacological management: Unless there are contraindications, angiotensin-converting enzyme (ACE) inhibitors are advised as first-line therapy for all patients with decreased left ventricular (LV) systolic function regardless of clinical symptoms. ACE medications have been proven to improve survival, decrease reinfarctions, and increase hospital stays in people who suffer from heart failure after the acute phase of myocardial infarction [102]. Renal function, serum electrolytes, especially potassium, and blood pressure (lying down and standing) should all be carefully monitored throughout the course of treatment. Angiotensin II type I receptor blockers (ARBs) may be used as an alternative to ACE inhibitors in patients with symptomatic chronic heart failure who cannot take ACE medications to reduce morbidity and mortality [103].

Inhibitors of the renin-angiotensin system should be co-administered with diuretics, which helps improve dyspnea and exercise intolerance because individuals with end-stage heart failure frequently exhibit indications of fluid retention or have a history of doing so. Due to their synergistic method of action, thiazides and loop diuretics can be utilized successfully in the event of a fluid overload that is resistant to treatment in end-stage heart failure. Patients with symptomatic stable systolic heart failure should get further treatment with adrenergic receptor blockers in the absence of contraindications, in addition to the conventional regimen of ACE inhibitors and diuretics [104,105].

Aldosterone receptor antagonists are advised in addition to adrenergic receptor blockers, ACE inhibitors, and diuretics in patients with advanced heart failure unless contraindicated because they are known to increase survival and morbidity. In symptomatic patients with heart failure with tachyarrhythmia caused by atrial fibrillation (AF) who have already received appropriate doses of beta-blockers, cardiac glycosides are recommended for heart rate management. The class III antiarrhythmic amiodarone may restore and maintain sinus rhythm or increase the achievement of electrical cardioversion in heart failure patients with atrial fibrillation (AF). Amiodarone is an effective treatment for the majority of supraventricular and ventricular arrhythmias in patients with heart failure [103, 104].

if write the contraindiCATION IT WILL BENIFICIAL

Surgical management: Cardiovascular resynchronization therapy (CRT) using biventricular pacing improves symptoms and exercise tolerance while lowering hospitalizations and mortality in patients with reduced LV function (ejaculation fraction (EF) 35%), left bundle branch block, sinus rhythm, or echocardiographic signs of ventricular dyssynchrony and QRS width 120 ms [108]. Patients with heart failure in NYHA classes III-IV with LVEF 35% and QRS width 120 ms were randomly assigned to receive the best pharmacological treatment alone, in combination with CRT, or in combination with implantable cardioverter-defibrillator (ICD). Importantly, although mortality was lower in both device arms, there was no discernible difference between CRT and CRT/ICD in terms of mortality [106, 107].

ICD implantation has been found to decrease mortality in cardiac arrest survivors and patients with persistent symptomatic ventricular tachyarrhythmias for secondary prevention of sudden cardiac death (SCD). ICD therapy is recommended for some patients with LVEF 30% after myocardial infarction (>40 days) and in patients with ischaemic and non-ischaemic heart failure (NYHA class II–III) with LVEF 35% to lower mortality for the primary prevention of SCD in heart failure patients receiving optimal pharmacological treatment [109, 110,111].

C**ardiogenic shock:** The complex disorder known as a cardiogenic shock (CS) is defined by end-organ hypoperfusion brought on by a decrease in cardiac output brought due to primary cardiac disease. The clinical manifestations of CS might range widely in terms of hemodynamic characteristics [112]. The common factor, though, is insufficient cardiac output necessitating medication and/or artificial circulatory support. A thorough examination of the etiology of CS is necessary for best-practice management in the CICU. Acute myocardial infarction and either acute or chronic heart failure continue to be the most frequent causes of CS. CS is typically compounded by multiorgan system dysfunction, regardless of the etiology, necessitating a multidisciplinary approach to management in an Intensive Care setting [113].

Pulmonary artery catheterization: The pathophysiology of CS is predisposed to metabolic disturbances and hemodynamic instability. Therefore, it's crucial to invasively monitor end-organ perfusion measurements in addition to systemic arterial pressures in order to accurately pinpoint the cause of the shock state. In a critical care situation, the pulmonary artery (PA) catheter is a crucial diagnostic tool that is frequently used to help determine the existence and type of CS as well as to direct treatment [114,115].

Pharmacological management: Inotropes boost cardiac output and contractility in CS. Vasopressors boost systemic vascular resistance by raising vascular tone, which raises blood pressure. Dobutamine, milrinone, norepinephrine, epinephrine, vasopressin, and dopamine are examples of frequently used vasotropes and inotropes. The two main inotropes utilized in a modern CICU are dobutamine and milrinone, and both promote myocardial contractility, albeit in distinct ways. In CS patients with hypotension, vasopressors such as norepinephrine, epinephrine, dopamine, and vasopressin are frequently utilized [116-118]

Non-pharmacological management:

Ultrafiltration: The critical care management of CS includes adjunct nonpharmacologic therapy. Elevated intracardiac filling pressures brought on by fluid and sodium retention by the kidneys as a consequence of neurohormonal activation are frequently seen in acute heart failure and CS [119]. The cornerstone of therapy to relieve congestion is diuretics. However, diuretic resistance can be brought on by proteinuria, reduced renal blood flow, and poor absorption. This vicious cycle is then exacerbated by increased congestion, which can then result in multiorgan dysfunction, including acute renal failure. Acute right ventricular failure may also enhance shock and end-organ failure, decrease left ventricular filling, increase ventricular interdependence, and worsen congestion linked to right ventricular distention [120,121].

Mechanical ventilation: In cases, of necessitating airway protection, or general hemodynamic instability, mechanical ventilation may be necessary. Physiologic objectives for oxygenation or ventilation in CS are not well CS caused by acute hypoxemia, increased labor of breathing, and decreased state of consciousness supported by evidence, despite the significant rate of respiratory failure needing mechanical ventilation. Clinicians need to be aware of how positive pressure ventilation affects the hemodynamics of the left and right ventricles as well as the best analgesics and sedatives to use in CS [122-124].

Acute coronary syndrome: Unstable angina (UA), non-ST elevated myocardial infarction (NSTEMI), and ST-elevated myocardial infarction (STEMI) are all cardiac ischemia conditions that fall under the umbrella term of acute coronary syndrome (ACS). A thorough evaluation of clinical characteristics, such as electrocardiogram (ECG) abnormalities and biochemical indicators of myocardial necrosis, is the foundation for the diagnosis and classification of ACS.

Initial management:

Early: To avoid potentially catastrophic clinical effects and alleviate persistent ischemia, it is critical to assess individuals with suspected ACS right away. It is important to do early risk stratification that takes into account a physical exam, patient's demographics, ECG, medical history, and cardiac biomarker measures.

Pharmacological management: (no mention of aspirin ?

Antithrombotic agents: A key component of the care of ACS is antiplatelet medication, which lowers the risk of thrombosis by preventing platelet release and aggregation [125].

Clopidogrel- Clopidogrel was a routine treatment for individuals presenting with ACS prior to the release of additional therapeutic medicines. A 2001 experiment that randomly allocated patients who presented with UA or NSTEMI to receive either clopidogrel or a placebo in addition to aspirin for a duration of 3–12 months was the first to show the efficacy of doing so. The primary endpoint of cardiovascular death, nonfatal MI, or stroke was observed to be decreased in the group given dual antiplatelet treatment (DAPT) [125].

Prasugrel- Prasugrel was associated with a substantial 2.2% absolute decrease in a nonfatal MI, a composite endpoint of cardiovascular death, or nonfatal stroke as compared to clopidogrel, according to a 2007 landmark trial comparing the two medications [126].

Ticagrelor- Comparing ticagrelor to clopidogrel, there was a 1.9% absolute reduction in the composite endpoint of vascular mortality, MI, or stroke [127].

Anticoagulants: Parenteral anticoagulants and antiplatelet medications are utilized during the initial therapy of ACS. During this time, parenteral anticoagulants such as fondaparinux, unfractionated heparin (UFH), low-molecular-weight heparin, or bivalirudin may be administered [128].

Adjuvant therapies: For patients presenting with NSTEMI, UA, or STEMI, oral β-blocker medication should be started within 24 hours of the event's beginning. By preventing the actions of catecholamines on β-receptors found in the heart, β-blockers lower myocardial contractility, sinus node rate, and AV node conduction velocity [129].

Valvular heart disease: In the etiology of acute decompensated heart failure, valvular dysfunction occurs as frequently as acute coronary syndromes. Over 10% of people over the age of 75 have significant valvular dysfunction, which is a prevalence that rises with age. Despite solid guidelines for treating valvular heart disease in the general population, there are few studies and guidelines on the treatment of these individuals, particularly in an Intensive Care unit (ICU) setting. When normal inotrope and vasopressor therapy fails to stabilize patients, a number of therapeutic alternatives have become accessible in the last ten years. These include mitral clipping, extracorporeal membrane oxygenation (ECMO), and balloon valvuloplasty in patients with severe aortic valve stenosis and assist devices. In cases of shock brought on by valvular dysfunction, these therapeutic options should be viewed as a bridge to surgical procedures because hemodynamic and stabilization of organ function are crucial for enabling valve repair or replacement, which is still the preferred course of action in this circumstance but is not always feasible in the acute setting [131].

Pericarditis: Clinical manifestations of pericardial disorders include cardiac tamponade, pericardial effusion, acute pericarditis, and constrictive pericarditis [132]. ECG/ ECho finding ?

Acute pericarditis: Inflammation of the pericardium causes the common disorder known as acute pericarditis, which can happen on its own or as a symptom of another systemic illness. Three main medications—NSAIDs, colchicine, and corticosteroids—have been the focus of medical treatment for viral or idiopathic acute pericarditis. Patients with myopericarditis have comparable treatment options and prognoses as those with acute pericarditis [132,133].

Constrictive pericarditis: The symptoms and constrictive characteristics of patients with temporary constrictive pericarditis brought on by pericardial inflammation may disappear with medical treatment alone. Surgery is considered the gold standard for treating chronic constrictive pericarditis [137,138].

Cardiac tamponade: Pericardial fluid builds up under pressure, which is a symptom of cardiac tamponade. The parietal pericardium moves less when the pericardial effusion enlarges. Tamponade happens when systemic venous return to the right atrium is compromised due to compression of all heart chambers brought on by elevated intrapericardial pressure [134,135]. A pericardiocentesis or surgical evacuation of pericardial fluid is urgently needed in cases of acute cardiac tamponade with hemodynamic compromise. Although meticulous hemodynamic surveillance with serial echocardiography and therapy of the underlying reason for tamponade may be appropriate in patients with hemodynamically stable individuals. Percutaneous catheter pericardiocentesis or surgical pericardiectomy can be used to drain the pericardial fluid from a patient with cardiac tamponade [136].

Myocarditis: Myocarditis is an inflammatory disease of the myocardium that can be developed as a result of an infection, which may be immune-mediated, or result from exposure to toxins. Acute, subacute, fulminant, and chronic types of myocarditis can occur. A month or less must pass between the onset of symptoms and the diagnosis to be considered acute myocarditis. A severe, fast-progressing form of acute myocarditis called fulminant myocarditis causes cardiogenic shock and necessitates the use of inotropes or mechanical circulatory support. Subacute myocarditis can also be referred to as resolving myocarditis whenever there is evidence of prior active myocarditis. It is characterized by continuous myocardial injury brought on by a chronic or recurring stimulus for myocardial inflammation. when symptoms last for a long time (more than a month) the condition is called chronic inflammatory myocardiopathy [139].

In cases of suspected myocarditis, the etiology and therapy may necessitate the participation of multiple specialists. If a particular cause is found, treatment is focused on the underlying aetiological process or condition, such as corticosteroids or other immunosuppressants in the event of immune-mediated disease or anti-infective medicines in the case of a curable infection [140]. Non-steroidal anti-inflammatory medicines (NSAIDs), which are a cornerstone of pericarditis therapy, are not advised in myocarditis, in part because of their inefficiency and risk for myocarditis exacerbation [141,142]. A temporary mechanical circulatory support device, such as venoarterial extracorporeal membrane oxygenation (VA-ECMO) and rotary blood pumps, may be used to temporarily sustain patients with considerable hemodynamic impairment or fulminant myocarditis. Patients with myocarditis whose heart failure or arrhythmias are resistant to these short-term treatments may be candidates for cardiac transplantation or the implantation of a left ventricular assist device. Such patients need to be discussed right away with a heart transplant facility [143].

Aortic dissection: the most common life-threatening disorder that affects the aorta is acute aortic dissection. The intima is torn, occasionally spreading to the media (entry tear), and the layers are divided during an acute aortic dissection. The deepest layer typically sheds in the direction of blood flow. As a result, a dissection membrane creates a false lumen that is isolated from the genuine lumen. The two lumina and dissection membranes frequently follow the blood flow in the aorta's craniocaudal direction in a spiral pattern [144].

The ascending aorta is not affected by type B aortic dissection, which has the entry tear distal to the outflow of the left subclavian artery. This is in contrast to type A aortic dissection, which affects the ascending aorta, according to the Stanford classification [144].

Pharmacotherapy: Delivery of morphine plus beta-blockers along with vasodilators or ACE inhibitors can result in pain alleviation and systolic blood pressure of 100 to 120 mm Hg. Massive hypertension typically necessitates the conjunction of many antihypertensives; monotherapy rarely works [145].

Surgery: It is imperative to do surgery on type A aortic dissection as soon as possible in order to stop a rupture or the onset of pericardial tamponade. Surgery on the aortic arch and ascending aorta is carried out to treat type A aortic dissection. In the Intensive Care unit, individuals with uncomplicated acute type B aortic dissection must be closely watched. Blood pressure management is crucial. In the event of immediate problems from type B aortic dissection, quick interventional or, rarely, surgical treatment may be taken into consideration. In cases of acute type B aortic dissection with complications, endovascular implantation of stent grafts is now the recommended method for treating distal mal perfusion or impending aortic rupture [146,147].

Vascular diseases: Despite a reduction in cardiovascular disease (CVD)-related mortality over the past three decades, CVD prevalence is still significant. Acute heart failure (AHF) accounts for 5.6% of all emergency hospitalizations in people over the age of 65 and has an inpatient death rate of 11%. 2. In the USA, one in five heart failure patients is hospitalized and admitted to an Intensive Care unit (ICU), and multiorgan failure complicated 31.7% of hospitalizations for cardiogenic shock (CS) brought on by acute myocardial infarction [148]. Therefore, the modern ICU must possess the knowledge and skills necessary to treat acute cardiovascular care across an expanding range and complexity of cardiovascular disorders, either as a presenting disease or as a comorbid illness in critically ill patients hospitalized for other reasons [149].

In order to prevent the development of permanent or irreparable non-cardiac organ dysfunction, general and specialized therapies should be carried out during the first 60–120 minutes of presentation in cardiovascular instability of any etiology [150].

Management of Airway and respiratory- Both as a cause of ICU admission and as a result of worsening cardiac failure in the ICU, associated respiratory impairment is frequent. To enable appropriate tissue oxygenation, arterial oxygen saturation must be restored to normal. Cardiogenic pulmonary edema prevents gas from passing through alveolar membranes, which contributes to hypoxia and hypercarbia and can negatively affect coronary perfusion and pulmonary vascular resistance (PVR). Through the recruitment of alveoli, redistribution of extravascular lung water, improvement of compliance, and surfactant synthesis, non-invasive positive pressure ventilation (NIPPV) lowers shunt and work of breathing [151].

Circulatory management- Myocardial depression can be made worse by the hypoxia and lactic acidosis brought on by CS, both directly and by reducing the response to vasopressors. Treatment for hypotension despite overt fluid excess is the first-line fluid challenge using a balanced solution. In the most severe cases, this frequently calls for the inclusion of vasoactive medications and consideration of suitability for MCS [152].

By optimizing CO and blood pressure, inotropes and vasopressors try to restore organ perfusion. The action of most vasoactive medications on the release and use of intracellular calcium is typical. The word "MCS" refers to a variety of apparatuses, such as extracorporeal membrane oxygenation, intra-aortic balloon pump, ventricular assist devices, and complete artificial hearts [153].

Refractory patients:

Heart transplantation- Heart transplantation is still the only effective treatment for eligible individuals with refractory heart failure, despite being the gold standard technique. Due to the quick advancement of underlying cardiac disease or the acute, irreversible signs of de novo illness, ICU admission is frequently the defining event that initiates an urgent examination. Organ failures and pulmonary hypertension may be stabilized and even returned to normal with the help of temporary or long-lasting ventricular assist devices [148].

Arrhythmias: Arrhythmias are a common problem that intensivists deal with. They are a significant cause of morbidity and prolonged hospital stays. The majority of patients with structural cardiac disease are at risk for arrhythmias. An insult such as infection, hypoxia, cardiac ischemia, an excess of catecholamines (endogenous or exogenous), or an electrolyte disturbance may be the cause of an arrhythmia in a particular patient. Correction of these abnormalities is part of management, along with medical treatment aimed at the arrhythmia itself [218].

Cardiac arrhythmias, which may be the main cause of ICU admission or a contingency in critically ill patients, put patients hospitalized in the Intensive Care unit (ICU) at a higher risk for developing them. Atrial fibrillation, atrial flutter, ventricular arrhythmias, and other supraventricular tachycardias (SVTs) are examples of tachyarrhythmias, and bradyarrhythmias (eg, junctional rhythm, sinus bradycardia, and atrioventricular [AV] conduction block) which make up the majority of arrhythmias in the Intensive Care unit (ICU).

Atrial fibrillation: AF, which can occur in up to 31% of ICU patients, is the most prevalent persistent arrhythmia in the general population. Hypotension, septic shock, the use of vasopressors or inotropes, electrolyte imbalance, fluid overload, heart failure, and postoperative status are some of the risk factors for AF in the ICU setting. Three techniques are used in the acute therapy of AF: rhythm control (cardioversion), anticoagulation, and rate control.

Cardioversion: Electrical cardioversion or pharmaceutical cardioversion are both options. In patients with AF who have a severe hemodynamic impairment (such as decompensated heart failure, hypotension), presumed to be connected to the arrhythmia, immediate electrical direct current (DC) cardioversion is recommended. Amiodarone and Ibutilide are the antiarrhythmic medications most frequently chosen in the Intensive Care unit (ICU). The choice of medication will depend on the underlying cardiac function. Although especially evaluated in ICU patients, intravenous ibutilide is said to have a 50% success rate [219]. CARDIOVERSION IN ACUTE OR CHRONIC AF

Rate control:

Anticoagulation: The risk of embolization in each patient is the basis for the general anticoagulant strategy. Warfarin, apixiban, dabigitran, and rivaroxiban are a few different types of oral anticoagulants. Any patient's anticoagulation choice must be considered against the possibility of bleeding.

Comapring Rate And Rythm Control Studies Eg: Race. Reafirm

Surgical

CABG: Cardiopulmonary bypass is commonly used during CABG procedures, which has a distinctive impact on the physiology of patients and might cause certain postoperative issues in some patients. By cycling the patient's venous blood through a mechanical oxygenator, cardiopulmonary bypass enables a motionless and bloodless surgical field while preserving tissue perfusion and blood oxygenation [149,150]. However, when blood comes into touch with the nonendothelialized surface of the bypass circuit, the body experiences a severe form of systemic inflammatory response syndrome (SIRS), which activates the coagulation system [151]. Heparin is frequently administered to prevent clotting, however, SIRS also causes significant fluid changes, abnormal capillary bed control, and tissue hypoperfusion despite water retention. Microemboli and SIRS-related hypoperfusion can harm organ systems and increase postoperative morbidity. In the weeks following surgery, patients may experience chest discomfort, shortness of breath, or dysregulation of blood pressure due to SIRS (fig 1) [152,153].

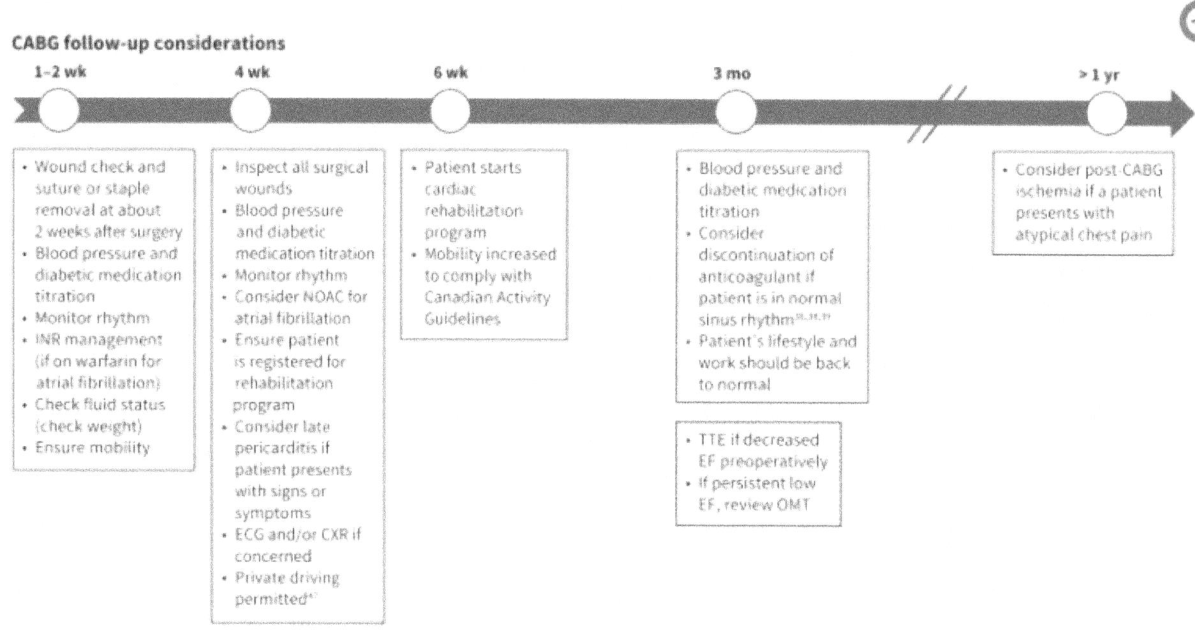

Fig E7: management of patients after CABG

Vascular disease: It can be very difficult to manage critical care for people who have had vascular surgery (fig 1). There is a considerable risk of serious postoperative consequences since this patient population has significant comorbidities combined with the extensive surgical insult brought on by vascular surgery. The successful treatment of patients undergoing massive vascular surgery depends on accurate preoperative medical risk classification and optimization, great surgical skill and anesthetic management, and attentive ICU care. In order to restore and maintain physiologic homeostasis while keeping a high index of suspicion for procedure-specific complications, the intensivist, and critical care team must be proactive [154]. ANTICOAGULATIOON

Post angioplasty: Patients with coronary stents who are admitted to the Intensive Care unit (ICU) may be more susceptible to stent thrombosis, a serious complication with a high morbidity and death rate. P2Y12 receptor antagonist and aspirin used together as dual antiplatelet medication considerably lower the risk of stent thrombosis, however, it might occasionally need to be stopped if bleeding occurs or invasive procedures with a high bleeding risk are required. If aspirin can be used in certain circumstances, it may offer some protection from problems. A short-acting antiplatelet drug, such as a small molecule glycoprotein IIb/IIIa inhibitor, may be beneficial if all antiplatelet therapy needs to be stopped. Close observation of patients with coronary stents may enable early detection and ICU-based therapy of any cardiac problems.

Postoperative critical care of surgical vascular patients by major systems

- Neurologic
  - Multimodal pain management
  - Monitoring for early signs of CVA and SCI
  - Maintain appropriate CSF pressure
  - Ensure adequate SCPP
- Respiratory
  - Early extubation when possible
  - Postextubation incentive spirometry and deep-breathing maneuvers
  - Lung protective ventilation strategy for ALI
  - Inspiratory muscle strength training to expedite ventilator weaning process
  - VAP-prevention bundle
- Cardiovascular
  - Monitoring for symptoms/signs of myocardial ischemia
  - Check myocardial biomarkers
  - Early resumption and/or starting aspirin, beta-blocker, statins
  - Avoid hypertension/hypotension
  - Acute limb ischemia (check peripheral pulses hourly by palpation or Doppler)
  - Monitoring for limb compartment syndrome
  - Daily surgical inspection of vascular surgery wounds
- Renal
  - Maintain euvolemia and adequate renal perfusion pressure
  - Avoid nephrotoxins
- Hematologic
  - Monitor for bleeding complications and retroperitoneal hematoma
  - Conservative blood transfusion strategy unless evidence of organ ischemia
  - Thromboembolic prophylaxis
- Gastrointestinal
  - Monitoring for early signs of mesenteric ischemia
  - Monitoring for abdominal compartment syndrome
  - Early resumption of oral feeding or early starting of enteral feeding
  - Stress gastritis prophylaxis

Figure E8: postoperative critical care of surgical vascular patients by major systems

ECMO VA: Extracorporeal membrane oxygenation (ECMO) use has grown significantly over the past ten years, and it is now regarded as a standard form of life-saving care in critical care medicine. Medical education, training, and experience are still absolutely necessary, nevertheless [155]. ECMO has historically been used to treat end-stage lung illness and circulatory collapse, but it is now also being used to treat right heart failure, as a stopgap measure before lung and heart transplantation, and as a rescue therapy for sepsis and post-organ transplantation [156]. Two of the most challenging conditions that can occur in the Intensive Care unit (ICU) which put patients at high risk for ICU mortality are hypoxic respiratory failure and/or cardiogenic shock. Cardiopulmonary bypass techniques, like ECMO, enable the provision of more aggressive lung rest methods and cardiovascular support than would otherwise be possible [157]. ECMO can provide different levels of assistance, including respiratory support only, respiratory support along with right ventricular support, and full cardiopulmonary support.

Today, with careful patient selection, ECMO is utilized as a preventive treatment for hypoxic respiratory failure and severe refractory cardiogenic shock to allow for recovery or serve as a bridge to transplant [158]. By sustaining systemic circulation until cardiac recovery, ECMO is used to assist the individual as a bridge to recovery, surgery, or another destination. ECMO is viewed as a bridge to LVAD therapy in individuals with end-stage heart failure or failure to improve. E-CPR, which helps to reestablish circulation following cardiac arrest, is another application of VA-ECMO [159,160].

Patients requiring VAD: Patients with end-stage heart failure survive longer thanks to left ventricular assist devices, whose use is on the rise. First-generation pulsatile devices have been replaced by continuous-flow left ventricular assist devices. Unique management issues are raised by these patients. Care must be made to sustain the right ventricle without assistance during the first few days after installation. To achieve the best left ventricular assist device settings and cardiac function, invasive blood pressure monitoring, echocardiography, and pulmonary artery catheterization are required. Anticoagulation is required to stop life-threatening thrombotic and embolic consequences, however, due to inherited bleeding disorders and prescribed anticoagulants, bleeding is a primary cause of morbidity. The device can be infected, which poses a life-threatening risk. In order to prevent seeding the device, all infections must be aggressively treated [161].

Monitoring: Since improving a patient's hemodynamics, temperature, ventilation, metabolism, and nutrition is the key to improving a patient's survival, monitoring is crucial to the daily treatment of ICU patients in critical care. The provision of oxygen to tissues in accordance with their metabolic requirements, in order to support mitochondrial respiration and, by extension, life, is the crucial endpoint. In this way, monitoring oxygenation and perfusion is necessary while putting any resuscitation plan into action. In an approach that was suitably named "goal-guided therapy," the growing idea has been to improve macrocirculation by first optimizing cardiac function in stages and then assessing the sufficiency of perfusion and oxygenation on specified parameters. On the other hand, maintaining a normal temperature is important and needs to be checked frequently. It involves serial evaluations of respiratory system mechanics, gas exchange, and the preparedness of patients for release from invasive positive pressure ventilation when it comes to respiratory surveillance of ventilated ICU patients. Additionally, the assessment of metabolic and nutritional care should enable control over blood glucose, blood sugar levels, and the supply of nutrients [162].

ECG interpretation: The Joint European Society of Cardiology/American College of Cardiology (ESC/ACC) updated the diagnostic standards for myocardial infarction (MI) in 2000. (UNIVERSAL DEFINITION OF MI) This was based on developments in the specific and sensitive biochemical marker cardiac troponin, which was used to diagnose myocardial injury [163]. The discovery of ischemia alterations on an electrocardiogram (ECG), pathologic findings, a rise and decline in biochemical markers like troponin, one of the classic ischemic symptoms, or a coronary artery intervention are used to make the diagnosis of MI. This definition presents various difficulties in the identification of MI in the Intensive Care unit (ICU). Because critically sick patients are commonly sedated, endotracheally intubated, or unconscious, ischemia symptoms are typically concealed by analgesia and are difficult to communicate. Second, many critically ill individuals with increased troponin levels have no signs of coronary thrombosis [164].

The ECG has become a more important diagnostic tool for identifying myocardial ischemia as a result of the limitations of MI in the ICU. When clinicians encounter a critically ill individual who simultaneously has an increased troponin level, the validity of ECG interpretation becomes a crucial factor [165]. An important feature of diagnostic testing is reliability, which is the degree to which measurement equipment gives reliable, stable, and uniform results during observational data under the same circumstances. Furthermore, accurate diagnostic test interpretation is required; in other words, an ECG is only effective in clinical practice if the interpretation of an ECG, performed on many occasions and by various observers, yields the same outcomes [166].

ECG basics and wave interpretation:

The electrocardiogram, often known as an ECG or EKG, is a non-invasive test that records an electrical trace of the heart from the body's surface. An important clinical application of the non-invasive diagnostic technique known as the electrocardiogram (ECG) is determining the severity of cardiovascular illnesses. ECG is being used more frequently to check on patients on antiarrhythmics and other medications, to evaluate patients before non-cardiac surgery, to screen people working in high-risk occupations, and to check on athletes. Given that cardiovascular illness is the leading cause of mortality, it is crucial for medical professionals to gain the skills and knowledge necessary to read ECGs in order to give the best care as soon as possible.

The purpose of electrocardiogram interpretation is to establish the normality or pathology of the ECG waves and intervals. The analysis of electrical signals provides a good estimate of heart pathology [167].

P-wave: On the ECG, it shows atrial depolarization. Right atrial and left atrial depolarization are represented by the first and second halves of the P wave, respectively. Atrial hypertrophy may be indicated by an aberrant P wave [168].

PR- interval: It comprises the lag at the AV node and measures the interval between the start of atrial depolarization and the commencement of ventricular depolarization. Various illnesses can result from variations in the PR interval. A first-degree AV block may be indicated by a long PR interval, whereas an enhanced AV conduction abnormality, such as a bypass tract, Wolf-Parkinson-White syndrome, or Lown-Ganong-Levine syndrome, may be indicated by a short PR interval [169].

R-wave: The electrical impulse that travels down the ventricles during depolarization is represented by this wave, which is the tallest in the QRS complex. R-wave progression refers to the R-gradual wave's amplitude increase as it progresses from right to left in the precordial leads. Numerous factors, such as anteroseptal MI in the past, left ventricular hypertrophy, improper lead placement, etc., might result in a decreased R-wave progression [176].

T-wave: This is ventricular repolarization in action. The effects of both cardiac and noncardiac factors, such as (hormonal and neurological). In leads with large R waves, it is typically positive [170].

ST segment: It shows when ventricular depolarization ends and ventricular repolarization starts. When observed in two or even more contiguous leads during an acute myocardial infarction, ST-elevation is extremely specific. In addition to these conditions, Prinzmetal angina, acute myocarditis, acute pericarditis, hyperkalemia, pulmonary embolism, and subarachnoid hemorrhage are also linked to ST elevation. An ST depression of more than 1 mm is frequently indicative of angina or myocardial ischemia [171].

QT interval: It signifies the beginning of ventricle depolarization and the conclusion of ventricle repolarization. Medications, congenital long QT syndrome, and electrolyte imbalances like hypomagnesemia and hypocalcemia are all prevalent causes of QT prolongation. Short QT syndrome, acidosis, hyperkalemia, hyperthermia, and hypercalcemia are all possible causes of a short QT interval (less than 360 milliseconds) [172].

U wave: The T wave is followed by a tiny wave. It stands for the papillary muscles' or Purkinje fibers' delayed repolarization. It frequently goes hand in hand with hypokalemia [173]

J wave: It is an aberrant ECG finding in hypothermia and is additionally known as the Osborn wave. At the junction of the QRS complex and ST segment, it appears as an additional deflection on the ECG [174].

Epsilon wave: It is a little positive deflection that is typically hidden near the end of the QRS complex and is a hallmark of arrhythmogenic right ventricular dysplasia [175].

Hemodynamic monitoring: Although the level of monitoring for each patient admitted to the ICU should be consistent, it might vary. Perhaps all that is needed for hemodynamically stable patients is continuous electrocardiographic (ECG) monitoring, routine non-invasive blood pressure checks, and peripheral pulse oximetry (peripheral oxygen saturation or SpO 2). An arterial line should be inserted for continuous invasive blood pressure monitoring and routine investigation of arterial blood gases in patients who are unstable or at risk of becoming unstable. Advanced hemodynamic assessment will be necessary to direct medical care if the patient's hemodynamic and/or respiratory state does not improve after the first resuscitation. We can determine whether vasopressors, fluid resuscitation, or inotropic medications are still necessary by monitoring CO and its constituents (preload, afterload, and contractility) [177].

Parameters used in CICU

CVP:

The right atrium or superior vena cava pressure is measured by central venous pressure (CVP) monitoring, typically with the help of a central venous catheter (CVC), also referred to as a central line. The effectiveness of cardiac preload and circulating blood volume can be assessed by CVP monitoring. In critical care situations, inserting a CVC to test CVP is an invasive approach to determining the fluid status of patients [178,179].

A CVC is a catheter whose tip is positioned within the right atrium, inferior vena cava, or the proximal third of the superior vena cava. Both proximal central veins and peripheral veins can be used to place these catheters [180]. The CVC can then be electronically connected to a cardiac monitor, permitting a transduced waveform and a continuously updated numerical value to be displayed together. As patients in all of these settings typically have a CVC already in place, which can readily be attached to a cardiac monitor to detect CVP, this is frequently feasible in critical care [181].

CVP is a measure of right ventricular PRELOAD and, to a lesser degree, left ventricular preload and is used to determine whether blood volume is adequate [182].

Additionally, CVP shows the venous return threshold and provides information on right ventricular function. CVP measures could therefore be useful in assisting with and directing fluid management [183].

Limitations: Critical care professionals frequently use CVP to help them decide whether to deliver intravenous (IV) fluid treatment. A systematic study found insufficient evidence for CVP monitoring in critical care and came to the conclusion that it was not a reliable indicator of fluid responsiveness. Accurate CVP measurement might be hampered by abnormal right atrial pressure in conditions such as atrial fibrillation, tricuspid regurgitation, atrioventricular block, chronic obstructive pulmonary disease, cardiac tamponade, and mechanical ventilation [181].

Complications: Since CVP screening is an invasive hemodynamic procedure, it necessitates stringent asepsis compliance and high-level competence. According to recent research, 5–19% of all patients experience mechanical difficulties, and 5-26.5% of those patients also experience catheter-associated infections and 2-26.3% thrombotic complications [183].

It is advised that the nurse keep an eye out for mechanical issues like dysrhythmias during catheter insertion, recognize patients who are at risk for pulmonary artery injury (like rupture) and infarction, and put preventive measures in place to lessen the potential dangers of catheter-induced pulmonary artery injury [184].

Arterial lines: the indwelling artery catheter (AC), a technique that is often and widely utilized in Intensive Care units (ICUs) but for which there is no proof of its impact on pertinent outcomes. In the

US, an AC is administered to about one-third of all ICU patients, with even higher usage in select subgroups [185]. This translates to about 2 million patients obtaining ACs per year and the exact number of AC therapies and catheters is probably substantially greater due to replacements and reinsertions. The main purposes of ACs are to monitor blood pressure and to assist in diagnostic blood tests, such as arterial blood gas analysis. These objectives don't, however, call for an AC [186]. Monitoring blood pressure is non-invasive. Phlebotomy or intermittent arterial puncture are two ways to acquire blood that will be used for laboratory testing [187].

Infections and arterial thrombosis are just two examples of the direct side effects of ACs. While AC devices resemble peripheral IV catheters in appearance, they are 2.5 times more likely to cause bloodstream infections. The lack of awareness of this risk may be due to both the observation that infected ACs hardly ever show symptoms of infection to the naked eye and the poor concordance between AC tip cultures and blood cultures obtained through the AC. Although the majority of the ischemia that results is transient, thrombosis due to ACs is not uncommon [188,189].

PA catheter: Through central venous access, a pulmonary artery catheter (PAC) is placed into the right portion of the heart and carried into the pulmonary artery. To aid in diagnosis and therapy, PAC measures cardiac output, stroke volume, intracardiac pressures, mixed venous oxygen saturation, and a number of other computed factors. The insertion of the line is mostly responsible for procedure complications. Cardiac arrhythmia, pulmonary hemorrhage and infarction, and related death from balloon tip rupture are rather infrequent consequences [190].

The catheter is not a kind of treatment, but rather a monitoring device that aids in diagnosis. After receiving proper training in the interpretation of data, specialists in the field should insert PACs to assist in treatment decisions for ICU patients. Critical hemodynamic information from a PAC includes cardiac output, intracardiac pressures, intrapulmonary pressures, and mixed venous oxygen saturation [191]. These variables, along with other derived variables derived from these measurements, are used to direct treatment for critically ill patients. These derived variables include right and left ventricular stroke work indices, pulmonary and systemic vascular resistance, right and left ventricular end-systolic and diastolic indices, arterial and venous oxygen content, right ventricular ejection fraction, oxygen delivery, oxygen consumption, and oxygen extraction ratio [190].

A PAC is a tool for both diagnosis and hemodynamic monitoring. Clinicians in cardiac catheterization labs, adult medical ICUs, and coronary care units (CCUs) employ the PAC. It is used to guide therapy and distinguish between distinct types of shock states in patients undergoing cardiothoracic surgery, including those undergoing coronary artery bypass graft (CABG, or bypass surgery), valvular surgery, and postoperative monitoring of critically ill patients [192].

Advantages: Many doctors still look for hemodynamic data throughout current clinical practice to treat critically ill patients. The effectiveness of the test has therefore been assessed by comparing a number of non-invasive monitoring equipment to PAC as the reference standard. Less invasive monitoring technologies are unable to reliably or continuously measure several hemodynamic variables, while PACs do. In addition to being used as a monitoring and data-gathering device, the PAC also offers the advantage of being a multi-lumen infusion port. Multiple drips are necessary for critically ill patients, and the standard of care nowadays is to establish central venous access using a CVC [193].

In addition to intracardiac screening, a PAC can also be implanted through central access and shares the same short-term difficulties as line insertion. The central venous oxygen saturation test (ScVO2) is another crucial procedure that heavily relies on the PAC. The treatment of patients experiencing septic shock and sepsis depends heavily on the measurement of ScVO2 [194].

Complications:

- those resulting from central venous access, including pneumothorax, air embolism, post-operative neuropathy (pain and feeling deficiency), and arterial puncture (air outside the lungs).
- those that result from using a catheter (right bundle branch block, complete heart block, and severe dysrhythmias).
- pulmonary infarction, pulmonary artery rupture, and venous thrombosis (clots in veins), which are caused by prolonged catheter occupancy [194].

CO monitoring: When a patient is severely unwell and at high risk for bleeding, hemodynamic instability, and significant fluid changes, cardiac output (CO) monitoring is a crucial tool. When a monitor is utilized in conjunction with the delivery of fluids and vasopressors to reach predetermined therapeutic objectives, thereby enhancing patient care and outcome, it is a crucial part of goal-directed therapy (GDT). Clinical evaluation and regular assessment are not reliable ways to evaluate CO. The Ficks principle, Doppler, thermodilution, bioimpedance, and pulse contour analysis are some of the techniques used for CO monitoring. Each approach has benefits and drawbacks of its own. An ideal CO monitoring should have a quick response time, be continuously operational, cost-effective, reproducible, and be slightly or completely non-invasive [195].

The following categories roughly classify CO monitoring techniques: There are three types of cardiac imaging: (1) invasive (intermittent bolus pulmonary artery thermodilution and continuous pulmonary artery thermodilution); (2) minimally invasive (lithium dilution CO (LiDCO), pulse contour analysis CO (PiCCO and FloTrac), transesophageal echocardiography (TEE); and (3) non-invasive (partial gas rebreathing, thoracic bioimpedance, and bioreactance, Photoelectric plethysmography, Doppler method, and endotracheal cardiac output monitor (ECOM) [195].

Invasive methods:

PAC- Dexter invented the pulmonary artery catheter (PAC), which Swan et al later adapted to evaluate central filling pressure and carbon monoxide (CO) levels. However, using it has been linked to a number of side effects, including pneumothorax, infection, arrhythmia, damage to the valve, rupture of the pulmonary artery, thrombosis resulting in embolism, and knotting [196].

Continuous measurement of CO by PAC- Continuous CO (CCO) is a variation of PAC that uses a catheter with a copper filament that stays in the right ventricle. The right heart's blood is intermittently heated by the filament, and a thermistor located close to the catheter's tip detects the resulting signal. On the monitor, the average CO measurement over time is shown. The main benefits of CCO over traditional PAC include the avoidance of repeated boluses, which lowers the risk of infection and operator error. Additionally, this catheter can be used to continuously evaluate systemic vascular resistance (SVR), stroke volume (SV), and mixed venous saturation [197].

Minimally invasive methods:

Pulse power analysis- This approach is predicated on the idea that changes in blood pressure relative to the mean have a direct impact on SV. Every eight hours and when significant hemodynamic changes call for calibration [198].

For continuous monitoring of SV and SV changes, the LiDCO system where pulse contour analysis combined with lithium indicator dilution (SVV). It is a minimally invasive procedure that was initially introduced in 1993 and calls for both an arterial catheter and a venous (central or peripheral) line. The arterial concentration is determined by drawing blood through a disposable lithium-sensitive sensor that has an ionophore that is only permeable to Li after a bolus of lithium chloride has been injected into the vein. Li dosage and area are used to determine CO in accordance with the concentration-time circulation. As quaternary ammonium residue produces electrode drift, it is not recommended for patients receiving Li treatment, and calibration is also impacted by neuromuscular blockers [198].

Pulse contour analysis- It is based on the idea that the SV is proportional to the area under the systolic component of the arterial pressure waveform. Erlanger and Hooker proposed that CO was proportional to arterial pulse pressure in their initial description of it in 1904 This technique divides the area from post-diastole to the conclusion of the ejection phase by the aortic impedance, which assesses stroke volume (SV). Additionally, it monitors pulse pressure change and stroke volume variation, both of which are helpful in predicting fluid responsiveness [199].

Non-invasive:

Partial gas rebreathing- The partial gas rebreathing monitor, also referred to as the NICO system, determines CO via the indirect Fick's principle. It is applied to individuals receiving mechanical ventilation who are intubated. At a steady state, the ratio of CO2 entering the airways through the pulmonary artery to CO is constant and equals the ratio of CO2 leaving the lungs by exhalation and the pulmonary veins [200].

The requirement for tracheal intubation with a fixed ventilator setting is a significant drawback. In patients with severe chest injuries, high CO situations,, large intrapulmonary shunt, and low minute ventilation, it is also not very accurate [200].

Thoracic bioimpedance- A non-invasive technique for measuring CO is thoracic bioimpedance (TEB). It was first used by astronauts in the 1960s. It is founded on the premise that the thorax functions as a cylinder that is perfused with fluid that has a particular resistance. The thorax's electrical resistance to a high frequency, low amplitude current is measured [201].

Thoracic bioreactance- Thoracic bioreactance is a variation of TEB that eliminates noise and outside sources of interference. It examines modifications in the electrical voltage signal's phase in relation to the current placed across the thorax. Electrical inductive and capacitive characteristics fluctuate as a result of intrathoracic volume changes [201]

Doppler- A probe is placed suprasternal to measure flow via the aorta or on the left chest to measure transpulmonary flow in portable, non-invasive Ultrasonic Cardiac Output Monitors. It makes use of the Doppler effect. The device's portability makes it ideal for usage in ERs, operating rooms, Intensive Care units, and even wards. It is a non-invasive gadget that may be utilized by skilled nursing personnel and serves as a crucial screening tool for cardiac surgery patients after surgery [202].

Thermodilution: It has been created a new thermodilution technique to monitor CO automatically and constantly. In order to identify a lo-cm thermal filament in the right ventricle (RV) while being used, pulmonary artery catheters (PACs) have been modified [203].

The thermal filament continuously delivers a safe amount of heat into the blood using a pseudorandom binary sequence without the use of any fluid injectate. A thermodilution "washout" curve is created by cross-correlating the temperature change that results with the input sequence in the pulmonary artery (PA) and detecting it downstream from there [203].

There is no need for an additional catheter positioning methodology because the PAC is inserted using the normal approach. The measurement process begins after the catheter is linked to the monitor. The initial CO measurement is generated and shown after a few minutes. The displayed CO is refreshed every 30 seconds to reflect the average flow over the past 3 to 6 minutes. There is no need for special user calibrating or catheter placement. The method for calculating volumetric fluid flow described here is based on stochastic system identification methods and conservation of mass, or thermodilution. This approach requires little user calibration, is simple to use, measures actual volumetric flow, and is not depending on vascular geometry [203].

Transpulmonary thermodilution: Many questions about a patient's hemodynamic treatment in the operating room or Intensive Care unit cannot be answered by a straightforward clinical examination. Particularly, arterial pressure only permits an approximation of cardiac output. Through cardiac output and other parameters, transpulmonary thermodilution is a technique that offers a complete hemodynamic examination.

Transpulmonary thermodilution periodically monitors cardiac output by analyzing the thermodilution curve that is obtained at the tip of an arterial catheter following the injection of a cold bolus into the venous circulation. The calibration of pulse contour analysis is made possible by this measure. This allows for continuous and real-time cardiac output monitoring, something the pulmonary artery catheter does not provide for. Beyond cardiac output, transpulmonary thermodilution offers a number of other factors. It calculates the four ventricular cavities' end-diastolic volume, which is a measure of cardiac preload. It provides an estimate of the united ventricles' systolic performance. Compared to the pulmonary artery catheter, it is more direct, but it does not allow for an accurate estimate of right and left heart performance.

Although it is quicker and easier to do than an echocardiogram, it does not give a complete assessment of the anatomy and functioning of the heart. The ability to measure extravascular lung water at the bedside, which quantifies the amount of pulmonary vascular permeability, and pulmonary edema which quantifies the severity of a pulmonary capillary leak, is a unique benefit of transpulmonary thermodilution [204].

Management of certain cases

Heart transplantation

Advanced heart failure is still only successfully treated with heart transplantation (HTx), and the survival and quality of life rates are quite good. The amount of organs accessible may be increased by using expanded donor criteria, obtaining hearts through donation after circulatory death, and transplanting patients using cutting-edge methods for organ preservation. After HTx, vigilant hemodynamic parameter monitoring is required since even little alterations in preload and afterload can have a negative impact on heart function and be challenging to cure. In addition to the usual monitoring, it is advised to perform continuous perioperative monitoring of systemic, pulmonary artery, and central venous pressure (CVP), as well as mixed venous oxygen saturation (SvO2), intermittent measurements of pulmonary capillary wedge pressure (PCWP), cardiac output, and left atrial pressure (LAP) [205].

Graft failure- Early primary graft dysfunction (PGD), which is defined as PGD identified within 24 hours following HTx, is linked to noticeably higher 30-day and 1-year mortality. In early PGD, the number of inotropes and mechanical assistance are utilized to classify the various types of dysfunction into left ventricular (LV), right ventricular (RV), and biventricular dysfunction. After HTx, LV failure is less frequent than RV failure, and LV systolic dysfunction might be an indication of subpar graft quality or acute rejection. One of the most serious side effects of HTx is isolated RV failure, which is a risk factor for mortality on its own. For chronotropic and inotropic stimulation of the denervated heart, inotropes are typically administered to patients. We frequently infuse isoproterenol for a minimum of twenty-four hours to decrease PVR and promote myocardial contraction and HR in order to prevent RV failure. Isoproterenol, milrinone, dobutamine, and dopamine are common ingredients in inotropic drugs [205].

Renal function- Acute kidney injury (AKI) after HTx is a frequent consequence, occurring at a rate of 25.6–50.2% and at a rate of 12.1-22.3% when dialysis is required. Post-HTx AKI is linked to decreased renal oxygen transport during CPB, bleeding/tamponade, venous congestion, postoperative RV failure, and the use of calcineurin inhibitors (CNI). Low-dose (50 ng/kg/min) atrial natriuretic peptide (ANP) infusion in early AKI post-HTx enhances renal blood flow and glomerular filtration rate and lowers the risk of dialysis in AKI following heart surgery [205].

Immunosuppression- Successful HTx requires effective immunosuppression, which has feared negative effects such as increased susceptibility to infections and cancer. It also protects against acute and chronic transplant rejection. Initiation therapy with anti-lymphocyte globulins or anti-thymocyte or interleukin-2 receptor antagonists, which is associated with greater long-term survival, is given to 51% of HTx recipients for severe immunosuppression immediately post-HTx [205].

Left ventricular failure: The pericardium, myocardium, and endocardium make up the heart. Heart failure can result from pathology in any of those structures. Left ventricular dysfunction results in inadequate blood flow to important body organs, which is known as left ventricular failure [206].

Management: Patients should be informed about the value of changing their lifestyles to better manage their disease. This includes limiting one's intake of salt and abstaining from narcotics, alcohol, and tobacco. It is crucial to treat the underlying cause of heart failure since certain disorders, such as alcohol-induced cardiomyopathies, tachycardia, or ischemia-induced cardiomyopathies, may be treatable by addressing the precipitating factors. Blood pressure must be tightly under control to stop further worsening. In addition to loop diuretics for volume overload, the pharmaceutical approach to treating HFrEF and HFpEF differs. Angiotensin-converting enzyme (ACE) inhibitors or angiotensin II receptor blockers (ARBs) combined with a beta blocker is the majority of treatment for HFrEF (carvedilol, metoprolol, or bisoprolol) [206,207].

Other drugs include hydralazine, nitrates, and inhibitors of the mineralocorticoid receptor, like ivabradine, spironolactone, and digoxin (as a last resort). In patients of African American descent, nitrates and hydralazine may be very effective. The mortality benefits of digoxin, diuretics, and ivabradine have not been demonstrated [207].

After receiving appropriate medical treatment, patients with severe symptoms and an ejection fraction under 35% should be referred for cardiac resynchronization therapy (CRT) or an implantable cardioverter-defibrillator (ICD), depending on the QRS width and the type of intraventricular conduction delay. Options for advanced cases include heart transplantation, continuous infusion of inotropic drugs like milrinone or dobutamine, and mechanical circulatory aid devices like LVAD [208].

Refractory arrhythmias:

Rapid diagnosis and action are frequently necessary for the disciplines of emergency medicine and critical care for particular conditions. It is good knowledge that assessment of the underlying cause and level of left ventricular function (dysfunction) is crucial in all individuals with tachyarrhythmias. Understanding the process that brought about the issue is essential for administering the proper medication for arrhythmias in Intensive Care patients. Antiarrhythmic medications may or may not be used therapeutically to treat cardiac arrest or atrial fibrillation. Any patient with atrial fibrillation has rhythm control as an alternative to sinus rhythm restoration as their main objective. The preventative use of antiarrhythmic medications in cardiac arrest victims has never been fully explored. There is currently no consensus on the appropriate time to administer antiarrhythmic medications—whether it is before or only after numerous defibrillation shocks have failed to restart circulation. One of the most crucial things is to employ automated external defibrillators to lower the rate of sudden cardiac death, both outside and within hospitals. However, it is now widely acknowledged that even when AEDs are installed in homes and used by family members, this therapy is unable to stop sudden death. To increase survival, more cardiac resuscitation techniques are necessary [210].

AICD:

Short-term management: ICD failure that manifests as unwarranted shocks necessitates immediate device investigation and reprogramming for short-term control. The patient's clinical state and underlying rhythm are taken into account while determining the short-term therapy of ICD lead failure. The magnet should be adhered to the skin with adhesive and put immediately over the device. Most of the time, the ICD emits an audible tone to signal adequate magnet placement. An ICD will lose its ability to detect when a magnet is attached to it (as long as the magnet remains applied). The application of a magnet won't change the device's pacing (bradycardia) settings [211].

Long-term management: First, the lead architecture and suspected lead failure mechanism need to be taken into account. This also applies to integrated bipolar leads with conductor fractures that involve the distal coil as well as leads with DF-4 connector pins. If there is a single fracture in the conductor of the ring electrode, only a new pace/sense lead needs to be installed. It might also be suitable to switch sensing electrodes utilizing still-functioning or abandoned lead components. Both methods might be more advantageous than inserting a fresh defibrillation lead. There is a theoretical worry about the current being shunted to the abandoned lead if there is an additional defibrillation coil placed in the heart [211].

Aortic dissection and repair: Patients undergoing vascular surgery have a number of comorbid conditions and are at significant risk for perioperative complications. Recent years have seen significant advancement in aortic repair surgery, with an increasing preponderance of endovascular procedures (EVAR). Endovascular treatment considerably lowers the likelihood of cardiac problems, but high-risk patients need postoperative ST-segment monitoring. The open aortic repair might herald an unacceptably high risk of respiratory problems, which might rule out surgery. An endovascular method considerably reduces this risk, thus whenever possible, endovascular repair should be performed without general anesthesia. Preoperative risk classification and secondary prevention are essential activities because preoperative renal function and postoperative kidney injury are significant predictors of short- and long-term outcomes. Open repair requires selective renal and distal aortic perfusion for intraoperative renal preservation. When compared to open repair, EVAR has reduced rates of postoperative renal failure, with a risk of acute kidney injury (AKI) that is about half as high and a demand for hemodialysis that is about one-third as high. Historically, the most notable and terrifying consequence of aortic surgery was spinal cord ischemia. Endovascular repair often results in less blood loss and less coagulopathy because it avoids significant aortic dissection and aortic cross-clamping [212].

Acute limb ischemia: Acute limb ischemia (ALI) is characterized by a sudden drop in limb perfusion that endangers limb viability and is a serious vascular emergency. If the clinical presentation happens within 14 days of the onset of symptoms, it is deemed acute. While collateral blood supply is frequently present in critical limb ischemia (CLI), also known as chronic limb-threatening ischemia (CLTI), ALI threatens limb viability in a relatively short amount of time because there is not enough time for new blood vessel formation to make up for the loss of perfusion [213].

Management: Vascular surgery, vascular medicine, and/or interventional therapy must be available around the clock due to the high amputation and fatality rates in ALI. Unfractionated heparin (UFH) is used as an immediate anticoagulant to stop thrombus growth and maintain microcirculation. Often, analgesic therapy is required. The various therapeutic approaches are discussed, including pharmacological (thrombolysis), interventional (thromboaspiration, mechanical thrombectomy, and stent implantation), established surgical (Fogarty thrombembolectomy, by-pass, endarterectomy, patch angioplasty, or combinations), and minor or major amputation when necessary. Additionally updated are postoperative management, reperfusion injury, compartment syndrome, and long-term care [213].

TAVR: As a method to medically treat aortic stenosis (AS) in high-risk patients, transcatheter aortic valve replacement (TAVR) is quickly gaining favor. TAVR is far less invasive than the conventional method of replacing an aortic valve with a median sternotomy. Patients having TAVR frequently have many comorbidities, and a specific set of problems that may become apparent in the Intensive Care unit may exacerbate their postoperative course (ICU) [214].

A sternotomy is not performed, cardiopulmonary bypass (CPB) is not required, and patients may be extubated in the operating room (OR) during TAVR, making it less invasive than classic aortic valve replacement (AVR). Despite being less invasive, TAVR has a distinct set of postoperative events and problems that have been documented over the past few years as the number of procedures has grown. While patients receiving TAVR share some ICU management concerns with patients undergoing classic

AVR, TAVR patients have additional ICU problems that the intensivist must be aware of and appropriately address [214].

WATCHMAN procedure: The inter-atrial septum is bridged using a transseptal cannula that is placed through the femoral vein and guided by a fluoroscope. The WATCHMAN Access Sheath and dilator are moved across the wire into the left atrium once access to the left atrium has been gained. A guidewire is then inserted into the upper pulmonary vein. The access sheath is gently inserted over a pigtail catheter into the distal section of the LAA after the guidewire is withdrawn. The entry sheath is prepared, the WATCHMAN Delivery System is inserted, and the device is gradually progressed. After then, the WATCHMAN gadget is introduced into the LAA. Transesophageal echocardiography (TEE) and fluoroscopy are used to check the device release criteria, and the device is then made available for use [215].

Left atrial appendage closure (LAAC) with Watchman seems to be a promising, secure, and efficient replacement for OAC. Current and upcoming studies should concentrate on comparing the safety and effectiveness of various LAAC devices, patient selection, different post-procedural antithrombotic regimens, head-to-head comparisons with NOAC, a better understanding of device-related thrombus, and the role of the LAA in the spread of non-valvular AF in order to solidify the position of Watchman [216].

ABG analysis: ABG analysis is one of the most frequently requested diagnostics in the ICU. When the results are likely to affect patient management, it is ideal to get an ABG sample. The evaluation of patient breathing, the necessity to quantify the response to therapeutic or diagnostic interventions, the monitoring of the severity and progression of a known disease process, and the assessment of acid-base balance are common indications for the ABG sample. ABG measurements that are repeated are linked to higher costs, blood loss, the spread of infection, and patient discomfort. In patients without an intra-arterial catheter, the requirement for numerous unpleasant punctures may result in significant blood loss. The arterial blood gas analysis is frequently requested as a routine test, and the ABG results typically do not alter patient management, which increases expense and resource usage. Since the majority of routine ABGs are performed without intervention, a tailored strategy might lower the incidence of incorrect ABGs [217].

References

100. Hoppe U C, Böhm M, Dietz R.*et al* Leitlinien zur Therapie der chronischen Herzinsuffizienz. *Z Kardiol* 200594488–509.Current recommendations of the German Cardiac Society for the treatment of chronic heart failure.

101. Swedberg K, Cleland J, Dargie H.*et al* Guidelines for the diagnosis and treatment of chronic heart failure: executive summary (update 2005): The Task Force for the Diagnosis and Treatment of Chronic Heart Failure of the European Society of Cardiology. *Eur Heart J* 2005261115–1140.Current ESC practice guidelines; compare with reference 1.

103. Hunt S A. ACC/AHA 2005 guideline update for the diagnosis and management of chronic heart failure in the adult: a report of the American College of Cardiology/American Heart Association Task Force on Practice Guidelines (Writing Committee to Update the 2001 Guidelines for the Evaluation and Management of Heart Failure). *J Am Coll Cardiol* 200546e1–82.Current ACC/AHA practice guidelines including comprehensive overview of the literature until 2005, together with references 1 and 2.

104. Cleland J G, Gemmell I, Khand A.*et al* Is the prognosis of heart failure improving? *Eur J Heart Fail* 19991229–241.

105. Böhm M, Werner N, Kindermann M. Drug treatment for chronic heart failure. *Clin Res Cardiol* 200695(suppl 4)36–56.

106. Flather M, Yusuf S, Kober L.*et al* Long-term ACE-inhibitor therapy in patients with heart failure or left-ventricular dysfunction: a systematic overview of data from individual patients. ACE-Inhibitor Myocardial infarction Collaborative Group. *Lancet* 20003551575–1581.Meta-analysis of clinical trials on the use of ACE inhibitors in heart failure.

107. Taylor A L, Ziesche S, Yancy C.*et al* Combination of isosorbide dinitrate and hydralazine in blacks with heart failure. *N Engl J Med* 20043512049–2057

108. Bristow M R, Saxon L A, Boehmer J.*et al* Comparison of Medical Therapy, Pacing and Defibrillation in Heart Failure (COMPANION) Investigators. Cardiac resynchronization therapy with or without implantable defibrillator in advanced chronic heart failure. *N Engl J Med* 20043502140–2150.First study to show that CRT improves mortality in heart failure.

109. Cleland J G, Daubert J C, Erdmann E.*et al* The effect of cardiac resynchronization on morbidity and mortality in heart failure. *N Engl J Med* 20053521539–1549.

110. Götze S, Butter C, Fleck E. Cardiac resynchronization therapy for heart failure—from experimental pacing to evidence-based therapy. *Clin Res Cardiol* 200695(suppl 4)18–35.

111. Lee D S, Green L D, Liu P P.*et al* Effectiveness of implantable defibrillators for preventing arrhythmic events and death. *J Am Coll Cardiol* 2003411573–1582.Meta-analysis of trials on secondary prevention of SCD.

112. Bohula EA, Katz JN, van Diepen S et al. Demographics, Care Patterns, and Outcomes of Patients Admitted to Cardiac Intensive Care Units: The Critical Care Cardiology Trials Network Prospective North American Multicenter Registry of Cardiac Critical Illness. JAMA Cardiol. 2019 Jul 24;

113. Holland EM, Moss TJ. Acute Noncardiovascular Illness in the Cardiac Intensive Care Unit. J Am Coll Cardiol. 2017 Apr 25;69(16):1999–2007.

114. Vallabhajosyula S, Dunlay SM, Prasad A et al. Acute Noncardiac Organ Failure in Acute Myocardial Infarction With Cardiogenic Shock. J Am Coll Cardiol. 2019 Apr 6;73(14):1781–91.

115. van Diepen S, Reynolds HR, Stebbins A et al. Incidence and outcomes associated with early heart failure pharmacotherapy in patients with ongoing cardiogenic shock. *Crit Care Med.* 2014 Feb;42(2):281–8.

116. Schumann J, Henrich EC, Strobl H et al. Inotropic agents and vasodilator strategies for the treatment of cardiogenic shock or low cardiac output syndrome. *Cochrane Database Syst Rev.* 2018 Jan 29;1 CD009669.

117. van Diepen S, Katz JN, Albert NM et al. Contemporary Management of Cardiogenic Shock: A Scientific Statement From the American Heart Association. *Circulation.* 2017 Oct 17;136(16):e232–e268.

118. Jentzer JC, Coons JC, Link CB, Schmidhofer M. Pharmacotherapy update on the use of vasopressors and inotropes in the Intensive Care unit. *J Cardiovasc Pharmacol Ther.* 2015 May;20(3):249–60.

119. Costanzo MR. Ultrafiltration in Acute Heart Failure. *Card Fail Rev.* 2019 Feb;5(1):9–18.

120. Zochios V, Jones N. Acute right heart syndrome in the critically ill patient. *Heart Lung Vessel.* 2014;6(3):157-70

121. Neri M, Villa G, Garzotto F et al. Nomenclature for renal replacement therapy in acute kidney injury: basic principles. *Crit Care.* 2016 Oct 10;20(1):318.

122. Costanzo MR, Guglin ME, Saltzberg MT et al. Ultrafiltration versus intravenous diuretics for patients hospitalized for acute decompensated heart failure. *J Am Coll Cardiol.* 2007 Feb 13;49(6):675–83.

123. Giglioli C, Landi D, Cecchi E et al. Effects of ULTRAfiltration vs. DIureticS on clinical, biohumoral and haemodynamic variables in patients with deCOmpensated heart failure: the ULTRADISCO study. *Eur J Heart Fail.* 2011 Mar;13(3):337–46.

124. Bart BA, Goldsmith SR, Lee KL et al. Ultrafiltration in decompensated heart failure with cardiorenal syndrome. *N Engl J Med.* 2012 Dec 13;367(24):2296–304. Heart Failure Clinical Research Network.

125. Sanofi Aventis. Clopidogrel (Plavix) package insert. Bridgewater NJ; 2013.

126. Eli Lilly and Company. Prasugrel (Effient) package insert. Indianapolis, IN; 2009.

127. Astra Zeneca LP. Ticagrelor (Brilinta) package insert. Wilmington, DE; 2011.

128. Yusuf S, Zhao F, Mehta SR, et al. Effects of clopidogrel in addition to aspirin in patients with acute coronary syndromes without ST-segment elevation. N Engl J Med 2001;345:494 –502.

129. Kezerashvili A, Marzo K, De Leon J. Beta blocker use after acute myocardial infarction in the patient with normal systolic function: When is it "ok" to discontinue? Curr Cardiol Rev. 2012;8:77– 84.

130. Køber L, Torp-Pedersen C, Carlsen JE, et al. A clinical trial of the angiotensin-converting-enzyme inhibitor trandolapril in patients with left ventricular dysfunction after myocardial infarction. Trandolapril Cardiac Evaluation (TRACE) Study Group. N Engl J Med 1995;333:1670 –1676.

131. Geppert A. Patienten mit Klappenvitium auf der Intensivstation [Patients in the Intensive Care unit with valvular diseases]. Med Klin Intensivmed Notfmed. 2013 Oct;108(7):555-60. German. doi: 10.1007/s00063-012-0140-z. Epub 2013 Sep 15. PMID: 24037458.

132. Spodick DH. Acute cardiac tamponade. *N Engl J Med.* 2003;349(7):684-690

133. Imazio M, Cecchi E, Demichelis B, et al. Myopericarditis versus viral or idiopathic acute pericarditis. *Heart* 2008;94(4):498-501

134. Troughton RW, Asher CR, Klein AL. Pericarditis. *Lancet* 2004;363(9410):717-727

135. Reddy PS, Curtiss EI, O'Toole JD, Shaver JA. Cardiac tamponade: hemodynamic observations in man. *Circulation* 1978;58(2):265-272

136. Kerber RE, Gascho JA, Litchfield R, Wolfson P, Ott D, Pandian NG. Hemodynamic effects of volume expansion and nitroprusside compared with pericardiocentesis in patients with acute cardiac tamponade. *N Engl J Med.* 1982;307(15):929-931.

137. Sagrista-Sauleda J, Permanyer-Miralda G, Candell-Riera J, Angel J, Soler-Soler J. Transient cardiac constriction: an unrecognized pattern of evolution in effusive acute idiopathic pericarditis. *Am J Cardiol.* 1987;59(9):961-966

138. Haley JH, Tajik AJ, Danielson GK, Schaff HV, Mulvagh SL, Oh JK. Transient constrictive pericarditis: causes and natural history. *J Am Coll Cardiol.* 2004;43(2):271-275.

139. Global Burden of Disease Study 2013 Collaborators . Global, regional, and national incidence, prevalence, and years lived with disability for 301 acute and chronic diseases and injuries in 188 countries, 1990-2013: a systematic analysis for the Global Burden of Disease Study 2013. *Lancet* 2015;386:743–800

140. Schultheiss HP, Khl U, Cooper LT. The management of myocarditis. *Eur Heart J* 2011;32:2616–25.

141. Cooper LT, Hare JM, Tazelaar HD. et al. Usefulness of immunosuppression for giant cell myocarditis. *Am J Cardiol* 2008;102:1535–9.

142. Khatib R, Reyes MP, Smith F, Khatib G, Rezkalla S. Enhancement of coxsackievirus B4 virulence by indomethacin. *J Lab Clin Med* 1990;116:116–20.

143. Ammirati E, Frigerio M, Adler ED. et al. Management of acute myocarditis and chronic inflammatory cardiomyopathy: an expert consensus document. *Circ Heart Fail* 2020;663–87.

144. Weigang, E., Nienaber, C. A., Rehders, T. C., Ince, H., Vahl, F., & Beyersdorf, F. (2008). Management of Patients With Aortic Dissection. *Deutsches Ärzteblatt International*, *105*(38), 639-645. https://doi.org/10.3238/arztebl.2008.0639

145. Borst HG. Aneurysma und Dissektion der Aorta ascendens und des Aortenbogens. In: Borst HG, Klinner W, Oelert H, editors. *Herzchirurgie: Die Eingriffe am Herzen und an den herznahen Gefäßen.* Berlin, Heidelberg, New York: Springer; 1991. pp. 434–463

146. Nienaber CA, Fattori R, Lund G, et al. Nonsurgical reconstruction of thoracic aortic dissection by stent-graft placement. *N Engl J Med.* 1999;340:1539–1545

147. Eggebrecht H, Nienaber CA, Neuhäuser M, et al. Endovascular stent-graft placement in aortic dissection: a meta-analysis. *Eur Heart J.* 2006;27:489–498.

148. Cook, D. J., Webb, S., & Proudfoot, A. (2022). Assessment and management of cardiovascular disease in the Intensive Care unit. *Heart*, *108*(5), 397-405. https://doi.org/10.1136/heartjnl-2019-315568

149. Bhatnagar P, Wickramasinghe K, Wilkins E, et al.. Trends in the epidemiology of cardiovascular disease in the UK. *Heart* 2016;102:1945–52. 10.1136/heartjnl-2016-309573

150. Adams KF, Fonarow GC, Emerman CL, et al.. Characteristics and outcomes of patients hospitalized for heart failure in the United States: rationale, design, and preliminary observations from the first 100,000 cases in the acute decompensated heart failure national registry (ADHERE). *Am Heart J* 2005;149:209–16. 10.1016/j.ahj.2004.08.005

151. Yancy CW, Jessup M, Bozkurt B. ACCF/AHA guideline for the management of heart failure: a report of the American College of Cardiology Foundation/American Heart Association Task Force on practice guidelines. *Circulation* 2013;2013:e240–327.

152. Ponikowski P, Voors AA, Anker SD, et al.. 2016 ESC Guidelines for the diagnosis and treatment of acute and chronic heart failure: The Task Force for the diagnosis and treatment of acute and chronic heart failure of the European Society of Cardiology (ESC)Developed with the special contribution of the Heart Failure Association (HFA) of the ESC. *Eur Heart J* 2016;37:2129–200. 10.1093/eurheartj/ehw128

153. Doll JA, Ohman EM, Patel MR, et al.. A team-based approach to patients in cardiogenic shock. *Catheter Cardiovasc Interv* 2016;88:424–33. 10.1002/ccd.26297.

154. Crimi, Ettore; Hill, Charles C. (2014). *Postoperative ICU Management of Vascular Surgery Patients. Anesthesiology Clinics, 32(3), 735–757.* doi:10.1016/j.anclin.2014.05.001

155. Rubenfeld GD, Caldwell E, Peabody E, . et al. Incidence and outcomes of acute lung injury. *N Engl J Med*. 2005. October 20; 353 16: 1685– 93.

156. Brower RG, Matthay MA, Morris A, . et al .; Acute Respiratory Distress Syndrome Network Ventilation with lower tidal volumes as compared with traditional tidal volumes for acute lung injury and the acute respiratory distress syndrome. *N Engl J Med*. 2000. May 4; 342 18: 1301– 8.

157. Brogan TV, Thiagarajan RR, Rycus PT, Bartlett RH, Bratton SL.. Extracorporeal membrane oxygenation in adults with severe respiratory failure: a multi-center database. *Intensive Care Med*. 2009. December; 35 12: 2105– 14.

158. Makdisi G, Wang IW. Extra Corporeal Membrane Oxygenation (ECMO) review of a lifesaving technology. *J Thorac Dis*. 2015. July; 7 7: E166– 76.

159. Napp LC, Kühn C, Hoeper MM, . et al. Cannulation strategies for percutaneous extracorporeal membrane oxygenation in adults. *Clin Res Cardiol*. 2016. April; 105 4: 283– 96.

160. Scherer M, Moritz A, Martens S.. The use of extracorporeal membrane oxygenation in patients with therapy refractory cardiogenic shock as a bridge to implantable left ventricular assist device and perioperative right heart support. *J Artif Organs*. 2009; 12 3: 160– 5.

161. Pratt AK, Shah NS, Boyce SW. Left ventricular assist device management in the ICU. Crit Care Med. 2014 Jan;42(1):158-68. doi: 10.1097/01.ccm.0000435675.91305.76. PMID: 24240731.

162. Kipnis, E., Ramsingh, D., Bhargava, M., Dincer, E., Cannesson, M., Broccard, A., Vallet, B., Bendjelid, K., & Thibault, R. (2011). Monitoring in the Intensive Care. *Critical Care Research and Practice*, *2012*. https://doi.org/10.1155/2012/473507

163. Lim, Wendy; Qushmaq, Ismael; Cook, Deborah J.; Devereaux, P J.; Heels-Ansdell, Diane; Crowther, Mark A.; Tkaczyk, Andrea; Meade, Maureen O.; Cook, Richard J. (2006). *Reliability of electrocardiogram interpretation in critically ill patients*. Critical Care Medicine, 34(5), 1338–1343.* doi:10.1097/01.ccm.0000214679.23957.90

164. Myocardial infarction redefined: A consensus document of the Joint European Society of Cardiology/American College of Cardiology Committee for the Redefinition of Myocardial Infarction. J Am Coll Cardiol 2000; 36: 959 –969

165. Ammann P, Maggiorini M, Bertel O, et al: Troponin as a risk factor for mortality in critically ill patients without acute coronary syndromes. J Am Coll Cardiol 2003; 41: 2004 –2009

166. Ammann P, Fehr T, Minder EI, et al: Elevation of troponin I in sepsis and septic shock. Intensive Care Med 2001; 27:965–969

167. Fye WB. A history of the origin, evolution, and impact of electrocardiography. Am J Cardiol. 1994 May 15;73(13):937-49.

168. Baranchuk A, Bayés de Luna A. The P-wave morphology: what does it tell us? Herzschrittmacherther Elektrophysiol. 2015 Sep;26(3):192-9.

169. PIPBERGER HV, TANENBAUM HL. [The P wave, P-R interval, and Q-T ratio of the normal orthogonal electrocardiogram]. Circulation. 1958 Dec;18(6):1175-80.

170. Zema MJ, Kligfield P. ECG poor R-wave progression: review and synthesis. Arch Intern Med. 1982 Jun;142(6):1145-8.

171. Channer K, Morris F. ABC of clinical electrocardiography: Myocardial ischaemia. BMJ. 2002 Apr 27;324(7344):1023-6.

172. de Bliek EC. ST elevation: Differential diagnosis and caveats. A comprehensive review to help distinguish ST elevation myocardial infarction from nonischemic etiologies of ST elevation. Turk J Emerg Med. 2018 Mar;18(1):1-10.

173. Tse G, Chan YW, Keung W, Yan BP. Electrophysiological mechanisms of long and short QT syndromes. Int J Cardiol Heart Vasc. 2017 Mar;14:8-13.

174. Levis JT. ECG Diagnosis: Hypothermia. Perm J. 2010 Fall;14(3):73.

175. Wang J, Yang B, Chen H, Ju W, Chen K, Zhang F, Cao K, Chen M. Epsilon waves detected by various electrocardiographic recording methods: in patients with arrhythmogenic right ventricular cardiomyopathy. Tex Heart Inst J. 2010;37(4):405-11.

176. Sattar, Y., & Chhabra, L. (2021). *Electrocardiogram*. PubMed; StatPearls Publishing. https://www.ncbi.nlm.nih.gov/books/NBK549803/

177. Huygh, J., Peeters, Y., Bernards, J., & G. Malbrain, L. N. (2015). Hemodynamic monitoring in the critically ill: An overview of current cardiac output monitoring methods. *F1000Research*, *5*. https://doi.org/10.12688/f1000research.8991.1

178. Adam SA, Osborne S, Welch J (eds). Critical care nursing: science and practice. 3rd edn. Oxford: Oxford University Press; 2017. https://doi.org/10.1093/ med/9780199696260.001.0001

179. American Association of Critical Care Nurses. AACN practice alert: pulmonary artery/central venous pressure monitoring in adults. AACN Adv Crit Care. 2020;31(1):41–48. https://doi.org/10.4037/aacnacc2020328

180. Bannon M, Heller SF, Rivera M. Anatomic considerations for central venous cannulation. Risk Manag Healthc Policy. 2011;4:27–39.

181. Bennett SR. Sepsis in the Intensive Care unit. Surgery (Oxf). 2015;33(11):565– 571. https://doi.org/10.1016/j.mpsur.2015.08.0024

182. Berlin DA, Bakker J. Starling curves and central venous pressure. Crit Care. 2015;19(1):55. https://doi.org/10.1186/s13054-015-0776-1

183. Chlabicz M, Kazimierczyk R, Lopatowska P et al. Fluid therapy in non-septic, refractory acute decompensated heart failure patients—the cautious role of central venous pressure. Adv Med Sci. 2019;64(1):37–43. https://doi. org/10.1016/j.advms.2018.11.001

184. Barry Hill;Catherine Smith; (2021). *Central venous pressure monitoring in critical care settings . British Journal of Nursing, (), –.* doi:10.12968/bjon.2021.30.4.230

185. Angus DC, Carlet J; 2002 Brussels Roundtable Participants. Surviving Intensive Care: a report from the 2002 Brussels Roundtable. Intensive Care Med . 2003; 29 (3): 368 - 377.

186. Zazzle t-shirts. Zazzle website. http://www.zazzle.ca/the_plural_of_ anecdote_is_not_data_tee_shirts-235279170565465750 . Accessed May 15, 2014.

187. Topol EJ. Nesiritide - not verifi ed . N Engl J Med . 2005; 353 (2): 113 - 116 .188. The EC/IC Bypass Study Group. Failure of extracranial-intracranial arterial bypass to reduce the risk of ischemic stroke. Results of an international randomized trial. N Engl J Med . 1985 ; 313 (19): 1191 - 1200.

189. Garland, Allan (2014). *Arterial Lines in the ICU. Chest, 146(5), 1155–1158.* doi:10.1378/chest.14-1212

190. Pulmonary Artery Catheter Consensus Conference Participants. Pulmonary Artery Catheter Consensus Statement. *Critical Care Medicine* 1997;25:910-25.

191. Shah MR, Hasselblad V, Stevenson LW, Binanay C, O'Connor CM, Sopko G, et al. Impact of pulmonary artery catheter in critically ill patients. Meta-analysis of randomized clinical trials. *JAMA* 2005;294:1664-70.

192. Wiener RS, Welch HG. Trends in the use of the pulmonary artery catheter in the United States, 1993-2004. *JAMA* 2007;298(4):423-9.

193. Zion MM, Balkin J, Rosenmann D, Goldbourt U, Reicher-Reiss H, Kaplinsky E, et al. Use of pulmonary artery catheters in patients with acute myocardial infarction. Analysis of experience in 5,841 patients in the SPRINT Registry. SPRINT Study Group. *Chest* 1990;98(6):1331-5.

194. Rajaram, S. S., Desai, N. K., Kalra, A., Gajera, M., Cavanaugh, S. K., Brampton, W., Young, D., Harvey, S., & Rowan, K. (2013). Pulmonary artery catheters for adult patients in Intensive Care. *The Cochrane Database of Systematic Reviews*, *2013*(2). https://doi.org/10.1002/14651858.CD003408.pub3

195. Mehta Y, Sharma KK. Double knot with formation of a double loop of pulmonary artery catheter. J Cardiothorac Anesth. 1990;**4**:149–150.

196. Linton RA, Band DM, Haire KM. A new method of measuring cardiac output in man using lithium dilution. Br J Anaesth. 1993;71:262–266.

197. Hofer CK, Cecconi M, Marx G, della Rocca G. Minimally invasive haemodynamic monitoring. Eur J Anaesthesiol. 2009;26:996–1002.

198. Funk DJ, Moretti EW, Gan TJ. Minimally invasive cardiac output monitoring in the perioperative setting. Anesth Analg. 2009;108:887–897.

199. Kubicek WG, Karnegis JN, Patterson RP, Witsoe DA, Mattson RH. Development and evaluation of an impedance cardiac output system. Aerosp Med. 1966;37:1208–1212.

200. Keren H, Burkhoff D, Squara P. Evaluation of a noninvasive continuous cardiac output monitoring system based on thoracic bioreactance. Am J Physiol Heart Circ Physiol. 2007;293:H583–H589.

201. CONMED Corporation. ECOM endotracheal cardiac output monitor. 2010. Available from:

202. Meyer S, Todd D, Wright I, Gortner L, Reynolds G. Review article: Non-invasive assessment of cardiac output with portable continuous-wave Doppler ultrasound. Emerg Med Australas. 2008;20:201–208.

203. Yelderman, Mark L.; Ramsay, Mike A.; Quinn, Michael D.; Paulsen, A.W.; McKown, Russel C.; Gillman, Paula H. (1992). *Continuous thermodilution cardiac output measurement in Intensive Care unit patients. , 6(3), 270–274.* doi:10.1016/1053-0770(92)90137-V

204. Monnet X, Teboul JL. Transpulmonary thermodilution: advantages and limits. Crit Care. 2017 Jun 19;21(1):147. doi: 10.1186/s13054-017-1739-5. PMID: 28625165; PMCID: PMC5474867.

205. Møller-Sørensen, H., Norum, H. M., & Ricksten, S.-E. (2019). 10 tips for Intensive Care management of transplanted heart patients. *Intensive Care Medicine*, *45*(3), 374–376. https://doi.org/10.1007/s00134-019-05545-w

206. Chahine, J., & Alvey, H. (2021, July 25). *Left Ventricular Failure*. PubMed; StatPearls Publishing. https://www.ncbi.nlm.nih.gov/books/NBK537098/

207. Yancy CW, Jessup M, Bozkurt B, Butler J, Casey DE, Drazner MH, Fonarow GC, Geraci SA, Horwich T, Januzzi JL, Johnson MR, Kasper EK, Levy WC, Masoudi FA, McBride PE, McMurray JJ, Mitchell JE, Peterson PN, Riegel B, Sam F, Stevenson LW, Tang WH, Tsai EJ, Wilkoff BL. 2013 ACCF/AHA guideline for the management of heart failure: executive summary: a report of the American College of Cardiology Foundation/American Heart Association Task Force on practice guidelines. Circulation. 2013 Oct 15;128(16):1810-52.

208. Yancy CW, Jessup M, Bozkurt B, Butler J, Casey DE, Colvin MM, Drazner MH, Filippatos GS, Fonarow GC, Givertz MM, Hollenberg SM, Lindenfeld J, Masoudi FA, McBride PE, Peterson PN, Stevenson LW, Westlake C. 2017 ACC/AHA/HFSA Focused Update of the 2013 ACCF/AHA Guideline for the Management of Heart Failure: A Report of the American College of Cardiology/American Heart Association Task Force on Clinical Practice Guidelines and the Heart Failure Society of America. Circulation. 2017 Aug 08;136(6):e137-e161.

209. Trappe, J. (2010). Treating critical supraventricular and ventricular arrhythmias. *Journal of Emergencies, Trauma and Shock*, *3*(2), 143-152. https://doi.org/10.4103/0974-2700.62114.

210. Kalahasty, G., & Ellenbogen, K. A. (2011). Management of the Patient With Implantable Cardioverter-Defibrillator Lead Failure. *Circulation*, *123*(12), 1352–1354. https://doi.org/10.1161/circulationaha.110.986828

211. Bradfield JS, Ajijola OA, Vaseghi M, Shivkumar K. Mechanisms and management of refractory ventricular arrhythmias in the age of autonomic modulation. Heart Rhythm. 2018 Aug;15(8):1252-1260. doi: 10.1016/j.hrthm.2018.02.015. Epub 2018 Feb 14. PMID: 29454137.

212. Paulis, S. D., Arlotta, G., Calabrese, M., Corsi, F., Taccheri, T., Antoniucci, M. E., Martinelli, L., Bevilacqua, F., Tinelli, G., & Cavaliere, F. (2022). Postoperative Intensive Care Management of Aortic Repair. *Journal of Personalized Medicine*, *12*(8). https://doi.org/10.3390/jpm12081351

213. Olinic, M., Stanek, A., Tătaru, A., Homorodean, C., & Olinic, M. (2019). Acute Limb Ischemia: An Update on Diagnosis and Management. *Journal of Clinical Medicine*, *8*(8). https://doi.org/10.3390/jcm8081215

214. Raiten, J. M., Gutsche, J. T., Horak, J., & Augoustides, J. G. (2012). Critical care management of patients following transcatheter aortic valve replacement. *F1000Research*, *2*. https://doi.org/10.12688/f1000research.2-62.v1

215. Möbius-Winkler S, Sandri M, Mangner N, Lurz P, Dähnert I, Schuler G. The WATCHMAN left atrial appendage closure device for atrial fibrillation. J Vis Exp. 2012 Feb 28;(60):3671. doi: 10.3791/3671. PMID: 22395336; PMCID: PMC3399494.

216. Wintgens LIS, Maarse M, Swaans MJ, Rensing BJWM, Van Dijk VF, Boersma LVA. The WATCHMAN left atrial appendage closure device for patients with atrial fibrillation: current status and future perspectives. Expert Rev Med Devices. 2020 Jul;17(7):615-626. doi: 10.1080/17434440.2020.1781615. Epub 2020 Jul 27. PMID: 32543911.

217. Chandran, J., Sriram, S., & Krishna, B. (2021). Clinical Utility of Arterial Blood Gas Test in an Intensive Care Unit: An Observational Study. *Indian Journal of Critical Care Medicine : Peer-reviewed, Official Publication of Indian Society of Critical Care Medicine*, *25*(2), 172-175. https://doi.org/10.5005/jp-journals-10071-23719.

218. Tracy C, Boushahri A. Managing arrhythmias in the Intensive Care unit. Crit Care Clin. 2014 Jul;30(3):365-90. doi: 10.1016/j.ccc.2014.03.009. PMID: 24996602.

219. Tarditi DJ, Hollenberg SM. Cardiac arrhythmias in the Intensive Care unit. Semin Respir Crit Care Med. 2006 Jun;27(3):221-9. doi: 10.1055/s-2006-945525. PMID: 16791756.

www.ingramcontent.com/pod-product-compliance
Ingram Content Group UK Ltd.
Pitfield, Milton Keynes, MK11 3LW, UK
UKHW062007290726
14090UKWH00022B/1440

9 789357 416559